D0781824

# REAL WORLD
# MICRO

## TWENTY-SECOND EDITION

**EDITED BY ROB LARSON, ALEJANDRO REUSS, BRYAN SNYDER, CHRIS STURR,**

**AND THE *DOLLARS & SENSE* COLLECTIVE**

# REAL WORLD MICRO, TWENTY-SECOND EDITION

Copyright © 2015 by Economic Affairs Bureau, Inc.

ISBN: 978-1-939402-19-6

All rights reserved. No portions of this book may be reproduced, stored in a retrieval system, or transmitted in any form or by any means, electronic, mechanical, photocopying, recording, or otherwise, except for brief quotations in a review, without prior permission from Economic Affairs Bureau.

Article 2.2: Copyright © Al Jazeera.
Articles 4.3, 5.4, 7.6, 8.2, 11.1: Copyright © Center for Economic and Policy Research (CEPR). Reprinted with permission.

Published by:
Economic Affairs Bureau, Inc. d/b/a *Dollars & Sense*
95 Berkeley St., 3rd floor, Boston, MA 02116
617-447-2177; dollars@dollarsandsense.org.
For order information, contact Economic Affairs Bureau or visit: www.dollarsandsense.org.

*Real World Micro* is edited by the *Dollars & Sense* Collective, which also publishes *Dollars & Sense* magazine and the classroom books *Microeconomics: Individual Choice in Communities, Real World Macro, Current Economic Issues, The Economic Crisis Reader, Real World Globalization, America Beyond Capitalism, Labor and the Global Economy, Real World Latin America, Real World Labor, Real World Banking and Finance, The Wealth Inequality Reader, The Economics of the Environment, Introduction to Political Economy, Unlevel Playing Fields: Understanding Wage Inequality and Discrimination, Striking a Balance: Work, Family, Life*, and *Grassroots Journalism*.

The 2015 *Dollars & Sense* Collective:
Betsy Aron, Nancy Banks, Nina Eichacker, Peter Kolozi, Lyden Marcellot, John Miller, Jawied Nawabi, Kevin O'Connell, Linda Pinkow, Alejandro Reuss, Dan Schneider, Zoe Sherman, Bryan Snyder, Chris Sturr, Jeanne Winner

Co-editors of this volume: Rob Larson, Alejandro Reuss, Bryan Snyder, and Chris Sturr
Design and layout: Alejandro Reuss

Printed in U.S.A

# CONTENTS

# INTRODUCTION

It sometimes seems that the United States has not one, but two economies. The first economy exists in economics textbooks and in the minds of many elected officials. It is a free-market economy, a system of promise and plenty, a cornucopia of consumer goods. In this economy, people are free and roughly equal, and each individual carefully looks after him- or herself, making uncoerced choices to advance his or her economic interests. Government is but an afterthought in this world, since almost everything that people need can be provided by the free market, itself guided by the reassuring "invisible hand."

The second economy is described in the writings of progressives, environmentalists, union supporters, and consumer advocates as well as honest business writers who recognize that real-world markets do not always conform to textbook models. This second economy features vast disparities of income, wealth, and power manifested in a system of class. It is an economy where employers have power over employees, where large firms have the power to shape markets, and where large corporate lobbies have the power to shape public policies. In this second economy, government sometimes adopts policies that ameliorate the abuses of capitalism and other times does just the opposite, but it is always an active and essential participant in economic life.

If you are reading this introduction, you are probably a student in an introductory college course in microeconomics. Your textbook will introduce you to the first economy, the harmonious world of free markets. *Real World Micro* will introduce you to the second.

## Why "Real World" Micro?

A standard economics textbook is full of powerful concepts. It is also, by its nature, a limited window on the economy. What is taught in most introductory economics courses today is in fact just one strand of economic thought—neoclassical economics. Fifty years ago, many more strands were part of the introductory economics curriculum, and the contraction of the field has imposed limits on the study of economics that can confuse and frustrate students. This is particularly true in the study of microeconomics, which looks at markets for individual goods or services.

*Real World Micro* is designed as a supplement to a standard neoclassical textbook. Its articles provide vivid, real-world illustrations of economic concepts. But beyond that, our mission is to address two major sources of confusion in the study of economics at the introductory level.

The first source of confusion is the striking simplification of the world found in orthodox microeconomics. Standard textbooks describe stylized economic

1

interactions between idealized buyers and sellers that bear scant resemblance to the messy realities of the actual economic activity that we see around us. There is nothing wrong with simplifying. In fact, every social science must develop simplified models; precisely because reality is so complex, we must look at it a little bit at a time in order to understand it. Still, these simplifications mystify and misrepresent actual capitalist social relations and excise questions of race, gender, and class from the analysis.

Mainstream economic analysis calls to mind the story of the tipsy party-goer whose friend finds him on his hands and knees under a streetlight. "What are you doing?" asks the friend. "I dropped my car keys across the street, and I'm looking for them," the man replies. "But if you lost them across the street, how come you're looking over here?" "Well, the light's better here." In the interest of greater clarity, economics often imposes similar limits on its areas of inquiry.

As the title *Real World Micro* implies, one of our goals is to confront mainstream microeconomic theory with a more complex reality to direct attention to the areas not illuminated by the streetlight, and particularly to examine how inequality, power, and environmental imbalance change the picture. The idea is not to prove the standard theory "wrong," but to challenge you to think about where the theory is more and less useful, and why markets may not operate as expected.

This focus on real-world counterpoints to mainstream economic theory connects to the second issue we aim to clarify. Most economics texts uncritically present key assumptions and propositions that form the core of standard economic theory. They offer much less exploration of a set of related questions: What are alternative propositions about the economy? Under what circumstances will these alternatives more accurately describe the economy? What differences do such propositions make? Our approach is not to spell out an alternative theory in detail, but to raise questions and present real-life examples that bring these questions to life. For example, textbooks carefully lay out "consumer sovereignty," the notion that consumers' wishes ultimately determine what the economy will produce. But can we reconcile consumer sovereignty with an economy where one of the main products in industries such as soft drinks, cars, and music is consumer desire itself? We think it is valuable to see ideas like consumer sovereignty as debatable propositions and that requires hearing other views in the debate.

In short, our goal in this book is to use real-world examples from today's economy to raise questions, stimulate debate, and dare you to think critically about the models in your textbook.

## What's in This Book

*Real World Micro* is organized to follow the outline of a standard economics text. Each chapter leads off with a brief introduction, including study questions for the entire chapter, and then provides several short articles from *Dollars & Sense* magazine and other sources that illustrate the chapter's key concepts.

Here is a quick overview:

**Chapter 1, Perspectives on Microeconomic Theory**, starts off the volume by taking a hard look at the strengths and weaknesses of actual markets, with special attention to weaknesses that standard textbooks tend to underemphasize.

**Chapter 2, Supply and Demand**, presents real-world examples of supply and demand in action. *Dollars & Sense* authors question the conventional wisdom on topics such as price volatility, affordability of essential goods like food (and issues of hunger), and price regulations like the minimum wage and rent control.

**Chapter 3, Consumers**, raises provocative questions about utility theory and individual consumer choice. What happens when marketers shape buyers' tastes? What happens when important information is hidden from consumers? How can consumer decisions include broader considerations like environmental sustainability or labor conditions? What roles should government play in consumer protection?

**Chapter 4, Firms, Production, and Profit Maximization**, illustrates how business strategies to maximize profits may come at the expense of the social good, and challenges students to think about different ways of organizing firms. The chapter considers issues like executive compensation, and the relation between the profit motive and essential goods like food and health care.

**Chapter 5, Market Failure I: Market Power**, explores market power and monopoly, just one example of the unequal power relationships that pervade our economic system. The chapter critiques market power in such industries as pharmaceuticals, banking, and agriculture, but also questions whether small business prevalence would be an improvement.

**Chapter 6, Market Failure II: Externalities**, addresses cases where processes of production, exchange, and consumption affect not only the parties to those transactions, but also third parties (especially negatively). It considers how public policy should address cases where such spillover effects create a divergence between private and social costs and benefits.

**Chapter 7, Labor Markets**, examines the ways in which labor-market outcomes can be affected by unionization, globalization, and a host of other factors largely left out of the standard supply-and-demand models. Among the issues discussed are the reasons for union decline, the causes of high unemployment today, the rise of "contingent" labor arrangements, and possible ways to improve labor conditions domestically and internationally.

**Chapter 8, The Distribution of Income and Wealth**, discusses the causes and consequences of inequality, countering the mainstream view that inequality is good for growth. The chapter examines the contours of inequality, with particular attention to race and gender. It questions conventional views attributing rising inequality to technological change and globalization, and considers the impact of a changing balance of power between workers and employers. And it dealw sith issues of wealth and poverty, both domestic and global.

**Chapter 9, Taxation**, explores issues of incomes, wealth, and taxation, including who actually pays taxes and at what rates. It also explores whether changes in taxes lead to changes in economic behavior and outcomes. This proposition is explored in the areas of taxes on high-income individuals and their effects on savings and investment, as well as taxes on financial transactions and effects on speculative activity. Finally, it discusses new controversies over growing inequality and the possibility of international taxation on accumulated wealth.

**Chapter 10, Trade and Development**, covers key issues in trade policy and the world economy. The chapter's articles question the value of free trade and foreign investment for development, consider the role of currency markets in global trade outcomes, address the impacts of globalization on workers (in both high-income and low-income countries), and discuss issues of development and environmental protection.

**Chapter 11, Policy Spotlight: Generational War?**, explores major policy and social issues related to "intergenerational equity"—the distribution of economic benefits and costs between generations, including the older versus the younger today and current generations versus those yet to be born. It considers issues including investments in education, pensions and Social Security, government debt, and climate change.

# Chapter 1

# PERPECTIVES ON MICROECONOMIC THEORY

## INTRODUCTION

Economics is all about tradeoffs. The concept of "opportunity cost" reminds us that in order to make a purchase, or even to make use of a resource that you control (such as your time), you must give up other possible purchases or other possible uses. Markets broaden the range of possible tradeoffs by facilitating exchange between people who do not know each other, and in many cases never meet at all. Think of buying a pair of athletic shoes in Atlanta from a company based in Los Angeles that manufactures shoes in Malaysia and has stockholders all over the world. As the idea of gains from trade suggests, markets allow many exchanges that make both parties better off.

But markets have severe limitations as well. The economic crisis that began in 2008 has made those limitations all too clear. Even lifelong free-marketeers such as former Federal Reserve chair Alan Greenspan have been forced to question their belief in the "invisible hand."

In the chapter's first article, economist Marty Wolfson critiques a mainstream "free market" ideology that views markets as delivering to each person their just rewards, based on their talent or effort. In fact, he argues, markets are often structured in ways that stack the deck in favor of the wealthy and powerful (Article 1.1).

Markets and price determination, in neoclassical economics, have been idealized into an elegant, utility-maximizing perfection. Chris Tilly, in "Shaking the Invisible Hand" (Article 1.2), uncovers the curious assumptions necessary to allow for the market mechanism to be the most efficient allocator of scarce resources. He provides us with eight "Tilly Assumptions" underlying perfectly functioning markets. If any of these assumptions is violated, then there is a possibility of "market failure," or less-than-optimal market results.

Alejandro Reuss provides us with a clear discussion of this idealized neoclassical view of exchange, with a particular focus on labor markets, in "Freedom, Equity, and Efficiency" (Article 1.3). Ideal neoclassical markets offer the promise of freedom of choice, equity (fairness), and efficiency, but often fail to deliver on all three counts. Reuss walks us through these neoclassical standards and contrasts them to the not-so-rosy reality of unrestrained labor-market competition.

In "Sharing the Wealth of the Commons" (Article 1.4), Peter Barnes focuses our attention on the oft-ignored forms of wealth that we do not own privately, but are held in various "commons." He challenges the way that conventional economists view the environment and other goods that are shared by many people.

Zoe Sherman (Article 1.5) turns Ronald Reagan's famous 1980 presidential-debate question—"Are you better off than you were four years ago?"— into a look at the changes in the quality of life in the United States in recent decades. She asks whether we're better off than we were forty years ago. Certainly, per capita income is higher (as mainstream economists would define being "better off")—but we also have rising inequality, increased burdens of work, greater insecurity, and serious problems of environmental sustainability.

An interview with economist Juliet Schor (Article 1.6) explores the causes behind U.S. consumerism. Schor looks beyond some of the "usual suspects"—like advertising—by linking the rise of consumerism to labor-market forces that have prevented the reduction of work time. She argues that future changes in U.S. con-suption behavior, and therefore long-term environmental sustainability, depend on reducing hours of work

## Discussion Questions

1. (General) What things should not be for sale? Beyond everyday goods and ser-vices, think about human bodies, votes, small countries, and other things that might be bought and sold. How do you draw the line between what should be bought and sold and what should not?

2. (General) If not markets, then what? What are other ways to organize eco-nomic activity? Which ways are most likely to resolve the problems brought up in this chapter?

3. (Article 1.1) Marty Wolfson argues that markets, far from being "free," are often rigged in favor of the wealthy and powerful. What are some examples?

4. (Article 1.2) Write out the eight "Tilly Assumptions" and corresponding realities using Tilly's exact terms for the assumptions. Are these assumptions reasonable?

5. (Article 1.2) For each of the eight "Tilly Assumptions," explain how the market mechanism would fail if the assumption were violated.

6. (Article 1.3) According to neoclassical theory, how do markets deliver "effi-cient" results if all "barriers" to exchange are removed? In what sense are these results "efficient"?

7. (Article 1.3) How is the word "freedom" defined by neoclassical economists? What freedoms do they argue workers lose under regulated labor markets? How does this compare to your idea of what kinds of freedoms are valuable?

8.  (Article 1.3) Does the unfettered operation of the market mechanism deliver "equity" to society? In your view, what would fair labor-market processes or outcomes look like?

9.  (Article 1.4) Peter Barnes says that we take for granted an enormous number of resources—including the natural environment, but also the laws and institutions that make economic activity possible. Is his point the same as saying that there are market failures, such as pollution externalities, that prevent markets from taking into account the full value of the environment?

10. (Article 1.5) What aspects of well-being does Sherman think are not very well captured by looking at economic growth alone?

11. (Article 1.6) Schor argues that, far from being the consequence of human beings' inherently insatiable wants, consumerism is the result of various social and institutional factors. What does she see as the key factors pushing people to consume more and more? What are the main reasons, in her view, that consumer behavior in the United States has differed from that in other countries?

*Article 1.1*

# "FREE MARKET" OUTCOMES ARE NOT FAIR—AND NOT FREE

**BY MARTY WOLFSON**
*November/December 2012*

**"S**ince 1980, the U.S. government has reduced its intervention in the U.S. economy, which has become much more of a free market. Conservatives applaud this development because they think that free-market outcomes reward talent and hard work; progressives object to the income inequality of free-market outcomes and want to use government tax and transfer policy to reduce inequality."

Most people, whether conservative or progressive, would probably agree with this statement. This framing of the issue, however, plays into a right-wing story in which conservatives are the defenders of (free) market outcomes, including the success of the rich who have made it "on their own"; meanwhile, the "dependent poor" look to the government for handouts. This has been a basic element of the right-wing playbook for a long time. Then-presidential candidate Mitt Romney was drawing on this narrative when he complained about the 47% of the U.S. population "who are dependent upon government ... who believe that government has a responsibility to care for them."

This view has two main themes: 1) Because the U.S. free-market economy rewards talent and hard work, the middle class should emulate the wealthy for their success, not vilify them; and 2) those who have been failures in the market want the government to take care of them by redistributing income from those who have been successful. We can see these themes play out on all sorts of political issues. They form, for example, the basis for the attacks on the Affordable Health Care Act (or "Obamacare"). Middle-class Americans, in the conservative view, are being taxed—forced to pay—to provide health insurance for those "unsuccessful" elements of the population who have not earned it themselves.

The conservative argument assumes that the outcomes we observe are the result of a free-market economy. However, the right-wing objective has not been to create a free market; it has been to rig government policy and the market so as to redistribute income towards large corporations and the wealthy.

For example, conservatives themselves want to use government policy to bring about a different distribution of income from what we have now—a distribution that is more favorable to corporations and the very rich. A central policy objective for conservatives, ever since the Reagan Administration, has been to cut taxes on the wealthy. And by cutting government revenue, they have been able to make the argument that government programs for the poor and the middle class need to be cut in order to balance the budget.

Also, conservatives have eliminated restrictions on corporations and protections for workers, consumers, and the environment. They have attacked barriers to international capital mobility, deregulated industries, and reduced government regulations aimed at ensuring a safe workplace and a healthy environment.

Because conservative policies have often taken the form of reducing government programs and regulations, the ideology of a free market has been useful in rationalizing them. Other conservative interventions, however, have been less able to fit into the free-market mold, and therefore are especially revealing of conservatives' genuine aims.

When the financial crisis of 2008 threatened the survival of the large banks, they were quick to ask for the government to intervene with a large bailout. The "right-to-work" law recently passed in Indiana, designed to deprive unions of financial resources, is an explicit rejection of a market outcome—the private agreement between management and union to require all workers to pay their "fair share" of the costs of union representation. "Free-trade" agreements, ostensibly designed to eliminate restrictions on the movement of goods and capital, have nonetheless continued to restrict the free movement of people. Even the repeal of financial regulations in the 1980s and 1990s, ostensibly a free-market endeavor, created the anti-competitive giant financial firms that demanded to be bailed out in 2008.

The realization that the economy is rigged to benefit the rich and large corporations takes away the force of the right-wing argument that progressives want to use government to "vilify" the "successful" and reward the "slothful and incompetent." When the game has been rigged, it is wrong to say that the market simply rewards talent and hard work, and the outcomes that result can hardly be called fair. When the market outcomes that we observe are unfair, we need to both change the rules for how the economy works and use the government to restore fairness. ❏

*Sources:* Dean Baker, *The End of Loser Liberalism: Making Markets Progressive* (2011); Transcript of Mitt Romney video, *Mother Jones*, September 17, 2012 (motherjones.com).

*Article 1.2*

# SHAKING THE INVISIBLE HAND

*The Uncertain Foundations of Free-Market Economics*

**BY CHRIS TILLY**
*November 1989; updated March 2011*

> "It is not from the benevolence of the butcher, the brewer or the baker that we expect our dinner, but from their regard to their own interest... [No individual] intends to promote the public interest... [rather, he is] led by an invisible hand to promote an end which was no part of his intention."
>
> —*Adam Smith, The Wealth of Nations, 1776*

Seen the Invisible Hand lately? It's all around us these days, propping up conservative arguments in favor of free trade, deregulation, and tax-cutting.

Today's advocates for "free," competitive markets echo Adam Smith's claim that unfettered markets translate the selfish pursuit of individual gain into the greatest benefit for all. They trumpet the superiority of capitalist free enterprise over socialist efforts to supplant the market with a planned economy, and even decry liberal attempts to moderate the market. Anything short of competitive markets, they proclaim, yields economic inefficiency, making society worse off.

But the economic principle underlying this fanfare is shaky indeed. Since the late 19th century, mainstream economists have struggled to prove that Smith was right—that the chaos of free markets leads to a blissful economic order. In the 1950s, U.S. economists Kenneth Arrow and Gerard Debreu finally came up with a theoretical proof, which many orthodox economists view as the centerpiece of modern economic theory.

Although this proof is the product of the best minds of mainstream economics, it ends up saying surprisingly little in defense of free markets. The modern theory of the Invisible Hand shows that given certain assumptions, free markets reduce the wasteful use of economic resources—but perpetuate unequal income distribution.

To prove free markets cut waste, economists must make a number of far-fetched assumptions: there are no concentrations of economic power; buyers and sellers know every detail about the present and future economy; and all costs of production are borne by producers while all benefits from consumption are paid for by consumers (see box for a complete list). Take away any one of these assumptions and markets can lead to stagnation, recession, and other forms of waste—as in fact they do.

In short, the economic theory invoked by conservatives to justify free markets instead starkly reveals their limitations.

## The Fruits of Free Markets

The basic idea behind the Invisible Hand can be illustrated with a story. Suppose that I grow apples and you grow oranges. We both grow tired of eating the same fruit all the time and decide to trade. Perhaps we start by trading one apple for one orange. This exchange satisfies both of us, because in fact I would gladly give up more than one apple to get an orange, and you would readily pay more than one orange for an apple. And as long as swapping one more apple for one more orange makes us both better off, we will continue to trade.

Eventually, the trading will come to a stop. I begin to notice that the novelty of oranges wears old as I accumulate a larger pile of them and the apples I once had a surplus of become more precious to me as they grow scarcer. At some point, I draw the line: in order to obtain one more apple from me, you must give me more than one orange. But your remaining oranges have also become more valuable to you. Up to now, each successive trade has made both of us better off. Now there is no further exchange that benefits us both, so we agree to stop trading until the next crop comes in.

Note several features of this parable. Both you and I end up happier by trading freely. If the government stepped in and limited fruit trading, neither of us would be as well off. In fact, the government cannot do anything in the apple/orange market that will make both of us better off than does the free market.

---

### Assumptions and Reality

The claim that free markets lead to efficiency and reduced waste rests on eight main assumptions. However, these assumptions differ sharply from economic reality. (Assumptions 1, 3, 4, and 5 are discussed in more detail in the article.)

ASSUMPTION ONE: *No market power.* No individual buyer or seller, nor any group of buyers or sellers, has the power to affect the market-wide level of prices, wages, or profits.

REALITY ONE: Our economy is dotted with centers of market power, from large corporations to unions. Furthermore, employers have an edge in bargaining with workers because of the threat of unemployment.

ASSUMPTION TWO: *No economies of scale.* Small plants can produce as cheaply as large ones.

REALITY TWO: In fields such as mass-production industry, transportation, communications, and agriculture, large producers enjoy a cost advantage, limiting competition.

ASSUMPTION THREE: *Perfect information about the present.* Buyers and sellers know everything there is to know about the goods being exchanged. Also, each is aware of the wishes of every other potential buyer and seller in the market.

REALITY THREE: The world is full of lemons—goods about which the buyer is inadequately informed. Also, people are not mind-readers, so sellers get stuck with surpluses and willing buyers are unable to find the products they want.

ASSUMPTION FOUR: *Perfect information about the future.* Contracts between buyers and sellers cover every possible future eventuality.

Adding more economic actors, products, money, and costly production processes complicates the picture, but we reach the same conclusions. Most of us sell our labor time in the market rather than fruit; we sell it for money that we then use to buy apples, oranges, and whatever else we need. The theory of the Invisible Hand tells us a trip to the fruit stand improves the lot of both consumer and seller; likewise, the sale of labor time benefits both employer and employee. What's more, according to the theory, competition between apple farmers insures that consumers will get apples produced at the lowest possible cost. Government intervention still can only make things worse.

This fable provides a ready-made policy guide. Substitute "Japanese autos" and "U.S. agricultural products" for apples and oranges, and the fable tells you that import quotas or tariffs only make the people of both countries worse off. Change the industries to airlines or telephone services, and the fable calls for deregulation. Or re-tell the tale in the labor market: minimum wages and unions (which prevent workers from individually bargaining over their wages) hurt employers and workers.

---

REALITY FOUR: Uncertainty clouds the future of any economy. Futures markets are limited.

ASSUMPTION FIVE: *You only get what you pay for.* Nobody can impose a cost on somebody else, nor obtain a benefit from them, without paying.

REALITY FIVE: Externalities, both positive and negative, are pervasive. In a free market, polluters can impose costs on the rest of us without paying. And when a public good like a park is built or roads are maintained, everyone benefits whether or not they helped to pay for it.

ASSUMPTION SIX: *Price is a proxy for pleasure.* The price of a given commodity will represent the quality and desirability and or utility derived from the consumption of the commodity.

REALITY SIX: "Conspicuous Consumption" (Veblen) and or "snob effects" will often distort prices from underlying utility and marketers will try to position commodities accordingly.

ASSUMPTION SEVEN: Self-interest only. In economic matters, each person cares only about his or her own level of well-being.

REALITY SEVEN: Solidarity, jealousy, and even love for one's family violate this assumption.

ASSUMPTION EIGHT: No joint production. Each production process has only one product.

REALITY EIGHT: Even in an age of specialization, there are plenty of exceptions to this rule. For example, large service firms such as hospitals or universities produce a variety of different services using the same resources.

—Chris Tilly and Bryan Snyder

## Fruit Salad

Unfortunately for free-market boosters, two major short-comings make a fruit salad out of this story. First, even if free markets perform as advertised, they deliver only one benefit—the prevention of certain economically wasteful practices—while preserving inequality. According to the theory, competitive markets wipe out two kinds of waste: unrealized trades and inefficient production. Given the right assumptions, markets ensure that when two parties both stand to gain from a trade, they make that trade, as in the apples-and-oranges story. Competition compels producers to search for the most efficient, lowest-cost production methods—again, given the right preconditions.

Though eliminating waste is a worthy goal, it leaves economic inequality untouched. Returning once more to the orchard, if I start out with all of the apples and oranges and you start out with none, that situation is free of waste: no swap can make us both better off since you have nothing to trade! Orthodox economists acknowledge that even in the ideal competitive market, those who start out rich stay rich, while the poor remain poor. Many of them argue that attempts at redistributing income will most certainly create economic inefficiencies, justifying the preservation of current inequities.

But in real-life economics, competition does lead to waste. Companies wastefully duplicate each other's research and build excess productive capacity. Cost-cutting often leads to shoddy products, worker speedup, and unsafe working conditions. People and factories stand idle while houses go unbuilt and people go unfed. That's because of the second major problem: real economies don't match the assumptions of the Invisible Hand theory.

Of course, all economic theories build their arguments on a set of simplifying assumptions about the world. These assumptions often sacrifice some less important aspects of reality in order to focus on the economic mechanisms of interest. But in the case of the Invisible Hand, the theoretical preconditions contradict several central features of the economy.

For one thing, markets are only guaranteed to prevent waste if the economy runs on "perfect competition": individual sellers compete by cutting prices, individual buyers compete by raising price offers, and nobody holds concentrated economic power. But today's giant corporations hardly match this description. Coke and Pepsi compete with advertising rather than price cuts. The oil companies keep prices high enough to register massive profits every year. Employers coordinate the pay and benefits they offer to avoid bidding up compensation. Workers, in turn, marshal their own forces via unionization—another departure from perfect competition.

Indeed, the jargon of "perfect competition" overlooks the fact that property ownership itself confers disproportionate economic power. "In the competitive model," orthodox economist Paul Samuelson commented, "it makes no difference whether capital hires labor or the other way around." He argued that given perfect competition among workers and among capitalists, wages and profits would remain the same regardless of who does the hiring. But unemployment—a persistent feature of market-driven economies—makes job loss very costly to workers. The sting my boss feels when I "fire" him by quitting my job hardly equals the setback I experience when he fires me.

## Perfect Information?

In addition, the grip of the Invisible Hand is only sure if all buyers and sellers have "perfect information" about the present and future state of markets. In the present, this implies consumers know exactly what they are buying—an assumption hard to swallow in these days of leaky breast implants and chicken à la Salmonella. Employers must know exactly what skills workers have and how hard they will work—suppositions any real-life manager would laugh at.

Perfect information also means sellers can always sniff out unsatisfied demands, and buyers can detect any excess supplies of goods. Orthodox economists rely on the metaphor of an omnipresent "auctioneer" who is always calling out prices so all buyers and sellers can find mutually agreeable prices and consummate every possible sale. But in the actual economy, the auctioneer is nowhere to be found, and markets are plagued by surpluses and shortages.

Perfect information about the future is even harder to come by. For example, a company decides whether or not to build a new plant based on whether it expects sales to rise. But predicting future demand is a tricky matter. One reason is that people may save money today in order to buy (demand) goods and services in the future. The problem comes in predicting when. As economist John Maynard Keynes observed in 1934, "An act of individual saving means—so to speak—a decision not to have dinner today. But it does not necessitate a decision to have dinner or to buy a pair of boots a week hence...or to consume any specified thing at any specified date. Thus it depresses the business of preparing today's dinner without stimulating the business of making ready for some future act of consumption." Keynes concluded that far from curtailing waste, free markets gave rise to the colossal waste of human and economic resources that was the Great Depression—in part because of this type of uncertainty about the future.

## Free Lunch

The dexterity of the Invisible Hand also depends on the principle that "You only get what you pay for." This "no free lunch" principle seems at first glance a reasonable description of the economy. But major exceptions arise. One is what economists call "externalities"—economic transactions that take place outside the market. Consider a hospital that dumps syringes at sea. In effect, the hospital gets a free lunch by passing the costs of waste disposal on to the rest of us. Because no market exists where the right to dump is bought and sold, free markets do nothing to compel the hospital to bear the costs of dumping—which is why the government must step in.

Public goods such as sewer systems also violate the "no free lunch" rule. Once the sewer system is in place, everyone shares in the benefits of the waste disposal, regardless of whether or not they helped pay for it. Suppose sewer systems were sold in a free market, in which each person had the opportunity to buy an individual share. Then any sensible, self-interested consumer would hold back from buying his or her fair share—and wait for others to provide the service. This irrational situation would persist unless consumers could somehow collectively agree on how extensive a sewer system to produce—once more bringing government into the picture.

Most orthodox economists claim that the list of externalities and public goods in the economy is short and easily addressed. Liberals and radicals, on the other hand, offer a long list: for example, public goods include education, health care, and decent public transportation—all in short supply in our society.

Because real markets deviate from the ideal markets envisioned in the theory of the Invisible Hand, they give us both inequality and waste. But if the theory is so far off the mark, why do mainstream economists and policymakers place so much stock in it? They fundamentally believe the profit motive is the best guide for the economy. If you believe that "What's good for General Motors is good for the country," the Invisible Hand theory can seem quite reasonable. Business interests, government, and the media constantly reinforce this belief, and reward those who can dress it up in theoretical terms. As long as capital remains the dominant force in society, the Invisible Hand will maintain its grip on the hearts and minds of us all. ❑

Article 1.3

# FREEDOM, EQUITY, AND EFFICIENCY
*Contrasting Views of Labor Market Competition*

**BY ALEJANDRO REUSS**
April 2012

The basic world-view of neoclassical economists is that, in markets, people engage voluntarily in exchanges with each other, and that this means market exchanges leave both parties better off. If someone cannot be forced to make a trade, they will only do so if it leaves them at least a little better off than they would have been otherwise. Left to their own devices, people will find and exhaust all the possibilities for trades that boost the overall social well-being. Policies that interfere with people's ability to make voluntary trades, then, can only subtract from the well-being of society as a whole.

The neoclassical narrative depends on many (often unspoken) *assumptions*. Individuals must be rational and self-interested. The assumption of "rationality" means they must act in ways that further their objectives, whatever these objectives may be. The assumption of "self-interest" means that, in making decisions, they must only take into account benefits and costs to themselves. They must have perfect information about all factors (past, present, and future) that could affect their decisions. Their actions must not affect any "third parties" (anyone other than those directly involved in the exchange and agreeing to its terms). There must be many buyers and sellers, so that no single buyer or seller (and no group of buyers or sellers colluding together) can impose the prices they want. Several other assumptions may also be important.

## The Neoclassical View

Implicitly, the neoclassical story appeals to ideas about freedom, equity (fairness), and efficiency. Very few people would say they are against any of these virtues, but different people embrace different definitions. Different people, for example, have different ideas about what people should have the freedom to do, and what "freedoms" would impinge on the freedoms, rights, or well-being of others. So really the issue is, when neoclassical economists say that unregulated market competition is desirable, for example, as a matter, of "freedom," what view of freedom are they basing this on?

### Freedom

By "freedom," neoclassical economists mean freedom from force or threat of force. They would recognize that someone making an exchange when threatened with violence—when confronted with "an offer they can't refuse," in the *Godfather* sense of that phrase—is not really engaging in a voluntary transaction. That person could very well make an exchange leaving them worse off than they would have been otherwise (except that they may have saved their own neck). On the other hand, suppose a person is faced only with very undesirable alternatives to engaging in a trade. Suppose they have "no choice" but to accept a job, because the alternative is to starve. Neoclassical economists would point out that these circumstances are not of the potential employer's making. It is quite unlike, in their view, conditions that are directly imposed by the other party (like having a gun held to one's head). If the impoverished worker accepts a job offer, even at a very low wage or under very bad working conditions, the neoclassical economist would argue that this is evidence that he or she really is made better off by the exchange. Restricting his or her freedom to engage in this exchange, in the neoclassical view, only makes him or her worse off.

## Equity

Neoclassical economists argue that restrictions on market competition can unfairly benefit some market participants (buyers or sellers) or potential market participants at the expense of others. This kind of equity concern enters into neoclassical theory in several ways:

First, restrictions on competition may affect the ability of different people (or firms) to participate in a market—to offer what they have for sale or to bid on what others offer for sale. Suppose that the government issues special licenses to some people or firms that permit them to engage in a certain trade, like driving a taxi, while denying such licenses to others. (Such policies create "barriers to entry," in the language of neoclassical economics.) Such restrictions are, in the neoclassical view, unfair to the unlucky (or less-influential) individuals or firms who do not receive licenses and so are locked out of the market.

Second, restrictions may affect the ability of different people to use whatever advantage they may have, to compete in a market. A price floor, for example, prevents lower-cost sellers from using their cost advantage (their willingness to accept a lower price) to compete in the market. In the neoclassical view, this favors higher-cost sellers at the expense of their lower-cost competitors.

Third, restrictions may affect the ability of sellers to fetch the highest price they can, constrained only by competition from other sellers, and of buyers to pay the lowest price they can, constrained only by bidding from other buyers. A price floor, by restricting producers from competing on price (preventing any from offering prices below the floor), may favor producers in general at the expense of consumers. By the same token, a price ceiling (a maximum legal price) may favor consumers at the expense of producers.

## Efficiency

In the neoclassical view, a resource is used "efficiently" as long as the benefit from using that resource is greater than the cost. Let's think about a company—say, an auto company—that has to decide how many machines to rent or how many workers to hire for its operations. It will consider how many extra cars it can produce if it rents one additional machine, or hires one additional worker. The company will figure out how much income it will get from the sale of those additional cars. That is, it will multiply the number of additional cars by the price it will get per car. Ultimately, it will compare this extra income against the rental cost paid for the machine, or the wage paid to the worker. The company will rent a machine, or hire a worker, as long as the extra income it gets is more than the additional cost it has to pay.

In the neoclassical view, this is "efficient" not only from the standpoint of the company, but from the standpoint of society as a whole. If the cost of using an extra machine or hiring an extra worker is less than value of the extra cars produced, the use of the machine or worker is also "efficient" from the standpoint of society as a whole.

There's just one more problem. In the neoclassical view, for private actors to make decisions that are also "efficient" form the standpoint of society as a whole, the prices they base their decisions on have to be the *right* prices. That is, each price has to reflect the true cost of a good to society as a whole. So how do we know, in this view, what is the "right price"?

## The "Right" Wage

Let's look at an example using, in the language of neoclassical economics, the "price of labor" (or wage). Suppose that the going wage in a certain place is $20 per hour. According to neoclassical economists, a company will hire a worker as long as the extra benefit it gets from each extra hour of labor (the extra units produced times the price the company gets per unit) is at least as much as the additional cost it pays for that extra hour of labor ($20). Suppose, however, that the wage was only this high because there were barriers to competition in the labor market. If the wage without barriers would have only been, say, $10, then a company would hire an extra worker as long as the extra benefit it got from each extra hour of labor was at least $10 per hour.

How do we know whether the "right" wage is $20 or $10? In the view of neoclassical economists, the right wage—like any other right price—reflects the true cost to society of the good involved (here, an hour of labor). The cost of labor is whatever pains the worker endures as a result of that hour of work. This includes having to show up for work, when one might prefer to be someone else, having to follow the employer's orders, when one would rather be "doing one's own thing," putting up with the conditions at work, which could be dangerous, unhealthy, or unpleasant, and so on. It is competition in the labor market that makes workers reveal what they really require to compensate them for the burdens of labor.

If the price of labor, due to barriers to labor-market competition, is "too high," then employers will use "too little" labor. If the wage is $20, due to barriers, then employers will not hire an extra hour of labor unless it results in the production of at least $20 of additional goods. As a result of the inflated price of labor, society will have turned its back on who-knows-how-many opportunities to get between $10 and $20 of goods at a true cost of $10 worth of labor. In other words, wages that are inflated by barriers to competition result in an "inefficient" use of resources.

## Critiques of the Neoclassical View

Economists associated with different schools of thought may use normative concepts like "freedom," "equity," or "efficiency," but mean something very different by these ideas than what neoclassical economists mean. (Some may choose not to use these terms, and instead invoke other normative concepts, like "justice," "equality," "the good life," and so on.) Here, however, we will focus on contrasts with the neoclassical views of freedom, equity, and efficiency described above.

## Freedom

Neoclassical economists emphasize workers' freedom of choice to accept low wages, long hours, bad working conditions, and so on. Workers would not accept those conditions, they argue, unless doing so would leave them better off than they would be otherwise. In this view, institutions like unions or policies like minimum-wage laws interfere with workers' freedom to make a deal that would leave them better off.

Many liberal and almost all radical economists, on the other hand, emphasize how the conditions that an individual will "freely" accept depend on the alternatives available to them. If the only alternative is to starve in the street, most people would work even very long hours, under very bad conditions, for very low pay. Instead of seeing these workers as having "freely" accepted such agreements, however, one could view them as lacking any real freedom to *refuse* these conditions.

Union contracts, minimum-wage laws, and other restraints on competition between workers do, indeed, restrict each individual worker's "freedom" to accept lower wages, worse conditions, and so on, just as neoclassical economists argue. However, this view ignores the benefit to each worker—that these institutions also *protect* each worker from other workers undercutting him or her. Instead of seeing restraints on labor competition as robbing workers of the freedom to accept lower wages or worse conditions, one can instead see them as giving workers the freedom to demand higher wages or better conditions.

## Equity

Barriers to labor-market competition, neoclassical economists argue, favor some workers at the expense of others and workers at the expense of consumers. An alternative view is that restraints on labor-market competition allow workers to get a better deal (higher pay, better conditions, etc.) from employers. The absence of these restraints, on the other hand, may result in higher profits for employers while relegating workers to lower pay and worse conditions. Which outcome one prefers depends on how one values benefits to one group of people (workers) compared to benefits to another (employers).

There are several reasons that someone might favor the interests of workers over those of employers, and therefore approve of changes that benefit workers even if these benefits come at the expense of employers:

1. Ideas of "fairness" based on social "custom" or "convention." In most societies where people work for wages, there are evolving ideas about what is a "fair" wage or "decent" living. Partly, such ideas may be based on what people have become accustomed to in the past. Partly, they may reflect expectations that conditions of life will improve over time, and especially from one generation to the next.

2. Commitment to greater economic and social equality. People who get most of their income from property (ownership of businesses, land or buildings, or financial wealth) are likely to be at the top of the income ladder. Most of the people at the bottom or in the middle, on the other hand, get most of their income from work. Therefore, changes that benefit workers as a group (at the expense of employers) tend to bring about a more equal distribution of income in society.

3. Ideas about who creates and deserves to keep society's wealth. Some "radical" economists argue that labor is the source of all new wealth produced in society. Owners of property take a piece of this wealth by controlling things (like farms, mines, factories, etc.) that everyone else needs in order to work and live. In this view, there is no such thing as a "fair" distribution of income between workers and employers, since the employing class exists only by virtue of taking part of what workers produce.

Much of the history of labor movements around the world centers on attempts to *restrain* competition between workers, to keep workers from undercutting each other on the wages or conditions they will accept, and therefore to benefit workers as a group. Unions, for example, are compacts by which each member agrees *not* to accept a lower wage or worse conditions than the other members. Unions also set conditions on hours, benefits, and conditions of work. No individual can bargain a lower wage or worse conditions, in order to get a job, and thereby force other workers to do the same. Labor legislation like the minimum-wage laws, maximum hours (or overtime) laws, and laws regulating labor conditions, likewise, all restrain competition between workers.

## Efficiency

We have already described one concept of efficiency used by neoclassical economists: The key idea is that resources are used if (and only if) the benefit to society is greater than the cost. Neoclassical economists also use another concept of efficiency: An efficient condition is one in which nobody can be made better off without making someone worse off. This definition, pioneered by the Italian neoclassical economist Vilfredo Pareto, is known as "Pareto efficiency." The two definitions are connected: If resources were being wasted (used inefficiently), they could be used to make someone better off without making anyone worse off.

Neoclassical economists call a *change* that makes some people better off without making anyone worse off a "Pareto improvement." There are very few changes in public policies, however, that make some people better off while literally making nobody worse off. Most policy changes, potentially affecting millions of people, make some people better off and others worse off. In these cases, neoclassical economists apply what they call the "compensation test." They compare the benefits to the "winners" from some change in public policy to the losses to the "losers." If the total gains are greater than the total losses, neoclassical economists argue, the winners could compensate the losers—and leave everyone at least a little better off.

In most cases where there are both winners and losers due to a change in public policy, however, the winners do not actually compensate the losers. These are not, then, actual efficiency improvements in the sense that some people are made better off while nobody is made worse off. Restraints on labor-market competition, for example, may benefit workers at the expense of their employers. (Eliminating such policies, meanwhile, may have the opposite effect.)

Judging whether these changes are for the better, then, involves weighing the benefits to some people against the losses to others. How one resolves such an issue depends on one's normative ideas, or values, about whose interests should take precedence. In other words—which side are you on? ❏

Article 1.4

# SHARING THE WEALTH OF THE COMMONS

**BY PETER BARNES**
*November/December 2004*

We're all familiar with private wealth, even if we don't have much. Economists and the media celebrate it every day. But there's another trove of wealth we barely notice: our common wealth.

Each of us is the beneficiary of a vast inheritance. This common wealth includes our air and water, habitats and ecosystems, languages and cultures, science and technologies, political and monetary systems, and quite a bit more. To say we share this inheritance doesn't mean we can call a broker and sell our shares tomorrow. It does mean we're responsible for the commons and entitled to any income it generates. Both the responsibility and the entitlement are ours by birth. They're part of the obligation each generation owes to the next, and each living human owes to other beings.

At present, however, our economic system scarcely recognizes the commons. This omission causes two major tragedies: ceaseless destruction of nature and widening inequality among humans. Nature gets destroyed because no one's unequivocally responsible for protecting it. Inequality widens because private wealth concentrates while common wealth shrinks.

The great challenges for the 21st century are, first of all, to make the commons visible; second, to give it proper reverence; and third, to translate that reverence into property rights and legal institutions that are on a par with those supporting private property. If we do this, we can avert the twin tragedies currently built into our market-driven system.

## Defining the Commons

What exactly is the commons? Here is a workable definition: The commons includes all the assets we inherit together and are morally obligated to pass on, undiminished, to future generations.

This definition is a practical one. It designates a set of assets that have three specific characteristics: they're (1) inherited, (2) shared, and (3) worthy of long-term preservation. Usually it's obvious whether an asset has these characteristics or not.

At the same time, the definition is broad. It encompasses assets that are natural as well as social, intangible as well as tangible, small as well as large. It also introduces a moral factor that is absent from other economic definitions: it requires us to consider whether an asset is worthy of long-term preservation. At present, capitalism has no interest in this question. If an asset is likely to yield a competitive return to capital, it's kept alive; if not, it's destroyed or allowed to run down. Assets in the commons, by contrast, are meant to be preserved regardless of their return.

This definition sorts all economic assets into two baskets, the market and the commons. In the market basket are those assets we want to own privately and manage for profit. In the commons basket are the assets we want to hold in common and manage for long-term preservation. These baskets then are, or ought to be, the yin and yang of economic activity; each should enhance and contain the other. The role of the state should be to maintain a healthy balance between them.

## The Value of the Commons

For most of human existence, the commons supplied everyone's food, water, fuel, and medicines. People hunted, fished, gathered fruits and herbs, collected firewood and building materials, and grazed their animals in common lands and waters. In other words, the commons was the source of basic sustenance. This is still true today in many parts of the world, and even in San Francisco, where I live, cash-poor people fish in the bay not for sport, but for food.

Though sustenance in the industrialized world now flows mostly through markets, the commons remains hugely valuable. It's the source of all natural resources and nature's many replenishing services. Water, air, DNA, seeds, topsoil, minerals, the protective ozone layer, the atmosphere's climate regulation, and much more, are gifts of nature to us all.

Just as crucially, the commons is our ultimate waste sink. It recycles water, oxygen, carbon, and everything else we excrete, exhale, or throw away. It's the place we store, or try to store, the residues of our industrial system.

The commons also holds humanity's vast accumulation of knowledge, art, and thought. As Isaac Newton said, "If I have seen further it is by standing on the shoulders of giants." So, too, the legal, political, and economic institutions we inherit—even the market itself—were built by the efforts of millions. Without these gifts we'd be hugely poorer than we are today.

To be sure, thinking of these natural and social inheritances primarily as economic assets is a limited way of viewing them. I deeply believe they are much more than that. But if treating portions of the commons as economic assets can help us conserve them, it's surely worth doing so.

How much might the commons be worth in monetary terms? It's relatively easy to put a dollar value on private assets. Accountants and appraisers do it every day, aided by the fact that private assets are regularly traded for money.

This isn't the case with most shared assets. How much is clean air, an intact wetlands, or Darwin's

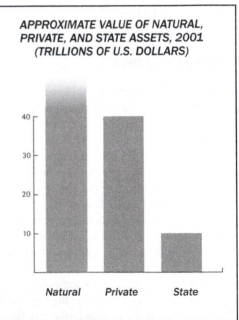

**APPROXIMATE VALUE OF NATURAL, PRIVATE, AND STATE ASSETS, 2001 (TRILLIONS OF U.S. DOLLARS)**

40

30

20

10

Natural     Private     State

theory of evolution worth in dollar terms? Clearly, many shared inheritances are simply priceless. Others are potentially quantifiable, but there's no current market for them. Fortunately, economists have developed methods to quantify the value of things that aren't traded, so it's possible to estimate the value of the "priceable" part of the commons within an order of magnitude. The surprising conclusion that emerges from numerous studies is that the wealth we share is worth more than the wealth we own privately.

This fact bears repeating. Even though much of the commons can't be valued in monetary terms, the parts that can be valued are worth more than all private assets combined.

It's worth noting that these estimates understate the gap between common and private assets because a significant portion of the value attributed to private wealth is in fact an appropriation of common wealth. If this mislabeled portion was subtracted from private wealth and added to common wealth, the gap between the two would widen further.

Two examples will make this point clear. Suppose you buy a house for $200,000 and, without improving it, sell it a few years later for $300,000. You pay off the mortgage and walk away with a pile of cash. But what caused the house to rise in value? It wasn't anything you did. Rather, it was the fact that your neighborhood became more popular, likely a result of the efforts of community members, improvements in public services, and similar factors.

Or consider another fount of private wealth, the social invention and public expansion of the stock market. Suppose you start a business that goes "public" through an offering of stock. Within a few years, you're able to sell your stock for a spectacular capital gain.

Much of this gain is a social creation, the result of centuries of monetary-system evolution, laws and regulations, and whole industries devoted to accounting, sharing information, and trading stocks. What's more, there's a direct correlation between the scale and quality of the stock market as an institution and the size of the private gain. You'll fetch a higher price if you sell into a market of millions than into a market of two. Similarly, you'll gain more if transaction costs are low and trust in public information is high. Thus, stock that's traded on a regulated exchange sells for a higher multiple of earnings than unlisted stock. This socially created premium can account for 30% of the stock's value. If you're the lucky seller, you'll reap that extra cash—in no way thanks to anything you did as an individual.

Real estate gains and the stock market's social premium are just two instances of common assets contributing to private gain. Still, most rich people would like us to think it's their extraordinary talent, hard work, and risk-taking that create their well-deserved wealth. That's like saying a flower's beauty is due solely to its own efforts, owing nothing to nutrients in the soil, energy from the sun, water from the aquifer, or the activity of bees.

## The Great Commons Giveaway

That we inherit a trove of common wealth is the good news. The bad news, alas, is that our inheritance is being grossly mismanaged. As a recent report by the advocacy group Friends of the Commons concludes, "Maintenance of the commons is terrible, theft is rampant, and rents often aren't collected. To put it bluntly, our common wealth—and our children's—is being squandered. We are all poorer as a result."

Examples of commons mismanagement include the handout of broadcast spectrum to media conglomerates, the giveaway of pollution rights to polluters, the extension of copyrights to entertainment companies, the patenting of seeds and genes, the privatization of water, and the relentless destruction of habitat, wildlife, and ecosystems.

This mismanagement, though currently extreme, is not new. For over 200 years, the market has been devouring the commons in two ways. With one hand, the market takes valuable stuff from the commons and privatizes it. This is called "enclosure." With the other hand, the market dumps bad stuff into the commons and says, "It's your problem." This is called "externalizing." Much that is called economic growth today is actually a form of cannibalization in which the market diminishes the commons that ultimately sustains it.

Enclosure—the taking of good stuff from the commons—at first meant privatization of land by the gentry. Today it means privatization of many common assets by corporations. Either way, it means that what once belonged to everyone now belongs to a few.

Enclosure is usually justified in the name of efficiency. And sometimes, though not always, it does result in efficiency gains. But what also results from enclosure is the impoverishment of those who lose access to the commons, and the enrichment of those who take title to it. In other words, enclosure widens the gap between those with income-producing property and those without.

Externalizing—the dumping of bad stuff into the commons—is an automatic behavior pattern of profit-maximizing corporations: if they can avoid any out-of-pocket costs, they will. If workers, taxpayers, anyone downwind, future generations, or nature have to absorb added costs, so be it.

For decades, economists have agreed we'd be better served if businesses "internalized" their externalities—that is, paid in real time the costs they now shift to the commons. The reason this doesn't happen is that there's no one to set prices and collect them. Unlike private wealth, the commons lacks property rights and institutions to represent it in the marketplace.

The seeds of such institutions, however, are starting to emerge. Consider one of the environmental protection tools the U.S. currently uses, pollution trading. So-called cap-and-trade programs put a cap on total pollution, then grant portions of the total, via permits, to each polluting firm. Companies may buy other firms' permits if they want to pollute more than their allotment allows, or sell unused permits if they manage to pollute less. Such programs are generally supported by business because they allow polluters to find the cheapest ways to reduce pollution.

Public discussion of cap-and-trade programs has focused exclusively on their trading features. What's been overlooked is how they give away common wealth to polluters.

To date, all cap-and-trade programs have begun by giving pollution rights to existing polluters for free. This treats polluters as if they own our sky and rivers. It means that future polluters will have to pay old polluters for the scarce—hence valuable—right to dump wastes into nature. Imagine that: because a corporation polluted in the past, it gets free income forever! And, because ultimately we'll all pay for limited pollution via higher prices, this amounts to an enormous transfer of wealth—trillions of dollars—to shareholders of historically polluting corporations.

In theory, though, there is no reason that the initial pollution rights should not reside with the public. Clean air and the atmosphere's capacity to absorb pollutants are "wealth" that belongs to everyone. Hence, when polluters use up these parts of the commons, they should pay the public—not the other way around.

## Taking the Commons Back

How can we correct the system omission that permits, and indeed promotes, destruction of nature and ever-widening inequality among humans? The answer lies in building a new sector of the economy whose clear legal mission is to preserve shared inheritances for everyone. Just as the market is populated by profit-maximizing corporations, so this new sector would be populated by asset-preserving trusts.

Here a brief description of trusts may be helpful. The trust is a private institution that's even older than the corporation. The essence of a trust is a fiduciary relationship. A trust holds and manages property for another person or for many other people. A simple example is a trust set up by a grandparent to pay for a grandchild's education. Other trusts include pension funds, charitable foundations, and university endowments. There are also hundreds of trusts in America, like the Nature Conservancy and the Trust for Public Land, that own land or conservation easements in perpetuity.

If we were to design an institution to protect pieces of the commons, we couldn't do much better than a trust. The goal of commons management, after all, is to preserve assets and deliver benefits to broad classes of beneficiaries. That's what trusts do, and it's not rocket science.

Over centuries, several principles of trust management have evolved.

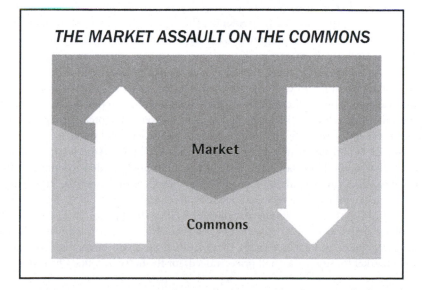

### THE MARKET ASSAULT ON THE COMMONS

Market

Commons

These include:

- Trustees have a fiduciary responsibility to beneficiaries. If a trustee fails in this obligation, he or she can be removed and penalized.
- Trustees must preserve the original asset. It's okay to spend income, but don't invade the principal.
- Trustees must assure transparency. Information about money flows should be readily available to beneficiaries.

Trusts in the new commons sector would be endowed with rights comparable to those of corporations. Their trustees would take binding oaths of office and, like judges, serve long terms. Though protecting common assets would be their primary job, they would also distribute income from those assets to beneficiaries. These beneficiaries would include all citizens within a jurisdiction, large classes of citizens (children, the elderly), and/or agencies serving common purposes such as public transit or ecological restoration. When distributing income to individuals, the allocation formula would be one person, one share. The right to receive commons income would be a nontransferable birthright, not a property right that could be traded.

Fortuitously, a working model of such a trust already exists: the Alaska Permanent Fund. When oil drilling on the North Slope began in the 1970s, Gov. Jay Hammond, a Republican, proposed that 25% of the state's royalties be placed in a mutual fund to be invested on behalf of Alaska's citizens. Voters approved in a referendum. Since then, the Alaska Permanent Fund has grown to over $28 billion, and Alaskans have received roughly $22,000 apiece in dividends. In 2003 the per capita dividend was $1,107; a family of four received $4,428.

What Alaska did with its oil can be replicated for other gifts of nature. For example, we could create a nationwide Sky Trust to stabilize the climate for future generations. The trust would restrict emissions of heat-trapping gases and sell a declining number of emission permits to polluters. The income would be returned to U.S. residents in equal yearly dividends, thus reversing the wealth transfer built into current cap-and-trade programs. Instead of everyone paying historic polluters, polluters would pay all of us.

Just as a Sky Trust could represent our equity in the natural commons, a Public Stock Trust could embody our equity in the social commons. Such a trust would capture some of the socially created stock-market premium that currently flows only to shareholders and their investment bankers. As noted earlier, this premium is sizeable—roughly 30% of the value of publicly traded stock. A simple way to share it would be to create a giant mutual fund—call it the American Permanent Fund—that would hold, say, 10% of the shares of publicly traded companies. This mutual fund, in turn, would be owned by all Americans on a one share per person basis (perhaps linked to their Social Security accounts).

To build up the fund without precipitating a fall in share prices, companies would contribute shares at the rate of, say, 1% per year. The contributions would be the price companies pay for the benefits they derive from a commons asset, the large, trusted market for stock—a small price, indeed, for the hefty benefits. Over time, the mutual fund would assure that when the economy grows, everyone benefits. The top 5% would still own more than the bottom 90%, but at least every American would have some property income, and a slightly larger slice of our economic pie.

## Sharing the Wealth

The perpetuation of inequality is built into the current design of capitalism. Because of the skewed distribution of private wealth, a small self-perpetuating minority receives a disproportionate share of America's nonlabor income.

Tom Paine had something to say about this. In his essay "Agrarian Justice," written in 1790, he argued that, because enclosure of the commons had separated so many people from their primary source of sustenance, it was necessary to create a functional equivalent of the commons in the form of a National Fund. Here is how he put it:

> There are two kinds of property. Firstly, natural property, or that which comes to us from the Creator of the universe—such as the earth, air, water. Secondly, artificial or acquired property—the invention of men. In the latter, equality is impossible; for to distribute it equally, it would be necessary that all should have contributed in the same proportion, which can never be the case …. Equality of natural property is different. Every individual in the world is born with legitimate claims on this property, or its equivalent.

Enclosure of the commons, he went on, was necessary to improve the efficiency of cultivation. But:

> The landed monopoly that began with [enclosure] has produced the greatest evil. It has dispossessed more than half the inhabitants of every nation of their natural inheritance, without providing for them, as ought to have been done, an indemnification for that loss, and has thereby created a species of poverty and wretchedness that did not exist before.

The appropriate compensation for loss of the commons, Paine said, was a national fund financed by rents paid by land owners. Out of this fund, every person reaching age 21 would get 15 pounds a year, and every person over 50 would receive an additional 10 pounds. (Think of Social Security, financed by commons rents instead of payroll taxes.)

## A Progressive Offensive

Paine's vision, allowing for inflation and new forms of enclosure, could not be more timely today. Surely from our vast common inheritance—not just the land, but the atmosphere, the broadcast spectrum, our mineral resources, our threatened habitats and water supplies—enough rent can be collected to pay every American over age 21 a modest annual dividend, and every person reaching 21 a small start-up inheritance.

Such a proposal may seem utopian. In today's political climate, perhaps it is. But consider this. About 20 years ago, right-wing think tanks laid out a bold agenda.

They called for lowering taxes on private wealth, privatizing much of government, and deregulating industry. Amazingly, this radical agenda has largely been achieved.

It's time for progressives to mount an equally bold offensive. The old shibboleths—let's gin up the economy, create jobs, and expand government programs—no longer excite. We need to talk about fixing the economy, not just growing it; about income for everyone, not just jobs; about nurturing ecosystems, cultures, and communities, not just our individual selves. More broadly, we need to celebrate the commons as an essential counterpoise to the market.

Unfortunately, many progressives have viewed the state as the only possible counterpoise to the market. The trouble is, the state has been captured by corporations. This capture isn't accidental or temporary; it's structural and long-term.

This doesn't mean progressives can't occasionally recapture the state. We've done so before and will do so again. It does mean that progressive control of the state is the exception, not the norm; in due course, corporate capture will resume. It follows that if we want lasting fixes to capitalism's tragic flaws, we must use our brief moments of political ascendancy to build institutions that endure.

Programs that rely on taxes, appropriations, or regulations are inherently transitory; they get weakened or repealed when political power shifts. By contrast, institutions that are self-perpetuating and have broad constituencies are likely to last. (It also helps if they mail out checks periodically.) This was the genius of Social Security, which has survived—indeed grown—through numerous Republican administrations.

If progressives are smart, we'll use our next New Deal to create common property trusts that include all Americans as beneficiaries. These trusts will then be to the 21st century what social insurance was to the 20th: sturdy pillars of shared responsibility and entitlement. Through them, the commons will be a source of sustenance for all, as it was before enclosure. Life-long income will be linked to generations-long ecological health. Isn't that a future most Americans would welcome? ❑

*Article 1.5*

# WHAT DOES IT MEAN TO BE "BETTER OFF"?

*Taking stock of how U.S. society has progressed or faltered over the last forty years.*

## BY ZOE SHERMAN
*November/December 2014*

In 1980, Ronald Reagan, trying to defeat Jimmy Carter's bid for a second term as president, asked, "Are you better off than you were four years ago?" A conservative turn in American politics was already underway and, campaigning on that question, Reagan rode the wave into the presidency. Forty years into the political epoch he symbolizes, and forty years into this magazine's history, we might well echo Reagan's question: Are you better off than you were forty years ago?

It is a deceptively simple question. What would it mean to be better off? Probably a lot of good things and a lot of bad things have happened to you in forty years (or however many of those years you've been alive) and to decide whether you are better off you would have to do some weighing. For many of us the final answer would be, "well, yes and no..." For any one person many of the then-vs.-now differences are largely a matter of the life cycle—maybe you were a child decades ago and an adult now. It really makes more sense to ask whether we as a society are better off that we were forty years ago.

The well-being of a society cannot be measured in a single dimension any more than a single person's well-being can. Assessments of our national well-being often begin—and too often end—with gross domestic product (GDP). Per capita GDP basically answers the question, "Are we collectively, on average, richer, as measured by the dollar value of the things we produce and sell to one another?" (This includes the government's provision of goods and services, even if they are not really "sold.")

Not only is GDP limited to measuring just one dimension of well-being—it doesn't even measure that dimension all that well. It fails to count the work we do for one another at home or in other non-monetized ways. It gives us only an aggregate with no information about how access to all those goods and services is distributed. And goods and bads get added together so long as they cost money and therefore generate income for someone—that is, a thousand dollars spent on cigarettes and treatments for emphysema add just as much to GDP as a thousand dollars spent on healthy foods and preventive medicine.

We'll certainly want to go beyond just GDP per capita, as we take a tour through various dimensions of well-being and take stock of how we have progressed or faltered since the first issue of this magazine came out in 1974.

## Income and Stuff

Though we know from the outset that we will not stop here, we may as well start in the traditional starting place: Changes in our national income, taking into account population growth and inflation. Real per capita GDP was $25,427 in 1974 (in 2009 U.S. dollars) and now it is almost double that at $49,810. A lot of that GDP growth represents more of the good stuff we already had in 1974 or cool, well-being-enhancing new stuff that we have now but didn't have then. I really like having a dishwasher and enough dishes that we don't have to wash the plates and forks after every meal (more of the already-invented good stuff). I am also awfully fond of my computer, Internet service, DVDs, and streaming video (cool new stuff).

But some of the higher production/higher income measured by GDP represents not-so-great things. Longer car commutes, for example, are costly and contribute to GDP through spending on gasoline, car repairs and replacement, and purchases of more cars per household. But long car commutes add nothing and likely subtract from the commuters' well-being. They also add pollutants to the air that affect us all.

Even if we subtract out the bads, the goods themselves can get to be too much of a good thing. Plenty of people know the experience of feeling that they are choking on stuff, crowded out of their living spaces by their belongings. Self storage ranks as the fastest growing segment of the commercial real estate industry since 1975. Self storage businesses brought in revenues of $24 billion dollars in 2013. Now, consider that the average size of a new single family home increased 57% from 1970 to the early 2000s. That means we spent $24 billion to store the things that we can't fit in our homes, even though many of our homes are bigger than ever! (See the interview with Juliet Schor in the September/October 2014 issue for a discussion of how we get trapped in this self-destructive overconsumption cycle.)

## Economic and Social Inequality

If the distribution of income had remained roughly the same over the last forty years, then the fact that per capita GDP nearly doubled would mean that everyone's income had nearly doubled. That's not what happened. Instead, those at the top of the income distribution have vastly more income than 40 years ago while those at the bottom have less. The real income of a household at the 20th percentile (above 20% of all house-holds in the income ranking) has scarcely budged since 1974—it was $20,000 and change then and is $20,000 and change now. For those below the 20th percentile, real income has fallen. The entire bottom 80% of households ranked by income now gets only 49% of the national pie, down from 57% in 1974. That means that the top 20% has gone from 43% to 51% of total income. Even within the top 20%, the distribution skews upward. Most of the income gains of the top 20% are concentrated in the top 5%; most of the gains of the top 5% are concentrated in the top 1%; most of the gains in the top 1% are concentrated in the top 0.1%.

By 1974, labor force participation rates were in the midst of a marked upward trend, driven largely by the entry of women into the paid labor force. Starting from a low of 59% in the early 1960s, the labor force participation rate passed 61% in 1974 and peaked at 67% in the late 1990s. Labor force participation has drifted back downward somewhat since then through a combination of baby boomer retirement and discouraged workers giving up on the labor force since the crisis that began in 2007, but it remains at 63%, still higher than in 1974. That means that even while more of us are participating in market work, the market is concentrating its rewards in a shrinking cabal of increasingly powerful hands.

More of us are working, but the share of national income that goes to ordinary workers is smaller. National income can be sorted into categories based on the route it takes to a person's pocket. One category of income—wages and salaries earned in return for work—is labor income. The other categories—profit, dividends, rent, interest—are all forms of income that result from owning. For many decades, the labor share of national income held fairly steady, but beginning in the mid-1970s it started falling. Economist James Heintz found that the share of the national income earned as private-business-sector wages (excluding executive compensation) fell from 58% in 1970 to 50% in 2010; the share that went to non-supervisory workers fell from 45% to 31%.

Even as hourly pay for a broad swath of people in the middle—between the 20th and 80th percentiles—has just about kept pace with inflation, the traditional tickets to the middle class have become more of a reach. Rising costs of higher education and housing have consigned many to a near-permanent state of debt peonage to maintain a tenuous grasp on middle-class social status, while others are blocked from access entirely.

While more employers now require a college degree before letting a job applicant set foot on the bottom rung of the career ladder, college tuitions have risen more than three times as fast as inflation since 1974. The total volume of outstanding student debt has passed $1 trillion—greater than even the volume of outstanding credit card debt.

Housing, too, has become more unaffordable. For white people who bought houses in the mid 20th century with the benefits of supportive government policies, a home was a secure form of both savings and shelter. (Discriminatory neighborhood redlining prevented most nonwhites from enjoying these benefits.) Within recent decades, however, home prices have risen faster than median incomes and deceptive lending practices trapped many home-buyers in unaffordable mortgages. For those who were lucky, and bought and sold at the right times, the housing bubble was a windfall. For many more, the home has become a millstone of debt and the threat of foreclose has rendered shelter uncertain.

The division of the national income pie may be more skewed, but do we all have an equal shot at finding our way into the charmed circle of plenty? The probability that a person who starts out in the bottom income quintile will make it into the top quintile has stayed remarkably constant since the mid twentieth century. A child born in the bottom quintile in 1971 had an 8.4% chance of making it to the top quintile; for a child born in 1986, the probability is 9.0%. Our national mythology notwithstanding, mobility is lower in the United States than in other comparably developed economies.

Now for some good news: although wealth and income disparities have worsened, we have made real strides in reducing disparities based on race and gender. Long-standing identity-based hierarchies have weakened, though they certainly have not disappeared. The narrowing of race and gender gaps in economic well-being owes everything to the social movements of the twentieth century. The gaps' persistence can be attributed both to differential impacts of ostensibly race- or gender-neutral policies and to our low levels of social mobility. The war on drugs and other "get tough on crime" polices really mean the mass incarceration of black men. "Welfare reform" withdrew much of whatever limited support there was for the intense labor—mostly women's—of raising children with minimal cash resources. Even as bigotry, in several forms, has lost explicit government sanction, the lack of social mobility casts the shadow of the more explicit inequities of the past longer and deeper.

Not only is income unequally distributed, it is also, for many, insecure. Having income is a good thing and helps to meet present needs. If there's some left over, present income might even help meet future needs. But confidence in future income

### Narrowing Race and Gender Gaps

The Civil Rights Movement, which achieved many of its judicial and legislative successes between 1954 (Brown v. Board of Education) and 1965 (Voting Rights Act), and the Women's Movement, whose judicial and legislative successes followed soon after (Title IX in 1972; Roe v. Wade in 1973) have reduced the role of outright, explicit discrimination. This is no small matter. Yet there are still wide gaps between white and nonwhite, especially black Americans in measures of economic well-being, and also gaps between men and women of all races.

|  | White Men | White Women | Black Men | Black Women |
|---|---|---|---|---|
| 1974 Median Income (in 2013 dollars) | 38,517 | 13,944 | 23,372 | 11,988 |
| 2013 Median Income (in 2013 dollars) | 40,122 | 23,780 | 24,855 | 20,044 |
| 1974 Unemployment rate | 3.5% | 5.1% | 7.4% | 8.8% |
| 2013 Unemployment rate | 6.2% | 5.7% | 12.9% | 11.3% |

**Sources:** Median income: Census Bureau, Current Population Survey, Table P02 (census.gov); Unemployment: Bureau of Labor Statistics (bls.gov).

The resources that would close the racial income gap are hard for individuals and families to come by. There is a strong correlation between educational attainment and future earnings, but black children on average get less from their public schools than white children get. The racial income gap has narrowed slightly between

matters to us a lot. We worry about whether we will be able to meet our needs tomorrow—and we have more reasons to worry now than ever.

Employment is a sometime thing: Workers on short-term contracts—like the majority of undergraduate college instructors who work on an adjunct basis—and the self-employed, whose income is also unpredictable, add up to 30% of the U.S. workforce with uncertain, episodic income. (See Gerald Friedman, "The Gig Economy," D&S, March/April 2014.) It is difficult to know exactly how the current level of job insecurity compares to 1974 because the Census Bureau only began systematic data collection on contingent labor in 1995. Median job tenure (years with one's current employer) has fallen for men over the past generation, though it has risen for women. Perhaps the feeling of greater insecurity is a result of men's paid work coming to resemble the precariousness of women's paid work, even while many families still think of a man's income as the mainstay.

The constant churn of a short-term-employment labor system means that for most who fall into poverty, poverty is not a permanent condition. By the mid-1970s, a decade into the War on Poverty, the poverty rate had fallen to 11%, but the reduction was not sustained. Since then, the poverty rate has fluctuated between 11% and 15% with no consistent long-term trend. Today, we are in a high poverty phase: somewhere in the neighborhood of 15% of the population is living in poverty during

1974 and now, but the median white household still has more than six times the wealth of the median nonwhite or Hispanic household. Low wealth reduces nonwhite families' ability to buy housing in better-funded public school districts or invest in college education—or in private K-12 substitutes if the public schools available to them are sub-par.

People with criminal convictions, once released, face enormous barriers to employment. For the more than one-in-six black men who have been incarcerated (a rate six times that for white men), a criminal record consigns them to the margins of the labor market. In some states, moreover, a felony conviction results in a permanent loss of voting rights and therefore the loss of one of the most powerful tools for political change.

The story for the gender gap in economic well-being is mixed. Women earn lower average incomes and suffer higher poverty rates than men (despite now graduating from college in greater numbers than men). But the female unemployment rate is, on average, lower than for men, and it has become less volatile; in the last few business-cycle downturns men have been more at risk of job loss than women.

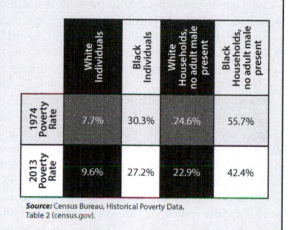

| | White Individuals | Black Individuals | White Households, no adult male present | Black Households, no adult male present |
|---|---|---|---|---|
| **1974 Poverty Rate** | 7.7% | 30.3% | 24.6% | 55.7% |
| **2013 Poverty Rate** | 9.6% | 27.2% | 22.9% | 42.4% |

**Source:** Census Bureau, Historical Poverty Data, Table 2 (census.gov).

any given month. While most spells of poverty last well under a year (6.6 months is the median), a large minority of the population cycles in and out of poverty. From January 2009 to December 2011, 31.6% of the population spent at least two consecutive months below the poverty line.

Families can fall into poverty for a number of reasons. Loss of employment, certainly, is a major cause. Another common precipitating event is the birth of a child—without guaranteed paid family leave, childbirth often means a simultaneous increase in household size (and expenses) and decrease in income. Health problems are another trigger for economic distress. Medical bills are the number-one cause of personal bankruptcy; even those who have health insurance may be unable to pay for their medical care. Insecurity is our constant companion.

## What Money Can't Buy

Many measures of our well-being cannot be viewed through the lens of income and the consumer spending it enables. A full life is not just made of purchased goods. Some of the most important gains in well-being are about the political and social gains achieved by social movements countering sexism and racism. The Civil Rights and Women's Liberation movements helped achieve an increase in economic well-being, sure, but also an increase in dignity and political power.

In the mid-1970s, marriage was still a strikingly unequal contract that subordinated wives to husbands. (Same-sex marriage was not permitted anywhere in the United States. Though there were already legal cases on the issue in the early 1970s, the courts upheld same-sex marriage bans.) The criminal laws did not grant married women a right to sexual autonomy and did little to protect their physical or emotional safety; rape laws contained exemptions in the case of husbands and domestic violence was largely hidden from view. But change was beginning. The women's movement brought attention to gender-based violence and built a network of support for survivors; the earliest rape crisis centers and emergency shelters are now marking their fortieth anniversaries, taking stock of the considerable progress we've made, and pressing on with the work that still needs to be done. By 1993, all states had changed their rape laws, withdrawing a husband's unlimited sexual access to his wife's body. In 1994, President Clinton signed into law the Violence Against Women Act, which devotes federal resources to the investigation and prosecution of violent crimes targeting women. Indeed, marriage contracts are now legally symmetrical (even if not yet symmetrical in practice)—and 33 states license marriages between any two unrelated adults, regardless of sex.

Not only are women safer at home than we were forty years ago, we have also claimed larger roles outside the home. Amendments made in 1972 to the Civil Rights Act expanded legal prohibitions on sex discrimination, including the Title IX provision prohibiting educational institutions receiving federal financial assistance from discriminating on the basis of sex. Protections against workplace discrimination are also stronger—the term "sexual harassment," unknown in 1974, is now recognized as a form of discrimination that can carry serious legal consequences. In the political arena, the number of women in Congress has more than tripled since the mid-seventies. Prior to 1974, only four women had ever served as state governors. Since then, 32 more women have held that office.

Important work combating racial discrimination was also underway forty years ago. The Equal Employment Opportunity Commission, responsible for enforcing the Civil Rights Act in the workplace, was not yet a decade old in 1974, still early in the process of setting legal precedent for documenting and opposing workplace discrimination, including the disguised discrimination of disparate impact (when a seemingly neutral rule disproportionately affects members of a protected group). The battle to make banks' mortgage lending data public was won in the mid-1970s, which then allowed organized (and ongoing) opposition to the "redlining" that the publicized data revealed. Twenty years after Brown v. Board of Education prohibited explicit, legally mandated school segregation, education activists in the mid-1970s pushed governments to take a more proactive role in school integration, albeit with mixed and in many places only temporary results.

## A Time for Every Matter

The good life for most of us means not just money to buy the stuff we need, but also plenty of time off the job to participate in social and civic life and to rest. The inequities of the labor market have divided us into two categories—the overworked and the underemployed. For those with consistent employment, the work is often too much work. Even as output per worker hour rises—meaning that, as a society we could increase our material standard of living while holding leisure time steady, or hold our material standard of living steady while increasing leisure time, we have instead increased average work hours per year. Hours of paid labor per employee were about the same in 2000 as in 1973, but since more people were in the paid labor force, the average number of hours per working age person rose from 1,217 to 1,396, equivalent to a full extra month of forty-hour workweeks.

One consequence is that we have a leisure shortage. Chronic sleep deprivation has become the norm. According to a study by the National Academy of Sciences, Americans' average amount of sleep fell by 20% over the course of the 20th century. Meanwhile, the unemployed and underemployed have hours on their hands that they either spend job hunting, in the endless sequence of bureaucratic tasks necessary to access the meager benefits available through the threadbare social safety net, or idle, their unclaimed hours more a burden than a gift. The supposed benefit of unemployment—leisure time to mitigate the loss of income—is not in evidence in the subjective well-being of the unemployed, who are more likely to suffer depression and family stress.

The time crunch resulting from more hours of paid work also squeezes our ability to keep up with the necessary unpaid work at home. Sociologist Arlie Hochschild was already noting in her research during the 1980s that dual-income households were giving up leisure or letting the standards of housework and at-home caregiving slip—often a mix of both. When a stay-at-home mother goes out to work for pay and reduces her hours of home production, the household's increase in cash income gets added to GDP but the household's loss of unpaid labor time is not subtracted. Or, if she hires a housecleaning service and a babysitter, the wages earned by the mother, the housecleaner, and the babysitter all get added to GDP, but the work done by the housecleaner and babysitter are substituting for unpaid work that was already being done. Correcting for the loss of home production that has accompanied the rise in female participation in the paid labor force requires us to revise downward the increase in output over the period 1959-2004—the largest hit came between 1959 and 1972 with the withdrawal of about 500 hours of household labor per year, a reduction of almost 20%.

## Common Resources and Public Goods

Just as mothers' labor is treated by official measures as a freely available resource, so are the gifts of nature. Nature is the source of the resources our lives depend on—trace back any production process and the earth's resources are there at the origin. Nature is also the sink into which all the refuse and byproducts of our production get dumped. Environmental concerns were at the core of another one of the 1970s' mass social movements. The first Earth Day was celebrated in 1970, and the Environmental Protection Agency (EPA) was created that same year. Concerns and activism around air pollution, water pollution, and the loss of biodiversity led, over the course of the 1970s, to the Clean Air, Clean Water, and Endangered Species Acts. Since the 1970s, the harms of an automotive culture have been lessened with emissions standards, fuel-efficiency standards, and the ban on leaded gasoline. Municipal recycling programs now divert tons of materials back into the human production cycle, reducing the strains on the planet as both a source of materials and as a sink for waste products.

---

### Private Wealth, Public Squalor

Just as we are depleting the gifts of nature, we are depleting or withdrawing many of the gifts we have collectively bestowed on ourselves, our publicly provided goods. We are consuming our public infrastructure—as seen dramatically in the 2004 failure of the levies in New Orleans during Hurricane Katrina and in the 2007 collapse of a bridge in Minneapolis.

Public goods can only be sustained if we each contribute. If we don't trust one another to contribute, we each feel the need to hoard our resources privately. When we hoard our resources privately, we discourage others from contributing, and our public goods wither.

The hoarding is especially extreme at the top of the income distribution. The top marginal tax rate has fallen from 70% in the 1970s to less than 40% today. The money not put into the common kitty instead pays for private substitutes—private schools (instead of public), private clubs (instead of public parks), gated communities (instead of neighborhoods that welcome visitors), and private security to defend these private goods against the claims of those who are excluded.

---

Over the past 40 years, we have made some important gains in how we make use of the gifts of nature, but our gains are nowhere near enough. Probably the most disastrous shortcoming of all is our collective failure to maintain the atmospheric balance. Since the middle of the twentieth century, we have known that an increased concentration of carbon dioxide ($CO_2$) in the atmosphere will cause dangerous climate change. Despite that, we have continued to emit $CO_2$ at a staggering rate. Even if we were to stop tomorrow, the effects on the global climate would play out at an accelerating rate for centuries. Several of the destabilizing shifts—melting of the polar ice caps, thawing of the arctic permafrost—are only in the early stages of "positive feedback loops," in which the result of some warming triggers more warming. Rising sea levels threaten coastal cities around the world. Severe storms will continue to increase in frequency. Wider year-to-year variations in temperature and rainfall will disrupt food production.

## Looking Backward, Looking Forward

When Reagan asked, "Are you better off than you were four years ago?" he predicted that many people would say "no" and that those who answered "no" would vote for change (not necessarily the kinds of change, as it turns out, that would solve their problems). We are still in the era that Reagan helped to usher in. How is it working for us? Are we better off now, or is it time for a change?

We have seen average income rise, though not as fast as it had in the post-World War II era. Many of the most important gains we have made, moreover, are not dependent on rising average income. The achievements of the Civil Rights and Women's Movements were about dismantling barriers to full participation in a society wealthy enough that it already could provide for all. Now rising income inequality is throwing up new barriers to inclusion.

There are enough ways in which we have lost ground that it must be time for a change. Not a change back—I would not trade the real gains we've made for a return to the so-called "Golden Age" of the 1940s-1970s—but a change that can carry us forward to a world we will still want to live in forty years from now.

The environmental crisis means that continuing with business as usual would sink us soon. Salvation can only come with a turn away from the fetish of GDP growth. About 40 years ago, research began systematically documenting the failure of rising average income to keep delivering rising levels of happiness (a phenomenon known as the "Easterlin paradox," for researcher Richard Easterlin). Unorthodox economists rethought the growth imperative: E.F. Schumacher wrote Small is Beautiful and Herman Daly penned Steady-State Economics. The kingdom of Bhutan famously rejected GDP and instituted instead the measurement of Gross National Happiness. All urged a turn away from defining well-being according to money incomes.

Once a society reaches a level of income that overcomes deprivation—when nobody need go hungry or homeless, nor suffer or die from preventable disease—more income has little affect on the dimensions of well-being that have intrinsic value.

Instead we must turn toward maximizing equality. In their book *The Spirit Level*, Richard Wilkinson and Kate Pickett demonstrate how consistently the empirical evidence shows that more equal societies have better social outcomes in many dimensions: including longer life expectancy, better educational outcomes, stronger environmental protection, lower rates of incarceration, obesity, and teen pregnancy. Perhaps—after forty more years of trying and failing to find our way to well-being through more and more market activity, in a quest for more and more income, which has been distributed more and more unequally—we are finally ready to set our priorities straight. It is equality and environmental sustainability that will allow for human flourishing. ❏

*Sources:* Self Storage Association (selfstorage.org); Margot Adler, "Behind the Ever-Expanding American Dream House," National Public Radio (npr.org); U.S. Census Bureau, Current Population Survey, Tables H-1 and H-2 (census.gov); Bureau of Labor Statistics, CPI Detailed Report, Data for August 2014 (bls.gov); Case-Shiller Home Price Index (us.spindices.com); Census Bureau, Table H-8 (census.gov); Jim Tankersley, "Economic mobility hasn't changed in a half-century in America, economists declare," Washington Post, Jan. 23, 2014 (washingtonpost.com); The Equality of Opportunity Project (equality-of-opportunity.org); U.S. Census 2012 Statistical Abstract, Table 721 (census.gov); NAACP, Criminal Justice Fact Sheet (naacp.org); Ibby Caputo, "Paying the Bills One Gig at a Time," WGBH, Feb. 1, 2012 (wgbh.org); Bureau of Labor Statistics, "Employee Tenure in 2014" (bls.gov); Ashley N. Edwards, "Dynamics of Economic Well-Being: Poverty, 2009-2011," Report Number: P70-137, January 2014 (census.gov); Moms Rising, Maternity/Paternity Leave (momsrising.org); Dan Mangan, "Medical Bills Are the Biggest Cause of US Bankruptcies: Study," CNBC, June 25, 2013 (cnbc.com); Christina LaMontagne, "NerdWallet Health finds Medical Bankruptcy accounts for majority of personal bankruptcies," March 26, 2014 (nerdwallet.com); Juliet Schor, "Sustainable Consumption and Worktime Reduction," Journal of Industrial Ecology, 2005; Edward Wolff, Ajit Zacharias, and Thomas Masterson, "Long-Term Trends in the Levy Institute Measure of Economic Well-Being (LIMEW), United States, 1959-2004," Levy Economics Institute of Bard College (levyinstitute.org); Nancy Folbre, The Invisible Heart, Chapter 3: "Measuring Success" (New Press, 2001); Environmental Protection Agency, "Earth Day and EPA History" (epa.gov); Environmental Protection Agency, Laws and Executive Orders (epa.gov).

*Article 1.6*

# THE FUTURE OF WORK, LEISURE, AND CONSUMPTION

## AN INTERVIEW WITH JULIET SCHOR
*May/June 2014*

**E**conomist Juliet Schor is known worldwide for her research on the interrelated issues of work, leisure, and consumption. Her books on these themes include The Overworked American: The Unexpected Decline of Leisure, The Overspent American: Upscaling, Downshifting, and the New Consumer, *and* Plenitude: The New Economics of True Wealth *(retitled* True Wealth *for its paperback edition). She is also a professor of sociology at Boston College.* —Eds.

**DOLLARS & SENSE**: We wouldn't expect patterns of work, leisure, and consumption to change overnight, but we're now more than half a decade into a profound crisis. Obviously it's had a big impact on employment, incomes, and so forth, but do you see any lasting changes emerging?

**JULIET SCHOR**: Some of the trends that were pretty significant before the crash have abated. I'm thinking most particularly about what I've called the "fast fashion model" of consumption—cheap imports of manufactured goods that people were acquiring at accelerating rates, the acceleration of the fashion cycle, and the cycle of acquisition and discard. The trend was people buying things, holding them for shorter and shorter periods of time and then discarding them either into some kind of household storage, into a waste stream, or into secondary markets. You had an amazing period of acquisition of consumer goods. I first started looking at this in the realm of apparel, but it was also in consumer electronics, ordinary household appliances, and pretty much across the board in consumer goods.

Of course, a lot of it was financed by debt or longer working hours, but manufactured goods just became so cheap. The idea that you could buy a DVD player for $19—and yes, people were trampling each other in the stores on Black Friday to get them—but that's just an extraordinary period. So that has changed, because the economics of that have changed. Going forward, I don't think we're going to see that level of availability of cheap goods that we saw before. So I think that cycle has slowed down.

The other big thing has been the bifurcation of the consumer market. That's something that's been going on for a long time—the falling out of the middle as a result of the decline of the middle class, the growth of a really low-end in the consumer market with dollar stores and a retail sector where even Walmart is considered expensive. The other side was the expansion of the hyper-luxury market.

Trends in income and wealth are reflected in the consumer sphere. There's more reluctance to take on debt, so debt-fueled consumer buying is lessened. There's also less availability of consumer credit for households now. The other big thing that I've been looking at is the rise of "alternative cultures" of consumption; that is, people moving out of the branded, advertised goods and the mass-produced lifestyles that dominated in the last couple of decades into more ecologically aware lifestyles with more artisanal and self-production.

**D&S**: Stepping back and looking more broadly at the emergence of this mass consumer culture in the United States after the Second World War, what do you see that are the key factors that are at the root of consumer capitalism in the United States? It seems a little facile to focus too narrowly on just advertising. Some scholars point to mass media images and what kinds of lifestyles people aspire to. Galbraith pointed more generally to the relentless stream of new products fueling new desires—the so-called "dependence effect." How do you see those influences, as well as others, sorting out?

**JS**: I don't want to completely dismiss factors like the old monopoly capital idea or the advertising and marketing story, which is that shortfalls of demand led to a big effort to get people to buy things, but I don't buy that story, for the most part. If you think about the postwar period, you had a labor market in which firms were unwilling to use productivity growth to reduce hours of work, and I wrote a book about that, *The Overworked American*. Part of that was about firms and why they don't want to do that. So in the post-war period, you have, from the labor market side, a situation where all productivity growth is getting channeled into income—into expansion of output—so it goes to wages and profits.

Now, of course, workers aren't getting the benefits of productivity growth, but in the post-war era, they did. There were contracts that were explicitly tied—3% productivity, 3% real wage growth. So that creates consumer demand, because that income is getting into people's pockets. Now you can ask the question: Why don't they save it? I don't think it's advertising, primarily, that determines why people didn't save more. There, I think, you have to look at social competition, and the fact that you have an unequal society in which how you live, what you buy, and what you have are important determinants of social position. Rising income gives you a constantly rising norm, and people consume to keep up with that norm. I think it would have played out more or less similarly if there weren't any advertising. The products might have been different but this sort of "consumer escalator," the fact that you have growing levels of consumption, is really coming much more from the production side. So in that way, I'm much more Marxian than Keynesian, I would say.

**D&S**: Turning to the contrast between the United States and other high-income capitalist countries, especially in terms of the shape of the labor movement and the role of the state: How did working hours get reduced in other countries? In France or Germany, for example, the average employed person works about 300 hours less per year than in the United States. So that strikes me as quite central, in your analysis, in terms of understanding consumption patterns in different countries.

**JS**: In the United States in the post-war period, the state devoted a lot of energy to the promotion of consumption, whether it was the highway system or suburbanization. That was in part out of a fear of the "Keynesian problem" of inadequate demand after the Second World War. In Europe, I guess I would point to two things. First, after the war, they had a supply-side problem, which was that they had to rebuild productive capacity rather than what we had, which was the demand-side problem. So our state was much more oriented to promoting consumption than European states, which were more oriented towards rebuilding their societies. In Europe, working hours continued to fall and they didn't in the United States.

That's the way you need to think about it—everybody was on a common trajectory of work-hours decline from about 1870. Of course, the United States was the leader in all of that. We had the shortest working hours and we were the first ones to put in reforms of working hours: The United States was the leader on no Sunday work, no Saturday work, etc. I think the factors are the role of trade unions—both that trade unions were much stronger in Europe and also that in the United States, trade unions turned against the reduction of working hours after the Second World War. That has to do mostly with the Cold War, and with the conservative nature of U.S. trade unions. So in the 1950s, the AFL-CIO became—"hostile" may be too strong a word—became extremely disinterested in the idea of shorter hours of work. That's something that did not happen in Europe.

The other thing is that the incentives facing firms in the United States were really different, in terms of U.S. employers having much higher per worker fixed costs, because of health insurance. There are some European countries where health insurance is provided at the firm level, but mostly not. In the United States that turns out to be a powerful disincentive to reduce working hours, and it becomes a powerful incentive for raising working hours. The growth in inequality, which is more pronounced in the United States, also raised working hours. I think those are the key factors which lead the United States and Europe to diverge quite rapidly on the issue of work time. That divergence turns out to have all sorts of very important consequences.

One of the things you have seen in the patterns of leisure time activities in the United States is you've got time-stressed households doing really money-intensive things like going to the Caribbean for three days, or spending a lot of money to "de-stress," or spending money to reward themselves for working so hard. So we definitely have quite a bit of that in the United States because work is so demanding and stressful and that shapes the leisure patterns. You get what economists call goods- or income-intensive leisure.

*D&S*: If we think of consumption behavior as social—as aiming to enhance a person's social status—can we think of any important social constraints on the amounts or patterns of consumption? If many people disapprove of polluting or wasteful forms of consumption, like the Hummer, can we observe a social constraint on that? Or, in what are very difficult economic times for a lot of people, is there any effect on people reining in unseemly levels of luxury consumption?

**JS**: Well, I'll start with the latter. I was reading about and experiencing people's reluctance to engage in ostentatious displays at the time of the crash, and in its early aftermath. I think, by now, that didn't last very long. One of the things about the most ostentatious stuff is that we're increasingly a gated society, so the wealthy are consuming lavishly outside of the view of the ordinary and the poor. There is certainly less celebration of it, and you see it less in the culture now than before the crash, for sure. The Hummers are a very interesting case. I have a friend who did research on the war between Hummer drivers and the Prius drivers, the Prius drivers being referred to as "pious" drivers by the Hummer folks. Now the Hummer vehicle has collapsed as a consumer product. Hummer drivers were subjected to a lot of social disapproval. It also became economically less-desirable when the price of gas went up.

There is definitely a rising ecological consciousness that is attempting to moralize consumption in ways that yield social approval or disapproval of low-carbon versus high-carbon lifestyles. It isn't mainstream yet. It's much more prevalent in highly educated groups, it tends to be more bicoastal, it's a kind of "forward trend" in the consumer culture. You do see more and more, as you move into the mainstream, people attempting to do more ecologically. I think there's widespread sentiment about that. Then, of course, you also have so many people who are just trying to make ends meet that they feel it is not possible for them to think about ecological impact. Of course, the irony is that the people who are just trying to make ends meet are the ones with the low carbon footprints, but the discourse of environmental impact is permeating through consumer culture.

*D&S*: Going back to something about advertising: It seems to have become more pervasive, both in terms of physical spaces that are filled with advertising and products advertised to users. In the last couple of decades, we've seen the advent of direct marketing of prescription pharmaceuticals, for example, directly to the people who will end up using them. There's a pushback, such as criticism of advertising to children, but it seems largely that there's widespread tolerance of this pervasiveness of advertising in daily life.

**JS**: This is a little counterintuitive, but part of why advertising has become so pervasive is that the core of advertising, which is television spots, have become so unimportant. People don't have to watch them anymore, and that's huge for advertisers. I think the 30- or 60-second TV spots are much more powerful than the kinds of things that advertisers have moved towards in terms of the spatial expansion of advertising. I think that advertising on the web is much less powerful. So, that's one of the paradoxes of advertising in the contemporary moment: the moment when advertising is much more pervasive in terms of space and place, is a moment when it's much less powerful. Advertisers have been able to move in a few directions that have been productive for them, like word of mouth advertising, and so forth, but those forms are also being delegitimized. People know the person sitting next to them in a bar telling them to drink this vodka might be paid by the company.

Prescription drugs are a big exception, because that came about as a regulatory change. Drug companies weren't allowed to advertise directly to consumers before. If it weren't for pharmaceuticals and ads directed at kids, the advertising industry would be in big trouble. Now the kid story is, I think, a little bit different than the adult story, in the sense that you have a much more powerful approach to children now than you did in the past. The approach to children, I think, is a lot more effective than the approach to adults, which I think is declining in effectiveness. So, you can see a theme in what I'm saying about advertising. Today, I would say I feel less worried about advertising than I did before I started studying it. I think people tune it out. I don't want to go too far on this, but to me it's not where the main action is in terms of what's driving consumer patterns.

**D&S:** We see some examples of people, in their purchasing decisions, transcending a kind of narrow consumer mentality: They're thinking about environmental impacts, say, in buying a hybrid or electric car. In terms of other products they may be thinking about labor conditions, such as buying fair trade goods or no sweatshop apparel or footwear. On the other hand, one might look at this as reinforcing a core aspect of consumerist capitalism: That whatever it is that you may want, it's for sale and you can buy it.

**JS:** There's a debate in sociology and the social sciences more generally—because there are other disciplines that have weighed in on this question—about the critique of ethical consumption, political consumption, green consumption. Some argue that it's actually detrimental because it leads people to think that this purchasing behavior can solve problems, and it leads them to be less likely to join in collective solutions to environmental problems, labor problems, poverty, and development in the global South.

I did a study of that, and I used two different data sets: One was a random sample survey of all Americans. The other was an intentional survey of people who are political or ethical consumers, or what we called "conscious consumers," with about 2,000 participants. What we found is that there are actually very high levels of correlation between people engaging in this kind of purchasing and being socially and politically involved in trying to solve these problems in collective ways. And we also looked at the time sequencing and found a group of people who are politically involved already and then you add on this "walk the talk" aspect—if you're going to be fighting sweatshops, then don't buy sweatshop clothing, and if you're concerned about environmental impacts then you don't want to be buying things that are at odds with your values.

So you have people who were political first, then extended to their purchasing behavior, and you have people who got into both at around the same time, and you have people who moved in the other direction—who first did the conscious consuming and then became politically active. Certainly the idea that becoming a "green consumer" undermines your likelihood of engaging in collective action around this is not at all supported by the data in the United States, and there have also been some studies in Europe that show the same thing.

I think the fact of the matter is that changing marketplace behavior in the kind of society we have today is an important component in a broad-based campaign, whether it's on the environment or labor conditions or whatever. We see a lot of the NGOs involved in campaigns that have a market-based dimension—and those have been some of the most successful campaigns in recent years—because it's so hard to get the state to act to do these things, because it is captured by business. People have turned to the market in part because it's an arena where it looks like you can have some results, at least in the short term.

Ultimately, can you stop climate change through consumer behavior and through just market behavior? Definitely not. Can you ensure good working conditions merely by market-oriented activity? Definitely not. To think that it's sufficient is the real mistake, but I don't think that most people who work in this field, who try to work on transforming consumer behavior, have such a naïve view.

**D&S**: We've already talked about ways in which consumption is connected to people's lives at work, and the availability of leisure time, as well as some changes in patterns of consumption related to broader social objectives. What kinds of changes in consumption—and in the forces shaping consumption—do you envision?

**JS**: Well, I have a hard time thinking about the future without orienting all of my thinking about climate, because I just don't see much of a positive future unless we can address climate change very significantly. And that means, for wealthy countries, pretty radical emissions cuts in a pretty short period of time. It actually means that for most countries. So, as I think about the future, I think about what we could do both to address climate change through radical emissions reductions and also increase social justice, reduce inequality, and start solving the enormous problems that we have in this country. My most recent book, *True Wealth*, is about how to do that. Obviously, we need to get onto a renewable energy system, there's no question about that. We need a carbon tax or carbon regulation, and that's stuff that is very well known. What is not understood, I don't think, is that we can't successfully address climate change with a model in which we continue to try to expand the size of the economy.

We're going to have to deal with working hours, because that's the only way to stop expanding the size of the economy in any sensible way. So the core of what we need to do is to get back on the trajectory of using productivity growth to reduce hours of work. And that then opens up incredible possibilities in terms of rebalancing the labor market, integrating the unemployed, and having a fairer distribution of hours. We're talking about the distribution of income, but not about the distribution of hours, which is one of the things that drives the distribution of income. So, fair access to the work that exists, giving people more time off from work, and doing much more as a society—and probably a lot on the local and community level—to ensure basic needs for people.

With declining work hours, people's incomes are pretty much stabilized, so you need to bring the incomes of the bottom up, and you need to bring the incomes of the top down. Part of that has to be a redistribution of work opportunity and creating community provisioning of basic needs, like publicly owned utilities which provide power and heat for people at reasonable prices, enhanced public transportation, more public provisioning of food. There are really interesting things going on in global-South countries bringing farmers and consumers together in local food economies that are not just about high-priced organic food, which is what we have here, but low-priced food that ensures food security for people. So, shorter hours, basic needs being met—including housing, education, healthcare—that's the direction I would like to see us go, and I think that really it all flows out from a kind of commitment to climate protection. It could all flow out from a commitment to basic needs, too. They really integrate.

Time use is central, and I think you get a totally different culture of consumption if people's incomes are on a basically stabilized trajectory and what they're getting is more and more free time. So, you have a new culture of consumption that is not about the acquisition of the new, it's not the "work and spend" pattern as I've called it, it's not "throw away" or media driven, it's more "true materialist," where you really pay attention to the things you have, and it's a kind of earthier consumption. ❏

# Chapter 2

# SUPPLY AND DEMAND

## INTRODUCTION

Textbooks tell us that supply and demand work like a well-oiled machine. The Law of Supply tells us that as the price of an item goes up, businesses will supply more of that good or service. The Law of Demand adds that as the price rises, consumers will choose to buy less of the item. Only one equilibrium price can bring businesses' and consumers' intentions into balance. Away from this equilibrium point, surpluses or shortages tend to drive the price back toward the equilibrium. Of course, government actions such as taxation or setting a price ceiling or floor can move the economy away from its market equilibrium, and create what economists call a "deadweight loss."

Marc Breslow argues that supply and demand do not always produce the best outcomes for society. He notes that the "price gouging" that we suffer during shortages or feared shortages—especially for hard-to-substitute goods like gasoline—is simply supply and demand at work (Article 2.1).

Timothy A. Wise and Marie Brill's "Fiddling in Rome While Our Food Burns" (Article 2.2) argues that the current demand for biofuels has significant negative unintended consequences—diverting agricultural resources away from food production and driving up food prices. It reminds readers the way that seemingly distinct markets are linked, and how factors that impact one market or industry can reverberate onto others.

The next two articles take on the mainstream textbook criticisms of price ceilings and price floors.

Economist Ellen Frank questions the textbook models' conclusion that rent controls (and other price ceilings) lead to permanent shortages. She maintains that rent control helps to equalize power between landlords and tenants, and also to assure a supply of affordable housing (Article 2.3).

Does raising the minimum wage cause layoffs, as mainstream models imply? Economist Jeannette Wicks-Lim says no, arguing that the minimum wage could go above $12 without causing substantial job loss (Article 2.4).

Finally, in "The Airfare Mystery" (Article 2.5), Arthur MacEwan argues that "supply and demand" is just a starting point for understanding what causes variation in air fares. We need to delve deeper, according to MacEwan, into issues of market power (does a particular airline monopolize a particular route?), price discrimination (are some buyers, like business travelers, charged more than others?), and government intervention (what roles do taxes and subsidies play?).

Taken together, these articles call into question the claims that markets always operate efficiently and lead to the best social allocation of resources. The articles also imply a constructive role for the "visible hand" of government.

## Discussion Questions

1.  (General) Several of these articles call for a larger government role in regulating supply and demand. What are some possible results of expanded government involvement, positive and negative? On balance, do you agree that government should play a larger role?

2.  (Article 2.1) Breslow says that shortages have different effects on prices in the short run and the long run. Explain the difference. How is this difference related to the concepts of elasticity of demand and elasticity of supply?

3.  (Article 2.2) Wise and Brill argues that policies promoting biofuels production have significant impacts on food prices. Why is this this the case?

4   (Article 2.3) Frank states that because modern rent-control laws are "soft," they do not lead to housing shortages. Explain. Do you agree with her reasoning?

5.  (Article 2.4) What is Wicks-Lim's argument against the claim that minimum-wage laws create unemployment?

6.  (Article 2.5) MacEwan sees "supply and demand" as a shorthand for the various kinds of forces operating in real-world markets. What kinds of influences does he describe that may affect air fares? Which have an impact mainly on the supply side? Which on the demand side?

*Article 2.1*

# PRICE GOUGING: IT'S JUST SUPPLY AND DEMAND

## BY MARC BRESLOW
*October 2000, updated May 2015*

Critics of the oil industry charge that the companies conspire to raise prices during shortages, ripping off consumers and gaining huge profits through illegal behavior. The industries respond that there is no conspiracy, prices rise due to the simple functioning of supply and demand in the market. The media debate the question: can evidence be found of a conspiracy? Or are rising prices simply due to increased costs as supplies are short? Politicians ask whether companies are guilty of illegal activity, and demand that investigations be opened.

What's going on? In reality, critics of the industries are missing the point of how a capitalist "free market" operates during times of shortages. The industry spokespersons are more on target in their explanations—but that doesn't mean what the companies are doing is okay. In fact, they *are* profiting at the expense of everyone who is forced to pay outrageous prices.

Both the media and public officials want to know whether rising costs of operation are causing the high prices, and therefore the companies are justified. Why? Because simple textbook economics says that in a competitive market we should get charged according to costs, with companies only making a "normal" profit. But a careful reading of the texts shows that this is only in the "long run" when new supplies can come into the market. In the short run, when a shortage develops, "supply and demand" can force prices up to unbelievable levels, especially for any product or service that is really a necessity. It doesn't have any relationship to the cost of supplying the item, nor does it take a conspiracy. The industry spokespeople are right that market pressures are the cause.

What confuses consumers is why a relatively small shortage can cause such a huge price jump, as it did for gasoline and electricity. Why, if OPEC reduces world oil supplies by only 1% or 2%, can the price of gasoline rise by perhaps 50%? Why shouldn't prices rise by the 1% or 2%? The answer lies in a common-sense understanding of what happens during a shortage. Everyone who owns a car, and still needs to get to work, drop the kids off at child care, and buy groceries, still needs to drive. In the short run, you can't sell your car for a more energy-efficient one, nor move someplace where public transit is more available, nor find a new day care center closer to home. Even if there are subways or buses available where you live, tight work and family time schedules probably make it difficult for you to leave the car at home.

So, as prices rise, everyone continues trying to buy as much gasoline as they did before (in technical terms, the "short-run price elasticity of demand" is very low). But there is 2% less gas available, so not everyone can get as much as they want. Prices will continue rising until some people drop out of the market, cutting back on their purchases because they simply can't afford to pay the higher prices. For something as essential to modern life as gasoline, this can take quite a price jump. If the price goes from $3.00 to $3.50 will you buy less? How about $4.00? Or $4.50? You can see the problem. Prices can easily rise by 50% before demand falls by the 2% needed for supply and demand to equalize.

Note that this situation has nothing to do with the costs of supplying gasoline, nor do oil companies in the United States have to conspire together to raise prices. All they have to do is let consumers bid for the available gasoline. Nothing illegal has taken place—OPEC is acting as a cartel, "conspiring," but the United States has no legal power over other countries. Profits can go up enormously, and they may be shared between OPEC, oil companies such as Exxon/Mobil and Royal Dutch Shell, and firms lower on the supply chain such as wholesalers and retail gas stations.

Housing is perhaps the worst of these situations, as no one should be forced to leave their home. But the "invisible hand" of the market will raise prices, and allocate housing, according to who has the greatest purchasing power, not who needs the housing. A highly-skilled computer programmer, moving into San Francisco from elsewhere, will get an apartment that some lesser-paid worker, maybe a public school teacher or a bus driver, has been living in, perhaps for many years.

In all these cases, the market has done what it does well—allocate sales to those who can afford to buy, without regard to need; and allocate profits to those who have a product in short supply, without regard to costs of production. The human costs to people of moderate- and low-incomes, who are priced out of the market, can be severe. But they can be prevented—by price controls that prevent price-gouging due to shortages. Such controls have been used many times in the United States—for rent in high-demand cities, for oil and gas during the "crises" of the 1970's, and for most products during World War II. Maybe it's time we made them a staple of sensible economic policy. ❑

*Resources:* "In Gas Prices, Misery and Mystery," Pam Belluck, *The New York Times*, 6/14/2000; "Federal action sought to cut power prices from May," Peter J. Howe, *The Boston Globe*, Aug. 24, 2000; "Industry Blames Chemical Additives for High Gas Prices," Matthew L. Wald, *The New York Times*, June 26, 2000.

*Article 2.2*

# FIDDLING IN ROME WHILE OUR FOOD BURNS

**BY MARIE BRILL AND TIMOTHY A. WISE**
*October 2013; Al Jazeera*

*This article first appeared on the Al Jazeera website, www.aljazeera.com.*
*Reprinted by permission.*

Rumor has it that the Roman emperor Nero played a fiddle and sang while Rome burned for five days in the Great Fire of 64 A.D. Nearly 2000 years later, at the very site where this devastating fire started so long ago, history is repeating itself, only the leaders doing the fiddling are delegates to the 40th meeting of the UN Committee on World Food Security (CFS). And what's burning is the world's food, in the engines of our cars.

Unfortunately this time, the fire didn't end in five days. Food-based biofuels have been burning for over a decade, the fires are growing in scale and intensity, and there is no end in sight.

It's not as if we haven't seen the warning signs. There have been three food price spikes in the last six years, with a wide range of studies implicating biofuels as a key driver of price volatility. How could it be otherwise? In the United States, 40% of our corn—fully 15% of the global corn supply—is now diverted to make ethanol, up from just 5% in 2000.

The food security impacts are multiple and severe. Because ethanol competes for corn with food and animal feed, it has a direct impact on the cost of food. Indeed, in 2008 global food prices doubled. This hurts poor consumers. Biofuels—from corn, sugar, soybeans, and other feedstocks—compete for land and water, putting added stress on scarce resources.

Most dramatically, biofuels producers have been key drivers of large-scale land acquisitions in African and other developing countries.

This is why the CFS put the issue of biofuels and food security on this year's agenda and commissioned an expert report to inform the decision. Indeed, the report confirmed the negative impacts of biofuels to date and recommended decisive action.

Our own report confirms that one of the main threats to our ability to feed the world in the future is the continued expansion of first generation biofuels.

No matter. At the CFS the fiddling began. Despite urgent statements from the floor about the negative impacts of biofuels on food security, the small group tasked to negotiate a set of principles and actions came up with weak principles and complete inaction. There was no acknowledgement of the negative impacts of biofuel policies and mandates in the United States and European Union, which have been instrumental in artificially stimulating and sustaining the biofuel industry.

Why the fiddling? Simple: the most powerful countries at the negotiating table were the same ones benefiting from the burning of food in our cars. Canada and the United States played the loudest, with the European Union, Brazil, and Argentina playing much the same tune. Only South Africa, a lonely voice, joined with civil society to speak for the victims of these policies.

Of course, the ones choosing the tune were powerful industry interests, from the biofuels companies themselves as well as the agribusiness firms capturing the benefits of high prices and subsidized demand for their products.

The CFS is supposed to be the principal international agency coordinating global responses to the food price crisis and dealing with the new realities of the rising and worrisome integration of food markets with fuel and financial markets. It has that clear mandate.

But instead of leading, the CFS decided to do nothing. The straightforward proposal that biofuels policies that harm food security should be reformed was categorically rejected. So too was any mention of the land and water impacts of runaway biofuels expansion.

The world is not waiting for the CFS to lead. Policy-makers around the world are beginning to contend with food-fuel competition. The U.S. Congress is under pressure to reform, or even repeal, its biofuels mandate. The European Union recently cut its own mandate in half, explicitly recognizing the negative impacts of food-based fuels.

Meanwhile, the fiddling continues, and the biofuels burn on.

More than 80 organizations from around the world signed an open letter urging the CFS to take action. Members of civil society formally involved in the CFS negotiations refused to endorse the resolution. "Small scale food producers have spoken powerfully here about the reality they are confronted with every day: that biofuels crops compete with their food production, for the land they till and for the water that sustains them," they stated in a press release. "[These] recommendations overwhelmingly defend the interests of the biofuels industry and legitimize violations of the right to food."

This no time for the CFS to fiddle in Rome. Our food is burning. In our cars. And hundreds of millions of people are going hungry. ❑

*Sources:* Food and Agriculture Organization of the United Nations, Committee on World Food Security – 40 Session, Oct. 7-11, 2013 (fao.org); Committee on World Food Security, "Biofuels and Food Security," 2013 (fao.org); Actionaid, "Rising to the Challenge: Changing Course to Feed the World in 2050" (actionaidusa.org).

*Article 2.3*

# DOES RENT CONTROL HURT TENANTS?

**BY ELLEN FRANK**
*March/April 2003*

> Dear Dr. Dollar:
> *What are the merits of the argument that rent control hurts tenants by limiting the incentives to create and maintain rental housing?*
> —Sarah Marxer, San Francisco, Calif.

The standard story of rent control, laid out in dozens of introductory economics textbooks, goes like this. In the housing market, landlords are willing to supply more rental units when prices are high, and tenants are willing to rent more units when prices are low. In an unregulated market, competition should result in a market-clearing price at which the number of apartments landlords are willing and able to provide just equals the number tenants are willing and able to rent. Thus, when prices are allowed to rise to their correct level, shortages disappear. Rent controls, in this story, disrupt the market mechanism by capping rents at too low a level. Artificially low rents discourage construction and maintenance, resulting in fewer available apartments than would exist without the controls. At the same time, low rents keep tenants in the area, searching for apartments that don't exist. The result: permanent housing shortages in rent-controlled markets.

What's wrong with this story? Just about everything.

First, the story ignores the unequal power that landlords and tenants exercise in an unregulated market. Boston College professor Richard Arnott notes that tenants are, for a number of reasons, averse to moving. This gives landlords inordinate pricing power even in a market where housing is not in short supply—and in areas where vacancy rates are low, land is scarce, and "snob zoning" commonplace, landlords can charge truly exorbitant prices. In Boston, rent controls were eliminated in 1997, and average apartment rents have since climbed nearly 100%. The city's spiraling rents show that without controls, landlords can—and do—gouge tenants.

Second, rent control opponents misrepresent the structure of controls. As practiced in the real world, rent control does not place fixed caps on rent. New York City enacted an actual rent freeze after World War II, and a small number of apartments still fall under this "old-law" rent control. But most rent-controlled apartments in New York and all controlled apartments in other U.S. cities fall under what Arnott calls "second generation" or "soft" controls, which simply restrict annual rent increases. Soft rent controls guarantee landlords a "fair return" on their properties and require that owners maintain their buildings. They allow landlords to pass along maintenance costs, and many allow improvement costs to be recouped on an accelerated schedule, making building upkeep quite lucrative.

Consequently, controlled apartments are not unprofitable. And as Occidental College professor and housing specialist Peter Dreier points out, landlords won't walk away as long as they are making a decent return. Residential landlords are not very mobile: they have a long-term interest in their properties, and only abandon them when *market* rents fall below even controlled levels as a result of poverty, crime, or economic depression. Rent controls themselves do not foster abandonment or poor maintenance.

Third, all second-generation rent control laws—enacted chiefly in the 1970s—exempted newly constructed buildings from controls. Thus, the argument that controls discourage new construction simply makes no sense. As for the oft-heard complaint that developers fear that rent controls, once enacted, will be extended to new buildings, the 1980s and 1990s construction booms in New York, Boston, San Francisco, and Los Angeles—all cities with controls—indicate that developers aren't all that worried. There is plenty of housing and construction in cities with and without rent controls.

Nevertheless, even in many cities with rent controls, there is a shortage of *affordable* apartments. Market housing costs have been rising faster than wages for at least two decades. That some apartments in New York and San Francisco are still affordable to low- and middle-income families is due primarily to rent control.

Indeed, limited as they might be, rent controls deliver real benefits. They prevent price-gouging and ration scarce apartments to existing tenants. The money tenants save in rent can be spent in the neighborhood economy, benefiting local businesses. Meanwhile, more secure tenants create neighborhoods that are stable, safe, and economically diverse. And rent controls are essential if tenants are to have credible legal protection against slumlords: the legal right to complain about lack of heat or faulty plumbing is meaningless if landlords can retaliate by raising rents.

There are many problems with the U.S. housing market. High prices, low incomes, and lack of public housing or subsidies for affordable housing all contribute to homelessness and housing insecurity in major American cities. Rent control is not the cause of these problems, nor is it the whole solution. But along with higher wages and expanded public housing, it is part of the solution. As Dreier puts it, "Until the federal government renews its responsibility to help poor and working-class people fill the gap between what they can afford and what housing costs to build and operate, rent control can at least help to keep a roof over their heads." ❏

***Resources:*** Richard Arnott, "Time for Revisionism on Rent Control?" *Journal of Economic Perspectives*, Winter 1995. Dreier and Pitcoff, "I'm a Tenant and I Vote," *Shelterforce*, July/August 1997 (nhi.org>.

Article 2.4

# HOW HIGH COULD THE MINIMUM WAGE GO?

*A 70% boost would help millions of workers, without killing jobs.*

## BY JEANNETTE WICKS-LIM
*July/August 2012*

The minimum wage needs a jolt—not just the usual fine-tuning—if it's ever going to serve as a living wage. Annual full-time earnings at today's $7.25 federal minimum wage are about $15,000 per year. This doesn't come anywhere near providing a decent living standard by any reasonable definition, for any household, least of all households with children. But among the seventeen states that either have active campaigns to raise their minimum wage or have raised them already this year, none have suggested raising the wage floor by more than 20%.

How high can the minimum wage go? As it turns out, a lot higher. Economists typically examine whether current minimum-wage laws hike pay rates up too high and cause employers to shed workers from their payrolls in response. But the current stockpile of economic research on minimum wages suggests that past increases have not caused any notable job losses. In other words, minimum wages in the United States have yet to be set too high. In fact, if we use past experience as a guide, businesses should be able to adjust to a jump in the minimum wage as great as 70%. That would push the federal minimum wage up to $12.30. In states with average living costs, full-time earnings at $12.30 per hour can cover the basic needs of the typical low-income working household (assuming both adults in two-adult households are employed).

Why is such a large increase possible? It's because minimum-wage hikes—particularly those in the 20-to-30% range adopted in the United States—impose very modest cost increases on businesses. This is true even for the low-wage, labor-intensive restaurant industry. And because these cost increases are so modest, affected businesses have a variety of options for adjusting to their higher labor costs that are less drastic than laying off workers.

Take, for example, the 31% rise in Arizona's state minimum wage in 2006, from $5.15 to $6.75. My colleague Robert Pollin and I have estimated that the average restaurant in Arizona could expect to see its costs rise between 1% and 2% of their sales revenue. What kind of adjustment would this restaurant need to make? A price hike of 1% or 2% would completely cover this cost increase. This would amount to raising the price of a $10.00 meal to $10.20.

To figure out what is the largest increase businesses can adjust to without laying off workers, we can take stock of what we know about how businesses have adjusted in the past and then figure out how much businesses can adjust along those lines.

Let's stick with the example of restaurants, since these businesses tend to experience the largest rise in costs. And let's start with a big increase in the minimum wage: 50%. If we add together all the raises mandated by such an increase in the minimum wage (assuming the same number of workers and hours worked), the raises employers would need to give workers earning wages above the minimum wage to maintain a stable wage hierarchy, and their higher payroll taxes, the total cost increase of a 50% minimum-wage hike would be 3.2% of restaurant sales.

The cost increase that these restaurants need to absorb, however, will actually be even smaller than 3.2% of their sales revenue. That's because when workers' wages rise, workers stay at their jobs for longer periods of time, saving businesses the money they would otherwise have spent on recruiting and training new workers. These savings range between 10% and 25% of the costs from raising the minimum wage. If the higher wage motivates workers to work harder, businesses would experience even more cost savings.

So what would happen if restaurants raised their prices to cover their minimum wage cost increases? One answer is that people may react to the higher prices by eating out less often and restaurant owners would lose business. With a large enough falloff in business, restaurants would have to cut back on their workforce. But it's unlikely that a price increase as small as 3% would stop people from eating out. Think about it: if a family is already willing to pay $40.00 to eat dinner out, it hardly seems likely that a price increase as small as $1.20 would to cause them to forgo all the benefits of eating out like getting together with family or friends and saving time in meal preparation, clean up, and grocery shopping.

Still, let's assume that a 3% price hike actually does influence people to eat out less. The key questions now are how much less and can restaurant owners make up their lost business activity? Economists have found that restaurant patrons do not react strongly to changes in menu prices (economists call this an "inelastic" demand). Estimates from industry research suggest that a price increase of 3% may reduce consumer demand by about 2%.

However, if these small price increases take place within a growing economy—even a slow-growing economy—restaurant owners will probably see basically no change in their sales. This is because as the economy expands and peoples' incomes rise, people eat out more. In an economy growing at a rate of 3% annually, which is slower than average for the U.S. economy, consumer demand for restaurant meals will typically rise by about 2.4%. This would boost sales more than enough to make up for any loss that restaurants may experience from a 3% price increase. In other words, consumers would still eat out more often even after a 50% minimum-wage hike.

After taking account of the ways that restaurants can adjust to the higher labor costs from a minimum wage hike, it turns out that the biggest minimum wage increase that restaurants can absorb while maintaining at least the same level of business activity is 70%. In 2004, Santa Fe, New Mexico, came close to this. Its citywide living-wage ordinance raised the wage floor by 65%—from $5.15 to $8.50. A city-commissioned report after it was put into effect found that "overall employment levels have been unaffected by the living wage ordinance."

However, even if the federal minimum rate were 70% higher, or $12.30, it would still fall short for two major groups of workers. First, one-worker families raising young children need generous income supports in addition to minimum wage earnings to help cover the high cost of raising children. Second, minimum-wage workers who live in expensive areas, such as New York City and Washington, D.C., require affordable housing programs.

A 70% minimum-wage hike is the biggest one-time increase that U.S. businesses can absorb without cutting jobs, but it's not the end of the story. In the future, the minimum wage can inch further upward. For example, it could rise in step with the expanding productive capacity of the U.S. economy, as it did in the 1950s and 1960s. A $12.30 minimum wage today rising each year with worker productivity would reach $17.00 in just over ten years (in 2011 dollars). This wage would be high enough so that a single parent with one child could support a minimally decent living standard. We would finally begin transforming the minimum wage into a living wage for all workers.

Policy discussions around the minimum wage need to move past the debate of whether or not it causes job loss. The evidence is clear: minimum wages, in the range of what's been adopted in the past, do not produce any significant job losses. Now it is time to focus on how we can use minimum wages to maximally support low-wage workers. Can we raise the minimum wage rate to a level we can call a living wage? By my reckoning, we can. ❑

**Sources:** Jeannette Wicks-Lim and Jeffrey Thompson, "Combining the Minimum Wage and Earned Income Tax Credit Policies to Guarantee a Decent Living Standard to All U.S. Workers" (Political Economy Research Institute, October 2010).

*Article 2.5*

# THE AIRFARE MYSTERY

## BY ARTHUR MacEWAN
*January/February 2014*

> Dear Dr. Dollar:
> *Boston is 3,280 air miles from London, only 27% further than the 2,580 air miles from Boston to San Diego. So why does a flight from Boston to London cost more than twice as much as a flight from Boston to San Diego, 100% more, for the same dates? Is it just supply and demand?* —Kathleen M. Gillespie, Lexington, Mass.

Airfares do seem to pose a mystery. Supply and demand may help explain things, but these are really little more than categories into which explanations can be placed. If someone says that the flights to London are so expensive because supply is limited relative to demand, we have no real explanation until we explain why supply is limited.

On the surface, the high price of flights on the Boston-London route suggests that this is a very profitable route. So why don't more airlines fly this route more often, expanding supply, to get a share of the profits?

Beneath the surface (on travel web sites), it turns out that a large part of the price difference between these two routes is not the actual payment to the airline, but taxes and fees. I found one Boston-London-Boston trip for $1,082, where taxes and fees accounted for $656 of that total. On the Boston-San Diego-Boston flight, however, taxes and fees accounted for only $33 out of the $436 cost.

In general, European governments charge much higher taxes and fees than is the case in the United States. From an environmental perspective, the Europeans are probably on the right track, as air travel is an especially polluting (greenhouse gas-creating) form of travel. The European governments, however, may simply be motivated by the opportunity to capture revenue.

There are seemingly strange airline fare differences within the United States that are not explained by tax and fee differences. For example, a non-stop round-trip Boston-Detroit flight (630 miles each way) costs about twice as much as a non-stop Boston-Chicago flight (860 miles each way)—$458 compared to $230 for the same times and dates.

This difference is explained by the fact that Delta has a lock on the Boston-Detroit route, while United, American, US Airways, and Jet Blue all fly the Boston-Chicago route. That is, Delta is a monopoly on the Boston-Detroit route and can charge high fares without facing competition. (Northwest used to control this route until it merged with Delta a couple of years ago.)

Why have no other airlines entered this apparently lucrative Boston-Detroit route? That's not clear. Perhaps Delta has long-term leases on Detroit airport gates. Or perhaps other airlines, recognizing the economic and population decline of Detroit, believe this market has limited potential. Whatever the reason, it is clear that monopoly control of this route is the issue.

Also, the Boston-Detroit fare portends an ominous future as airline mergers reduce competition further. Following the Delta-Northwest merger, Continental and United came together. American Airlines and US Airways have also been moving toward a merger. In August, however, the federal government acted to block the move. "According to the Justice Department," reported the *New York Times*, the proposed merger "would substantially reduce competition in over 1,000 city pairs served by the two airlines."

While monopolistic situations and taxes and fees explain some of the "mystery" of airline fares, there is more. Flights and times that are heavily used by business travelers tend to have high fares because business travelers are less concerned about the price. This is partly because they often have limited flexibility, but also because airfares are deductible as a cost of business—i.e., the taxpayers pick up part of the tab.

Also, on a flight with the same airline, prices can change dramatically within a day or even within hours. Trying to book a flight one evening, the cheapest ticket I could find was about $600, but by the next morning I got the ticket for about $300. I suspect that in this case the airline (using computer-based forecasting) recognized that the flight was not filling up and therefore reduced the price to attract more customers.

And things can work in the other direction. Making a reservation at the last minute, the potential passenger is often faced with a very high fare because the airline views the traveler as having little flexibility. For example, if I make a reservation to fly Boston-Chicago-Boston, leaving tomorrow and returning two days later, the fare would be over $900, as compared to the $230 I would pay if I made the reservation a few weeks in advance.

So, yes, supply and demand can help explain the variation in airfares. But to really understand what is going on we need to know a good deal more. ❏

*Sources:* "Airline Merger Mania," *New York Times*, June 22, 2013; James B. Stewart, "For Airlines, It May Be One Merger Too Many," *New York Times*, Aug. 16, 2013.

# Chapter 3

# CONSUMERS

## INTRODUCTION

The "two economies" described in the introduction to this book—the textbook economy and the economy portrayed by critics of the status quo—come into sharp contrast when we consider the theory of consumer choice. In the textbook model of consumer choice, rational individuals seek to maximize their well-being by choosing the right mix of goods to consume and allocating their "scarce" resources accordingly. They decide for themselves how much they would enjoy various things, and make their choices based on full information about their options. More of any good is always better, but diminishing marginal utility says that each additional unit of a good consumed brings less additional enjoyment than the one before. The theory attempts to assess the utility of each individual uniquely. Yet, we soon discover that it is difficult if not impossible to "measure pleasure" for a single individual and impossible to compare utility between individuals.

The first article in this chapter contends that the idea of consumer sovereignty—that consumer wishes determine what gets produced—does not fit the facts. Helen Scharber notes, in "The 800-Pound Ronald McDonald in the Room" (Article 3.1), how the advertising that saturates our daily lives constantly creates new wants. In recent years, advertisers have been increasingly targeting children in order to convince them to nag their parents into buying products they suddenly "need."

Deborah M. Figart's "Underbanked and Overcharged" (Article 3.2) argues that low-income communities are ill-served by both conventional banks and "alternative financial service providers" (AFSPs), such as check-cashing outlets. Low-income areas may lack convenient nearby outlets for conducting financial transactions, and community members typically face high fees and interest rates from both banks and AFSPs. Figart points to a possible solution: recent proposals for the revival of "postal banks" operated by the U.S. Postal Service.

Zoe Sherman's "When the Public Square is in Cyberspace" (Article 3.3.) is a story about corporate power. The telecommunications giants are the "gatekeepers" to the Internet, and want to be able to use that power, already highly profitable, to wring as much money out of users as possible. They have lobbied to eliminate net neutrality—the rule that all packets of information have to be treated equally, facing equal delay when the Net is congested—so they can charge a premium for privileged access to something that ought to be a public space and a bastion of democracy.

The next two articles focus on ways that consumers may bring more broadly social-minded concerns to their purchasing decisions, and the pitfalls they sometimes face. Today, consumers are increasingly conscious of environmental problems, and many are willing to pay premium prices for recycled, less-polluting, or otherwise "green" goods. In "Way Beyond Greenwashing" (Article 3.4), however, Jonathan Latham documents the way that corporate "greenwashing" stands in the way of informed consumer decisions. "Big Conservation" organizations, he argues, sell "indulgences" to global agribusiness corporations over the issue of habitat destruction, allowing the companies to appear more environment-friendly than they really are.

In "Campus Struggles Against Sweatshops Continue" (Article 3.5), Sarah Blaskey and Phil Gasper turn our attention to activism around global labor conditions. They show how how people on the consumption side, in this case students and faculty at U.S. colleges and universties, have banded together with workers on the other side of the world to fight "sweatshop" conditions in apparel production.

In the chapter's final article, "How to Take on the Card Sharks—and Win!" (Article 3.6), Jim Campen describes a rare case of successful consumer-protection regulation in recent U.S. history. Credit card regulation has reined in what were widely seen as deceptive and abusive practices, designed to extract as much money in fees and fines as possible from unsuspecting card holders.

## Discussion Questions

1. (Article 3.1) Standard consumer theory still applies if advertising is simply a way to inform consumers. But critics suggest that advertising shapes our tastes and desires. Think of some of your recent purchases. For which purchases was advertising primarily a source of information, and for which was it more of a taste-shaper?

2. (Article 3.1) According to Scharber, what are the negative impacts of advertising directed at children? Would you support a law banning advertising to young children? Why or why not?

3. (Article 3.2) Why might private for-profit enterprises not supply desired services at affordable prices, as in the case of financial services in low-income communities? Is the establishment of public service providers a good solution?

4. (Article 3.3) Mainstream microeconomic theory includes the concept of "market power," meaning that a particular buyer or seller is able to influence market prices (contrary to the first "Tilly assumption," Article 1.2). How does Sherman's analysis take into account the existence of market power? Does it take into account power in other senses as well?

5. (Articles 3.4 and 3.5) How can consumers overcome the problem of "asymmetric information" in making purchases? Consider cases when consumers are interested

in something (like environmental impact or labor conditions) that they cannot directly observe from the product itself.

6. (Article 3.5) Why might people on the consumption side of a market (like apparel buyers) consider factors other than product price and quality in their purchasing decisions? Do you think changes in purchasing behavior are enough to bring about social change, in terms of things like labor conditions and environmental impacts of production methods?

7. (Articles 3.6) Why does Campen think that government regulation was called for in the case of credit cards? Do you agree?

*Article 3.1*

# THE 800-POUND RONALD McDONALD IN THE ROOM

## BY HELEN SCHARBER
*January 2007*

When your child's doctor gives you advice, you're probably inclined to take it. And if 60,000 doctors gave you advice, ignoring it would be even more difficult to justify. Last month, the American Academy of Pediatrics (AAP) issued a policy statement advising us to limit advertising to children, citing its adverse effects on health. Yes, banning toy commercials might result in fewer headaches for parents ("Please, please, pleeeeeeease, can I have this new video game I just saw 10 commercials for????"), but the AAP is more concerned with other health issues, such as childhood obesity. Advertising in general—and to children specifically—has reached astonishingly high levels, and as a country, we'd be wise to take the doctors' orders.

Advertising to kids is not a new phenomenon, but the intensity of it is. According to Juliet Schor, author of *Born to Buy*, companies spent around $100 million in 1983 on television advertising to kids. A little more than 20 years later, the amount earmarked for child-targeted ads in a variety of media has jumped to at least $12 billion annually. That's over $150 per boy and girl in the U.S. And it's not as though kids only see ads for action figures and sugary cereal; the other $240 billion spent on advertising each year ensures that they see ads for all kinds of products, everywhere they go. According to the AAP report, "the average young person views more than 3,000 ads per day on television, on the Internet, on billboards, and in magazines." Ads are also creeping into schools, where marketers have cleverly placed them in "educational" posters, textbook covers, bathroom stalls, scoreboards, daily news programs, and bus radio programming.

If advertising to children is becoming increasingly ubiquitous, it's probably because it's becoming increasingly profitable. Once upon a time, kids didn't have as much market power as they do today. The AAP report estimates that kids under 12 now spend $25 billion of their own money annually, teenagers spend another $155 billion, and both groups probably influence around $200 billion in parental spending. Not too surprising, considering that 62 percent of parents say their children "actively participate" in car-buying decisions, according to a study by J.D. Power & Associates. Marketers are also becoming more aware of the long-term potential of advertising to children. While they may not be the primary market now, they will be someday. And since researchers have found that kids as young as two can express preferences for specific brands, it's practically never too early to begin instilling brand loyalty.

But while small children have an incredible memory for commercial messages, they may not have developed the cognitive skills necessary to be critical of them. In 2004, the American Psychological Association (APA) also called for setting limits on advertising to kids, citing research that "children under the age of eight are unable to critically comprehend televised advertising messages and are prone to accept advertiser messages as truthful, accurate and unbiased." Many people take offense at the idea that we might be manipulated by marketing. Aren't we, after all, intelligent enough to make up our own minds about what to buy? The research cited by the APA, however, shows that children are uniquely vulnerable to manipulation by advertising. Marketers therefore should not be allowed to prey on them in the name of free speech.

Such invasive advertising to children is not only an ethical problem. The American Academy of Pediatrics cited advertising's effects on health through the promotion of unhealthy eating, drinking and smoking as the main motivation for setting limits. Children's health issues certainly merit attention. The Center for Disease Control, for example, has found that the prevalence of overweight children (ages 6 to 11) increased from 7 percent in 1980 to about 19 percent in 2004, while the rate among adolescents (ages 12 to 19) jumped from 5 percent to 17 percent. In addition to physical health problems, Schor argues that extensive marketing has negative effects on children's emotional well being. In her research for Born to Buy, Schor found links between immersion in consumer culture and depression, anxiety, low self esteem and conflicts with parents. The big push to consume can also lead to financial health problems, as many Americans know all too well, with credit card debt among 18 to 24-year-olds doubling over the past decade.

Not even the staunchest critics of marketing to children would argue that advertisements are completely at fault for these trends. Yet, the commercialization of nearly everything is negatively affecting children's well being in rather profound ways. Why, then, is hardly anyone paying attention to the 800-pound Ronald McDonald in the room? Perhaps it's because advertising appears to be a necessary evil or a fair tradeoff—maybe little Emma's school couldn't afford a soccer team without Coke on the scoreboard, for example. Or perhaps some would argue that parents who don't approve of the commercial culture should limit their kids' exposure to it. Increasingly invasive marketing techniques make it practically impossible to simply opt out of commercial culture, though. Thus, decisions to limit marketing to children must be made by the country as a whole. Sweden, Norway, Greece, Denmark, and Belgium have already passed laws curbing kid-targeted advertising, and according to 60,000 pediatricians, if we care about the health of our kids, we should too. ❏

*Sources:* American Association of Pediatrics, Policy Statement on Children, Adolescents, and Advertising, December 2006 (pediatrics.aappublications.org/cgi/content/full/118/6/2563); American Psychological Association, "Television Advertising Leads to Unhealthy Habits in Childen" February 2004 (releasees/childrenads.html); Jennifer Saranow, "Car makers direct more ads at kids," *Wall Street Journal*, November 9th, 2006 (www.commercialexploitation.org/news/ carmakers.html); David Burke, "Two-year olds branded by TV advertising" (www.whitedot.org/ issue/isssory.aps?slug=Valkenburg); Center for a New American Dream, *Kids and Commercialism* (www.newdream.org/kids/);; Juliet Schor, Born to Buy: The Commercialized Child and the New Consumer Culture (New York: Scribner, 2004); Center for Disease Control, "Facts about Childhood Overweight" www.cdc.gov/Healthy Youth/overweight/index.html).

*Article 3.2*

# UNDERBANKED AND OVERCHARGED
Creating Alternatives to the "Alternative Financial Service Providers"

## BY DEBORAH M. FIGART
*July/August 2014*

**D**riving down Atlantic Avenue, the main commercial thoroughfare in Atlantic City, N.J., one can easily count at least three times as many check-cashing outlets as banks. At these stores, you can cash your paycheck or government check (for a fee), send a wire transfer to a relative or friend overseas, or pay some bills.

Many traditionally African-American neighborhoods and poor census tracts, like this one, do not have a single bank nearby. The U.S. banking system is working for well-heeled customers. It isn't working for poor people.

Over 30 million households—more than one in four—are unbanked or underbanked. That means they have no access to traditional banking services or that they have a bank account but also rely on Alternative Financial Service Providers (AFSPs). According to the Federal Deposit Insurance Corporation's 2011 FDIC National Survey of Unbanked and Underbanked Households, the number of financially excluded households has increased since the publication of its first survey in 2009, with the number of unbanked alone increasing by over 800,000. The incidence of financial exclusion is highest among households that are African-American, Hispanic, lower-income, younger, or less-educated (see Figure 1).

The FDIC asked people why they had never had a bank account or why they had closed any prior account. Some reasons are listed in Figure 2. (Respondents were able to select more than one option.) Since the exact language of the FDIC's survey choices changed between 2009 and 2011, four reasons from the 2009 survey are included for further information.

**FIGURE 1: PERCENTAGES OF HOUSEHOLDS, BY CHARACTERISTIC OF HOUSEHOLDER, UNBANKED OR UNDERBANKED, 2011**

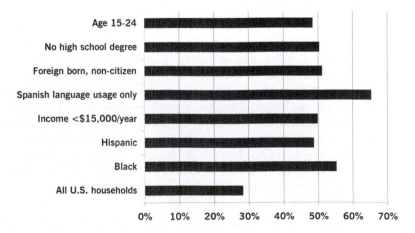

The responses suggest how difficult it is to survive at the lower end of the income distribution. Living paycheck to paycheck, the unbanked feel they do not have enough money to open and maintain a bank account, especially if there is a minimum balance requirement or the bank charges low-balance fees. The survey also reveals social barriers to being a bank customer. If your primary language is not spoken at the bank, for example, then you may feel banks are unwelcoming. This is one reason that over half of immigrant/non-citizen households, and that nearly two-thirds of households where only Spanish is spoken, are unbanked or underbanked

Logistical problems can be a major barrier. "Do I have the proper documents to open an account?" "Is there a bank near me that is convenient?" Banks and savings-and-loans ("thrifts") are under-represented in minority and low-income areas, and AFSPs cluster in those communities. (Scholars who study the issue call this the "spatial void hypothesis.") These spatial voids have only intensified since the 2008 financial crisis, as mainstream banks have ostensibly become more risk-averse—at least regarding low- and moderate-income households and communities.

Alternative financial services are big business in the United States, with an FDIC estimate of $320 billion in annual revenues. The sheer number of check-cashing outlets, payday lenders, auto-title lenders, and issuers of loans on anticipated tax refunds—over 13,000 according to the trade association Financial Service Centers of America—places them nearly on par numerically with banks and credit unions. (Combined, banks and credit unions number almost 15,000, according to the FDIC and National Credit Union Association.)AFSPs are not a "fringe" phenomenon in another sense—many are owned by large mainstream banks that have sought to profit in the market niches left unexploited by regular banking.

In states where check-cashing stores are regulated, fees are clearly posted in business locations, so it is fairly easy to determine the costs to customers. For example, cashing a

**FIGURE 2: SOME REASONS HOUSEHOLDS DO NOT HAVE AN ACCOUNT OR CLOSED THEIR ACCOUNT, 2011 AND 2009**

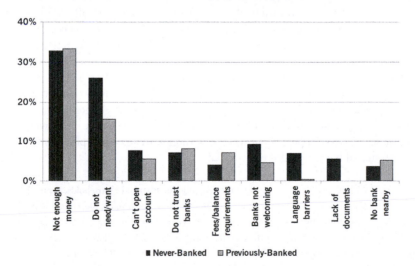

*Note:* The last four categories appeared only in the 2009 survey.

government check (or direct deposit services for these checks) costs 1-3% of the face value of the check. Paychecks from businesses typically carry a 1-5% fee. Determining the typical fees for transaction services in mainstream banks is more difficult because of complicated fee structures that are dependent upon minimum balances. For people with limited needs for transaction services, and who would risk low balance penalties if they used a mainstream bank, AFSPs may in fact be a reasonable alternative.

Fees for transaction services, however, pale in comparison to the cost of credit. To make ends meet, 12 million Americans rely on short-term payday loans each year, at interest rates of about 300-750% (annual percentage rate, or APR). (Thirty-five states allow payday lending.) For the average borrower, a two-week payday loan stretches into five months of debt, with total interest payments greater than the amount of the loan. Wanting in on the action, big banks have issued payday loans to their own customers.–terming them "deposit-advance loans," presumbaly to make them sound more legitimate.

With increased pressure from the new Consumer Financial Protection Bureau (CFPB) and the FDIC, the greedy practices of payday lenders, especially those operating on the internet, are gradually being investigated and curtailed. Now, banks are pulling back from deposit-advance loans. They are also beginning to cut off accounts for payday lenders and are allowing bank customers to halt automatic withdrawals to payday lending companies. What a difference the Dodd-Frank financial-regulation law and the CFPB are beginning to make.

U.S. Senator Elizabeth Warren (D-MA) wants to take the solutions to financial exclusion one step further, beyond regulatory protections against harmful lending and transaction practices. In a recent Huffington Post opinion piece, she urges a serious consideration of postal banks, backing a new report from the U.S. Postal Service (USPS) Office of the Inspector General. The Postal Service, she argues, could partner with banks to offer basic services, including bill paying, check cashing, and small loans.

The idea has precedents. The United States had a postal savings system for accepting and insuring small deposits from 1911 to 1967. The government was thought to be a safe place to stash savings. Savers were paid interest on money that the postal service accepted and redeposited in local banks. After World War II, banks offered higher interest rates to compete for deposits and postal deposits fell. The convenience of the local post office faded in importance as Americans increasingly enjoyed access to cars.

But the idea of postal banks is once again garnering widespread support (44% in favor vs. 37% opposed in a recent YouGov/Huffington Post poll). For millions of Americans, the local post office is one of the geographically closest retail outlets. Unlike private financial-service providers subject to patchy state-by-state regulations, federal postal banks would be regulated in all U.S. states. They would help ease the spatial void in poorer communities and guard against exploitative practices by unregulated banking "alternatives." ❑

*Sources:* 2011 FDIC National Survey of Unbanked and Underbanked Households, September 2012; FDIC National Survey of Unbanked and Underbanked Households, December 2009; Sen. Elizabeth Warren, "Coming to a Post Office Near You: Loans You Can Trust?" Huffington Post Blog, Feb. 1, 2014 (huffingtonpost.com); Office of the Inspector General, U.S. Postal Service, "Providing Non-Bank Financial Services for the Underserved," Report Number RARC-WP-14-2007, Jan. 27, 2014; Pew Charitable Trusts reports on Payday Lending in America (pewstates.org).

*Article 3.3*

# WHEN THE PUBLIC SQUARE IS IN CYBERSPACE
*Why Democracy Demands Net Neutrality*

## BY ZOE SHERMAN
*July/August 2014*

It is sometimes hard to remember how young the Internet really is. Many of the people I know first ventured online (starting with email) around 1995. For the technologically savvy, the Internet was a cool thing to play around with, but it was peripheral to most of the world's communications, commerce, and governance. Now, in less than one generation, it has become all but impossible to participate fully in many aspects of U.S. society without using the Internet, and this is also true to varying degrees around the world.

The Internet has become a layer of the public square. Because it now mediates our access to the cultural, economic, and political realms, its infrastructure matters. A lot. The structure of the Internet has deep implications for democracy. And that structure is not fixed. New rules being considered by the Federal Communications Commission (FCC)—under a heavy lobbying effort by the giant telecommunications companies—now threaten to change the architecture of the Internet in dangerous ways.

Since the Internet is a component of the public sphere, we should hold it to the ideal of freedom of expression. For this ideal to be fully meaningful, it must include not just the "negative freedom" from interference with the act of speaking, but also the "positive freedom" of access to other listeners and other voices. A democratic ideal of freedom of expression requires the practical ability to participate in public conversation.

The Internet has tremendous democratic potential. Its user-to-user architecture enables people to both speak and listen in ways that one-way-transmission technologies of print and broadcast media do not. Recognizing the role of Internet access in enabling full social participation, the Telecommunications Act of 1996 assigned the FCC the task of monitoring "whether advanced telecommunications capability ... [reaches] all Americans in a reasonable and timely fashion." The Act defined a slow connection as a problem that should be remedied. According to the FCC's most recent progress report, in 2012, 19 million Americans, mostly in rural areas, did not yet have access to broadband service. Of those living where broadband was offered, only 40% subscribed. Those who did not cited a variety of reasons, including inability to afford it. Still, most of us find one way or another to get online.

Now, the big internet service providers (ISPs)—telecom giants like Time-Warner, Comcast, and Verizon—want to change the price and speed structure. Under the current system, all of the data that any subscriber uploads or downloads is treated equally. When traffic is light, it all gets to its destination equally quickly. When traffic strains the capacity of the network, all data is at equal risk of delay. What the telecom companies would like to do, and what the FCC is poised to let them do, is charge a premium for priority service.

The telecom companies are the gatekeepers to the public square of cyberspace. They supply the physical infrastructure through which we make contact with one another. Those wires and fiber optic cables and wifi signals are valuable to us not as things-in-themselves but as conduits to the people on the other side. The telecom companies, standing between users, are positioned to shake us down, in exchange for letting us reach one another. It is a hugely profitable position to hold, and it would be an even more profitable position under the proposed rule changes. (Their proposal makes for strange bedfellows—you and I, and web-content companies like Netflix and Google, would all be subject to the shakedown.)

The position of gatekeeper is, or should be, a public trust. That is, in theory, why we have the FCC setting rules. If we allow differential pricing, we will be increasing the already staggering power of money, amplifying the voices of those who can pay, and further diminishing the democratic meaning of freedom of expression—understood as equal access for all. Indeed, these rule changes are only being considered because money already buys so much influence. Michael Powell is a former chairman of the FCC and a current big-money lobbyist for the cable industry. Tom Wheeler is the current chairman of the FCC and a former big-money lobbyist for the cable industry. Oh, and Wheeler was also a big contributor to Obama's presidential campaign before the President appointed him to the FCC.

The FCC received nearly 700,000 comments on the proposed rule changes via their website and e-mail. Most people can't afford a lobbyist to bend Wheeler's ear in person, but at least their emails are guaranteed to travel over the Internet just as fast as any other information—for now. ❏

*Sources:* Lawrence Lessig, *The Future of Ideas* (Random House, 2001); Stephen Breyer, *Active Liberty* (Alfred A. Knopf, 2005); Federal Communications Commission, *Eighth Broadband Progress Report*, 2012.

Article 3.4

# WAY BEYOND GREENWASHING

*Have corporations captured "Big Conservation"?*

## BY JONATHAN LATHAM
*March/April 2012*

I magine an international mega-deal. The global organic food industry agrees to support international agribusiness in clearing as much tropical rainforest as they want for farming. In return, agribusiness agrees to farm the now-deforested land using organic methods, and the organic industry encourages its supporters to buy the resulting timber and food under the newly devised "Rainforest Plus" label. There would surely be an international outcry.

Virtually unnoticed, however, even by their own membership, the world's biggest wildlife conservation groups have agreed to exactly such a scenario, only in reverse. Led by the World Wide Fund for Nature (WWF, still known as the World Wildlife Fund in the United States), many of the biggest conservation nonprofits including Conservation International and the Nature Conservancy have already agreed to a series of global bargains with international agribusiness. In exchange for vague promises of habitat protection, sustainability, and social justice, these conservation groups are offering to greenwash industrial commodity agriculture.

The big conservation nonprofits don't see it that way, of course. According to WWF's "Vice President for Market Transformation" Jason Clay, the new conservation strategy arose from two fundamental realizations.

The first was that agriculture and food production are the key drivers of almost every environmental concern. From issues as diverse as habitat destruction to over-use of water, from climate change to ocean dead zones, agriculture and food production are globally the primary culprits. To take one example, 80-90% of all fresh water extracted by humans is for agriculture, according to the UN Food and Agriculture Organization's "State of the World's Land and Water" report.

This point was emphasized once again in an analysis published in the scientific journal *Nature* in October 2011. The lead author of this study was Professor Jonathan Foley. Not only is Foley the director of the University of Minnesota-based Institute on the Environment, but he is also a science board member of the Nature Conservancy.

The second crucial realization for WWF was that forest destroyers typically are not peasants with machetes but national and international agribusinesses with bulldozers. It is the latter who deforest tens of thousands of acres at a time. Land clearance on this scale is an ecological disaster, but Claire Robinson of Earth Open Source points out it is also "incredibly socially destructive," as peasants are driven off their land and communities are destroyed. According to the UN Permanent Forum on Indigenous Issues, 60 million people worldwide risk losing their land and means of subsistence from palm plantations.

By about 2004, WWF had come to recognize the true impacts of industrial agriculture. Instead of informing their membership and initiating protests and boycotts, however, they embarked on a partnership strategy they call "market transformation."

## Market Transformation

With WWF leading the way, the conservation nonprofits have negotiated approval schemes for "Responsible" and "Sustainable" farmed commodity crops. According to WWF's Clay, the plan is to have agribusinesses sign up to reduce the 4-6 most serious negative impacts of each commodity crop by 70-80%. And if enough growers and suppliers sign up, then the Indonesian rainforests or the Brazilian Cerrado will be saved.

The ambition of market transformation is on a grand scale. There are schemes for palm oil (the Roundtable on Sustainable Palm Oil; RSPO), soybeans (the Round Table on Responsible Soy; RTRS), biofuels (the Roundtable on Sustainable Biofuels), Sugar (Bonsucro) and also for cotton, shrimp, cocoa and farmed salmon. These are markets each worth many billions of dollars annually and the intention is for these new "Responsible" and "Sustainable" certified products to dominate them.

The reward for producers and supermarkets will be that, reinforced on every shopping trip, "Responsible" and "Sustainable" logos and marketing can be expected to have major effects on public perception of the global food supply chain. And the ultimate goal is that, if these schemes are successful, human rights, critical habitats, and global sustainability will receive a huge and globally significant boost.

The role of WWF and other nonprofits in these schemes is to offer their knowledge to negotiate standards, to provide credibility, and to lubricate entry of certified products into international markets. On its UK website, for example, WWF offers its members the chance to "Save the Cerrado" by emailing supermarkets to buy "Responsible Soy." What WWF argues will be a major leap forward in environmental and social responsibility has already started. "Sustainable" and "Responsible" products are already entering global supply chains.

## Reputational Risk

For conservation nonprofits these plans entail risk, one of which is simple guilt by association. The Round Table on Responsible Soy (RTRS) scheme is typical of these certification schemes. Its membership includes WWF, Conservation International, Fauna and Flora International, the Nature Conservancy, and other prominent nonprofits. Corporate members include repeatedly vilified members of the industrial food chain. As of January 2012, there are 102 members, including Monsanto, Cargill, ADM, Nestle, BP, and UK supermarket ASDA.

That is not the only risk. Membership in the scheme, which includes signatures on press-releases and sometimes on labels, indicates approval for activities that are widely opposed. The RTRS, for example, certifies soybeans grown in large-scale chemical-intensive monocultures. They are usually genetically modified organisms (GMOs). They are mostly fed to animals. And they originate in countries with hungry populations. When, according to an ABC News poll, 52% of Americans think GMOs are unsafe and 93% think GMOs ought to be labeled, for example, this is a risk most organizations dependent on their reputations probably would not consider.

The remedy for such reputational risk is high standards, rigorous certification, and watertight traceability procedures. Only credibility at every step can deflect the seemingly obvious suspicion that the conservation nonprofits have been hood-winked or have somehow "sold out."

So, which one is it? Are "Responsible" and "Sustainable" certifications indicative of a genuine strategic success by WWF and its fellows, or are the schemes nothing more than business as usual with industrial-scale greenwashing and a social-justice varnish?

## Low and Ambiguous Standards

The first place to look is the standards themselves. The language from the RTRS standards (see sidebar), to stick with the case of soy, illustrates the tone of the RTRS principles and guidance.

There are two ways to read these standards. The generous interpretation is to recognize that the sentiments expressed are higher than what is actually practiced in many countries where soybeans are grown, in that the standards broadly follow common practice in Europe or North America. Nevertheless, they are far lower than organic or fair-trade standards; for example, they don't require crop rotation, or prohibit pesticides. Even a generous reading also needs to acknowledge the crucial point that adherence to similar requirements in Europe and North America has contaminated wells, depleted aquifers, degraded rivers, eroded the soil, polluted the oceans, driven species to extinction, and depopulated the countryside—to mention only a few well-documented downsides.

There is also a less generous interpretation of the standards. Much of the content is either in the form of statements, or it is merely advice. Thus section 4.2 reads: "Pollution is minimized and production waste is managed responsibly." Imperatives, such as: "must," "may never," "will," etc., are mostly lacking from the document. Worse, key terms such as "pollution," "minimized," "responsible," and "timely" (see sidebar) are left undefined. This chronic vagueness means that both certifiers and producers possess effectively infinite latitude to implement or judge the standards. They could never be enforced, in or out of court.

---

### The Round Table on Responsible Soy Standards

RTRS standards (version 1, June 2010) cover five "principles." Principle 1: Legal Compliance and Good Business Practices. Principle 2: Responsible Labour Conditions. Principle 3: Responsible Community Relations. Principle 4: Environmental Responsibility. Principle 5: Good Agricultural Practice.

Language typical of the standards includes, under Principle 2 (Responsible Labour Conditions), section 2.1.1 states: "No forced, compulsory, bonded, trafficked, or otherwise involuntary labor is used at any stage of production," while section 2.4.4 states, "Workers are not hindered from interacting with external parties outside working hours."

Under Principle 3 (Responsible Community Relations), section 3.3.3 states: "Any complaints and grievances received are dealt with in a timely manner."

Under Principle 4 (Environmental Responsibility), section 4.2 states: "Pollution is minimized and production waste is managed responsibly," and section 4.4 states: "Expansion of soy cultivation is responsible."

Under Principle 5 (Good Agricultural Practice), Section 5.9 states: "Appropriate measures are implemented to prevent the drift of agrochemicals to neighboring areas."

## Dubious Verification and Enforcement

Unfortunately, the flaws of RTRS certification do not end there. They include the use of an internal verification system. The RTRS uses professional certifiers, but only those who are members of RTRS. This means that the conservation nonprofits are relying on third parties for compliance information. It also means that only RTRS members can judge whether a principle was adhered to. Even if they consider it was not, there is nothing they can do, since the RTRS has no legal status or sanctions.

The "culture" of deforestation is also important to the standards. Rainforest clearance is often questionably legal, or actively illegal, and usually requires removing existing occupants from the land. It is a world of private armies and bribery. This operating environment makes very relevant the irony under which RTRS members, under Principle 1, volunteer to obey the law. The concept of volunteering to obey the law invites more than a few questions. If an organization is not already obeying the law, what makes WWF suppose that a voluntary code of conduct will persuade it? And does obeying the law meaningfully contribute to a marketing campaign based on responsibility?

Of equal concern is the absence of a clear certification trail. Under the "Mass Balance" system offered by RTRS, soybeans (or derived products) can be sold as "Responsible" that were never grown under the system. Mass Balance means vendors can transfer the certification quantity purchased, to non-RTRS soybeans. Such an opportunity raises the inherent difficulties of traceability and verification to new levels.

## How Will Certification Save Wild Habitats?

A key stated goal of WWF is to halt deforestation through the use of maps identifying priority habitat areas that are off-limits to RTRS members. There are crucial questions over these maps, however. First, even though soybeans are already being traded, the maps have yet to be drawn up. Secondly, the maps are to be drawn up by RTRS members themselves. Thirdly, RTRS maps can be periodically redrawn. Fourthly, RTRS members need not certify all of their production acreage. This means they can certify part of their acreage as "Responsible," but still sell (as "Irresponsible"?) soybeans from formerly virgin habitat. This means WWF's target for year 2020 of 25% coverage globally and 75% in WWF's "priority areas" would still allow 25% of the Brazilian soybean harvest to come from newly deforested land. And of course, the scheme cannot prevent non-members, or even non-certified subsidiaries, from specializing in deforestation.

These are certification schemes, therefore, with low standards, no methods of enforcement, and enormous loopholes. Pete Riley of UK GM Freeze dubs their instigator the "World Wide Fund for naïveté" and believes "the chances of Responsible soy saving the Cerrado are zero." Claire Robinson of Earth Open Source agrees: "The RTRS standard will not protect the forests and other sensitive ecosystems. Additionally, it greenwashes soy that's genetically modified to survive being sprayed with quantities of herbicide that endanger human health and the environment." There is even a website (www.toxicsoy.org) dedicated to exposing the greenwashing of GMO soy.

Many other groups apparently share that view. More than 250 large and small sustainable farming, social justice, and rainforest preservation groups from all over the world signed a "Letter of Critical Opposition to the RTRS" in 2009. Signatories included the Global Forest Coalition, Friends of the Earth, Food First, the British Soil Association and the World Development Movement.

Other commodity certifications involving WWF have also received strong criticism. The Mangrove Action Project in 2008 published a "Public Declaration Against the Process of Certification of Industrial Shrimp Aquaculture" while the World Rainforest Movement issued "Declaration against the Roundtable on Sustainable Palm Oil (RSPO)," signed by 256 organizations in October 2008.

## What Really Drives Commodity Certification?

Commodity certification is in many ways a strange departure for conservation nonprofits. In the first place the big conservation nonprofits are more normally active in acquiring and researching wild habitats. Secondly, these are membership organizations, yet it is hard to envisage these schemes energizing the membership. How many members of the Nature Conservancy will be pleased to find that their organization has been working with Monsanto to promote GM crops as "Responsible"? Indeed, one can argue that these programs are being actively concealed from their members, donors, and the public. From their advertising, their websites, and their educational materials, one would presume that poachers, population growth and ignorance are the chief threats to wildlife in developing countries. It is not true, however, and as WWF's Jason Clay and the very existence of these certification schemes make clear, senior management knows it well.

In public, the conservation nonprofits justify market transformation as cooperative; they wish to work with others, not against them. However, they have chosen to work preferentially with powerful and wealthy corporations. Why not cooperate instead with small farmers' movements, indigenous groups, and already successful standards, such as fair-trade, organic and non-GMO? These are causes that could use the help of big international organizations. Why not, with WWF help, embed into organic standards a rainforest conservation element? Why not cooperate with your membership to create engaged consumer power against habitat destruction, monoculture, and industrial farming? Instead, the new "Responsible" and "Sustainable" standards threaten organic, fair-trade, and local food systems—which are some of the environmental movement's biggest successes.

One clue to the enthusiasm for "market transformation" may be that financial rewards are available. According to Nina Holland of Corporate Europe Observatory, certification is "now a core business" for WWF. Indeed, WWF and the Dutch nonprofit Solidaridad are currently receiving millions of euros from the Dutch government (under its Sustainable Trade Action Plan) to support these schemes. According to the plan, 67 million euros have already been committed, and similar amounts are promised.

## The Threat From the Food Movement

Commodity-certification schemes like RTRS can be seen as an inability of global conservation leadership to work constructively with the ordinary people who live in and around wild areas of the globe; or they can be seen as a disregard for fair-trade and organic labels; or as a lost opportunity to inform and energize members and potential members as to the true causes of habitat destruction; or even as a cynical moneymaking scheme. These are all plausible explanations of the enthusiasm for certification schemes and probably each plays a part. None, however, explains why conservation nonprofits would sign up to schemes whose standards and credibility are so low. Especially when, as never before, agribusiness is under pressure to change its destructive social and environmental practices.

The context of these schemes is that we live at an historic moment. Positive alternatives to industrial agriculture, such as fair trade, organic agriculture, agro-ecology, and the System of Rice Intensification, have shown they can feed the planet, without destroying it, even with a greater population. Consequently, there is now a substantial international consensus of informed opinion that industrial agriculture is a principal cause of the current environmental crisis and the chief obstacle to hunger eradication.

This consensus is one of several roots of the international food movement. As a powerful synergism of sustainability, social-justice, sustainability, food-quality, and environmental concerns, the food movement is a clear threat to the long-term existence of the industrial food system. Incidentally, this is why big multinationals have been buying up ethical brands.

Under these circumstances, evading the blame for the environmental devastation of the Amazon, Asia, and elsewhere, undermining organic and other genuine certification schemes, and splitting the environmental movement must be a dream come true for members of the industrial food system. A true cynic might surmise that the food industry could hardly have engineered it better had they planned it themselves.

## Who Runs Big Conservation?

To guard against such possibilities, nonprofits are required to have boards of directors whose primary legal function is to guard the mission of the organization and to protect its good name. In practice, for conservation nonprofits this means overseeing potential financial conflicts and preventing the organization from lending its name to greenwashing.

So, who are the individuals guarding the mission of global conservation nonprofits? U.S.-WWF boasts (literally) that its new vice-chair was the last CEO of Coca-Cola, Inc. (a member of Bonsucro) and that another board member is Charles O. Holliday Jr., the current chairman of the board of Bank of America, who was formerly CEO of DuPont (owner of Pioneer Hi-Bred International, a major player in the GMO industry). The current chair of the executive board at Conservation International is Robert Walton, better known as chair of the board of Wal-Mart (which now sells "sustainably sourced" food and owns the supermarket chain ASDA). The boards of WWF and Conservation International do have more than a sprinkling of members with conservation-related careers. But they are heavily outnumbered by business representatives. On the board of Conservation International, for example, are GAP, Intel, Northrop Grumman, JP Morgan, Starbucks, and UPS, among others.

The Nature Conservancy's board of directors has only two members (out of 22) who list an active affiliation to a conservation organization in their board CV (Prof. Gretchen Daly and Cristian Samper, head of the U.S. Museum of Natural History). Only one other member even mentions among his qualifications an interest in the subject of conservation. The remaining members are like Shona Brown, who is an employee of Google and a board member of Pepsico, or Meg Whitman, the current president and CEO of Hewlett-Packard, or Muneer A. Satter, a managing director of Goldman Sachs.

So, was market transformation developed with the support of these boards or against their wishes? The latter is hardly likely. The key question then becomes: Did these boards in fact instigate market transformation? Did it come from the very top?

## Never Ending

Leaving aside whether conservation was ever their true intention, it seems highly unlikely that WWF and its fellow conservation groups will leverage a positive transformation of the food system by bestowing "Sustainable" and "Responsible" standards on agribusiness. Instead, it appears much more likely that, by undermining existing standards and offering worthless standards of their own, habitat destruction and human misery will only increase.

Market transformation, as envisaged by WWF, nevertheless might have worked. However, WWF neglected to consider that successful certification schemes start from the ground up. Organic and fair-trade began with a large base of committed farmers determined to fashion a better food system. Producers willingly signed up to high standards and clear requirements because they believed in them. Indeed, many already were practicing high standards without certification. But when big players in the food industry have tried to climb on board, game the system and manipulate standards, problems have resulted, even with credible standards like fair-trade and organic. At some point big players will probably undermine these standards. They seem already to be well on the way, but if they succeed their efforts will only have proved that certification standards can never be a substitute for trust, commitment and individual integrity.

The only good news in this story is that it contradicts fundamentally the defeatist arguments of the WWF. Old-fashioned activist strategies, of shaming bad practice, boycotting products, and encouraging alternatives, do work. The market opportunity presently being exploited by WWF and company resulted from the success of these strategies, not their failure. Multinational corporations, we should conclude, really do fear activists, non-profits, informed consumers, and small producers all working together. ❑

**Sources:** Jonathan A. Foley et al. "Solutions for a Cultivated Planet" *Nature*, October 2011 (Nature.com); Jason Clay, "Economics, Behavior and Biodiversity Loss: Sustainability as a Pre-competitive Issue," March 25, 2011 (youtube.com); Food and Agriculture Organization of the United Nations, "Scarcity and degradation of land and water: growing threat to food security," November 28, 2011 (fao.org); State of the World's Land and Water Resources for Food and Agriculture (SOLAW), November 28, 2011 (fao.org); Mat McDermott, "More Dirty Deforestation: 55% of Indonesia's Logging Illegal + Cargill's Two Hidden Palm Oil Plantations," May 6, 2010 (treehugger.com); Earth Open Source (earthopensource.org); United Nations (UN; un.org); Roundtable on Sustainable Palm Oil (RSPO; rspo.org); Round Table on Responsible Soy (RTRS; responsiblesoy.org); Roundtable on Sustainable Biofuels (rsb.epfl.ch); Bonsucro (Bonsucro.com); WWF, "Save the Cerrado: What's happening in the Cerrado?" (wwf.org. uk); Gary Langer, "Behind the Label, Many Skeptical of Bio-engineered Food," June 19, 2001 (abcnews.com); Round Table on Responsible Soy, "Why certifying under the RTST Standard?" (responsiblesoy.org); Natural Resources Defense Council, "Atrazine: Poisoning the Well," May 2010 (nrdc.org); The *Capital-Journal* Editorial Board, "Time for action on rural depopulation," July 28, 2011 (cjonline.com); "State of the World's Indigenous Peoples Report, Chapter 7: Emerging Issues," January 2010 (un.org); "A Brief History of Rubber" (rainforests.mongabay.com); "Letter of critical opposition to the Round Table on Responsible Soy," April 2009 (bangmfood. org); Global Forest Coalition (globalforestcoalition.org); Public Declaration Against the Process of Certification of Industrial Shrimp Aquaculture, November 3, 2008 (mangroveactionproject. org); World Rainforest Movement, "Declarations against the Roundtable on Sustainable Palm Oil (RSPO) in Defence of Human Rights, Food Sovereignty," September 2008 (wrm.org); System of Rice Intensification (SRI-Rice; sri.ciifad.cornell.edu); Sarah Hills, "Coca-Cola snaps up first Bonsucro certified sugarcane," June 22, 2011 (foodnavigator.com); "Wal-Mart Unveils Global Sustainable Agriculture Goal," October 14, 2010 (walmartstores.com); "Largest Corporate Dairy, Biotech Firm and USDA Accused of Conspiring to Corrupt Rulemaking and Pollute Organics," January 23, 2012 (cornucopia.org); Dutch Ministry of Agriculture, "Nature and Food Quality Sustainable Food: Public Summary of Policy Document" (government.nl); Jonathan Latham and Allison Wilson, "How the Science Media Failed the IAASTD," April 7, 2008 (independentsciencenews.org).

*Article 3.5*

# CAMPUS STRUGGLES AGAINST SWEATSHOPS CONTINUE

*Indonesian workers and U.S. students fight back against Adidas.*

## BY SARAH BLASKEY AND PHIL GASPER
*September/October 2012*

Abandoning his financially ailing factory in the Tangerang region of Indonesia, owner Jin Woo Kim fled the country for his home, South Korea, in January 2011 without leaving money to pay his workers. The factory, PT Kizone, stayed open for several months and then closed in financial ruin in April, leaving 2,700 workers with no jobs and owed $3.4 million of legally mandated severance pay.

In countries like Indonesia, with no unemployment insurance, severance pay is what keeps workers and their families from literal starvation. "The important thing is to be able to have rice. Maybe we add some chili pepper, some salt, if we can," explained an ex-Kizone worker, Marlina, in a report released by the Worker Rights Consortium (WRC), a U.S.-based labor-rights monitoring group, in May 2012.

Marlina, widowed mother of two, worked at PT Kizone for eleven years before the factory closed. She needs the severance payment in order to pay her son's high school registration fee and monthly tuition, and to make important repairs to her house.

When the owner fled, the responsibility for severance payments to PT Kizone workers fell on the companies that sourced from the factory—Adidas, Nike, and the Dallas Cowboys. Within a year, both Nike and the Dallas Cowboys made severance payments that they claim are proportional to the size of their orders from the factory, around $1.5 million total. But Adidas has refused to pay any of the $1.8 million still owed to workers.

Workers in PT Kizone factory mainly produced athletic clothing sold to hundreds of universities throughout the United States. All collegiate licensees like Adidas and Nike sign contracts with the universities that buy their apparel. At least 180 universities around the nation are affiliated with the WRC and have licensing contracts mandating that brands pay "all applicable back wages found due to workers who manufactured the licensed articles." If wages or severance pay are not paid to workers that produce university goods, then the school has the right to terminate the contract.

Using the language in these contracts, activists on these campuses coordinate nationwide divestment campaigns to pressure brands like Adidas to uphold previously unenforceable labor codes of conduct.

Unpaid back wages and benefits are a major problem in the garment industry. Apparel brands rarely own factories. Rather, they contract with independent manufacturers all over the world to produce their wares. When a factory closes for any reason, a brand can simply take its business somewhere else and wash its hands of any responsibilities to the fired workers.

Brands like Nike and Russell have lost millions of dollars when, pressed by United Students Against Sweatshops (USAS), universities haver terminated their contracts. According to the USAS website, campus activism has forced Nike to pay severance and Russell to rehire over 1,000 workers it had laid off, in order to avoid losing more collegiate contracts. Now many college activists have their sights set on Adidas.

At the University of Wisconsin (UW) in Madison, the USAS-affiliated Student Labor Action Coalition (SLAC) and sympathetic faculty are in the middle of a more than year-long campaign to pressure the school to terminate its contract with Adidas in solidarity with the PT Kizone workers.

The chair of UW's Labor Licensing Policy Committee (LLPC) says that Adidas is in violation of the code of conduct for the school's licensees. Even the university's senior counsel, Brian Vaughn, stated publicly at a June LLPC meeting that Adidas is "in breach of the contract based on its failure to adhere to the standards of the labor code." But despite the fact that Vaughn claimed at the time that the University's "two overriding goals are to get money back in the hands of the workers and to maintain the integrity of the labor code," the administration has dragged its feet in responding to Adidas.

Instead of putting the company on notice for potential contract termination and giving it a deadline to meet its obligations as recommended by the LLPC, UW entered into months of fruitless negotiations with Adidas in spring of 2012. In July, when these negotiations had led nowhere, UW's interim chancellor David Ward asked a state court to decide whether or not Adidas had violated the contract (despite the senior counsel's earlier public admission that it had). This process will delay a decision for many more months--perhaps years if there are appeals.

Since the Adidas campaign's inception in the fall of 2011, SLAC members have actively opposed the school's cautious approach, calling both the mediation process and the current court action a "stalling tactic" by the UW administration and Adidas to avoid responsibility to the PT Kizone workers. In response, student organizers planned everything from frequent letter deliveries to campus administrators, to petition drives, teach-ins, and even a banner drop from the administration building that over 300 people attended, all in hopes of pressuring the chancellor (who ultimately has the final say in the matter) to cut the contract with Adidas.

While the administration claims that it is moving slowly to avoid being sued by Adidas, it is also getting considerable pressure from its powerful athletics director, Barry Alvarez, to continue its contract with Adidas. As part of the deal, UW's sports programs receive royalties and sports gear worth about $2.5 million every year.

"Just look at the money—what we lose and what it would cost us," Alvarez told the *Wisconsin State Journal*, even though other major brands would certainly jump at the opportunity to replace Adidas. "We have four building projects going on. It could hurt recruiting. There's a trickle-down effect that would be devastating to our whole athletic program."

But Tina Treviño-Murphy, a student activist with SLAC, rejects this logic. "A strong athletics department shouldn't have to be built on a foundation of stolen labor," she told Dollars & Sense. "Our department and our students deserve better.".

Adidas is now facing pressure from both campus activists in the United States and the workers in Indonesia--including sit-ins by the latter at the German and British embassies in Jakarta. (Adidas' world headquarters are in Germany, and the company sponsored the recent London Olympics.) This led to a meeting between their union and an Adidas representative, who refused to admit responsibility but instead offered food vouchers to some of the workers. The offer amounted to a tiny fraction of the owed severance and was rejected as insulting by former Kizone workers.

In the face of intransigence from university administrations and multinational companies prepared to shift production quickly from one location to another to stay one step ahead of labor-rights monitors, campus activism to fight sweatshops can seem like a labor of Sisyphus. After more than a decade of organizing, a recent fundraising appeal from USAS noted that "today sweatshop conditions are worse than ever."

Brands threaten to pull out of particular factories if labor costs rise, encouraging a work environment characterized by "forced overtime, physical and sexual harassment, and extreme anti-union intimidation, even death threats," says Natalie Yoon, a USAS member who recently participated in a delegation to factories in Honduras and El Salvador.

According to Snehal Shingavi, a professor at the University of Texas, Austin who was a USAS activist at Berkeley for many years, finding ways to build links with the struggles of the affected workers is key. "What I think would help the campaign the most is if there were actually more sustained and engaged connections between students here and workers who are in factories who are facing these conditions," Shingavi told *Dollars & Sense*. Ultimately, he said, only workers' self-activity can "make the kind of changes that I think we all want, which is an end to exploitative working conditions."

But in the meantime, even small victories are important. Anti-sweatshop activists around the country received a boost in September, when Cornell University President David Skorton announced that his school was ending its licensing contract with Adidas effective October 1, because of the company's failure to pay severance to PT Kizone workers. The announcement followed a sustained campaign by the Sweatfree Cornell Coalition, leading up to a "study in" at the president's office. While the contract itself was small, USAS described the decision as the "first domino," which may lead other campuses to follow suit. Shortly afterwards, Oberlin College in Ohio told Adidas that it would not renew its current four-year contract with the company if the workers in Indonesia are not paid severance.

Perhaps just as significant are the lessons that some activists are drawing from these campaigns. "The people who have a lot of power are going to want to keep that power and the only way to make people give some of that up is if we make them," Treviño-Murphy said. "So it's really pressure from below, grassroots organizing, that makes the difference. We see that every day in SLAC and I think it teaches us to be not just better students but better citizens who will stand up to fight injustice every time." ❏

*Sources:* Worker Rights Consortium, "Status Update Re: PT Kizone (Indonesia)," May 15, 2012 (workersrights.org); Andy Baggot, "Alvarez Anxiously Awaits Adidas Decision," *Wisconsin State Journal*, July 13, 2012 (host.madison.com); United Students Against Sweatshops (usas.org), PT Kizone update, June 15, 2012 (cleanclothes.org/urgent-actions/kizoneupdate).

Article 3.6

# HOW TO TAKE ON THE CARD SHARKS—AND WIN!

*New consumer-protection legislation has reined in predatory credit card lending.*

**BY JIM CAMPEN**
*November/December 2013*

In the early 2000s, credit card companies, like other lenders, decided that there was lots of money to be made by exploiting vulnerable consumers. Up to that point, the credit card industry was a somewhat boring business that made its money by charging high—but not exorbitant—interest rates to borrowers who it judged likely to be able to make their monthly payments on time. Then, however, the giant banks that provide the bulk of the nation's credit cards switched to a business model based on what Elizabeth Warren, then a professor at Harvard Law School, memorably termed "tricks and traps." These were spelled out in the almost impossible-to-understand small print of the multi-page "agreements" that the banks provided to their customers. Anyone who did manage to read to the end found that the "agreement" allowed the credit card company to change any of its terms "at any time, for any reason."

The unfair and exploitative practices of the credit card companies, affecting millions of households, soon became widely known. Five years ago, it was almost impossible to avoid the avalanche of news articles, radio and TV reports, and Internet postings about them. Today, such stories are few and far between. This isn't because the media became bored with the story. It's because a powerful consumer movement publicized the abuses, built a strong campaign, and won two important legislative victories.

## Tricks and Traps

Millions of consumers were enticed with offers of cards with "promotional" interest rates as low as 0% for the first few months and regular interest rates of between 12% and 14% after that, but ended up paying far more. They were slapped with late fees averaging over $33 each time their monthly payment arrived even one day late, even if the due date fell on a Sunday and their payment arrived on Monday. They faced stiff over-limit fees—sometimes multiple charges for a number of small purchases on the same day—if their charges exceeded their credit limit by even a single dollar, even though borrowers were generally not aware that they had exceeded their limit or that the credit card companies would authorize over-limit charges.

Most devastatingly, both of these minor mistakes were among those that could result in their interest rate being switched to a much higher "penalty rate." Some card companies adopted the policy of "universal default" whereby even a problem on an unrelated account (for example, being late on an electric bill) could result in a cardholder being subject to the penalty rate. By 2007, the average penalty rate was 16.9 percentage points higher than the regular interest rate, meaning that a 13% rate would jump to 29.9%.

Worst of all, the penalty rate applied not only to future purchases, but also to money already borrowed. For a household with the average 2008 credit card balance, about $10,700, this would result in additional interest charges of more than $1,800 per year. Once a household fell into this trap, it was almost impossible to get out—which is just the way the banks liked it.

Many of those trapped were low- and middle-income families who used their credit cards to pay for basic living expenses and unexpected medical bills. One recent survey, by the liberal policy organization Dēmos, found that two-fifths of such lower-income families used their credit cards in this way. Many other victims were college students, on their own for the first time, who fell prey to aggressive marketing on college campuses and ended up with debt that they couldn't repay as well as a damaged credit rating.

## A Consumer Victory: The Credit CARD Act of 2009

As the credit card industry's abuses grew and spread, millions of outraged consumers demanded change. Led by a coalition of national consumer advocacy groups —including the Center for Responsible Lending, the Consumer Federation of America, Consumers Union, the National Consumer Law Center, and U.S. PIRG —a powerful grassroots movement pushed Congress to take action. The industry argued that the proposed legislation that eventually became the Credit Card Accountability, Responsibility, and Disclosure Act (known as the CARD Act) would end up hurting consumers by raising the cost and reducing the availability of credit card borrowing.

But credit card abuses were so widespread and so offensive that politicians were unwilling to defend them in the light of day. Although many Republicans worked behind the scenes to derail or weaken the bill, when the CARD Act came up for its final votes in May 2009, it passed overwhelmingly in both the Senate (90-5) and the House of Representatives (361-54).

The CARD Act effectively outlaws the worst of the credit card industry's tricks and traps. Most importantly, it prohibits retroactive interest rate increases on existing balances unless a borrower has missed two consecutive monthly payments on the account. And not only that: when a borrower is hit with a penalty rate, the company is required to restore the original interest rate if and when the borrower succeeds in making six consecutive on-time payments.

Late fees have been reduced by requiring that consumers have at least 21 days to make their payments, that payments due on a Sunday or holiday be regarded as on time if they arrive the next business day, that payments be due the same date each month, and that the fees be "reasonable and proportional." Over-limit fees are banned unless a cardholder opts-in to allow approval of charges over their credit limit, and are limited to one fee per month. The initial rate offered on a new account cannot be raised during the first year, and after that the borrower must be provided with 45-day advance notice and given the opportunity to cancel the card and pay off the existing balance over five years.

Credit card companies are prohibited from opening a new account or increasing a borrower's credit limit without assessing the consumer's ability to make timely loan payments. Those under 21 are given special protection from predatory credit card lenders by a prohibition on sending pre-approved offers of credit without advance permission, a ban on marketing on college campuses, and a new rule that no one under 21 years of age can get a card without either proving an independent ability to make the required monthly payments or obtaining a co-signer over 21.

## Consumers Win Again: The CFPB

The enactment of the CARD Act was a major accomplishment. But simply passing laws doesn't make a difference unless those laws are enforced. And prohibiting existing abusive practices can't protect consumers against the credit card companies' endless ability to come up with imaginative new abuses that get around the law. The title of a December 2009 report from the Center for Responsible Lending spelled out the problem: "Dodging Reform: As Some Credit Card Abuses are Outlawed, New Ones Proliferate."

That's why a second consumer legislative victory—ensuring that the financial reform law passed in July 2010 (the Dodd-Frank Act) mandated the establishment of a Consumer Financial Protection Bureau (CFPB)—was perhaps even more important than the CARD Act itself.

The CFPB, which came into existence in July 2011, is charged not only with writing and enforcing the regulations that implement the CARD Act and other consumer-protection laws, but also with monitoring the operation of consumer-credit markets and taking action against unfair, deceptive, or abusive acts and practices. It seeks to improve consumers' ability to understand prices and risks upfront when shopping for credit, and to offer them a one-stop location for submitting complaints and seeking remedies for problems with credit card providers.

## The Fruits of These Victories

That the CARD Act has produced major benefits for consumers, with none of the dire consequences predicted by the industry, has been documented in numerous reports and studies. For example, the group Consumer Action noted that while complaints about credit cards were regularly the number one reason for calls to its consumer hotline before 2009, they are no longer even among the top ten.

The most comprehensive assessment to date of the Act's impact on consumers and on the industry is provided by a major report released by the CFPB in October 2013. This report found that the average late fee had gone down from $33 to $27 and that over-limit fees had essentially disappeared. Together, these two changes were saving consumers an estimated $4 billion per year.

The CFPB also found that, while credit remains readily available to those with the ability to repay, the number of 18- to 20-year-olds with at least one credit card had fallen by half. (Meanwhile, of course, student loans have soared. These loans have their own problems, but at least their interest rates are much lower than those on credit cards and no repayment is required while students remain in school.)

The CFPB's publicly available consumer complaint database recorded over 36,000 complaints about credit cards in its first two years of operation, resulting in monetary payments to about 6,500 consumers, and increased public scrutiny of card-company performance. J. D. Power's 2013 *Credit Card Satisfaction Study* showed that customer satisfaction had risen every year since 2010, to the highest level since the study began in 2007.

The CFPB's report also highlighted areas where consumers continue to suffer from abusive practices of the credit card industry and promised to address these issues in a timely manner. In one of these areas—the selling of "add-on" products that purport to offer debt protection and identity protection—the CFPB has already required three big lenders (Chase, Capital One, and Discover) to refund over $700 million to consumers and to pay over $100 million in fines for deceptive marketing and charging for services that were never actually provided.

## Crying Wolf

Data on what's happened during the three and one-half years since passage of the CARD Act demonstrate beyond any doubt what consumer advocates said at the time: that banks were "crying wolf," rather than warning of real dangers, when they predicted that the pending legislation would cause the cost of credit card borrowing to soar and their own profitability to plummet.

It is theoretically possible that all of the CARD Act's consumer benefits from the lower fees and rates noted earlier could have been offset by increases in other charges. This is what Jamie Dimon, CEO of JPMorgan Chase, was predicting when he said that "If you're a restaurant and you can't charge for the soda, you're going to charge more for the burger." But the CFPB investigated this possibility by measuring what it calls the "total cost of credit"—that is, it added up all fees and interest charges paid by credit card borrowers and calculated what percentage this represented of the total amount of credit card debt outstanding. The CFPB found that the total cost of credit declined from 16.4% in the last quarter of 2008 to 14.4% in the last quarter of 2012. It is impossible to know how much of this reduction is a result of the CARD Act, but it is crystal clear that predictions of an increase in borrowing costs were wrong.

Another October 2013 study on the impact of the CARD Act, this one by four academic economists, concluded that the resulting fee reductions have saved consumers $21 billion per year "with no evidence of an offsetting increase in interest charges or a reduction in access to credit." The savings were particularly great for the riskiest borrowers. While the fee reductions amounted to 2.8% of total credit card balances annually, they came to over ten percent of their credit card balances for the 17% of borrowers who were in the highest risk category as measured by their credit scores at the time they opened their accounts.

Did the consumer benefits from the CARD Act come at the expense of lender profitability? It's possible to get a remarkably clear answer to this question because the FDIC reports quarterly on the performance of different kinds of banks, categorized by specialization or size, and one of its categories consists of "credit card lenders." It turns out that all but one of the six largest credit card lenders (who together account for over two-thirds of total credit card balances) do their lending though separate banks that specialize in credit cards. This is true for Bank of

America, Chase, Capital One, Discover, and American Express; the only exception is Citibank.

Since 2010, "credit card banks" has been the most profitable single category, using the two measures of profitability reported by the FDIC—return on assets (ROA) and return on equity (ROE). In 2012, ROA was 3.14% for credit card banks, more than triple the 1.00% for all banks; ROE was 20.97% for credit card banks, more than double the 8.92% for all banks. The results for 2012 are very similar to those for 2011 and for the first half of 2013, and also to those for 2007, before the onset of the financial crisis and economic downturn.

Perhaps the credit card companies had been outsmarting themselves. A business model based on "tricks and traps" that aggressively pushed money into the hands of borrowers who lacked the ability to repay their debts may have worked in the short run, but ultimately was disastrous to the lenders themselves. Lending money only to those with the ability to repay it would seem like simple common sense. It's too bad that financial hardship for millions of borrowers, an act of Congress, and a new federal agency was necessary to make these lenders behave sensibly. ❑

**Sources:** The CARD ACT Report, October 1, 2013 (consumerfinance.gov); Sumit Agarwal, et al., "Regulating Consumer Financial Products: Evidence from Credit Cards"; Center for Responsible Lending (responsiblelending.org); Federal Deposit Insurance Corporation (FDIC), *Quarterly Banking Profile* (fdic.gov); Peter Dreier and Donald Cohen, "Credit Sharks Crying Wolf," The Cry Wolf Project, May 2009 (crywolfproject.org).

# Chapter 4

# FIRMS, PRODUCTION, AND PROFIT MAXIMIZATION

## INTRODUCTION

How do producers make decisions? Textbooks describe a process that is rational, benign, and downright sensible. There is one best—least costly and most profitable—way to produce any given amount of goods or services. Given a particular scale of operations, there is one most profitable amount to produce. Businesses adjust their total output and the mix of inputs at the margin until they achieve these most profitable outcomes. They pay the going wage for labor, just as they pay the going price for any input. And when businesses have achieved the lowest possible costs, market competition ensures that they pass on savings to consumers.

This chapter describes a reality that is a bit more complicated, and in some ways uglier, than the textbook model. Very large companies are not the passive price-takers of neoclassical lore but do in fact affect the market-wide level of prices, profits, and wages, and manufacture their own demand. Thus, large corporations are the very embodiment of market power (volating Tilly Assumption #1, Article 1.2).

James Boyce opens the discussion, in "Pursuing Profits—Or Power?" (Article 4.1), by questioning the assumption that the firm seels to maximize profits alone. In Boyce's view, a great deal of business behavior (especially political behavior) suggests that corporate decision-makers often put the pursuit of power above profits.

Alejandro Reuss follows with a primer on corporations (Article 4.2). He describes the ways that corporations are "special"—that is, different from other capitalist enterprises—and why they have become the dominant form of business organization in many countries. He concludes by discussing how corporations' economic power—their control over investment and employment—can translate into political power.

Next, Dean Baker takes a look at the factors behind skyrocketing executive compensation at large corporations. In "Corporate Cronyism: The Secret to Overpaid CEOs" (Article 4.3), Baker argues that it is not CEOs' indiviual productivity, but rather their relationship to other corporate directors, that explains the executive-pay mystery.

In Article 4.4, "What's Good for Wal-Mart ...," John Miller provides a salient example of firms' market power. He suggests that there may not be just "one best way" for retail businesses, but rather two: a "high road" based on high levels of service, skilled, decently paid employees, and higher prices, as exemplified by the business model at Costco; and a "low road" that offers low prices, no frills, and a low-paid, high-turnover workforce, which is Walmart's business model. Despite Walmart's growth and its position as the world's largest retailer, the author questions whether the business model has in fact proven beneficial for the U.S. economy as a whole.

In the next article, "Vultures in the E.R." (Article 4.5), Nicole Aschoff details how firms can profit at the expense of the social good. Aschoff focuses her attention on private-equity firms' increasingly common acquisition of hospitals. This may be profitable for the firms, she argues, while coming at the expense of patient care and sometimes jeopardizing the long term viability of the hospitals themselves.

Mark Paul and Emily Stephens (Article 4.6) describe the growing phenomenon of community supported agriculture (CSA), an alternative model for small-farm financing in which consumers pay for a share of farm produce at the beginning of the growing season. Paul and Stephens take a sympathetic but not uncritical look at CSA's potential for reestablishing a direct relationship between farmers and eaters.

The final essay is economist Nancy Folbre's look at an alternative way of structuring the firm, "Co-op Economics" (Article 4.7). Folbre looks not only at the strength of workers' cooperatives, in which the workers are also the owners of the firm, but also the problems that they face in growing and becoming more widespread.

## Discussion Questions

1. (General) The authors of the articles in this chapter present various firm strategies as a choice, rather than an imperative. How does this compare with the standard microeconomic analysis of business decision-making?

2. (General) Miller suggests that we should change the rules of the competitive game to steer businesses toward better treatment of workers. Present-day capitalism already has some such rules (such as those forbidding slavery). What rule changes do articles in this chapter propose? What do you think of these proposals?

3. (Article 4.1) Boyce argues that firms frequently put power before profits. If greater power goes hand in hand with higher profits, how can we tell what aim firms are actually pursuing?

4. (Article 4.2) How do corporations differ from other capitalist firms? How should the fact that corporations are chartered by the government, and shareholders given special protections by law (such as limited liability), affect our attitudes about government regulation of corporate operations?

5. (Article 4.3) Mainstrem neoclassical theory claims that, whatever CEOs' compensation, it must be justified by their contributions to production, or firms would not be willing to pay it. How does Baker dispute this view?

6.  (Article 4.4) John Miller implies that there is more than one "best" way to organize production. Do you agree? If other ways of organizing production are equally good, why are certain ways dominant, at least in particular industries?

7.  (Article 4.4) According to Cervantes (sidebar), how does Costco keep prices low while following very different labor practices?

8.  (Article 4.5) Neoclassical economists argue that competitive markets align private incentives with the social good. Why does Aschoff think this is not the case with private-equity firms? Is this a special case, or does this point to a broader problem with the neoclassical view?

9.  (Articles 4.5) Aschoff describes ways corporations can profit that are formally legal but, in her view, socially harmful. When does the pursuit of profits cross the line? Would you draw the line at law-breaking, or are there some legal business practices—in addition to illegal ones—that you consider unacceptable?

10. (Article 4.6) Paul and Stephens describe community supported agriculture, a relationship where consumers purchase farm "shares" directly from farmers at the beginning of the growing season. This both eliminates the role of food wholesalers and retailers (as intermediaries between food producers and consumers) and the reliance of farmers on credit. Do you see these changes as desirable? Could they become the norm, rather than the exception? Why or why not?

11. (Article 4.7) Folbre proposes a dramatically different power structure at the level of the individual firm, with workers democratically contolling the enterprises where they work. Why does she think that this alternative structure could be desirable for workers and for society? If it is so desirable, why is it not more common?

*Article 4.1*

# PURSUING PROFITS—OR POWER?

## BY JAMES K. BOYCE
*July/August 2013*

**D**o corporations seek to maximize profits? Or do they seek to maximize power? The two may be complementary—wealth begets power, power begets wealth— but they're not the same. One important difference is that profits can come from an expanding economic "pie," whereas the size of the power pie is fixed. Power is a zero-sum game: more for me means less for you. And for corporations, the pursuit of power sometimes trumps the pursuit of profits.

Take public education, for example. Greater investment in education from pre- school through college could increase the overall pie of well-being. But it would narrow the educational advantage of the corporate oligarchs and their privately schooled chil- dren—and diminish the power that comes with it. Although corporations could benefit from the bigger pie produced by a better-educated labor force, there's a tension between what's good for business and what's good for the business elite.

Similarly, the business elite today supports economic austerity instead of full-employment policies that would increase growth and profits. This may have something to do with the fact that austerity widens inequality, while full employ- ment would narrow it (by empowering workers). If we peel away the layers of the onion, at the core again we find that those at the top of the corporate pyramid put power before profits.

As one more example, consider the politics of government regulation. Corporations routinely pass along to consumers whatever costs they incur as a result of regulation. In the auto industry, for instance, the regulations that mandated seat belts, catalytic converters, and better fuel efficiency added a few hundred dollars to car prices. They didn't cut automaker profit margins. If the costs of regulation are ultimately borne by the consumer, why do they face such stiff resistance from the corporations? The answer may have less to do with profits than with power. Corporate chieftains are touchy about their "management prerogatives." They sim- ply don't like other folks telling them what to do.

In a famous 1971 memorandum to the U.S. Chamber of Commerce, future Supreme Court Justice Lewis Powell wrote, "The day is long past when the chief executive office of a major corporation discharges his responsibility by maintain- ing a satisfactory growth of profits." To counter what he described as an attack on the American free-enterprise system by labor unions, students, and consumer advo- cates, Powell urged CEOs to act on "the lesson that political power is necessary; that power must be assiduously cultivated; and that when necessary, it must be used aggressively and with determination." He was preaching to a receptive choir.

The idea that firms single-mindedly maximize profits is an axiom of faith of neoclassical Econ 101, but alternative theories have a long history in the broader profession. Thorstein Veblen, John Maynard Keynes, and Fred Hirsch all saw an individual's position relative to others as a key motivation in economic behavior.

Today a sound-bite version of this idea is encountered on bumper stickers: "He Who Dies with the Most Toys Wins."

In his 1972 presidential address to the American Economics Association, titled "Power and the Useful Economist," John Kenneth Galbraith juxtaposed the role of power in the real-world economy to its neglect in orthodox economics: "In eliding power—in making economics a nonpolitical subject—neoclassical theory ... destroys its relation with the real world."

On the free-marketeer side of the ideological spectrum, the pursuit of power is depicted as a pathology distinctive to the State. "Chicago school" economist William Niskanen theorized that public-sector bureaucrats seek to maximize the size of their budgets, taking this as a proxy for "salary, perquisites of the office, public reputation, power, patronage, ease of managing the bureau, and ease of making changes." He called this "the peculiar economics of bureaucracy."

But the pursuit of power isn't unique to government bureaucracies. It's commonplace in corporate bureaucracies, too. In his presidential address, Galbraith made the connection: "Between public and private bureaucracies—between GM and the Department of Transportation, between General Dynamics and the Pentagon—there is a deeply symbiotic relationship."

Recognizing the real-world pursuit of power not only helps us understand behavior that otherwise may seem peculiar. It also redirects our attention from the dichotomy between the market and the state toward a more fundamental one: the divide between oligarchy and democracy. ❏

***Sources:*** Sarah O'Connor, "OECD warns of rising inequality as austerity intensifies," *Financial Times*, May 15, 2013 (ft.com); Lewis F. Powell, Jr., "Confidential Memorandum: Attack on American Free Enterprise System," Aug. 23, 1971 (law.wlu.edu); John Kenneth Galbraith, "Power and the Useful Economist," *American Economic Review*, March 1973; William A. Niskanen, "The Peculiar Economics of Bureaucracy," *American Economic Review*, May 1968.

Article 4.2

# WHAT ARE CORPORATIONS?

**BY ALEJANDRO REUSS**
April 2012

When people use the word "corporation," they are usually referring to certain private, for-profit businesses, especially the largest businesses in the United States or other capitalist economies. When we think of corporations, we usually think of "big business." Besides size, people often picture other features of corporations when they hear the word. A corporation can have many shareholders—all part-owners of the company—instead of being owned by a single owner or a couple of partners. A corporation has a board of directors, elected by some or all of the shareholders, which may direct the overall way the corporation is managed. The board usually hires a few top executives, who then make decisions about how the corporation in managed on a day-to-day basis.

Corporations do not have to be large. There are corporations of all different sizes. Even a small company with a few employees could be a corporation. There are some large companies that are not corporations, but the very largest companies, which may have hundreds of thousands of employees and may sell billions of dollars of goods each year, are almost always corporations. Various different kinds of businesses can be corporations, including manufacturing companies (such as General Motors), retail companies (like Wal-Mart), or financial companies (like Bank of America or Liberty Mutual).

Even though some not for-profit entities are also—legally speaking—corporations, people usually use the word "corporation" as shorthand for for-profit companies like General Motors or Wal-Mart. A corporation, in this sense, is a particular type of capitalist enterprise—a "capitalist corporation."

## What Is a Capitalist Enterprise?

By "capitalist enterprise," we just mean a private, for-profit business whose owners employ other people in exchange for wages. By this definition, a private business where a "self-employed" owner works, but which does not hire other people for wages, is not a capitalist enterprise.

In the United States and other similar economies, relatively few people are business owners. Farm workers do not usually own the farms where the work. Miners do not usually own the mines. Factory workers usually do not own the factories. People who work in shops or offices usually do not own those businesses. Most workers do not own the buildings where they go to work, the materials or tools they use, or the products they produce. Instead, they work for pay at capitalist enterprises that are owned by others.

Workers get paid a wage or salary by the owner of the business, who in turn owns whatever the worker produces using the materials and tools provided. The owners of a business, of course, do not usually want the goods that employees produce, but want to sell these goods. If a capitalist enterprise cannot sell these goods for more than what it cost to produce them, it cannot make a profit.

Even a business that makes a profit may not stay in business for very long if the profit is less than "normal" (whatever that may be). The owners may decide that it is not worth investing in that business, if it is possible for them to make a larger profit in another business. In addition, businesses that make higher profits can reinvest these profits to expand and modernize, and may put the less profitable business at a competitive disadvantage in the future. Therefore, owners of capitalist enterprises are under competitive pressure to make the most profit they can.

## How Are Corporations Special?

In many ways, capitalist corporations are like other capitalist enterprises. However, corporations are also defined by their special legal status, which makes them different from other capitalist enterprises. Corporations are granted a "charter" by the government, which means that the corporation exists as a legal entity. (In the United States, state governments grant corporate charters.)

All the things that make corporations different from other capitalist enterprises are determined by government policy. Corporate law creates certain special privileges for corporations that other businesses do not have. It also imposes special obligations on corporations (especially those whose shares are bought and sold on the stock market). The most important of these special characteristics are "limited liability," the "fiduciary responsibility" of management to the corporation's shareholders, "public disclosure" requirements, and the corporate "governance" structure.

### Limited Liability

If a corporation cannot pay its debts, it can declare bankruptcy, and the people it owes can get paid off from the sale of its assets, like the buildings or machinery it owns. If the proceeds are not enough to pay off all the debts, however, the shareholders are not responsible (not "liable") to pay the rest. This is what we mean by the term "limited liability." Someone who buys stock in a corporation is risking whatever they paid for the stock, but cannot lose more than this amount. If the corporation goes bankrupt, the shareholders' stock becomes worthless, but the shareholders cannot be forced, legally, to pay whatever debts the corporation has left unpaid.

The justification usually given for the legal principle of limited liability is that it promotes economic growth and development. The idea is that, if companies were limited to what an individual or family, or perhaps a couple of partners, could scrape together to start a business, they would not be able to operate at the scale that modern corporations do. They would not have enough money to buy expensive machinery, let alone buy large factories or put together huge assembly lines.

Even if the reason given for limited liability is to fuel economic growth, however, we should remember that this is also a big favor from the government for the people who own shares in corporations. First, limited liability means that the government gives the shareholders of a corporation a certain kind a protection from other people's claims against it. Second, it means that corporations may take bigger risks in hopes of bigger profits, since the shareholders that they are not on the hook for all the corporation's liabilities if these risks do not pay off.

## Fiduciary Responsibility

A single person who fully owns an entire company (known as a "privately held" company) can use the company's funds for whatever he or she likes, whether that is expanding the company's operations or buying luxury cars. In contrast, corporate executives receive a salary and other compensation (often lavish, in the case of large companies) decided by the board of directors or a committee of the board. They are legally free to spend this income as they wish.

Corporate executives also control how company funds are spent, but are not free to treat corporate funds as their own. This means that the chief executive of a company is not legally entitled to use company funds to remodel his or her house, buy fancy cars, take expensive vacations, and so on. Of course, executives still fly on private jets, take "business trips" to exotic locales, enjoy fancy "business dinners," and so on, but they have to justify these as necessary costs of doing business. If shareholders think that executives have failed in their fiduciary responsibility, they can actually sue the company.

Some legal scholars and economists have extended this idea to the logical extreme that corporate managers are legally obligated to the shareholders and only the shareholders. In this view, management decisions must be guided by the sole objective of enhancing "shareholder value" (in effect, the profitability of the corporation, and therefore the value of an ownership stake in it). This means that they cannot put other people's interests ahead of those of the shareholders. According to the "shareholder value" doctrine, if managers decide to pay workers more than they really have to, they are giving away the company's (that is, the shareholders') money. Likewise, they have no legal duty to the broader community, beyond abiding by the law. They do not have to "give back," say, by funding schools, libraries, or parks in the communities where they operate.

The shareholder value doctrine is not new, and it is not just something that pro-business comentators have made up. The doctrine was clearly articulated no later than 1919, in a Supreme Court opinion (*Dodge v. Ford Motor Company*) no less. However, in practice, the courts have been reluctant to intervene in disputes between shareholders and management (in effect, declining to open up the can of worms of deciding what the right business decisions would be).

## Public Disclosure

Corporations that sell shares of stock on the stock market are called "publicly traded corporations." Each time a corporation sells a share of its stock to an individual or another company, it raises some money. This is one way the company can finance its operations. In actual fact, most stock sales do not involve a corporation selling stock to a member of the public, but one member of the public selling shares to another (that is, resale of shares that a corporation had previously issued). Therefore, most stock sales do not result in any money going to the corporation that originally issued it.

By law, publicly traded companies have to disclose certain business information. They have to file forms with the government listing their officers (board members and top executives), the officers' compensation (salaries and other benefits), the company's profits or losses, and other information. The idea behind disclosure requirements is to protect shareholders or people who might consider purchasing shares in a company, often referred to as the "investing public."

In practice, corporate "insiders" (board members, top executives, etc.) have much more information about the financial condition of a corporation than members of the public. This has led to well-publicized scandals in recent years, such as the Enron case. Corporate executives sold the stock they owned when the price was high, knowing that in reality the company was not as profitable as the public thought, and that the stock price would soon plummet.

## Corporate Governance

When an individual buys a share (or many shares) of a corporation, he or she gets certain property rights. Shareholders are not legally entitled to receive a share of the company's profits each year. The company management decides how much of this money to pay out to shareholders (as "dividends") and how much to keep. A corporation might keep cash reserves, use profits to buy existing businesses, use them to expand its existing operations (for example, by buying or renting additional factory or office buildings, buying new machinery, hiring additional workers, etc.). It is not necessarily preferable for shareholders to receive all or most of the company's profit for a year in the form of dividends. By using "retained earnings" to expand, a corporation may increase in overall value. This increases the value of an ownership share in the company (the value of the stock that shareholders own).

Shareholders have the right to sell their shares if and when they wish. This gives them a stake in the profitability of the corporation, since the price of a share (on the stock exchange) is likely to go higher the more profitable the company is. A shareholder who does not want to be a part owner of the company anymore is not entitled to sell back the shares to the company, nor to take "their" piece of the company with them. The corporation is not required to give the shareholder any tangible asset—the shareholder cannot claim any particular thing owned by the corporation—nor is the corporation forced to sell off tangible assets in order to pay a shareholder who does not want his or her shares anymore. This way, shareholders come and go, but the corporation itself stays intact.

Shareholders also have a say in the governance structure of the corporation. You can think of a corporation as a political entity, like a small (or, in some cases, not so small) country. Shareholders are like the citizens. They are entitled to attend annual shareholder meetings, where they can address questions or comments to the corporation's directors (board members) and executives. Shareholders are entitled to vote in elections to the board of directors (except for those holding certain classes of "nonvoting" or "preferred" stock). They can even run for election to the board of directors, if they so wish.

Corporate elections are different from government elections. First, in corporate elections, only shareholders are allowed to vote. The decisions made by a corporation's management may affect many other people—workers, people in communities where the corporation has operations, etc.. However, if they are not shareholders in the corporation, they are not entitled to vote. In addition, in corporate elections, different shareholders do not get the same number of votes. Rather, each shareholder gets a number of votes equal to the number of shares he or she owns (excluding nonvoting stock). Someone who owns one share gets one vote; 10 shares, 10 votes; 100 shares, 100 votes.

In practice, a large shareholder does not need to own anywhere near a majority of the shares to effectively control a company. People who own very few shares in a company, if disgruntled with the management, are more likely to just sell their shares than to devote a lot of time and energy to getting the management replaced. Relatively small shareholders, in fact, usually just sign away their voting rights to other, larger shareholders. This way, a very wealthy individual may have effective control of a company even though he or she "only" owns, say, 5% of the total shares. Keep in mind that 5% of the stock in the largest corporate giants could be worth billions of dollars.

## Corporations, Economic Power, and Political Power

Large corporations are certainly among the most powerful entities in the U.S. economy and politics. We can start by classifying the power of large corporations into economic power, on the one hand, and political power, on the other. Economic power has to do with the ability of large corporations to dictate to others (other businesses, workers, etc.) the conditions under which they will do business. Political power has to do with their ability to get what they want from the government, including both favors they can get from the government and influence over the overall direction of government policy.

Mainstream or "neoclassical" economists do not talk about economic power very much. Mostly, they talk about "market" economies as if nobody exercised any power over anyone else—buyers and sellers engaging in voluntary exchanges, each free from any kind of coercion from other buyers or sellers. The main form of economic power neoclassical economists do talk about is "market power"—basically, the ability of a seller (or buyer) to dictate higher (or lower) prices to others, because of a lack of competition.

In the view of radical political economists, employers as a group have economic power in a different sense. Most of the economic activity in capitalist economies depends on the economic decisions made by capitalist enterprises, such as how much output to produce, how many people to hire, whether to buy new machines or new buildings (this is what economists mean by "investment"), and so on. If capitalist employers decide not to hire people to produce goods and services, many people will be unemployed. Tax collections will be low, and governments are likely to experience budget deficits, unless they dramatically cut spending. Moreover, if capitalist enterprises are not hiring, unemployment is high, and many people are afraid of losing their jobs, the party in power probably will not survive the next election.

If the owners and managers of capitalist enterprises do not like the kinds of economic policies the government is putting in place, they may decide not to hire or invest. In some cases, where capitalists feel very threatened by government policies, they may actually do this with the conscious political aim of bringing down the government. More often, a decline in employment and investment can arise from a simple decline in "business confidence." The owners and managers of capitalist enterprises become pessimistic about being able to sell their goods at a profit, and make a business decision to cut back on production, employment, and investment. The effect, however, can still be to force the government to bend over backwards to maintain profitable conditions for business, in order to avoid an economic downturn. This way, the economic power of capitalist enterprises over the whole economy can result in their getting the kinds of government policies that favor them. ❏

*Article 4.3*

# CORPORATE CRONYISM: THE SECRET TO OVERPAID CEOs

## BY DEAN BAKER
*February 2014; Truthout*

I t's hardly a secret that the heads of major corporations in the United States get mind-bending paychecks. While high pay may be understandable when a top executive turns around a failing company or vastly expands a company's revenue and profit, CEOs can get paychecks in the tens or hundreds of millions even when they did nothing especially notable.

For example, Lee Raymond retired from Exxon-Mobil in 2005 with $321 million. (That's 22,140 minimum wage work years.) His main accomplishment for the company was sitting at its head at a time when a quadrupling of oil prices sent profits soaring. Hank McKinnel walked away from Pfizer in 2006 with $166 million. It would be hard to identify his outstanding accomplishments.

But you don't have to be mediocre to get a big paycheck as a CEO. Bob Nardelli pocketed $240 million when he left Home Depot after six years. The company's stock price had fallen by 40% in his tenure, while the stock its competitor Lowe's had nearly doubled. And then we have the CEOs in the financial industry, heads of huge banks like Lehman's, Bear Stearns, and Merrill Lynch, or the insurer AIG. These CEOs took their companies to the edge of bankruptcy or beyond and still walked away with hundreds of millions of dollars in their pockets.

It's not hard to write contracts that would ensure that CEO pay bear a closer relationship to the company's performance. For example, if the value of Raymond's stock incentives at Exxon were tied to the performance of the stock of other oil companies (this can be done) then his going away package probably would not have been one-tenth as large. Also, there can be longer assessment periods so that it's not possible to get rich by bankrupting a company.

If anyone were putting a check on CEO pay, these sorts of practices would be standard, but they aren't for a simple reason. The corporate directors who are supposed to be holding down CEO pay for the benefit of the shareholders are generally buddies of the CEOs.

Corporate CEOs often have considerable input into who sits on their boards. (Some CEOs sit on the boards themselves.) They pick people who will be agreeable and not ask tough questions.

For example, corporate boards probably don't often ask whether they could get a comparably skilled CEO for lower pay, even though top executives of major companies in Europe, Japan, and South Korea earn around one-tenth as much as CEOs in the United States. Of course this is the directors' job. They are supposed to be trying to minimize what the company pays their top executives in the same way that companies try to cut costs by outsourcing production to Mexico, China, and elsewhere.

But friends don't try to save money by cutting their friends' pay. And when the directors themselves are pocketing hundreds of thousands of dollars a year for attending 4-10 meetings, there is little incentive to take their jobs seriously.

Instead we see accomplished people from politics, academia, and other sectors collecting their pay and looking the other way. For example, we have people like Erskine Bowles who had the distinction of sitting on the boards of both Morgan Stanley and General Motors in the years they were bailed out by the government. And we have Martin Feldstein, the country's most prominent conservative economist, who sat on the board of insurance giant AIG when it nearly tanked the world's financial system. Both Bowles and Feldstein were well-compensated for their "work."

Excessive CEO pay matters not only because it takes away money that rightfully belongs to shareholders, which include pension funds and individuals with 401(k) retirement accounts. Excessive CEO pay is important because it sets a pattern for pay packages throughout the economy. When mediocre CEOs of mid-size companies can earn millions or tens of millions a year, it puts upward pressure on the pay of top executives in other sectors.

It is common for top executives of universities and private charities to earn salaries in the millions of dollars because they can point to executives of comparably sized companies who earn several times as much. Those close in line to the boss also can expect comparably bloated salaries. In other words, this is an important part of the story of inequality in the economy.

To try to impose the checks that don't currently exist, the Center for Economic and Policy Research (CEPR) has created Director Watch. This site will highlight directors like Erskine Bowles and Martin Feldstein who stuff their pockets while not performing their jobs.

CEPR also worked with the Huffington Post to compile a data set that lists the directors for the Fortune 100 companies, along with their compensation, the CEOs' compensation, and the companies' stock performance. This data set is now available at the Huffington Post as Pay Pals.

Perhaps a little public attention will get these directors to actually work for their hefty paychecks. The end result could be to bring a lot of paychecks for those at the top back down to earth. ❑

*Article 4.4*

# WHAT'S GOOD FOR WAL-MART . . .

## BY JOHN MILLER
*January/February 2006*

> "Is Wal-Mart Good for America?"
>
> It is a testament to the public relations of the anti-Wal-Mart campaign that the question above is even being asked.
>
> By any normal measure, Wal-Mart's business ought to be noncontroversial. It sells at low costs, albeit in mind-boggling quantities. ...
>
> The company's success and size ... do not rest on monopoly profits or price-gouging behavior. It simply sells things people will buy at small markups and, as in the old saw, makes it up on volume. ... You may believe, as do service-workers unions and a clutch of coastal elites—many of whom, we'd wager, have never set foot in Wal-Mart—that Wal-Mart "exploits" workers who can't say no to low wages and poor benefits. You might accept the canard that it drives good local businesses into the ground, although both of these allegations are more myth than reality.
>
> But even if you buy into the myths, there's no getting around the fact that somewhere out there, millions of people are spending billions of dollars on what Wal-Mart puts on its shelves. No one is making them do it. ... Wal-Mart can't make mom and pop shut down the shop anymore than it can make customers walk through the doors or pull out their wallets.
>
> What about the workers? ... Wal-Mart's average starting wage is already nearly double the national minimum of $5.15 an hour. The company has also recently increased its health-care for employees on the bottom rungs of the corporate ladder.
>
> —*Wall Street Journal* editorial, December 3, 2005

"Who's Number One? The Customer! Always!" The last line of Wal-Mart's company cheer just about sums up the *Wall Street Journal* editors' benign view of the behemoth corporation. But a more honest answer would be Wal-Mart itself: not the customer, and surely not the worker.

The first retail corporation to top the Fortune 500, Wal-Mart trailed only Exxon-Mobil in total revenues last year. With 1.6 million workers, 1.3 million in the United States and 300,000 offshore, Wal-Mart is the largest private employer in the nation and the world's largest retailer.

Being number one has paid off handsomely for the family of Wal-Mart founder Sam Walton. The family's combined fortune is now an estimated $90 billion, equal to the net worth of Bill Gates and Warren Buffett combined.

But is what's good for the Walton family good for America? Should we believe the editors that Wal-Mart's unprecedented size and market power have redounded not only to the Walton family's benefit but to ours as well?

## Low Wages and Meager Benefits

Working for the world's largest employer sure hasn't paid off for Wal-Mart's employees. True, they have a job, and others without jobs line up to apply for theirs. But that says more about the sad state of today's labor market than the quality of Wal-Mart jobs. After all, less than half of Wal-Mart workers last a year, and turnover at the company is twice that at comparable retailers.

Why? Wal-Mart's oppressive working conditions surely have something to do with it. Wal-Mart has admitted to using minors to operate hazardous machinery, has been sued in six states for forcing employees to work off the books (i.e., unpaid) and without breaks, and is currently facing a suit brought by 1.6 million current and former female employees accusing Wal-Mart of gender discrimination. At the same time, Wal-Mart workers are paid less and receive fewer benefits than other retail workers.

Wal-Mart, according to its own reports, pays an average of $9.68 an hour. That is 12.4% below the average wage for retail workers even after adjusting for geography, according to a recent study by Arindrajit Dube and Steve Wertheim, economists at the University of California's Institute of Industrial Relations and long-time Wal-Mart researchers. Wal-Mart's wages are nearly 15% below the average wage of workers at large retailers and about 30% below the average wage of unionized grocery workers. The average U.S. wage is $17.80 an hour; Costco, a direct competitor of Wal-Mart's Sam's Club warehouse stores, pays an average wage of $16 an hour.

Wal-Mart may be improving its benefits, as the *Journal*'s editors report, but it needs to. Other retailers provide health care coverage to over 53% of their workers, while Wal-Mart covers just 48% of its workers. Costco, once again, does far better, covering 82% of its employees. Moreover, Wal-Mart's coverage is far less comprehensive than the plans offered by other large retailers. Dube reports that according to 2003 IRS data, Wal-Mart paid 59% of the health care costs of its workers and dependents, compared to the 77% of health care costs for individuals and 68% for families the average retailer picks up.

A recent internal Wal-Mart memo leaked to the *New York Times* confirmed the large gaps in Wal-Mart's health care coverage and exposed the high costs those gaps impose on government programs. According to the memo, "Five percent of our Associates are on Medicaid compared to an average for national employees of 4 percent. Twenty-seven percent of Associates' children are on such programs, compared to a national average of 22 percent. In total, 46 percent of Associates' children are either on Medicaid or are uninsured."

A considerably lower 29% of children of all large-retail workers are on Medicaid or are uninsured. Some 7% of the children of employees of large retailers go uninsured, compared to the 19% reported by Wal-Mart.

Wal-Mart's low wages drag down the wages of other retail workers and shutter downtown retail businesses. A 2005 study by David Neumark, Junfu Zhang, and Stephen Ciccarella, economists at the University of California at Irvine, found that Wal-Mart adversely affects employment and wages. Retail workers in a community with a Wal-Mart earned 3.5% less because Wal-Mart's low prices force other businesses to lower prices, and hence their wages, according to the Neumark study. The same study also found that Wal-Mart's presence reduces retail employment by 2% to 4%. While other studies have not found this negative employment effect, Dube's research also reports fewer retail jobs and lower wages for retail workers in metropolitan counties with a Wal-Mart. (Fully 85% of Wal-Mart stores are in metropolitan counties.) Dube figures that Wal-Mart's presence costs retail workers, at Wal-Mart and elsewhere, $4.7 billion a year in lost earnings.

In short, Wal-Mart's "everyday low prices" come at the expense of the compensation of Wal-Mart's own employees and lower wages and fewer jobs for retail workers in the surrounding area. That much remains true no matter what weight we assign to each of the measures that Wal-Mart uses to keep its costs down: a just-in-time inventory strategy, its ability to use its size to pressure suppliers for large discounts, a routinized work environment that requires minimal training, and meager wages and benefits.

## How Low are Wal-Mart's Everyday Low Prices?

Even if one doesn't subscribe to the editors' position that it is consumers, not Wal-Mart, who cause job losses at downtown retailers, it is possible to argue that the benefit of Wal-Mart's low prices to consumers, especially low-income consumers, outweighs the cost endured by workers at Wal-Mart and other retailers. Jason Furman, New York University economist and director of economic policy for the 2004 Kerry-Edwards campaign, makes just such an argument. Wal-Mart's "staggering" low prices are 8% to 40% lower than people would pay elsewhere, according to Furman. He calculates that those low prices on average boost low-income families' buying power by 3% and more than offset the loss of earnings to retail workers. For Furman, that makes Wal-Mart "a progressive success story."

But exactly how much savings Wal-Mart affords consumers is far from clear. Estimates vary widely. At one extreme is a study Wal-Mart itself commissioned by Global Insight, an economic forecasting firm. Global Insight estimates Wal-Mart created a stunning savings of $263 billion, or $2,329 per household, in 2004 alone.

At the other extreme, statisticians at the U.S. Bureau of Labor Statistics found no price savings at Wal-Mart. Relying on Consumer Price Index data, the BLS found that Wal-Mart's prices largely matched those of its rivals, and that instances of lower prices at Wal-Mart could be attributed to lower quality products.

Both studies, which rely on the Consumer Price Index and aggregate data, have their critics. Furman himself allows that the Global Insight study is "overly simplistic" and says he "doesn't place as much weight on that one." Jerry Hausman, the M.I.T. economist who has looked closely at Wal-Mart's grocery stores, maintains that the CPI data that the Bureau of Labor Statistics relies on systematically miss the savings offered by "supercenters" such as Wal-Mart. To show the difference between prices at Wal-Mart and at other grocers, Hausman, along with Ephraim Leibtag, USDA Economic Research Service economist, used supermarket scanner data to examine the purchasing patterns of a national sample of 61,500 consumers from 1988 to 2001. Hausman and Leibtag found that Wal-Mart offers many identical food items at an average price about 15%-25% lower than traditional supermarkets.

While Hausman and Leibtag report substantial savings from shopping at Wal-Mart, they fall far short of the savings alleged in the Global Insight study. The Hausman and Leibtag study suggests a savings of around $550 per household per year, or about $56 billion in 2004, not $263 billion. Still, that is considerably more than the $4.7 billion a year in lost earnings to retail workers that Dube attributes to Wal-Mart.

But if "Wal-Mart hurts wages, not so much in retail, but across the whole country," as economist Neumark told *BusinessWeek*, then the savings to consumers from Wal-Mart's everyday low prices might not outweigh the lost wages to all workers. (Retail workers make up just 11.6% of U.S. employment.)

Nor do these findings say anything about the sweatshop conditions and wages in Wal-Mart's overseas subcontractors. One example: A recent Canadian Broadcasting Corporation investigative report found that workers in Bangladesh were being paid less than $50 a month (below even the United Nation's $2 a day measure of poverty) to make clothes for the Wal-Mart private label, Simply Basic. Those workers included ten- to thirteen-year-old children forced to work long hours in dimly lit and dirty conditions sewing "I Love My Wal-Mart" t-shirts.

## Making Wal-Mart Do Better

Nonetheless, as Arindrajit Dube points out, the relevant question is not whether Wal-Mart creates more savings for consumers than losses for workers, but whether the corporation can afford to pay better wages and benefits.

Dube reasons that if the true price gap between Wal-Mart and its retail competitors is small, then Wal-Mart might not be in a position to do better—to make

### The Costco Alternative? Wall Street Prefers Wal-Mart

In an April 2004 online commentary, *BusinessWeek* praised Costco's business model but pointed out that Costco's wages cause Wall Street to worry that the company's "operating expenses could get out of hand." How does Costco compare to low-wage Wal-Mart on overhead expenses? At Costco, overhead is 9.8% of revenue; at Wal-Mart, it is 17%. Part of Costco's secret is that its better paid workers are also more efficient: Costco's operating profit per hourly employee is $13,647; each Wal-Mart employee only nets the company $11,039. Wal-Mart also spends more than Costco on hiring and training new employees: each one, according to Rutgers economist Eileen Appelbaum, costs the company $2,500 to $3,500. Appelbaum estimates that Wal-Mart's relatively high turnover costs the company $1.5 to $2 million per year.

Despite Costco's higher efficiency, Wall Street analysts like Deutsche Bank's Bill Dreher complain that "Costco's corporate philosophy is to put its customers first, then its employees, then its vendors, and finally its shareholders. Shareholders get the short end of the stick." Wall Street prefers Wal-Mart's philosophy: executives first, then shareholders, then customers, then vendors, and finally employees.

In 2004, Wal-Mart paid CEO Lee Scott $5.3 million, while a full-time employee making the average wage would have received $20,134. Costco's CEO Jim Senegal received $350,000, while a full-time average employee got $33,280. And *BusinessWeek* intimates that the top job at Costco may be tougher than at Wal-Mart. "Management has to hustle to make the high-wage strategy work. It's constantly looking for ways to repackage goods up its wage and benefit gap and still maintain its price advantage. But if Wal-Mart offers consumers only minor price savings, then its lower wages and benefits hardly constitute a progressive success story that's good for the nation.

If Wal-Mart's true price gap is large (say, the 25% price advantage estimated by Hausman), then Wal-Mart surely is in a position to do better. For instance, Dube calculates that closing Wal-Mart's 16% overall compensation gap with other large retailers would cost the company less than 2% of sales. Raising prices by two cents on the dollar to cover those increased compensation costs would be "eminently absorbable," according to Dube, without eating away much of the company's mind-boggling $10 billion profit (2004).

Measures that set standards to force Wal-Mart and all big-box retailers to pay decent wages and provide benefits are beginning to catch on. Chicago, New York City, and the state of Maryland have considered or passed laws that would require big-box retailers to pay a "living wage" or to spend a minimum amount per worker-hour for health benefits. The Republican board of Nassau County on Long Island passed an ordinance requiring that all big-box retailers pay $3 per hour toward health care. Wal-Mart's stake in making sure that such proposals don't become law or spread nationwide goes a long way toward explaining why 80% of Wal-Mart's $2 million in political contributions in 2004 went to Republicans.

Henry Ford sought to pay his workers enough so they could buy the cars they produced. Sam Walton sought to pay his workers so little that they could afford to shop nowhere else. And while what was good for the big automakers was probably never good for the nation, what is good for Wal-Mart, today's largest employer, is undoubtedly bad for economic justice. ❏

---

into bulk items, which reduces labor, speeds up Costco's just-in-time inventory, and boosts sales per square foot. Costco is also savvier ... about catering to small shop owners and more affluent customers, who are more likely to buy in bulk and purchase higher-margin goods."

Costco's allegedly more affluent clientele may be another reason that its profit per employee is higher than Wal-Mart's and its overhead costs a lower percentage of revenue. However, Costco pays its employees enough that they could afford to shop there. As the *BusinessWeek* commentary noted, "the low-wage approach cuts into consumer spending and, potentially, economic growth."

—*Esther Cervantes*

| Average Hourly Wage | | Percentage of U.S. Workforce in Unions | | Employees Covered by Company Health Insurance | | Employees Who Leave After One Year | |
|---|---|---|---|---|---|---|---|
| Wal-Mart | Costco | Wal-Mart | Costco | Wal-Mart | Costco | Sam's Club* | Costco |
| $9.68 | $16.00 | 0.0% | 17.9% | 48% | 82% | 21% | 6% |
| * Sam's Club is the Wal-Mart unit that competes directly with Costco. | | | | | | | |

***Sources:*** "Is Wal-Mart Good for America?" *Wall Street Journal*, 12/3/05; "Gauging the Wal-Mart Effect," *WSJ*, 12/03/05; Arindrajit Dube & Steve Wertheim, "Wal-Mart and Job Quality—What Do We Know, and Should We Care?" 10/05; Jason Furman, "Wal-Mart: A Progressive Success Story," 10/05; Leo Hindery Jr., "Wal-Mart's Giant Sucking Sound," 10/05; A. Bernstein, "Some Uncomfortable Findings for Wal-Mart," *Business Week* online, 10/26/05, and "Wal-Mart: A Case for the Defense, Sort of," *Business Week* online, 11/7/05; Dube, Jacobs, and Wertheim, "The Impact of Wal-Mart Growth on Earnings Throughout the Retail Sector in Urban and Rural Counties," *Institute of Industrial Relations Working Paper*, UC Berkeley, 10/05; Dube, Jacobs, and Wertheim, "Internal Wal-Mart Memo Validates Findings of UC Berkeley Study," 11/26/05; Jerry Hausman and Ephraim Leibtag, "Consumer Benefits from Increased Competition in Shopping Outlets: Measuring the Effect of Wal-Mart," 10/05; Hausman and Leibtag, "CPI Bias from Supercenters: Does the BLS Know that Wal-Mart Exists?" *NBER Working Paper No. 10712*, 8/04; David Neumark, Junfu Zhang, and Stephen Ciccarella, "The Effects of Wal-Mart on Local Labor Markets," *NBER Working Paper No. 11782*, 11/05; Erin Johansson, "Wal-Mart: Rolling Back Workers' Wages, Rights, and the American Dream," American Rights at Work, 11/05; Wal-Mart Watch, "Spin Cycle"; CBC News, "Wal-Mart to cut ties with Bangladesh factories using child labour," 11/30/05; National Labor Committee, "10 to 13-year-olds Sewing 'I Love My Wal-Mart' Shirts," 12/05; Global Insight, "The Economic Impact of Wal-Mart," 2005.

*Article 4.5*

# VULTURES IN THE E.R.
*Private-equity firms target the U.S. health-care industry.*

## BY NICOLE ASCHOFF
*January/February 2013*

Public anger over increasing economic polarization and frustration with the seemingly unassailable power of big finance coalesced for a brief moment last summer in the public shaming of Bain Capital, the private-equity firm formerly run by Mitt Romney. Popular journalists like *Rolling Stone*'s Matt Taibbi turned their attention to the activities of powerful, secretive private equity firms, connecting the dots between private-equity investment and job loss, and people got mad. But, as with the leveraged-buyout kings of the 1980s, after the election furor subsided, Bain and its private-equity brethren dropped back under the radar, returning to business as usual.

However, the nature of "business as usual" for private equity warrants another look. Private-equity (PE) firms like Bain, Cerberus, Blackstone, Warburg Pincus, and Kohlberg, Kravis and Roberts (KKR) operate in nearly every sector of the economy, including manufacturing, business and financial services, food, entertainment, and health care. Cutthroat tactics, job loss, and bankruptcy are common themes in the PE world.

Health care is a particularly popular sector for PE firms. After a decline following the 2008 financial crisis, PE investment in health care has rebounded, both in the United States and globally. In particular, medical technology, pharmaceuticals, and medical services (like hospitals and nursing homes) are seeing sharp increases in PE investment. According to a recent report by Bain, the value of global private-equity deals in health care was over $30 billion in 2011, double the investment of 2010.

Growing PE interest in low-profit, or no-profit, sectors like hospitals may come as a surprise to many who assume that private investors prefer to channel their money toward industries with rapid growth or high profit potential, like medical technology and pharmaceuticals. But private-equity firms are not like most investors. Unlike venture capitalists, who bet their own money on the success of a company, in most cases private-equity firms put very little of their own capital into their investments, and instead arrange for outside investors (like pension funds) and the firm being taken over to fund the investment. The PE firms make their money from fees and dividends, which are often debt-financed by the acquired firm. This unique feature of private-equity firms means that any company with steady cash flow (or even just a substantial potential cash flow) is a possible target for acquisition.

The growing appetite for hospital takeovers by PE firms has its roots in the ongoing struggle for survival experienced by many hospitals. Hospitals—particularly small, community hospitals and those serving poor populations—are under intense pressure due to declining Medicare/Medicaid reimbursement rates, new government demands for technological upgrades, increasing numbers of under- and uninsured patients, and restricted access to credit markets. According to the American Hospital Association (AHA), roughly 30% of non-profit hospitals are operating at a loss. Many more hospitals find themselves breaking even each year, but unable to borrow and make investments to keep up with increasing costs and regulation.

The precarious financial situation of many community hospitals has led to a wave of mergers and acquisitions in recent years by for-profit hospital corporations and larger non-profit systems. Community hospitals believe that being absorbed by a larger hospital or hospital chain will result in improved access to capital to make necessary upgrades and maintain their patient base. Meanwhile, big, for-profit, and non-profit hospitals view the acquisition of smaller, community hospitals as an easy way to increase market share and improve economies of scale.

This consolidation trend is similar to the one that occurred in the hospital sector in the 1990s, but with one significant difference—the increasing role of PE investors. PE investors are betting that the growing needs of the baby-boomer generation, in combination with the Affordable Care Act, which will dramatically expand health-insurance coverage (an estimated 15-20 million new insured by 2014, and an additional 15 million by 2016), will create new profit opportunities. For example, in 2006, KKR, Bain, and Merrill Lynch acquired the mammoth Hospital Corporation of America (HCA), a for-profit hospital chain that owns hundreds of hospitals in the United States and England, for $31.6 billion. PE firms are also snapping up non-profit, community hospitals. In December 2010, Vanguard Health (owned at the time by Blackstone), bought the Detroit Medical Center for $1.3 billion. In the same year, Cerberus Capital Management paid $830 million to acquire the Caritas Christi chain of hospitals from the Archdiocese of Boston, folding the hospitals into a new, for-profit entity called Steward Health Care System. Although the AHA estimates that less than 20% of community hospitals are investor-owned, the number is growing rapidly. Josh Kosman, an expert on PE investment, estimates that half of the biggest for-profit hospital chains are now owned by private-equity firms.

One of the strategies followed by PE-backed, for-profit hospital chains like Vanguard and Steward is to gain control over urban market share by aggressively acquiring hospital groups. This strategy is a departure from earlier, more scattered, and somewhat opportunistic, acquisition patterns by for-profit hospital chains like HCA and Essent. Vanguard's purchase of Detroit Medical Center gave it control over 13.4% of Detroit's total market, while its 2010 purchase of Westlake Hospital and West Suburban Medical Center in Illinois gave it 47% of acute care inpatient beds in the immediate health planning area. Steward's recent acquisitions, including its purchase of the Caritas chain, give it control over a quarter of eastern Massachusetts acute care beds.

## What's the Difference?

All hospitals are facing similar market conditions and are concerned with minimizing costs and increasing revenues. So what is the difference between not-for-profit systems like Partners, for-profit hospital chains such as Tenet and LifePoint, and PE-owned hospital chains like Steward? A recent report issued by the Congressional

Budget Office suggests that there is little difference in the behavior of non-profit and for-profit hospitals. The report found that not-for-profit hospitals on average provide slightly higher levels of uncompensated care than for-profit hospitals, while for-profit hospitals, on average, serve poorer populations with higher rates of people living with little or no health insurance.

However, Jill Horwitz, a professor at the University of Michigan, argues that nonprofit hospitals and for-profit hospitals exhibit important differences in the types of care they offer. For-profit firms emphasize surgical and acute care services, and cardiac and diagnostic services, while non-profit hospitals often provide less lucrative care such as mental health services, drug-and-alcohol treatment programs, and trauma-and-burn centers. When non-profit hospitals are converted into for-profits, they often discontinue or decrease these crucial, but less-profitable, services.

PE-backed hospital firms are particularly likely to jettison less-profitable services given their shorter investment timelines. Like most PE investments, PE firms' hospital acquisitions tend to last a short period (around five years). Then, the PE firm either takes the acquired firm public (offers stock for sale to the general public) or re-sells to other PE firms. For example, HCA was owned by two PE firms (KKR and Bain) for five years before a March 2011 initial public offering of stock (IPO), while Vanguard was owned by Morgan Stanley and Blackstone before going public in June 2011. The PE owners' goal during this period of time is to quickly increase profits and cash flow, enabling the PE firm to collect its fees and dividends, often by accessing credit and bond markets.

This investment timeline pushes PE firms to look for simple, and relatively fast, ways to increase revenues, such as eliminating less-profitable services. For example, in 2004, Vanguard's Weiss Hospital in Chicago failed a spot inspection for maternity-ward security. Staff failed to stop undercover inspectors from removing a baby (actually, for the purpose of the inspection, just an infant doll) from the ward without authorization. Rather than resolve the issue through increased staffing and a reexamination of hospital policy, Vanguard simply closed the maternity wing in 2007, eliminating a vital service for the surrounding community.

At the Vanguard-acquired Phoenix Memorial Hospital, located in a predominately urban, poor area of Phoenix, the company announced the closure of the emergency room despite earlier promises to the contrary. After a public outcry, Vanguard shelved the plan, but just a few years later closed the entire hospital and leased out the space. In the meantime, Vanguard invested heavily in surgical and ambulatory services at a nearby hospital in Phoenix's wealthier western suburbs.

In addition to reducing less-profitable services, PE-owned hospitals look for other ways to increase profits. These include centralizing and improving billing, records management, and financial services, and reducing staff, particularly registered nurses. In late 2011, nurses organized by the Massachusetts Nurses Association (MNA) gathered at Cerberus headquarters in New York to protest cuts of registered nurses on duty at Steward's Morton Hospital in southeastern Massachusetts. Since Steward's creation in 2010, the MNA and Steward have been at loggerheads. The MNA argues that Steward has cut the level of registered nurses to dangerously low levels at a number of its hospitals, including psychiatric units like the one at Carney Hospital in Boston, and has cut back on basics for patients. Nurses at Holy Family Hospital in northeastern Massachusetts complained that they were not allowed to give patients even a cup of coffee, while nurses at Norwood Hospital (in Norwood, Mass., south of Boston) brought loaves of bread to their floor to protest decreased food for patients. Nurses at Merrimack Valley Hospital, also in northeastern Massachusetts, claimed that administrators were turning down the temperature of electric blankets for chemotherapy patients to save pennies. The MNA and Steward are also fighting an ongoing battle over the MNA's pension plan. The MNA argues that Steward has refused to honor the pension agreement the union made with Caritas Christi, the former owner of the Steward chain, prior to the PE firm's 2010 acquisition.

PE-owned hospitals also engage in less-visible strategies to boost profits such as increasing lucrative surgical procedures. In 2005, the former chief compliance officer at the PE-owned Iasis hospital chain filed a complaint under the False Claims Act, alleging that doctors at St. Luke's Medical Center in Phoenix were installing a specific kind of heart implant—the intra-aortic pump—at ten times the normal rate. The alleged motive? Iasis could bill patients an additional $1000. In a 2012 exposé, the *New York Times* reported that an internal HCA memo showed that the company performed 1,200 cardiac procedures on patients without significant heart disease. The whistleblower, a registered nurse at a Florida HCA hospital, was fired for reporting the abuse.

## The Biggest Difference: The Debt Trap

While service and staffing cuts, deteriorating patient care, and potentially unethical medical practices are easy to find at PE-owned hospitals and deserve urgent attention, they are not uniformly present at all PE-owned hospitals, and are also present at many non-PE-owned hospitals, both for-profit and non-profit. There is, however, another much bigger problem particular to PE hospital ownership.

PE firms are often portrayed as "turnaround" specialists and are viewed by many, including the hospitals themselves, as white knights bringing desperately needed investment and credit access. The problem with this view is that PE firms do not actually earn their money by turning around companies and making them successful. A PE firm's return on investment has little relation to whether the acquired hospital succeeds through improved patient care or increased cash flow. Instead, PE firms recoup their investment through fees (management fees, transaction fees, selling fees, etc.) from both the acquired firm and outside institutional investors. In fact, unlike other kinds of investment firms, PE firms generally put only a small percentage of the total equity down themselves, instead getting outside investors to cover the bulk of the initial equity investment. So even if the PE firm's investment fails to yield the imagined profits, the PE firm still earns a profit, or loses little or no money, because the risk is shouldered by outside investors, and in many cases, the acquired firm itself.

The primary source of risk for hospitals being acquired by PE firms is the debt load that comes with PE ownership. PE firms use the acquired hospital as a vehicle to earn profits by forcing it to sell bonds or shares, or take on bank debt, to pay the PE firm fees and dividends. For example, in January 2010, Vanguard took on $1.76

billion in debt, of which $300 million went to pay dividends to Blackstone. In June 2010, the hospital chain issued an additional $250 million in bonds and, in January 2011, the company recapitalized again. It paid a grand total of $775 million in debt-funded dividends to its PE sponsors between January 2010 and summer 2011.

When PE-backed hospital chains like Vanguard and HCA go public, they (and their PE sponsor) are able to make huge profits from their initial public offerings (IPOs). HCA raked in a record $3.8 billion at its 2011 IPO, but the money from the IPO went directly to chip away at the huge debt HCA incurred under KKR and Bain ownership. In the spring of the previous year, HCA's PE owners borrowed $2.5 billion to pay themselves a dividend, and then followed up in December with a junk-bond sale to pay themselves another nearly $2 billion dividend. As a result, under PE ownership, hospital companies like Vanguard and HCA, and all the community hospitals they have acquired along the way, become buried under a mountain of debt that stays with them long after their PE sponsor has moved on to other investments.

High levels of debt make hospitals vulnerable to changes in the industry as well as broader economic shifts. When credit markets are loose and the economy is growing, hospitals can manage their debt by issuing bonds to cover interest payments or by tapping revolving lines of credit from banks, enabling a steady inflow of funds. But these safety valves quickly disappear during broader economic downturns. A contraction in credit markets can make it difficult or impossible for hospitals to service debt by accessing new sources of liquidity. At the same time, because hospitals are saddled with so much debt, profits are channeled toward servicing the debt rather than building up cash reserves or making long-term investments in patient care or technology. This weakens the hospitals' ability to adjust to industry or economic shifts and makes them more likely to end up in bankruptcy.

The pitfalls associated with PE ownership have, in some cases, led to pushback against PE hospital acquisitions. For example, when Steward attempted to acquire Florida's non-profit Jackson Health System in 2011, it was met with public outcry from Miami residents and local politicians and was forced to back out of the deal. Unions have also been vocal opponents. In 2010, Council 31 of AFSCME in Chicago fought hard against the sale of Westlake Hospital and West Suburban Medical Center to Vanguard Health Systems, but ultimately failed to prevent the sale. Some states have attached conditions to deals involving the transformation of non-profit hospitals to for-profit, PE-owned entities. Michigan's attorney general forced Vanguard to agree to continue existing operations and services at the Detroit Medical Center for ten years after the 2010 purchase date, including commitments to charity care and research. However, the Michigan deal is exceptional, and most PE-hospital acquisitions come with few restrictions on the sale or closure of facilities.

The future of PE investment in hospitals depends on a number of factors, including the cost and availability of credit, health care legislation, and the public response to PE ownership. PE interest in the hospital sector hinges on cheap credit. If credit markets contract, and PE firms find it harder to arrange financing for their investment deals, they may lose interest in health care and instead restrict their investments to more profitable ventures. However, growing demand for health care, in the context of increased hospital obligations and restrictions as a result of the Affordable Care Act, may make community hospitals more vulnerable, and actually increase their attractiveness as takeover targets. Ultimately, the most promising avenue for restricting, or ideally, preventing PE takeovers of hospitals is to publicly scrutinize their behavior and demand alternative forms of financial support for the hospitals, doctors, and nurses struggling to provide affordable, high-quality care. ❑

*Sources:* Tim van Biesen and Karen Murphy, "Global Healthcare Private Equity Report 2012," Bain & Company, 2012; Advisen, "Private equity and hospitals: providence or problem," OneBeacon Professional Insurance, 2011; Lisa Goldstein, "New forces driving rise in not-for-profit hospital consolidation," Moody's Investor Service, 2012; Josh Kosman, *The Buyout of America: How Private Equity Will Cause the Next Great Credit Crisis* (New York: Portfolio, 2009); Congressional Budget Office, "Nonprofit hospitals and the provision of community benefits," Dec., 2006; Jill Horwitz, "Making Profits And Providing Care: Comparing Nonprofit, For-Profit, And Government Hospitals," *Health Affairs*, 24 (3), May 2005; Reed Abelson and Julie Creswell, "Hospital Chain Inquiry Cited Unnecessary Cardiac Work," *New York Times*, Aug. 6, 2012.

*Article 4.6*

# COMMUNITY SUPPORTED AGRICULTURE
*A Chance to Revitalize Farming?*

**BY MARK PAUL AND EMILY STEPHENS**
*March/April 2015*

Have you tried the locavore bahn mi sandwich? How about that fantastic hakurei rabe pasta with organic heirloom beans and pasture-raised eggs? For years, our community supported agriculture (CSA) farm has been sending recipes encouraging us to incorporate our weekly vegetable pick-up, ranging from tomatoes and potatoes to kolrabi and okra, into home-cooked meals and dinner conversations with friends. CSA farms are in fashion, with a near three-fold increase in their numbers across the nation over the past five years. They're bucking the trend: during the same time period, the total number of U.S. farms has decreased by over 100,000, with the largest losses seen among small farms. While the growth of community supported agriculture is an exciting development, the revitalization of agriculture should not be equated blindly with small, local, or family farms. Rather, it has to incorporate a breadth of goals to sustain the farmer, the worker, the eater, and the environment.

First off, what is community supported agriculture? Originally, CSA farms set out to align the interests of community members—seeking fresh, sustainable, local food—with farmers—seeking to support themselves by farming on small plots of land and engaging in high-diversity, labor-intensive production. Given their available inputs, farmers decided how many families they could provide sustenance for during the season, determined the cost of production (including a living wage for the farmer), and then divided total farm costs among the families who then became "shareholders" of the farm. Shareholders paid for their portion of the farms' operation prior to the start of the season, providing working capital for the farms to purchase inputs at the beginning of the growing season—thereby eliminating the farms' dependency on credit from financial institutions.

In the original model, how much did the produce cost the shareholder? That's a tricky question. Shareholders didn't receive a fixed amount of produce for their payment; rather, they received a weekly share of the harvest. This innovative agreement between the farm and the shareholder may have laid the fertile groundwork necessary for revitalizing farming in the United States, but is it leading us in the right direction?

In a capitalist economy, the market is a force to be reckoned with, on par with the droughts, hurricanes, and frosts that often keep farmers up at night. While U.S. farm policy has intentionally led to the expulsion of farmers from agriculture, the 1984 Economic Report of the President called the transition to industrial agriculture "the most successful example of agricultural development in the world." But at what cost? Researchers Leo Horrigan, Robert S. Lawrence, and Polly Walker find that industrial agriculture is gobbling up fossil fuels, water, and topsoil at rates far beyond the capacity of our planet to sustain. Furthermore, industrial agriculture has resulted in dangerous levels of biodiversity loss, while simultaneously being associated with detrimental effects to human health. A recent article in the journal

*Science* argues that under the current system, "[f ]arm productivity and economic viability are vulnerable to resource scarcities, climate change, and market volatility." This doesn't need to be the case.

Alternatives are possible. CSA advocates, as part of the local food movement, are working to build consumer demand for alternative agricultural systems by creating what *New York Times* author Randy Kennedy calls "deeper-than-commerce connection[s] between people who make things and people who buy them." From humble beginnings, CSA farms have aimed to meet the needs of farmers, consumers, and surrounding communities by incorporating issues such as environmental sustainability, workers' rights, and food justice. This contrasts greatly with the industrial food system, which ignores externalities, focusing solely on producing the most food at the lowest cost.

In theory, CSA farms are positioned to overcome many of the challenges faced by small, diversified farming operations that are striving to produce food sustainably and equitably. Through non-traditional agreements with shareholders, the unique needs of these farms can be met:

- • Access to land: community relations and a socially and environmentally just farming model can help farms acquire land through community land trusts.
- • Working capital: shareholder payment in advance of the growing season ensures farms are provided with the necessary capital to purchase inputs.A living wage: the complete cost of production, including farmers' labor, is used to determine a fair price for the share.
- • Guaranteed market: through the purchase of shares, shareholders provide the farm with a secure market for their produce.
- • Risk hedging: shareholders purchase a share of the season's harvest rather than a fixed amount of food, ensuring that the farmer is compensated at a fixed level regardless of shocks such as extreme weather events or crop failure.

Additionally, the needs of consumers, or shareholders, are met through a weekly supply of fresh, local produce and the opportunity to know and support their farmer. Finally, community supported agriculture can improve the well-being of a community through the preservation of open space, support of a healthy environment, and provision of living-wage jobs.

While this brief outline provides an idealist vision of CSA farms, how are things really working?

Upon conducting interviews and a survey with CSA farmers in western Massachusetts, it is clear that the model is struggling to fulfill its original goals. While for many, the original ideals are still there, farmers seem to be stuck at a crossroads. They simply can't sell their shares for enough money to fulfill the fundamental CSA goal of providing a living wage to farmers. Encouragingly, a previous study found CSA shares were not only cheaper than buying organically grown produce at regional chains, but also cheaper than buying conventionally grown produce at any store. Despite the cost-effectiveness of a CSA share, perhaps overall spending on produce has an upper limit that farmers are encountering. Many of the farmers explained that they couldn't raise prices any more, as there is fierce competition between CSA farms to both maintain and grow their customer base. Additionally, farmers were frustrated that their CSA shares were not accessible to low-income consumers, placing farmers and the entire local food movement in a moral bind.

Yet the movement continues to grow. Farmers, particularly young people and women—who have historically been underrepresented among farmers— continue to flock to community supported agriculture. As the number of CSA farms increases, the ideas encompassed by community supported agriculture have become more pliable. A recent NPR report, entitled "What Is Community Supported Agriculture? The Answer Keeps Changing," brings to light just how varied the concept can be, resulting in the dilution of its original meaning and a decrease in its potential to revitalize agriculture. As with the organic movement, CSA farms are undergoing a form of conventionalization. For many farms, community supported agriculture is little more than a marketing ploy. While farms engaged exclusively in community supported agriculture are protected from market pressures, today many CSA farms are hybrids, selling some produce through their CSA but also relying on a traditional capitalist market. These CSA farms seem to be the most removed from the original values such as risk sharing, community relations, and sustainability. Clearly, not all CSA farms are the same, but for consumers aren't labels like "CSA" supposed to simplify their daily purchases? As one CSA farmer put it, "people feel if it is a local farm then it has got all this integrity. But there are local farms around here that use GMO crops and are spraying the crap out of their fields. It's just not the same thing."

Although the phrase "community supported agriculture" is no longer a guarantee of environmental stewardship or social equity, one benefit is that it encourages real relationships and understanding between farmers and consumers. Accountability is built into the system; both farmers and consumers feel a sense of responsibility for the other's well-being. While shareholders can't make assumptions about the values supported by their farm, they have an opportunity to directly ask the expert, their farmer. Through the elimination of distance, CSA bypasses the need for consistent labeling, providing the consumer with the opportunity to understand far more about how their food is grown than any label can convey. There are no easy solutions for the revitalization of agriculture, but these conversations, should people choose to have them, are a step in the right direction. ❏

*Sources:* USDA, "2012 Census of Agriculture" (agcensus.usda.gov); Committee for Economic Development, "An Adaptive Program for Agriculture," 1962; J. P. Cooley and D. A. Lass, "Consumer benefits from community supported agriculture membership," *Review of Agricultural Economics* (1998); Local Harvest: Real Food, Real Farmers, Real Community (localharvest.org); L. Horrigan, et al., "How sustainable agriculture can address the environmental and human health harms of industrial agriculture," *Environmental Health Perspectives* (2002); D. Lass, et al., "Community supported agriculture entering the 21st century: Results from the 2001 national survey," Department of Resource Economics, University of Massachusetts (2003); J. Reganold, et al., "Transforming US agriculture," Science (2003); M. Ritchie and K. Ristau, "US farm policy," *World Policy Journal* (1986); Randy Kennedy, " 'Buy Local' Gets Creative," *New York Times*, Aug. 4, 2013; Ted Burnham, "What Is Community Supported Agriculture? The Answer Keeps Changing," NPR, March 29, 2012 (npr.org).

*Article 4.7*

# CO-OP ECONOMICS

*What can economics teach us about the challenges and potential of cooperation?*

## BY NANCY FOLBRE

*September/October 2013*

I teach economics, a discipline largely inhabited by people skeptical of human potential for cooperation. But I live in a small New England town and work in a university environment that are, for the most part, cooperative. If I eat lunch on campus, I buy it from a student-managed, democratically run business that offers the tastiest, healthiest, cheapest provisions available. If I need to buy bread or milk on the way home, I pull into the Leverett Village Co-op. If my car needs attention, it goes to a worker-owned business, Pelham Auto, where I know both service managers by name. My money sits at the Five College Federal Credit Union, where it earns more interest and gains me better service than I've ever gotten at any other bank.

About four years ago, I began to weave economic theory more closely into my everyday life. The threads began coming together when Adam Trott and Michael Johnson, two members of the local Valley Alliance of Worker Cooperatives, reached out to tell me about their efforts to promote locally owned and democratically managed firms.

Although we lived in the same community, they found me as a result of a short post I wrote for the *New York Times'* "Economix" blog, describing a collaborative agreement between the United Steel Workers and the largest worker-owned business in the world, Mondragón Corporation. It seemed ironic, but also encouraging, that we first connected online, and that it might be possible to go from the global to the local and then back again.

Even in our cooperative-rich area of Western Massachusetts, Adam and Michael explained, most potential worker/owners knew virtually nothing about the principles involved (beyond liking the general idea). Why couldn't a public university provide better education and training for students potentially interested in starting up or joining a worker-owned business? Of course it could, and should. We decided to try to make that happen.

In a collaborative process that involved interested faculty and graduate students, as well as representatives from the Valley Alliance, we developed a new upper-division economics course and designed a Certificate Program for Applied Economic Research on Cooperative Enterprises centered on a summer research internship with a local cooperative.

Here, I want to share some of the ideas and opinions I've formed in the process of developing this program, which we believe could be a good model for other colleges and universities.

## History Matters

Most people, including most college students, seem to think that cooperatives are a counter-cultural leftover from the 1960s, a niche phenomenon confined to hip neighborhoods and college towns. The economic history of the United States is typically portrayed as the steady march of corporate capitalism, trampling all other institutional forms. Many on the right see it as a march of progress; many on the left, as a march of doom.

Ironically, the traditional left preoccupation with corporate capitalism may simply feed the beast—overstating its hegemonic role, as though it can't be contained until the revolution comes. J.K. Gibson-Graham makes this point persuasively in *The End of Capitalism (As We Knew It)*: What we call "capitalism" involves many different creatures. Families, communities, non-profit organizations, and the state actually account for a larger share of economic activity—broadly defined—than capitalist firms.

Though standard economics texts hardly mention them, consumer cooperatives and worker-owned businesses have shaped our history. Their influence, however, has been uneven, greater in some industries and regions than others.

Marxist scholars have often associated cooperatives with the so-called "utopian socialists"—whom they have traditionally considered well-meaning but misguided. Efforts to establish alternative businesses have often been labeled a form of co-optation less politically virtuous than trade-union organizing or socialist political parties. Yet cooperative efforts have typically been closely linked to and complementary with larger anti-corporate organizing efforts. In a fascinating article entitled "Toward an Organizationally Diverse American Capitalism? Cooperative, Mutual, and Local, State-Owned Enterprise," sociologist Mark Schnaiberg traces the history of cooperative marketing efforts in the grain and dairy industries, originally dominated by large monopsonies that used their market power to pay farmers as little as possible. (A monopsony is a single buyer that dominates a market, just as a monopoly is a single seller.) When farmers successfully started up cooperatives, other members of the community also became more likely to organize on their own behalf.

Even when cooperative enterprises represent only a small proportion of market transactions in a local community, they often exercise a disproportionate influence, disciplining capitalist enterprises or pioneering innovations that are later adopted by them. Local food cooperatives were the first to begin marketing organic and local produce, and large supermarket chains gradually followed suit. Local credit unions have made it harder for large banking institutions to charge excessive fees. Worker-owned businesses have pulled the small-business community in a more progressive direction, serving as a counterweight to large, footloose firms.

By demonstrating the viability of businesses aimed to serve larger social goals, cooperatives have altered our economic ecology.

## Culture Matters

As an economist, I was trained to emphasize the difference between for-profit and non-profit firms. But that difference may be less significant than the moral and cultural values central to the definition of cooperative enterprises.

Consumer cooperatives seek to provide high-quality products at minimal cost. Worker-owned businesses need to generate profits both to pay themselves and to finance investment. Both, however, are committed to seven "cooperative principles" (see box, p. 211) that include democracy and concern for community.

In this respect, cooperative enterprises can be seen as a subset of efforts to develop a solidarity economy, which also includes non-profit businesses and community organizations. They are also closely aligned with "buy local" efforts that urge consumers to shop in locally owned stores and build a local supply chain (for instance, by patronizing restaurants utilizing locally grown products).

Not that it's always clear how "concern for community" should be defined. Almost by their very nature as small, decentralized businesses, co-ops prioritize those with whom they are most likely to come into contact. But local solidarity is not automatically consistent with broader forms of solidarity. In fact, it risks a kind of parochialism that could lead to happy little enclaves embedded in a larger economy built on hierarchy and exploitation.

On the other hand, co-op culture can promote values that may lead people toward other forms of positive engagement, with the goal of steadily expanding the cooperative reach and linking many kinds of progressive efforts together. Co-op ventures also offer people the opportunity to build something new, rather than merely trying to tear down something old.

---

### The Seven Cooperative Principles

Cooperatives around the world generally operate according to the same core principles and values, adopted by the International Co-operative Alliance (www.ica.coop) in 1995. Cooperatives trace the roots of these principles to the first modern cooperative, founded in Rochdale, England, in 1844.

1. **Voluntary and Open Membership**: Cooperatives are voluntary organizations, open to all people able to use its services and willing to accept the responsibilities of membership, without gender, social, racial, political or religious discrimination.
2. **Democratic Member Control**: Cooperatives are democratic organizations controlled by their members—those who buy the goods or use the services of the cooperative—who actively participate in setting policies and making decisions.
3. **Members' Economic Participation**: Members contribute equally to, and democratically control, the capital of the cooperative. This benefits members in proportion to the business they conduct with the cooperative rather than on the capital invested.
4. **Autonomy and Independence**: Cooperatives are autonomous, self-help organizations controlled by their members. If the co-op enters into agreements with other organizations or raises capital from external sources, it is done so based on terms that ensure democratic control by the members and maintains the cooperative's autonomy.
5. **Education, Training and Information**: Cooperatives provide education and training for members, elected representatives, managers and employees so they can contribute effectively to the development of their cooperative. Members also inform the general public about the nature and benefits of cooperatives.
6. **Cooperation among Cooperatives**: Cooperatives serve their members most effectively and strengthen the cooperative movement by working together through local, national, regional and international structures.
7. **Concern for Community**: While focusing on member needs, cooperatives work for the sustainable development of communities through policies and programs accepted by the members.

*From the National Cooperative Business Association, International Year of Cooperatives (usa2012.coop).*

The commitment to democratic decision-making distinguishes worker-owned businesses from other institutional forms that aim to enlarge economic goals (such as the new "social benefit" corporate charters) or to help incentivize workers (such as profit-sharing or employee-stock-ownership plans). This commitment reflects a cultural value—as well as a political principle. Other shared values encouraging respect and concern for others may help lubricate the democratic process by making collective decision-making less contentious.

Democratic values and skills may grow stronger in communities where they are consistently exercised, explaining why some regions of the world seem to foster more cooperative enterprises than others. The famous Mondragón cooperatives grew up in the Basque area of northern Spain, among people who felt embattled and impoverished by their minority status and strengthened by their progressive Catholic traditions. Many small cooperatives have prospered in northern Italy, an area with a long history of labor radicalism and a strong Communist Party. In Canada, the province of Quebec has successfully encouraged the cooperative provision of social services under the banner of the "social economy."

In the United States, cooperatives have often helped improve living standards in African-American communities, from a cooperative shipyard in 1860s Baltimore, to a co-op buying club in Depression-era Gary, Ind., to the Common Ground Collective in post-Katrina New Orleans. As Jessica Gordon-Nembhard and Ajowa Nzinga point out (see *Dollars & Sense*, July/August 2006), a common history of economic exclusion and hardship can foster cooperation.

Public policies have also played a role in developing these epicenters of cooperative development. But culture is surely one of the factors shaping the political alignments that generate such policies.

## Efficiency Matters

Economists often overstate the value of efficiency, or define it in excessively narrow terms. But that doesn't mean it's not important. Efficiency is an important arbiter of success in competition and, in the world we live in, co-operators need to compete. Since competition between firms is, to some extent a "team sport," successful cooperation among team members can prove advantageous.

Democratically managed firms may be more efficient than others, even from the relatively narrow perspective of costs and benefits. The British economist John Stuart Mill made this argument in the mid-19th century, pointing out that workers who were also owners would be likely to work harder and smarter than those merely paid an hourly wage.

This issue never received much attention from early-twentieth-century Marxists convinced of the virtues of central planning. However, it came to the fore with Yugoslavian experiments in worker self-management in the mid-20th century and has since had a big impact on progressive economic thinking—in part because it helps frame a critique of both the traditional family firm and the modern corporation.

A long-standing favorite of neoclassical economists is an argument, developed by economists Armen Alchian and Harold Demsetz, that workers will have a tendency to shirk on the job unless they are overseen by an owner who can capture any profits (or "residual") left over after the workers are paid. This gives the "residual claimant" an incentive to crack the whip and make them work as hard as possible. Ownership in most modern corporations is highly fragmented, but owners presumably hire managers—from the chief executive officer or CEO down to supervisors and foremen—to fulfill this disciplinary role.

Radical economist Samuel Bowles effectively rebuts this argument, pointing out that it is difficult and costly to monitor effort. Workers seeking to resist capitalist exploitation may be especially likely to shirk unless managers can find a way to either secure their loyalty or threaten them with costly job loss.

Unfortunately, worker ownership alone doesn't necessarily solve this incentive problem. Workers either have to be really good at monitoring one another's efforts (so that no one can free ride without being sanctioned), or they have to feel such strong solidarity toward one another that no one even tries to free ride. (The latter is preferable, since it's often hard for a collective to fire someone who is slacking off.)

Other tensions among owner-workers can arise. For instance, young owner-workers have a stronger incentive to reinvest firm profits to increase their future earnings than older owner-workers, who would prefer to retain more earnings and/or fund their pensions. The success of a worker-owned enterprise depends on the ability of worker-owners to anticipate and creatively respond to such conflicts of interest. But the process of doing so—negotiating and resolving differences of opinion—can itself be quite costly, in two ways.

First, democratic decision-making can be quite time-consuming, especially if based on rules of consensus. Worker-owned firms generally treat time in meetings as part of their paid work, and the time they devote to it can cut down on directly productive activities.

Second, democratic decision-making can prove emotionally costly, as when good friends disagree about important matters and find it difficult to accommodate one another. On the other hand, conflict avoidance—such as a desire not to discipline a fellow worker who is also a friend—can also lower efficiency. This problem can be described as a "second order" free-rider problem—that is, a reluctance to openly point to or discourage free riding.

Representative democracy and delegation to a manager can help minimize these problems, but also at some cost. Majority rule can alienate the minority, and unstable factions can lead to lack of continuity in decision-making.

Worker-owned firms will be more likely to prosper if they cultivate an awareness of decision-making problems and develop the institutional structures and skills necessary to over-come them.

Here comes the Catch-22. Neither our educational system nor most employers do much to help people develop democratic management skills, so there's a big start-up problem. If we could just create more opportunities for people to develop and practice such skills, worker-owned businesses could enjoy more success.

Efficiency gains can also come at the macro level. Worker-owned businesses that get off the ground tend to be more stable than other small businesses, in part because workers have an incentive to hang in over the long haul, even if revenue slumps. This can buffer the effects of recession on the economy as a whole.

Most importantly, worker-owned businesses depend more on positive incentives than on the threat of job loss. Unlike employer-owned businesses, they don't rely on the labor discipline imposed by a high unemployment rate. And consistently high unemployment rates are among the most inefficient features of our current economic system.

## Collaboration Matters

For all the reasons given above, the cooperative movement may need to reach a certain critical mass before it can really take off. More collaboration among cooperatives—and between cooperatives and other institutions such as public universities—could make a big difference.

Relatively few worker-owned businesses are started up in a given year, leading some to speculate that they are inherently less expansionary than capitalist firms (for the simple reason that worker-owners care about more than the rate of return on their capital investment). They also care about the quality of their work life and their place in the community. Some of the decision-making problems described above, moreover, may be more easily solved in small firms where everyone knows everyone else. Expansion can lead to complications.

However, collaboration and expansion could help worker-owned businesses in several ways. First, it could help them gain access to more and better financing. By definition, worker-owned firms can't sell equity shares in their business (because all owners must be workers). They can develop other forms of self-financing, including bonds that can be especially attractive to socially responsible investors. But they can also develop ways of pooling resources and helping to finance one another. Each firm belonging to the Valley Alliance of Worker Coops sets aside a percentage of its profits to promote local cooperative development. One can even imagine a kind of franchise model in which one firm could spin off smaller firms, which could become financially independent, but remain closely allied.

Second, vertical networking along the supply chain could increase efficiency and the ability to compete with large conglomerate capitalist enterprises. International networking among cooperatives holds particular promise, because it advances a larger fair-trade agenda, and also helps escape parochialism. Many examples of this kind of networking exist, such as the People's Market at UMass-Amherst buying only cooperatively produced coffee and actively seeking other cooperatively produced goods and services.

Third, more networking could help develop the distinctive managerial and decision-making skills described above. Indeed, the more worker-owners gain experience in different types of firms, the richer the skills they bring to the task of democratic management. And the more visible worker-owners become, the more young people are likely to become attracted to new prospects for more socially meaningful and economically rewarding work.

Finally, the more worker-owned businesses and other cooperative enterprises expand, the easier it becomes to build political coalitions and implement policies that promote their efforts. These synergies help explain how regional economies in the Basque area of Spain, northern Italy, and the Canadian province of Quebec have evolved.

A worker-owned business is what economists call a "microeconomic structure." But its ultimate success may depend on its ability to change the macroeconomic structure, which can, in turn, improve its microeconomic efficiency. Even a small cooperative firm can help a community enhance its standard of living and quality of life. More importantly, however, it can provide a catalyst for social and political changes that not only bring more and more worker-owned businesses into being, but also enable them to compete more effectively with capital-owned firms.

That's why worker-owned businesses fit the description of what the 20th-century Italian theorist and revolutionary Antonio Gramsci called a "non-reformist reform" and what sociologist Erik Olin Wright terms a "real utopia." Take another look at those seven cooperative principles. They offer a pretty good guide to running not just a business, but a whole society. ❏

**Sources:** J.K. Gibson-Graham, *The End of Capitalism (As We Knew It)* (University of Minnesota Press, 2006); Mark Schnaiberg, "Toward an Organizationally Diverse American Capitalism? Cooperative, Mutual, and Local, State-Owned Enterprise," *Seattle University Law Review*, Vol. 34, No. 4 (2011); Jessica Gordon-Nembhard and Ajowa Nzinga, "African-American Economic Solidarity," *Dollars & Sense*, July/August 2006; Erik Olin Wright, *Envisioning Real Utopias* (Verso, 2010).

# Chapter 5

# MARKET FAILURE I: MARKET POWER

## INTRODUCTION

With monopoly, we finally encounter a situation in which most economists, orthodox and otherwise, agree that unfettered markets lead to an undesirable outcome. If a firm is able to create a monopoly, it faces a downward-sloping demand curve—that is to say, if it reduces output, it can charge a higher price. Economists argue that competitive forces tend to undermine any monopoly, but failing this, they support antitrust policy as a backstop. The concept of monopoly not only points to an important failing of markets, but it opens the door to thinking about many possible market structures other than perfect competition, including oligopoly, in which a small group of producers dominates the market. Monopoly and oligopoly are examples of market structures in which firms wield "market power" (violating Tilly Assumption #1—see Article 1.2). That is, individual firms can affect the market-wide level of prices, profits, and wages. Market power alters how markets function from the ideal of perfect competition and delivers significantly less optimal results.

We begin this chapter with another seminal article by Chris Tilly, "Is Small Beautiful? Is Bigger Better? Small and Big Businesses Both Have Their Drawbacks" (Article 5.1). This article walks through the pluses and minuses of large and small businesses, and finds both wanting.

The current financial crisis has provided particularly egregious examples of what happens when we institute *laissez-faire* (hands-off) regulatory regimes, especially in the area of finance. In "A Brief History of Mergers and Antitrust Policy" (Article 5.2), Edward Herman provides a long-term context for the discussion, reviewing the history of U.S. antitrust law over the last century. He also criticizes economists for justifying a hands-off policy toward big business mergers over the last few decades.

Next, Arthur MacEwan discusses the relevance of the concept of "monopoly capital" in an age of globalized competition (Article 5.3). MacEwan finds that firm size and market concentration have continued to grow throughout the era of globalization and that large firms still exhibit extraordinary market power.

In "Want Free Trade? Open the Medical and Drug Industry to Competition" (Article 5.4), Dean Baker describes how companies in this sector are protected from market competition. Doctors are protected form international competition, even as "free trade" agreements have put blue-collar workers squarely in competition with workers all over the world. Meanwhile, pharmaceutical companies enjoy monopoly protections lasting decades, thanks to patents, without a significant counterweight from government price regulation.

The last two articles look at two examples of the exercise of market power today. Rob Larson's "Not Too Big Enough" (Article 5.5) explores the phenomenon of the "too big to fail" banks as an expression of market power. Elizabeth Fraser and Anuradha Mittal's "Seeds of Change" (Article 5.6) explain how the world seed market is dominated by a handful of corporations, but also how national governments are pushing back and a global movement against the seed giants is growing.

## Discussion Questions

1. (Article 5.1) List the pros and cons of large and small businesses that Tilly discusses. How does this compare with the problems associated with market structure that your textbook mentions? Be sure to compare Tilly's list of small-business flaws with what your textbook has to say about small business.

2. (Articles 5.1 and 5.2) In what ways do these articles show that corporations control "the marketplace of ideas"? What are the possible consequences? What, if anything, should be done about it?

3. (Article 5.3) Mainstream economists view competition among many small firms as a prerequisite for "efficient" market outcomes. Some touted globalization as a way to increase competition and benefit consumers. What problems, if any, result from the large size and market dominance of a few global firms? Should this change our view of globalization in any way?

4. (Article 5.4) Baker argues that trade agreements have protected U.S. doctors and pharmaceutical companies from international competition. Why do you think this has been the case, when other kinds of workers and industries have borne the full brunt of global competition? Would policies to reduce the prices charged by the medical sector be desirable? What policies?

5. (Articles 5.5) What is "moral hazard?" How does this concept relate to "too big to fail"? If the public cannot allow some firms to fail, is there anything that can replace the "discipline of the market" in restraining those companies' behavior?

6. (Article 5.6) If farmers purchase seeds voluntarily from seed companies, does this mean that the farmers are made better off in the deal? If this is the case, is there any cause for criticism of the dominance of a few giant companies over the seed market?

Article 5.1

# IS SMALL BEAUTIFUL? IS BIG BETTER?

*Small and big businesses both have their drawbacks.*

**BY CHRIS TILLY**
*July/August 1989, revised April 2002*

**B**eginning in the late 1980s, the United States has experienced a small, but sig-nificant boom in small business. While big businesses have downsized, small enterprises have proliferated. Should we be glad? Absolutely, declare the advocates of small business. Competition makes small businesses entrepreneurial, innovative, and responsive to customers.

Not so fast, reply big business's boosters. Big corporations grew big because they were efficient, and tend to stay efficient because they are big—and thus able to invest in research and upgrading of technology and workforce skills.

But each side in this debate omits crucial drawbacks. Small may be beautiful for consumers, but it's often oppressive for workers. And while big businesses wield the power to advance technology, they also often wield the market power to bash com-petitors and soak consumers. In the end, the choices are quite limited.

## Big and Small

Is the United States a nation of big businesses, or of small ones? There are two con-ventional ways to measure business size. One is simply to count the number of employees per firm. By this measure, small businesses (say, business establishments with less than 20 employees) make up the vast majority of businesses (Table 1). But they provide only a small fraction of the total number of jobs.

The other approach gauges market share—each firm's share of total sales in a given industry. Industries range between two extremes: what economists call "perfect com-petition" (many firms selling a standardized product, each too tiny to affect the market price) and monopoly (one business controls all sales in an industry). Economy-wide, as with employment, small businesses are most numerous, but control only a small slice of total sales. Sole proprietorships account for 73% of established businesses, far out-numbering corporations, which are 20% of the total (the remainder are partnerships). But corporations ring up a hefty 90% of all sales, leaving sole proprietors with only 6%. It takes a lot of mom and pop stores to equal General Motors' 1999 total of $177 billion in sales.

Industry by industry, the degree of competition varies widely. Economists con-sider an industry concentrated when its top four companies account for more than 40% of total sales in the industry (Table 2). At the high end of the spectrum are the cigarette, beer, and aircraft industries, where four firms account for the bulk of U.S. production.

No market comes close to meeting the textbook specifications for perfect competition, but one can still find industries in which a large number of produc-ers compete for sales. The clothing and restaurant industries, for example, remain relatively competitive. Overall, about one-third of U.S. goods are manufactured in concentrated industries, about one fifth are made in competitive industries, and the rest fall somewhere in between.

## Beating the Competition

Those who tout the benefits of small, competitive business make a broad range of claims on its behalf. In addition to keeping prices low, they say the quality of the product is constantly improving, as companies seek a competitive edge. The same desire, they claim, drives firms toward technological innovations, leading to productivity increases.

The real story is not so simple. Competition does indeed keep prices low. Believe it or not, clothing costs us less—in real terms—than it cost our parents. Between 1960 and 1999, while the overall price level and hourly wages both increased nearly sixfold, apparel prices didn't even triple. And small businesses excel at offering variety, whether it is the ethnic restaurants that dot cities or the custom machine-tool work offered by small shops. Furthermore, however powerful small business lobbies may be in Washington, they do not influence the legislative process as blatantly as do corporate giants.

But those low prices often have an ugly underside. Our sportswear is cheap in part because the garment industry increasingly subcontracts work to sweatshops—whether they be export assembly plants in Haiti paying dollar-a-day wages, or the "underground" Los Angeles stitcheries that employ immigrant women in virtual slavery. Struggling to maintain razor-thin profit margins, small businesses cut costs any way they can—which usually translates into low wages and onerous working conditions.

"There is a rule of survival for small business," Bill Ryan, president of Ryan Transfer Corporation, commented some years ago. "There are certain things you want to have [in paying workers] and certain things you can afford. You had better go with what you can afford." Bottom line, workers in companies employing 500 or more people enjoy average wages 30% higher than their counterparts in small businesses.

Part of this wage gap results from differences other than size—unionization, the education of the workforce, the particular jobs and industries involved. But University of Michigan economist Charles Brown and his colleagues

### TABLE 1:
### SMALL BUSINESS NATION?

**Most businesses are small, but most employees work for big businesses**

| Company size (number of employees) | Percent of all firms | Percent of all workers |
|---|---|---|
| 1–4 | 54% | 6% |
| 5–9 | 20% | 8% |
| 10–19 | 13% | 11% |
| 20–49 | 8% | 16% |
| 50–99 | 3% | 13% |
| 100–249 | 2% | 16% |
| 250–499 | 0.4% | 10% |
| 500–999 | 0.2% | 7% |
| 1,000 or more | 0.1% | 13% |

Note: "Businesses" refers to establishments, meaning business locations.

Source: County Business Patterns, 1998.

controlled for all these differences and more, and still found a 10% premium for big business's employees. A note of caution, however: Other recent research indicates that this wage bonus is linked to long-term employment and job ladders. To the extent that corporations dissolve these long-term ties—as they seem to be rapidly doing—the pay advantage may dissolve as well.

Small business gurus make extravagant claims about small businesses' job-generation capacity. An oft-quoted 1987 report by consultant David Birch claimed that businesses with fewer than 20 employees create 88% of new jobs. The reality is more mundane: over the long run, businesses with 19 or fewer workers account for about one quarter of net new jobs. One reason why Birch's statistics are misleading is that new small businesses are created in great numbers, but they also fail at a high rate. The result is that the *net* gain in jobs is much smaller than the number created in business start-ups.

For companies in very competitive markets, the same "whip of competition" that keeps prices down undermines many of competition's other supposed benefits. The flurry of competition in the airline industry following deregulation, for example, hardly resulted in a higher quality product. Flying became temporarily cheaper, but also less comfortable, reliable, and safe.

Technological innovation from competition is also more myth than reality. Small firms in competitive industries do very little research and development. They lack both the cash needed to make long-term investments and the market power to guarantee a return on that investment. In fact, many of them can't even count on surviving to reap the rewards: only one-third to one-half of small business startups survive for five years, and only about one in five makes it to ten years. A 1988 Census Bureau survey concluded that in manufacturing, "technology use is positively correlated with plant size." Agriculture may be the exception that proves the rule. That highly competitive industry has made marked productivity gains, but its research is supported by the taxpayer, and its risks are reduced by government price supports.

Of course, the biggest myth about competition is that it is in any way a "natural state" for capitalism. In fact, in most markets the very process of competing for high profits or a bigger market share tends to create a concentrated, rather than a competitive, market structure.

### TABLE 2: WHO COMPETES, WHO DOESN'T

| Industry | Percent of sales by top four firms |
|---|---|
| Light truck and utility vehicle manufacturing | 96% |
| Breweries | 91% |
| Home center stores | 91% |
| Breakfast cereal manufacturing | 78% |
| General book stores | 77% |
| Credit card issuing | 77% |
| Lawn equipment manufacturing | 62% |
| Cable providers | 63% |
| Computer and software stores | 51% |
| Sock manufacturing | 30% |
| Hotels and motels (excl. casinos) | 22% |
| Gas stations | 9% |
| Real estate | 4% |
| Bars | 2% |

Source: 2002 Economic Census.

This process occurs in several ways. Big firms sometimes drive their smaller competitors out of business by selectively cutting prices to the bone. The smaller firms may lack the financial resources to last out the low prices. In the 1960s, several of IBM's smaller competitors sued it for cutting prices in a pattern that was designed to drive the smaller firms out of the market. Large corporations can also gain a lock on scarce resources: for example, large airlines like United and American operate the comprehensive, computerized information and reservation systems that travel agents tap into—and you can bet that each airline's system lists their own flights first. Or businesses may exploit an advantage in one market to dominate another, as Microsoft used its control of the computer operating system market to seize market share for its Internet browser.

Other firms eliminate competitors by buying them out—either in a hostile takeover or a friendly merger. Either way, a former competitor is neutralized. This strategy used to be severely limited by strict antitrust guidelines that prohibited most horizontal mergers—those between two firms that formerly competed in the same market. The Reagan administration's team at the Justice Department, however, loosened the merger guidelines significantly in the early 1980s. Since that time, many large mergers between former competitors have been allowed to go through, most notably in the airline industry.

## The Power of Concentration

Concentration, then, is as natural to market economies as competition. And bigness, like smallness, is a mixed bag for us as consumers and workers. For workers, bigness is on the whole a plus. Whereas competition forces small businesses to be stingy, big firms are on average more generous, offering employees higher wages, greater job security, and more extensive fringe benefits. In 1993, 97% of businesses with 500 or more workers provided health insurance; only 43% of businesses with 25 or fewer employees did so. Large firms also provide much more employee training. The strongest unions, as well, have historically been in industries where a few firms control large shares of their markets, and can pass along increased costs to consumers—auto, steel, and tires, for example. When profits are threatened, though, firms in concentrated markets also have more resources with which to fight labor. They are better able to weather a strike, oppose unionization, and make agreements with rivals not to take advantage of each other's labor troubles. In addition, large companies, not surprisingly, score low on workplace autonomy.

What about consumers? Corporations in industries where there are few competitors may compete, but the competitive clash is seldom channeled into prolonged price wars. The soft drink industry is a classic example. David McFarland, a University of North Carolina economist, likens soft drink competition to professional wrestling. "They make a lot of sounds and groans and bounce on the mat, but they know who is going to win," he remarked.

Coke and Pepsi introduce new drinks and mount massive ad campaigns to win market share, but the net result is not lower prices. In fact, because competition between industry giants relies more on product differentiation than price, companies pass on their inflated advertising expenses to consumers. In the highly concentrated breakfast cereal market, the package frequently costs more than the contents. And of every dollar you pay for a box, nearly 20 cents goes for advertising.

It takes resources to develop and market a new idea, which gives large corporations distinct advantages in innovation. The original idea for the photocopier may have come from a patent lawyer who worked nights in his basement, but Xerox spent $16 million before it had a product it could sell. RCA invested $65 million developing the color television. RCA could take this gamble because its dominance in the television market ensured that it would not be immediately undercut by some other firm.

But market dominance can also translate into complacency. The steel industry illustrates the point. A few major producers earned steady profits through the 1950s and 1960s but were caught off-guard when new technologies vaulted foreign steel-makers to the top of the industry in the 1970s. Similarly, when IBM dominated the computer industry in the 1960s and early 1970s, innovation proceeded quite slowly, particularly compared to the frantic scramble in that industry today. With no competitors to worry about, it was more profitable for IBM to sit tight, since innovation would only have made its own machines obsolete.

And large corporations can also put their deep pockets and technical expertise to work to short-circuit public policy. In the 1980s, when Congress changed corporate liability laws to make corporate executives criminally liable for some kinds of offenses, General Electric's lobbyists and legal staff volunteered to help draft the final regulations, in order to minimize the damage.

Big businesses sometimes hide their lobbying behind a "citizen" smokescreen. The largest-spending lobby in Washington in 1986 was Citizens for the Control of Acid Rain. These good citizens had been organized by coal and electric utility companies to oppose tighter pollution controls. Along the same lines, the Coalition for Vehicle Choice (now, who could be against that?) was set up by Ford and General Motors in 1990 to fight higher fuel efficiency standards.

## Concentration or Conglomeration

Over the last couple of decades, the mix of big and small businesses has changed, but the changes are small and—at first glance—contradictory. Over time, employment has shifted toward smaller firms, though the shift has been subtle, not revolutionary. Meanwhile, the overall level of industry-by-industry sales concentration in the economy has increased, but only slightly. As older industries become more concentrated, newer, more competitive ones crop up, leaving overall concentration relatively steady. In his book *Lean and Mean*, economist Bennett Harrison points out that there is actually no contradiction between the small business employment boomlet and big firms' continued grip on markets. Big businesses, it turns out, are orchestrating much of the flowering of small business, through a variety of outsourcing and subcontracting arrangements.

But if industry-by-industry concentration has changed little over the decades, conglomeration is a different matter. Corporate ownership of assets has become much more concentrated over time, reflecting the rise in conglomerates—corporations doing business in a variety of industries. Five decades ago, the top 200 manufacturing firms accounted for 48% of all sales in the U.S. economy. By 1993, the 200 biggest industrial businesses controlled 65% of sales.

Most mainstream economists see these groupings as irrelevant for the competitive structure of the economy. Antitrust laws place no restrictions on firms from different industries banding together under one corporate roof. But sheer size can easily affect competition in the markets of the individual firms involved. A parent company can use one especially profitable subsidiary to subsidize start-up costs for a new venture, giving it a competitive edge. And if one board of directors controls major interests in related industries, it can obviously influence any of those markets more forcefully.

A case in point is the mega-merger of Time Inc. and Warner, which will soon be joining with America Online. The resulting conglomerate will control massive sections of the home entertainment business, bringing together Time's journalists, film and television producers, and authors, Warner's entertainment machine, which includes Home Box Office, the nation's largest pay television channel, and AOL's huge share of the Internet access market. The conglomerate can influence the entertainment business from the initial point—the actors, writers, and directors—up to the point where the finished products appear on people's televisions or computers. Conglomeration also multiplies the political clout of large corportions. No wonder Disney and other entertainment giants have also hopped on the conglomeration bandwagon.

## Choose Your Poison

Competition, concentration, or conglomeration: The choice is an unsavory one indeed. Opting for lots of tiny, competing firms leaves labor squeezed and sacrifices the potential technological advantages that come with concentrated resources. Yet the big monopolies tend to dominate their markets, charge high prices, and waste countless resources on glitzy ad campaigns and trivial product differentiation. And the big conglomerate firms, while not necessarily dominant in any single market, wield a frightening amount of political and economic power, with budgets larger than those of most countries.

Of course, we don't have much to say about the choice, no matter how much "shopping for a better world" we engage in. Market competition rolls on—sometimes cutthroat, other times genteel. Industries often start out as monopolies (based on new inventions), go through a competitive phase, but end up concentrating as they mature. As long as bigness remains profitable and the government maintains a hands-off attitude, companies in both competitive and concentrated industries will tend to merge with firms in other industries. This will feed a continuing trend toward conglomeration. Since bigness and smallness both have their drawbacks, the best we can do is to use public policies to minimize the disadvantages of each. ❏

**Sources:** *Lean and Mean: The Changing Landscape of Corporate Power in the Age of Flexibility*, Bennett Harrison, 1994; *Employers Large and Small*, Charles Brown, James Hamilton, and James Medoff, 1990.

Article 5.2

# A BRIEF HISTORY OF MERGERS AND ANTITRUST POLICY

## BY EDWARD HERMAN
*May/June 1998*

Government efforts to prevent or break up monopolies are called antitrust policy. They assume that when a few companies dominate an industry, this weakens competition and hurts the public by reducing production, raising prices, and slowing technical advance. Antitrust has gone through cycles during this century. In some years, strongly pro-business presidencies (usually Republican) have allowed businesses to merge at will. These have often been followed by "reform" administrations, which tend to restrain, but not to reverse, concentrations of corporate power.

The federal government first took on a strong antitrust role with the Sherman Act of 1890, which outlawed monopoly and efforts to obtain it. In 1914 the Clayton Act also put restrictions on stock purchases and interlocking directorates that would reduce competition. This legislation responded to public anger and fears about "trusts," which brought separate firms under common control. Most notorious were Rockefeller's Standard Oil Trust and James Duke's American Tobacco Company, which employed ruthless tactics to drive their competitors out of business.

Early on the antitrust laws also treated organized labor as a "monopoly," and were used in breaking the Pullman strike in 1892. In 1908, the Supreme Court awarded damages to an employer against whom unions had organized a secondary boycott. This led to the Clayton Act exempting unions from its restrictions.

Otherwise, the federal government only minimally enforced the Sherman Act until Theodore Roosevelt was elected in 1900. Then in 1911 the Supreme Court decided that both the Standard Oil and American Tobacco trusts were "bad trusts," and ordered their dismantling. But in 1920 the Court refused to condemn the U.S. Steel consolidation, because it was a "good trust" that didn't attack its smaller rivals. This began a long period when the Antitrust Division and the courts approved mergers that produced industries with a few dominant firms, but which were "well-behaved." And in the 1920s, Republicans virtually ended antitrust enforcement.

## The Golden Age

Franklin Roosevelt revived antitrust during 1938 to 1941, and antitrust law had its golden age from 1945 to 1974, fueled by a liberal Supreme Court, anti-merger legislation passed in 1950, and mildly progressive enforcement (though less so in the Republican years). During this period Alcoa's monopoly over aluminum production was broken (1945), and the Court found the tobacco industry guilty of "group monopoly" (1946), although the companies were only assessed a modest fine.

During the 1960s, when antitrust law blocked mergers among companies in the same industry, businesses adapted by acquiring firms in unrelated industries. Many such "conglomerate" mergers took place during 1964-68, when Lyndon Johnson was president. Companies like International Telephone and Telegraph, Ling-Temco-Vought, Gulf & Western, Tenneco, and Litton Industries grew rapidly.

## The Reagan-Bush Collapse

Antitrust policy went into recession around 1974, then plunged during the presidencies of Ronald Reagan and George H. W. Bush. They aggressively dismantled antitrust, imposing drastic cuts in budgets and manpower, installing officials hostile to the antitrust mission, and failing to enforce the laws. During 1981-89, the Antitrust Division of the Justice Dept. challenged only 16 of over 16,000 pre-merger notices filed with them.

Despite his high-profile contest with Microsoft, Bill Clinton largely accepted the conservative view that most mergers are harmless. During his two terms, federal authorities approved or ignored many giant mergers. These included Westinghouse's buyout of CBS, the joining of "Baby Bells" Bell Atlantic and Nynex, and the combination of Chemical Bank and Manufacturers Hanover. During 1997 alone, 156 mergers of $1 billion or more, and merger transactions totalling more than *$1 trillion*, passed antitrust muster.

Clinton's failure to attack giant mergers rests nominally on the alleged efficiency of large firms and the belief that globalized markets make for competition. FTC head Robert Pitofsky said, "this is an astonishing merger wave," but not to worry because these deals "should be judged on a global market scale, not just on national and local markets."

But the efficiency of large size—as opposed to the profit-making advantages that corporations gain from market power and cross-selling (pushing products through other divisions of the same company)—is eminently debatable. And many markets are not global—hospitals, for example, operate in local markets, yet only some 20 of 3,000 hospital mergers have been subjected to antitrust challenge. Even in global markets a few firms are often dominant, and a vast array of linkages such as joint ventures and licensing agreements increasingly mute global competition.

The Clinton administration's failure to contest many giant mergers did not rest only on intellectual arguments. It also reflected political weakness and an unwillingness to oppose powerful people who fund elections and own or dominate the media. This was conspicuously true of the great media combinations—Disney and Cap-Cities/ABC, and TimeWarner and Turner—and the merger of Boeing and McDonnell-Douglas, which involved institutions of enormous power, whose mergers the stock market greeted enthusiastically.

## The Economists Sell Out

Since the early 1970s, powerful people and corporations have funded not only elections but conservative economists, who are frequently housed in think-tanks such as the American Enterprise, Hoover, and Cato Institutes, and serve as corporate consultants in regulatory and anti-trust cases. Most notable in hiring economic consultants have been AT&T and IBM, which together spent hundreds of millions of dollars on their antitrust defenses. AT&T hired some 30 economists from five leading economics departments during the 1970s and early 1980s.

Out of these investments came models and theories downgrading the "populist" idea that numerous sellers and decentralization were important for effective competition (and essential to a democratic society). They claimed instead that the market can do it all, and that regulation and antitrust actions are misconceived. First, theorists showed that efficiency gains from mergers might reduce prices even more than monopoly power would cause them to rise. Economists also stressed "entry," claiming that if mergers did not improve efficiency any price increases would be wiped out eventually by new companies entering the industry. Entry is also the heart of the theory of "contestable markets," developed by economic consultants to AT&T, who argued that the ease of entry in cases where resources (trucks, aircraft) can be shifted quickly at low cost, makes for effective competition.

Then there is the theory of a "market for corporate control," in which mergers allow better managers to displace the less efficient. In this view, poorly-managed firms have low stock prices, making them easy to buy. Finally, many economists justified conglomerate mergers on three grounds: that they function as "mini capital markets," with top managers allocating capital between divisions of a single firm so as to maximize efficiency; that they reduce transaction costs; and that they are a means of diversifying risk.

These theories, many coming out of the "Chicago School" (the economics department at the University of Chicago), suffer from over-simplification, a strong infusion of ideology, and lack of empirical support. Mergers often are motivated by factors other than enhancing efficiency—such as the desire for monopoly power, empire building, cutting taxes, improving stock values, and even as a cover for poor management (such as when the badly-run U.S. Steel bought control of Marathon Oil).

Several researchers have questioned the supposed benefits of mergers. In theory, a merger that improves efficiency should increase profits. But one study by Dennis Mueller, and another by F. W. Scherer and David Ravenscraft, showed that mergers more often than not have reduced returns to stockholders. A study by Michael Porter of Harvard University demonstrated that a staggering 74% of the conglomerate acquisitions of the 1960s were eventually sold off (divested)—a good indication that they were never based on improving efficiency. William Shepherd of the University of Massachusetts investigated the "contestable markets" model, finding that it is a hypothetical case with minimal applicability to the real world.

Despite their inadequacies, the new apologetic theories have profoundly affected policy, because they provide an intellectual rationale for the agenda of the powerful. ❏

*Sources:* "Competition Policy in America: The Anti-Antitrust Paradox," James Brock, *Antitrust Bulletin*, Summer 1997; "The Promotional-Financial Dynamic of Merger Movements: A Historical Perspective," Richard DuBoff and Edward Herman, *Journal of Economic Issues*, March 1989; "Antimerger Policy in the United States: History and Lessons," Dennis C. Mueller, *Empirica*, 1996; "Dim Prospects: effective competition in telecommunications, railroads and electricity," William Shepherd, *Antitrust Bulletin*, 1997.

*Article 5.3*

# MONOPOLY CAPITAL AND GLOBAL COMPETITION

## BY ARTHUR MacEWAN
*September/October 2011*

> Dear Dr. Dollar:
> *Is the concept of monopoly capital relevant today, considering such things as global competition?*
>                                        —Paul Tracy, Oceanside, Calif.

In 1960, the largest 100 firms on *Fortune* magazine's "annual ranking of America's largest corporations" accounted for 15% of corporate profits and had revenues that were 24% as large as GDP. By the early 2000s, each of these figures had roughly doubled: the top 100 firms accounted for about 30% of corporate profits and their revenues were over 40% as large as GDP.*

The banking industry is a prime example of what has been going on: In 2007 the top ten banks were holding over 50% of industry assets, compared with about 25% in 1985.

If by "monopoly capital" we mean that a relatively small number of huge firms play a disproportionately large role in our economic lives, then monopoly capital is a relevant concept today, even more so than a few decades ago.

Global competition has certainly played a role in reshaping aspects of the economy, but it has not altered the importance of very large firms. Even while, for example, Toyota and Honda have gained a substantial share of the U.S. and world auto markets, this does not change the fact that a small number of firms dominate the U.S. and world markets. Moreover, much of the rise in imports, which looks like competition, is not competition for the large U.S. firms themselves. General Motors, for example, has established parts suppliers in Mexico, allowing the company to pay lower wages and hire fewer workers in the states. And Wal-Mart, Target, and other large retailers obtain low-cost goods from subcontractors in China and elsewhere.

Economics textbooks tell us that in markets dominated by a few large firms, prices will be higher than would otherwise be the case. This has generally been true of the auto industry. Also, this appears to be the case in pharmaceuticals, telecommunications, and several other industries.

Wal-Mart and other "big box" stores, however, often do compete by offering very low prices. They are monopsonistic (few buyers) as well as monopolistic (few sellers). They use their power to force down both their payments to suppliers and the wages of their workers. In either case—high prices or low prices—large firms are exercising their market power to shift income to themselves from the rest of us.

Beyond their operation within markets, the very large firms shift income to themselves by shaping markets. Advertising is important in this regard, including, for example, the way pharmaceutical firms effectively create "needs" in pushing their products. Then there is the power of large firms in the political sphere. General

Electric, for example, maintains huge legal and lobbying departments that are able to affect and use tax laws to reduce the firm's tax liability to virtually nothing. Or consider the success of the large banks in shaping (or eliminating) financial regulation, or the accomplishments of the huge oil companies and the military contractors that establish government policies, sometimes as direct subsidies, and thus raise their profits. And the list goes on.

None of this is to say that everything was fine in earlier decades when large firms were less dominant. Yet, as monopoly capital has become more entrenched, it has generated increasingly negative outcomes for the rest of us. Most obvious are the stagnant wages and rising income inequality of recent years. The power of the large firms (e.g., Wal-Mart) to hold down wages is an important part of the story. Then there is the current crisis of the U.S. economy—directly a result of the way the very large financial firms were able to shape their industry (deregulation). Large firms in general have been prime movers over recent decades in generating deregulation and the free-market ideology that supports deregulation.

So, yes, monopoly capital is still quite relevant. Globalization does make differences in our lives, but globalization has in large part been constructed under the influence and in the interest of the very large firms. In many ways globalization makes the concept of monopoly capital even more relevant. ❑

* The profits of the top 100 firms (ranked by revenue) were quite low in 2010, back near the same 15% of total profits as in 1960, because of huge losses connected to the financial crisis incurred by some of the largest firms. Fannie Mae, Freddie Mac, and AIG accounted for combined losses of over $100 billion. Also, the revenues of all firms are not the same as GDP; much of the former is sales of intermediate products, but only sales of final products are included in GDP. Thus, the largest firms' revenues, while 40% as large as GDP, do not constitute 40% of GDP.

Article 5.4

# WANT FREE TRADE?
Open the Medical and Drug Industry to Compeititon

## BY DEAN BAKER
November 2013; The Guardian Unlimited

Free trade is like apple pie, everyone is supposed to like it. Economists have written thousands of books and articles showing how everyone can gain from reducing trade barriers. While there is much merit to this argument, little of it applies to the trade pacts that are sold as "free-trade" agreements.

These deals are about structuring trade to redistribute income upward. In addition, these agreements also provide a mechanism for over-riding the democratic process in the countries that are parties to the deals. They are a tool whereby corporate interests can block health, safety, and environmental regulations that might otherwise be implemented by democratically elected officials. This is the story with both the Trans-Pacific Partnership (TPP) now being negotiated by General Electric, Merck, and other major corporations who have been invited to the table, as well as the European Union-United States (EU-U.S.) trade agreement.

But trade agreements don't have to be designed to make the rich richer. It is possible to envision trade deals that actually would liberalize trade. NAFTA and it successors were designed to push down the wages of manufacturing workers by making it as easy as possible to set up operations overseas. This put U.S. steelworkers and autoworkers in direct competition with the low-wage workers in the developing world, pushing down wages of manufacturing workers in the United States, and by reducing the number of manufacturing jobs, the wages of less educated workers more generally.

This is all very simple and straightforward. But suppose that instead of designing trade deals to give us cheaper manufacturing workers we designed trade deals to give us cheaper doctors. In the United States, we pay our doctors almost twice as much as the average in other wealthy countries, and almost three times as much as in countries like Sweden or Norway. Suppose we structured a trade deal to get our doctors' pay in line with pay in other wealthy countries.

If we could save an average of $100,000 per doctor, this would translate to savings of roughly $85 billion a year, which would come to more than $1 trillion over the next decade. Throw in dentists and a few other highly paid professions and we would be talking real money. Just the savings on doctors' pay would come to more than $12,000 for an average family of four over ten years. This dwarfs the potential gains that are projected even by supporters of the trade agreements now being negotiated.

But we can be sure that freer trade in physicians' services will not be on the agenda in these trade deals. While the United States brings in Stem workers, nurses, and even teachers from other countries in order to keep their wages down in the United States, no one in a policy position will talk about doing the same with doctors.

The reason is very simple: doctors have lots of money and power. Roughly a third of them can be found in the top 1%, and nearly all would be in the top 3% of the income distribution.

Of course, trade can be used to bring down prices in other areas as well. The United States pays close to twice as much for its prescription drugs as people in other wealthy countries. This is the deliberate result of a patent policy that gives unchecked monopolies to drug companies for decades. In contrast, every other wealthy country couples patent monopolies with price controls, negotiated prices or some other policy that limits the extent to which drug companies can exploit their monopoly.

The United States could simply change its patent policy, but with that route being politically blocked, it could in principle use free trade to bring about the same result. With the country spending over $300 billion a year on drugs at present, the potential gains here also could be well over $1 trillion over the course of a decade.

The industry will claim that lower drug prices will hurt the incentive to develop new drugs, but we can switch to more modern and efficient methods for financing research. By raising prices by tens or even hundreds of times above their free market price, drug patents create the same sort of distortions and waste that we would expect from tariffs of several thousand percent. It's not hard to envision a system that leads to less waste and corruption.

There are many other areas where trade could, in principle, be used to bring about gains for large segments of the U.S. population as well as its trading partners. Unfortunately, we are not likely to see trade agreements that will produce such broad gains. This has nothing to do with trade per se, it has due to with the fact that these trade deals are developed and negotiated by corporate interests for corporate interests.

With the drug companies sitting at the negotiating table at the TPP, does anyone think the deal will actually lower drug prices? Do we expect good rules regulating fracking when the oil and gas industries are writing them? And will the big banks working on the financial section produce good rules for regulating finance?

Yes, free trade can benefit the country as a whole. But the trade deals we will see in the next year have nothing to do with free trade, they are just one more item on the agenda for redistributing wealth upward. ❏

# NOT TOO BIG ENOUGH
*Where the big banks come from.*

**BY ROB LARSON**
*April 2010*

The government bailout of America's biggest banks set off a tornado of public anger and confusion. When the House of Representatives initially rejected the bailout bill, the *Wall Street Journal* attributed it to "populist fury," and since then the public has remained stubbornly resentful over the bailout of those banks considered "too big to fail." Now, the heads of economic policy are trying to gracefully distance themselves from bailouts, claiming that future large-scale bank failures will be avoided by stronger regulation and higher insurance premiums.

Dealing with the collapse of these "systemically important banks" is a difficult policy issue, but the less-discussed issue is how the banking industry came to this point. If the collapse of just one of our $100 billion megabanks, Lehman Brothers, was enough to touch off an intense contraction in the supply of essential credit, we must know how some banks became "too big to fail" in the first place. The answer lies in certain incentives for bank growth, which after the loosening of crucial industry regulations drove the enormous waves of bank mergers in the last thirty years.

## Geographical Growth

Prior to the 1980s, American commercial banking was a small-scale affair. State-chartered banks were prohibited by state laws from running branches outside their home state, or sometimes even outside their home county. Nationally chartered banks were likewise limited, and federal law allowed interstate acquisitions only if a state legislature specifically decided to permit out-of-state banks to purchase local branches. No states allowed such acquisition until 1975, when Maine and other states began passing legislation allowing at least some interstate banking. The trend was capped in 1994 by the Riegle-Neal Act, which removed the remaining restrictions on interstate branching and allowed direct cross-state banking mergers.

This geographic deregulation allowed commercial banks to make extensive acquisitions, in state and out. When Wells Fargo acquired another large California bank, Crocker National, in 1986 it was the largest bank merger in U.S. history. Since "the regulatory light was green," a single banking company could now operate across the uniquely large U.S. market, opening up enormous new opportunities for economies of scale in the banking industry.

Economies of scale are savings that companies enjoy when they grow larger and produce more output. The situation is similar to a cook preparing a batch of cookies for a Christmas party, and then preparing a batch for New Year's while all the ingredients and materials are already out. Producing more output (cookies) in one afternoon is more efficient than taking everything out again later to make the New Year's batch separately. In enterprise, this corresponds to spreading the large costs of startup investment over more and more output, and is often thought of as lower per-unit costs as the level of production increases. In other words, there's less effort per cookie if you make them all at once. Economies of scale, when present in an industry, create a strong incentive for firms to grow larger, since profitability will improve. But they also give larger, established firms a valuable cost advantage over new competitors, which can put the brakes on competition.

Once unleashed by the policy changes, these economies of scale played a major role in the industry's seemingly endless merger activity. "In order to compete, you need scale," said a VP for Chemical Bank when buying a smaller bank in 1994. Of course, in 1996 Chemical would itself merge with Chase Manhattan Bank.

---

### Economies of Scale in Banking and Finance

Economies of scale are savings that companies benefit from as they grow larger and produce more output. While common in many industries, in banking and finance, these economies drove bank growth after industry deregulation in the 1980s and 90s. Some of the major scale economies in banking are:

- **Spreading investment over more output.** With the growth in importance of large-scale computing power and sophisticated systems management, the costs of setting up a modern banking system are very large. However, as a firm grows it can "spread out" the cost of that initial investment over more product, so that its cost per unit decreases as more output is produced.

- **Consolidation of functions.** The modern workforce is no stranger to the mass firings of "redundant" staff after mergers and acquisitions. If one firm's payroll staff and computer systems can handle twice the employees with little additional expense, an acquired bank may see its payroll department harvest pink slips while the firm's profitability improves. When Citicorp merged with the insurance giant Travelers Group in 1998, the resulting corporation laid off over 10,000 workers—representing 6% of the combined company's total workforce and over $500 million in reduced costs for Citigroup. This practice can be especially lucrative in a country like the United States, with a fairly unregulated labor market where firms are quite free to fire. Despite the economic peril inflicted on workers and their families, this consolidation is key to increasing company efficiency post-merger. Beyond back-office functions, core profit operations may also benefit from consolidation. When Bank of America combined its managed mutual funds into a single fund, it experienced lower total costs, thanks to trimming overhead from audit and prospectus mailing expenses. Consolidating office departments in this fashion can yield savings of 40% of the cost base of the acquired bank.

- **Funding mix.** The "funding mix" used by banks refers to where banks get the capital they then package into loans. Smaller institutions, having only limited deposits from savers, must "purchase funds" by borrowing from other institutions. This increases the funding cost of loans for banks, but larger banks will naturally have access to larger pools of deposits from which to arrange loans. This funding cost advantage for larger banks relative to smaller ones represents another economy of scale.

- **Advertising.** The nature of advertising requires a certain scale of operation to be viable. Advertising can reach large numbers of potential customers, but if a firm is small or local, many of those customers will be too far afield to act on the marketing. Large firm size, and especially geographic reach, can make the returns on ad time worth the investment.

Spreading big investment costs over more output is the main source of generic economies of scale, and in banking, the large initial investments are in sophisticated computer systems. The cost of investing in new computer hardware and systems development is now recognized as a major investment obstacle for new banks, although once installed by banks large enough to afford them, they are highly profitable. The *Financial Times* describes how "the development of bulk computer processing and of electronic data transmission…has allowed banks to move their back office operations away from individual branches to large remote centers. This had helped to bring real economies of scale to banking, an industry which tradition-ally has seen diseconomies set in at a very modest scale."

Economies of scale are common in manufacturing, and in the wake of deregulation the banking industry was also able to exploit a number of them. Besides spreading out the cost of computer systems, economies of scale may be present in office consolidation, in the funding mix used by banks, and in adver-tising (see sidebar).

## Industry-to-Industry Growth

*BusinessWeek*'s analysis is that the banking industry "has produced large competi-tors that can take advantage of economies of scale…as regulatory barriers to inter-state banking fell," although not until the banks could "digest their purchases." The 1990s saw hundreds of bank purchases annually and hundreds of billions in acquired assets.

But an additional major turn for the industry came with the Gramm-Leach-Bliley Act of 1999 (GLB), which further loosened restrictions on bank growth, this time not geographically but industry-to-industry. After earlier moves in this direc-tion by the Federal Reserve, GLB allowed for the free combination of commercial banking, insurance, and the riskier field of investment banking. These had been separated by law for decades, on the grounds that the availability of commercial credit was too important to the overall economy to be tied to the volatile world of investment banking.

GLB allowed firms to grow further, through banks merging with insurers or investment banks. The world of commercial credit was widened, and financial merg-ers this time exploited economies of scope—where production of multiple products jointly is cheaper than producing them individually. As commercial banks, invest-ment banks, and insurers have expanded into each others' fields in the wake of GLB, their different lines of business can benefit from single expenses—for example, banks perform research on loan recipients that can also be used to underwrite bond issues. Scope economies such as these allow the larger banks to both run a greater profit on a per-service basis and attract more business. Thanks to the convenience of "one stop shopping," Citigroup now does more business with big corporations, like IT giant Unisys, than its component firms did pre-merger.

Exploiting economies of scope to diversify product lines in this fashion can also help a firm by reducing its dependence on any one line of business. Bank of America weathered the stock market downturn of 2001 in part because its corporate debt underwriting business was booming. Smaller, more specialized banks can become "one-trick ponies" as the *Wall Street Journal* put it—outdone by larger competitors with low-cost diversification thanks to scope economies.

These economies of scope are parallel to the scale economies, since both required deregulatory policy changes to be unleashed. Traditionally, banking wasn't seen as an industry with the strong economies of scale seen in, say, manufacturing. But the deregulation and computerization of the industry have allowed these firms to realize returns to greater scale and wider scope, and this has been a main driver of the endless acquisitions in the industry in recent decades.

## Market Power

The enormous proportions that the banking institutions have taken on following deregulation have meant serious consequences for market performance. A number of banks have reached sufficient size to exercise market power—the ability of firms to influence prices and to engage in anticompetitive behavior. The market power of our enormous banks allows them to take positions as price leaders in local markets, where large firms use their dominance to elevate prices (i.e., increase fees and rates on loans, and decrease interest rates on deposits). Large firms can do this because smaller firms may perceive that lowering their prices to take market share could be met by very drastic reductions in prices from the larger firm in retaliation. Large firms, having deeper pockets, may be able to withstand longer periods of operating at a loss than the smaller firms.

Small banks are likely to perceive that the colossal size and resources of the megabanks make them unprofitable to cross—better to follow along and charge roughly what the dominant, price-leading firm does. Empirical research by Federal Reserve Board senior economist Steven Pilloff supported this analysis, finding that the arrival of very large banks in local markets tended to increase bank profitability for reasons of price leadership, due to the larger banks' economies of scale and scope, financial muscle, and diversification.

Examples of the use of banking industry market power are easy to find. Several bills now circulating in Congress deal with the fees retail businesses pay to the banks and the credit card companies. When consumers make purchases with their Visas or MasterCards, an average of two cents of each dollar goes not to the retailer but to the credit card companies that run the payment network and the banks that supply the credit. These "interchange fees" bring in over $35 billion in profit in the United States alone, and they reflect the strong market power of the banks and credit card companies over the various big and small retailers. The 2% charge comes to about $31,000 for a typical convenience store, just below the average per-store yearly profit of $36,000, and this has driven a coalition of retailers to press for congressional action.

Visa has about 50% of the credit card market (including debit cards), and MasterCard has 25%, which grants them profound market power and strong bargaining positions. Federal Reserve Bank of Kansas City economists found the United States "maintains the highest interchange fees in the world, yet its costs should be among the lowest, given economies of scale and declining cost trends." The *Wall Street Journal*'s description was that "these fees...have also been paradoxically tending upward in recent years when the industry's costs due to technology and economies of scale have been falling." Of course, there's only a paradox if market power is omitted from the picture. The dominant size and scale economies of the banks and the credit card oligopoly allow for high prices to be sustained—bank muscle in action against a less powerful sector of the economy. The political action favored by the retailers includes proposals for committees to enact price ceilings or (interestingly) collective bargaining by the retailers. As is often the case, the political process is the reflection of the different levels and positions of power of various corporate institutions, and the maneuvering of their organizations.

Market power brings with it a number of other advantages. A powerful company is likely to have a widespread presence, make frequent use of advertising, and be able to raise its profile by contributing to community organizations like sports leagues. This allows the larger banks to benefit from stronger brand identity—their scale and resources make customers more likely to trust their services. This grants a further advantage in the form of customer tolerance of higher prices due to brand loyalty.

## Political Clout

Crucially, large firms with market power are free to participate meaningfully in politics—using their deep pockets to invest in electoral campaigns and congressional lobbying. The financial sector is among the highest-contributing industries in the United States, with total 2008 campaign contributions approaching half a billion dollars, according to the Center For Public Integrity. So it's unsurprising that they receive so many favors from the government, since they fund the careers of the decision-making government personnel. This underlying reality is why influential Senator Dick Durbin said of Congress, "The banks own the place."

Finally, banks may grow so large by exploiting scale economies and market power that they become "systemically important" to the nation's financial system. In other words, the scale and interconnectedness of the largest banks is considered to have reached a point where an abrupt failure of one or more of them may have "systemic" effects—meaning the broader economic system will be seriously impaired. These "too big to fail" banks are the ones that were bailed out by act of Congress in the fall 2008. Once a firm becomes so enormous that the government must prevent its collapse for the good of the economy, it has the ultimate advantage of being free to take far greater risks. Riskier investments come with higher returns and profits, but the greater risk of collapse that accompanies them will be less intimidating to huge banks that have an implied government insurance policy.

Some analysts have expressed doubt that such firms truly are too large to let fail, and that the banks have pulled a fast one. It might be pointed out in this connection that in the past the banks themselves have put their money where their mouths are—they have paid out of pocket to rescue financial institutions they saw as too large and connected to fail. An especially impressive episode took place in 1998, when several of Wall Street's biggest banks and financiers agreed to billions in emergency loans to rescue Long Term Capital Management. LTCM was a high-profile hedge fund that borrowed enormous sums of capital to make billion-dollar gambles on financial markets.

America's biggest banks aren't in the habit of forking over $3.5 billion of good earnings, but they had loaned heavily to LTCM and feared losing their money if the fund went under. The Federal Reserve brought the bankers together, and in the end, they paid up to bail out their colleagues, and the *Wall Street Journal* reported that it was the Fed's "clout, together with the self-interest of several big firms that already had lent billions of dollars to Long-Term Capital, that helped fashion the rescue." Interestingly, the banks insisted on real equity in the firm they were pulling out of the fire, and they gained a 90% stake in the hedge fund. Comparing this to the less-valuable "preferred stock" the government settled for in its 2008 bailout package of the large banks is instructive. The banks also got a share of control in the firm they rescued, again in stark contrast to the public bailout of some of the same banks.

## Even Bigger?

In fact, the financial crisis and bailout led only to further concentration of the industry. The crisis gave stronger firms an opportunity to pick up sicker ones in another "wave of consolidation," as *BusinessWeek* put it. And a large part of the government intervention itself involved arranging hasty purchases of failing giants by other giants, orchestrated by the Federal Reserve. For example, the Fed helped organize the purchase of Bear Stearns by Chase in March 2008 and the purchase of Wachovia by Wells Fargo in December 2008. Even the bailout's "capital infusions" were used for further mergers and acquisitions by several recipients. The Treasury Department was "using the bailout bill to turn the banking system into the oligopoly of giant national institutions," as the *New York Times* reported.

The monumental growth of the largest banks owes a lot to the industry's economies of scale and scope, once regulations were relaxed so firms could exploit them. While certainly not unique to finance, these dynamics have brought the banks to such enormous size that their bad bets can put the entire economy in peril. Banking therefore offers an especially powerful case for the importance of these economies and the role of market power, since it's left the megabanks holding all the cards.

In fact, many arguments between defenders of the market economy and its critics center on the issue of competition vs. power—market boosters reliably insist that markets mean efficient competition, where giants have no inherent advantage over small, scrappy firms. However, the record in banking clearly shows that banks have enjoyed a variety of real benefits from growth. The existence of companies of great size and power is a quite natural development in many industries, due to the appeal of returns to scale and power. This is why firms end up with enough power to influence government policy, or such absurd size that they can blackmail us for life support.

And leave us crying all the way to the bank. ❑

*Sources:* Judith Samuelson and Lynn Stout, "Are Executives Paid Too Much?" *Wall Street Journal*, February 26, 2009; Tom Braithwaite, "Geithner Presses Congress for Action on Reform," *Financial Times*, September 23, 2009; Phillip Zweig, "Intrastate Mergers Between Banking Giants Might Not Be Out of the Question Anymore," *Wall Street Journal*, March 25, 1986; Bruce Knecht, "Chemical Banking plans acquisition of Margaretten," *Wall Street Journal*, May 13, 1994; Eric Weiner, "Banks Will Post Good Quarterly Results," *Wall Street Journal*, January 10, 1997; Gabriella Stern, "Four Big Regionals To Consolidate Bank Operations," *Wall Street Journal*, July 22, 1992; "Pressure for change grows," *Financial Times*, September 27, 1996; Tracy Corrigan and John Authers, "Citigroup To Take $900 million charge: Cost-cutting Program to Result in Loss of 10,400 Jobs," *Financial Times*, December 16, 1998; Eleanor Laise, "Mutual-Fund Mergers Jump Sharply," *Wall Street Journal*, March 9, 2006; Steven Pilloff, "Banking, commerce and competition under the Gramm-Leach-Bliley Act," *The Antitrust Bulletin*, Spring 2002; David Humphrey, "Why Do Estimates of Bank Scale Economies Differ?" *Economic Review* of Federal Reserve Bank of Richmond, September/October 1990, note four; Michael Mandel and Rich Miller, "Productivity: The Real Story," *BusinessWeek*, November 5, 2001; John Yang, "Fed Votes to Give 7 Bank Holding Firms Additional Power in Securities Sector," *Wall Street Journal*, July 16, 1987; "Banking Behemoths—What Happens Next: Many companies Like to Shop Around For Their Providers of Financial Services," *Wall Street Journal*, September 14, 2000; Carrick Mollenkamp and Paul Beckett, "Diverse Business Portfolios Boost Banks' Bottom Lines," *Wall Street Journal*, July 17, 2001; *Journal of Financial Services Research*, "Does the Presence of Big Banks Influence Competition in Local Markets?" May 1999; "Credit-Card Wars," *Wall Street Journal*, March 29, 2008; *Economic Review* of the Federal Reserve Bank of Kansas City, "Interchange Fees in Credit and Debit Card Markets: What Role for Public Authorities," January-March 2006; "Credit Where It's Due," *Wall Street Journal*, January 12, 2006; Keith Bradsher, "In One Pocket, Out the Other," *New York Times*, November 25, 2009; Center For Public Integrity, Finance/Insurance/ Real Estate: Long-Term Contribution Trends, opensecrests.org; Dean Baker, "Banks own the U.S. government," *Guardian*, June 30, 2009; Anita Raghavan and Mitchell Pacelle, "To the Rescue? A Hedge Fun Falters, So the Fed Persuades Big Banks to Ante Up," *Wall Street Journal*, September 24, 1998; Theo Francis, "Will Bank Rescues Mean Fewer Banks?" *BusinessWeek*, November 25, 2008; Joe Nocera, "So When Will Banks Give Loans?" *New York Times*, October 25, 2008.

*Article 5.6*

# SEEDS OF CHANGE

*Corporate Power, Grassroots Resistance, and the Battle Over the Food System*

## BY ELIZABETH FRASER AND ANURADHA MITTAL
*Mach/April 2015*

For most of history, farmers have had control over their seeds: saving, sharing, and replanting them with freedom. Developments in the course of the 20th century, however, have greatly eroded this autonomy. Legal changes, ranging from the Plant Variety Protection Act (1970) in the United States to the World Trade Organization's Agreement on Trade-Related Aspects of Intellectual Property Rights (TRIPS), have systematically eroded farmers' rights to save seeds for future use. By the end of 2012, Monsanto had sued 410 farmers and 56 small farm businesses in the United States for patent infringement, winning over $23 million in settlements. Here, we describe some of the key developments further intensifying corporate control over the food system. It is not, however, all bleak news. Civil society groups are using everything from grassroots protest to open-source licensing to ensure that the enclosure and privatization of seeds comes to an end.

## Corporations Have Consolidated Their Control

In 2011, just four transnational agri-businesses—Monsanto, Dupont Pioneer, Syngenta, and Vilmorin (Groupe Limagrain)—controlled 58% of the commercial seed market. Four—Syngenta, Bayer CropScience, BASF, and Dow AgroSciences—controlled 62% of agrochemicals worldwide. The top six companies controlled 75% of all private plant breeding research, 60% of commercial seed sales, and 76% of the global agrochemical market. This consolidation of power has been aided by a large string of mergers and acquisitions, leading the Canada-based Action Group on Erosion, Technology and Concentration (ETC Group) to conclude that "there just aren't many seed companies left to buy."

The World Bank, too, has played a role in this increased consolidation. In 2014, a report from the Oakland Institute provided details on the World Bank's efforts to open African markets to private seed companies. (Full disclosure: The authors of this article both work at the Oakland Institute.) The report, titled "The World Bank's Bad Business with Seed and Fertilizer in African Agriculture," paints a stark picture of the possible consequences of these actions: removing farmers' rights to save seeds and implementing intellectual property claims over seeds does not improve food security, but rather undermines farmers' autonomy and further increases profits for the existing seed oligopoly.

## Supposed Benefits of Genetically Modified (GM) Seeds Have Not Materialized

Two arguments often put forward in favor of GM seeds are the need to feed the world's burgeoning population and the potential for these new seeds to reduce overall pesticide use. Neither of these claims promulgated by industry have proved true. Globally, we are currently producing more than enough food to adequately feed our population. However, that food isn't being distributed fairly, and malnutrition remains staggering—805 million people worldwide. As the Canadian Biodiversity Action Network reminds us in its report "Will GM Crops Feed the World?" hunger is not usually a result of low food production, but rather a result of poverty. This points to a greater need to address issues of inequality, distribution, and access.

Arguments that genetically modified crops could reduce overall agrochemical use also remain unfounded, with the rise of herbicide-resistant weeds requiring more and more chemical cocktails for the GM crops to remain productive. A report from Food and Water Watch, "Superweeds: How Biotech Crops Bolster the Pesticide Industry," notes that herbicide use on GM crops in the United States did initially fall in the late 1990s; however, once resistance in GM crops to the herbicide glyphosate (marketed by Monsanto under the trade name "RoundUp") developed, total herbicide use skyrocketed, leading to greater net herbicide use over time.

## Large Agribusinesses Have Spent Millions to Defeat Labelling Ballot Measures

In the past few years, large agribusinesses have worked to defeat numerous U.S. state ballot measures intended to enforce the labelling of GM foods. Of the $46 million spent to defeat an anti-GM labelling campaign in the state of California in 2013, over $8 million came from Monsanto alone. Ballot measures in Washington State (2012), Colorado (2014), and Oregon (2014) met similar fates, with large agribusinesses outspending pro-labelling campaigns by a wide margin. In Vermont, state legislation to enforce GM labelling was approved in mid-2014 and is scheduled to come into force in early 2016. However, the Grocery Manufacturers Association (supported by corporations including Monsanto, Coca-Cola, and Starbucks) is now suing the state, alleging that the law would violate the U.S. Constitution in various ways. This further demonstrates the power wielded by large agribusinesses, even in the face of widespread consumer (and legislative) pressure.

## Activists Are Developing New "Open Source" Options for Seeds

One positive development is the April 2014 launch of the Open Source Seed Initiative (OSSI), a group "dedicated to maintaining fair and open access to plant genetic resources worldwide." Jack Kloppenburg, a member of OSSI's board of directors, has written extensively about the potential modification of open-source licensing (which is used widely in software development, and led to the development of Linux, the vastly popular operating system) to seeds and other plant materials. Kloppenburg advocates a new type of plant licensing that makes plant materials a) widely available, b) modifiable by any actor, and c) distributable provided the same terms of the original license carry forward. These principles mirror those developed by the open-source technology movement, and it is anticipated that these licenses will lead to the creation of a "protected commons"—preventing the patenting of this material in the future. While the group is far from challenging the agribusiness seed cartel, initiatives like this are beginning to provide a way to legally protect plant genetic material from corporate capture.

## Resistance to GM Crops Has Increased

The mobilization against the use of GM crops has gained momentum in recent years. In 2013, the global "March Against Monsanto" was estimated to have brought over two million citizens to the streets, across six continents, 52 nations, and 48 states of the United States. After an extended period of protests, anti-GM protesters celebrated a victory in 2014, when the Chilean government withdrew a bill that would have allowed large agribusinesses like Monsanto to patent seeds in the country. (With falling demand for GM seeds in South America, Monsanto's profits fell 34%, according to the company's most recent quarterly report. Whether the falling demand was a result of global resistance, falling corn prices, or both is unclear).

Mexico imposed a ban on genetically modified corn in 2013, days after worldwide protests against Monsanto and the whole genetically modified organism (GMO) industry. This made Mexico a key front in the global battle against corporate giants that bring in GMOs and "genetic pollution"—the transfer of GMO genetic codes into other plants (as by cross-pollination). Last year, a Mexican judge revoked Monsanto's planting permit, which had allowed the company to sow more than 253,000 hectares of land across seven states. The ruling followed complaints from beekeepers in the state of Yucatán that Monsanto's planned planting of GM soybeans, made to withstand RoundUp, would decimate the bee population and demolish the honey industry.

China has maintained a strong stance against GM products, leading to lawsuits against seed companies like Syngenta, which released a GM seed variety to farmers before it had been approved in the country. While China has recently begun approving more GM seed and crop varieties, mandatory labelling laws also look likely to pass.

## What Do These Developments Demonstrate?

On one hand, our global food system continues to be dominated by agribusiness giants, who use their power to quash legislation designed to protect consumer and farmer interests, with little demonstration of the benefits of their genetically modified products. At the same time, despite the power wielded by corporations, resistance is growing. In many cases, agribusiness has met this resistance with outspending and overwhelming legal challenges. But in countries like Chile and Mexico, victories have been won, and promising new alternatives like the Open Source Seed Initiative are creating new ways of protecting plant material going forward. The growing awareness of and mobilization against the corporatization of food cannot be denied. Movements around organic standards, Fair Trade, farmers' markets, and community supported agriculture have made huge gains over the last ten years. The next ten years have to build on these successes to reclaim seed sovereignty, to challenge the power of agribusinesses over our land and food system, and to increase popular engagement, advocating for the health of our planet and our food. ❑

*Sources:* Center for Food Safety and Save Our Seeds, "Seed Giants vs. U.S. Farmers", 2013 (www. centerforfoodsafety.org); ETC Group, "Putting the Cartel before the Horse ...and Farm, Seeds, Soil, Peasants, etc.: Who Will Control Agricultural Inputs, 2013?" September 2013 (etcgroup. org); Anuradha Mittal and Haley F. Kaplan, with Alice Martin-Prével and Frédéric Mousseau, "The World Bank's Bad Business with Seed and Fertilizer in African Agriculture," The Oakland Institute, 2014 (oaklandinstitute.org); Canadian Biotechnology Action Network (CBAN), "Will GM Crops Feed the World?" October 2014 (cban.ca); Global Food Politics, "Agricultural Biotechnology and the Use of Herbicides in US Agriculture," Dec. 1, 2013 (globalfoodpolitics. wordpress.com); Evan Fraser, "10 Things You Need to Know About the Global Food System," *The Guardian* (theguardian.com); Food and Water Watch, "Superweeds: How Biotech Crops Bolster the Pesticide Industry," July 2013 (foodandwaterwatch.org); Andrew Pollack, "After Loss, the Fight to Label Modified Food Continues," *New York Times*, Nov. 7, 2012 (nytimes.com); Luke Runyon, "Colorado, Oregon Reject GMO Labeling," NPR, Nov. 5, 2014 (npr.org); Peter Moskowitz, "In GMO labeling fight, all eyes on Vermont," Aljazeera America, Dec. 1, 2014 (america.aljazeera.com); Open Source Seed Initiative (opensourceseedinitiative.org); "Challenging Monsanto: Over two million march the streets of 436 cities, 52 countries," RT, May 24, 2013 (rt.com); Andrea Germanos, "'Monsanto Law' Brings Uproar to Chile," Common Dreams, Aug. 19, 2013 (commondreams.org); Belinda Torres-Leclercq, "Government Withdraws Controversial 'Monsanto Law' from Congress," *Santiago Times*, March 18, 2014 (santiagotimes.cl); "Monsanto Earnings Fall 34% After a Year of Global Protests," *The Guardian*, Jan. 7, 2014 (theguardian.com); The Global Diary, "China's Hard Line on Biotech Burns US Hay," Dec. 15, 2014 (theglobaldiary. com); "Syngenta Facing Dozens of Lawsuits Over GMO Seed," Nov. 18, 2014 (thonline.com); Zhang Yi and Zhong Nan, "Mandatory GM Food Labeling a Step Closer," *China Daily*, Dec. 23, 2014 (chinadaily.com).

# Chapter 6

# MARKET FAILURE II: EXTERNALITIES

## INTRODUCTION

**M**arkets sometimes fail. Mainstream economists typically focus on cases in which existing markets fail to facilitate exchanges that would make both parties better off. When a factory pollutes the air, people downwind suffer a cost. They might be willing to pay the polluter to curb emissions, but there is no market for clean air. In cases like this, one solution is for the government to step in with regulations that ban industries from imposing pollution costs on others. The same goes when private markets do not provide sufficient amounts of public goods, such as vaccines, from which everyone benefits whether they contribute to paying for them or not. Again, government must step in. But what percentage of pollution should industries be required to eliminate? How much should be spent on public health? To decide how much government should step in, economists propose cost-benefit analysis, suggesting that the government weigh costs against benefits, in much the same way a firm decides how many cars to produce.

Orthodox economists typically see market failures as fairly limited in scope. In fact, they deny that many negative consequences of markets are market failures at all. When workers are paid wages too low to meet their basic needs, economists do not usually call their poverty and overwork market failures, but "incentives" to get a higher-paying job. When economists do recognize market failures, most argue that they are best solved by markets themselves. So pollution, for example, should be reduced by allowing firms to trade for the right to pollute. Finally, orthodox economists worry about government failure—the possibility that government responses to market failures may cause more problems than they solve. They conclude that the "invisible hand" of the market works pretty well, and that the alternatives, especially the "visible hand" of the state, will only make matters worse.

In "Pricing the Priceless: Inside the Strange World of Cost-Benefit Analysis" (Article 8.1), Lisa Heinzerling and Frank Ackerman point out key flaws in the use of cost-benefit analysis to guide government action. While weighing the costs of a course of action (like pollution limits) against the benefits has a superficial plausibility, cost-benefit analysis fails to clarify the nature of public choices. It fails, for example, to account for all relevant costs or benefits, it downgrades the importance of the future, and it does not deal with the problem of how costs and benefits are distributed.

The most common complaint from industry and their legions of lobbyists is that there is a rigid trade-off between environmental protection and employment. In "The Phantom Menace: Environmental Regulations are Not 'Job Killers'"(Article 6.2), Garrett-Peltier shows this is a false dichotomy. Enforcing environmental rules and "going green" not only might not cost net jobs, but in fact might create significant new employment, especially in weaning ourselves off hydrocarbon fuels.

In his article "Frackonomics: The Science and Economics of the Gas Boom" (Article 6.3), economist Rob Larson looks at the environmental impacts of this controversial new form of natural-gas extraction. He finds harms including everything from toxic pollution to increased seismic instabiliy. Moreover, he argues, these problems are not well dealt with by neoclassical economics' usual prescription of strengthened private-property rights.

Stephanie Welcomer, Mark Haggerty, and John Jemison take us inside Maine farming, and farmers' varied reactions to the climate change (Article 6.4). Almost all farmers, they note, are making adaptations to deal with new and increasingly volatile weather conditions. Few, however, speak directly about global climate change, much less the need for climate policy to avert more severe change in the future. Welcomer, Haggerty, and Jemison suggest that, sooner rather than later, farmers must confront this reality more directly.

James K. Boyce's "Climate Policy as Wealth Creation" (Article 6.5) notes that the atmosphere is currently treated as a free dumping ground for carbon pollution. The richest dump the most, and the fossil-fuel companies profit in the bargain. The vision Boyce proposes is clear and profound—the atmosphere belongs to us all "in equal and common measure," and the key to addressing the climate crisis is the development of a system of public property rights over it.

## Discussion Questions

1.  (Article 6.1) Lisa Heinzerling and Frank Ackerman point out a number of flaws in cost-benefit analysis. These weaknesses suggest that the cost-benefit approach will work better in some situations, worse in others. Describe when you would expect it to work better or worse, and explain.

2.  (Article 6.1) Make a list of types of goods that are harder to put a price on (valuate) than others. Why is it so hard to price these types of goods?

3.  (Article 6.2) Do environmental regulations "kill jobs"? Is this a false dichotomy? If so, why? Why is the concept "net jobs" important here?

4.  (Article 6.3) What are the main harms, in Larson's view, from gas extraction by hydraulic fracturing ("fracking")? What are some possible solutions? Why does Larson doubt the viability of solutions based purely on private property and private legal action?

5.  (Article 6.4) Welcomer, Haggerty, and Jemison suggest that many farmers recognize their own need to adapt to a changing climate, yet few advocate for policies to address climate change. If climate change is already costly to farmers, why would they not actively support measures to avert further impacts?

6.  (Article 6.5) Some commentators argue that environmental regulations, such as a carbon tax or other carbon price, would reduce economic growth—and so be a form of wealth destruction. Boyce argues, on the contrary, that climate policy can be a form of "wealth creation." What does he mean by this? Do you agree?

Article 6.1

# PRICING THE PRICELESS
*Inside the Strange World of Cost-Benefit Analysis*

**BY LISA HEINZERLING AND FRANK ACKERMAN**
*March/April 2003*

How strictly should we regulate arsenic in drinking water? Or carbon dioxide in the atmosphere? Or pesticides in our food? Or oil drilling in scenic places? The list of environmental harms and potential regulatory remedies often appears to be endless. In evaluating a proposed new initiative, how do we know if it is worth doing or not? Is there an objective way to decide how to proceed? Cost-benefit analysis promises to provide the solution—to add up the benefits of a public policy and compare them to the costs.

The costs of protecting health and the environment through pollution control devices and other approaches are, by their very nature, measured in dollars. The other side of the balance—calculating the benefits of life, health, and nature in dollars and cents—is far more problematic. Since there are no natural prices for a healthy environment, cost-benefit analysis creates artificial ones. Researchers, for example, may ask a cross-section of the affected population how much they would pay to preserve or protect something that can't be bought in a store. The average American household is supposedly willing to pay $257 to prevent the extinction of bald eagles, $208 to protect humpback whales, and $80 to protect gray wolves.

Costs and benefits of a policy, however, frequently fall at different times. When the analysis spans a number of years, future costs and benefits are *discounted,* or treated as equivalent to smaller amounts of money in today's dollars. The case for discounting begins with the observation that money received today is worth a little more than money received in the future. (For example, if the interest rate is 3%, you only need to deposit about $97 today to get $100 next year. Economists would say that, at a *3% discount rate,* $100 next year has a *present value* of $97.) For longer periods of time, or higher discount rates, the effect is magnified. The important issue for environmental policy is whether this logic also applies to outcomes far in the future, and to opportunities—like long life and good health—that are not naturally stated in dollar terms.

## Why Cost-Benefit Analysis Doesn't Work

The case for cost-benefit analysis of environmental protection is, at best, wildly optimistic and, at worst, demonstrably wrong. The method simply does not offer the policy-making panacea its adherents promise. In practice, cost-benefit analysis frequently produces false and misleading results. Moreover, there is no quick fix, because these failures are intrinsic to the methodology, appearing whenever it is applied to any complex environmental problem.

*It puts dollar figures on values that are not commodities, and have no price.*
Artificial prices have been estimated for many benefits of environmental regulation. Preventing retardation due to childhood lead poisoning comes in at about $9,000 per lost IQ point. Saving a life is ostensibly worth $6.3 million. But what can it mean to say that one life is worth $6.3 million? You cannot buy the right to kill someone for $6.3 million, nor for any other price. If analysts calculated the value of life itself by asking people what it is worth to them (the most common method of valuation of other environmental benefits), the answer would be infinite. The standard response is that a value like $6.3 million is not actually a price on an individual's life or death. Rather, it is a way of expressing the value of small risks of death. If people are willing to pay $6.30 to avoid a one in a million increase in the risk of death, then the "value of a statistical life" is $6.3 million.

*It ignores the collective choice presented to society by most public health and environmental problems.*
Under the cost-benefit approach, valuation of environmental benefits is based on individuals' private decisions as consumers or workers, not on their public values as citizens. However, policies that protect the environment are often public goods, and are not available for purchase in individual portions. In a classic example of this distinction, the philosopher Mark Sagoff found that his students, in their role as citizens, opposed commercial ski development in a nearby wilderness area, but, in their role as consumers, would plan to go skiing there if the development was built. There is no contradiction between these two views: as individual consumers, the students would have no way to express their collective preference for wilderness preservation. Their individual willingness to pay for skiing would send a misleading signal about their views as citizens.

It is often impossible to arrive at a meaningful social valuation by adding up the willingness to pay expressed by individuals. What could it mean to ask how much you personally are willing to pay to clean up a major oil spill? If no one else contributes, the clean-up won't happen regardless of your decision. As the Nobel Prize-winning economist Amartya Sen has pointed out, if your willingness to pay for a large-scale public initiative is independent of what others are paying, then you probably have not understood the nature of the problem.

*It systematically downgrades the importance of the future.*
One of the great triumphs of environmental law is that it seeks to avert harms to people and to natural resources in the future, and not only within this generation, but in future generations as well. Indeed, one of the primary objectives of the National Environmental Policy Act, which has been called our basic charter of environmental protection, is to nudge the nation into "fulfill[ing] the responsibilities of each generation as trustee of the environment for succeeding generations."

The time periods involved in protecting the environment are often enormous—even many centuries, in such cases as climate change, radioactive waste, etc. With time spans this long, any discounting will make even global catastrophes seem trivial. At a discount rate of 5%, for example, the deaths of a billion people 500 years from now become less serious than the death of one person today. Seen in this way, discounting looks like a fancy justification for foisting our problems off onto the people who come after us.

*It ignores considerations of distribution and fairness.*
Cost-benefit analysis adds up all the costs of a policy, adds up all the benefits, and compares the totals. Implicit in this innocuous-sounding procedure is the assumption that it doesn't matter who gets the benefits and who pays the costs. Yet isn't there is an important difference between spending state tax revenues, say, to improve the parks in rich communities, and spending the same revenues to clean up pollution in poor communities?

The problem of equity runs even deeper. Benefits are typically measured by willingness to pay for environmental improvement, and the rich are able and willing to pay for more than the poor. Imagine a cost-benefit analysis of locating an undesirable facility, such as a landfill or incinerator. Wealthy communities are willing to pay more for the benefit of not having the facility in their backyards; thus, under the logic of cost-benefit analysis, the net benefits to society will be maximized by putting the facility in a low-income area. In reality, pollution is typically dumped on the poor without waiting for formal analysis. Still, cost-benefit analysis rationalizes and reinforces the problem, allowing environmental burdens to flow downhill along the income slopes of an unequal society.

## Conclusion

There is nothing objective about the basic premises of cost-benefit analysis. Treating individuals solely as consumers, rather than as citizens with a sense of moral responsibility, represents a distinct and highly questionable worldview. Likewise, discounting reflects judgments about the nature of environmental risks and citizens' responsibilities toward future generations.

These assumptions beg fundamental questions about ethics and equity, and one cannot decide whether to embrace them without thinking through the whole range of moral issues they raise. Yet once one has thought through these issues, there is no need then to collapse the complex moral inquiry into a series of numbers. Pricing the priceless just translates our inquiry into a different language, one with a painfully impoverished vocabulary. ❏

*This article is a condensed version of the report* Pricing the Priceless, *published by the Georgetown Environmental Law and Policy Institute at Georgetown University Law Center. The full report is available on-line at www. ase.tufts.edu/gdae. See also Ackerman and Heinzerling's book on these and related issues,* Priceless: Human Health, the Environment, and the Limits of the Market, *The New Press, January 2004.*

*Article 6.2*

# THE PHANTOM MENACE
*Environmental regulations are not "job-killers."*

## BY HEIDI GARRETT-PELTIER
*July/August 2011*

Polluting industries, along with the legislators who are in their pockets, consistently claim that environmental regulation will be a "job killer." They counter efforts to control pollution and to protect the environment by claiming that any such measures would increase costs and destroy jobs. But these are empty threats. In fact, the bulk of the evidence shows that environmental regulations do not hinder economic growth or employment and may actually stimulate both.

One recent example of this, the Northeast Regional Greenhouse Gas Initiative (RGGI), is an emissions-allowance program that caps and reduces emissions in ten northeast and mid-Atlantic states. Under RGGI, allowances are auctioned to power companies and the majority of the revenues are used to offset increases in consumer energy bills and to invest in energy efficiency and renewable energy. A report released in February 2011 shows that RGGI has created an economic return of $3 to $4 for every $1 invested, and has created jobs throughout the region. Yet this successful program has come under attack by right-wing ideologues, including the Koch brothers-funded "Americans for Prosperity"; as a result, the state of New Hampshire recently pulled out of the program.

The allegation that environmental regulation is a job-killer is based on a mischaracterization of costs, both by firms and by economists. Firms often frame spending on environmental controls or energy-efficient machinery as a pure cost—wasted spending that reduces profitability. But such expenses should instead be seen as investments that enhance productivity and in turn promote economic development. Not only can these investments lead to lower costs for energy use and waste disposal, they may also direct innovations in the production process itself that could increase the firm's long-run profits. This is the Porter Hypothesis, named after Harvard Business School professor Michael Porter. According to studies conducted by Porter, properly and flexibly designed environmental regulation can trigger innovation that partly or completely offsets the costs of complying with the regulation.

The positive aspects of environmental regulation are overlooked not only by firms, but also by economists who model the costs of compliance without including its widespread benefits. These include reduced mortality, fewer sick days for workers and school children, reduced health-care costs, increased biodiversity, and mitigation of climate change. But most mainstream models leave these benefits out of their calculations. The Environmental Protection Agency, which recently released a study of the impacts of the Clean Air Act from 1990 to 2020, compared the effects of a "cost-only" model with those of a more complete model. In the version which only incorporated the costs of compliance, both GDP and overall economic welfare were expected to decline by 2020 due to Clean Air Act regulations. However, once the costs of compliance were coupled with the benefits, the model showed that both GDP and economic welfare would increase over time, and that by 2020 the economic benefits would outweigh the costs. Likewise, the Office of Management and Budget found that to date the benefits of the law have far exceeded the cost, with an economic return of between $4 and $8 for every $1 invested in compliance.

Environmental regulations do affect jobs. But contrary to claims by polluting industries and congressional Republicans, efforts to protect our environment can actually create jobs. In order to reduce harmful pollution from power plants, for example, an electric company would have to equip plants with scrubbers and other technologies. These technologies would need to be manufactured and installed, creating jobs for people in the manufacturing and construction industries.

The official unemployment rate in the United States is still quite high, hovering around 9%. In this economic climate, politicians are more sensitive than ever to claims that environmental regulation could be a job-killer. By framing investments as wasted costs and relying on incomplete economic models, polluting industries have consistently tried to fight environmental standards. It's time to change the terms of the debate. We need to move beyond fear-mongering about the costs and start capturing the benefits. ❑

*Article 6.3*

# FRACKONOMICS
*The Science and Economics of the Gas Boom*

## BY ROBERT LARSON
*July/August 2013*

Between 1868 and 1969, Cleveland's Cuyahoga River caught fire at least ten times, including one blaze that reached the Standard Oil refinery where storage tanks detonated. Ultimately, the seemingly impossible and unnatural phenomenon of burning water came to represent the dangers of unregulated industrial development and generated popular support for the environmental laws of the 1970s, including the Clean Water Act and the Safe Drinking Water Act.

Today the unsettling sight of burning water has returned, from a new industry that is exempt from both these laws. In homes near installations using the drilling technique known as hydraulic fracturing, or "fracking," the tap water has been known to ignite with the touch of a lighter. The industry is relatively new, so the scientific literature yields only tentative results and provisional research conclusions. But the early research suggests fracking has serious negative consequences for public health and local ecology, from flaming tap water to toxic chemicals to ground tremors. Industry spokesmen insist that the negative side-effects of fracking are insignificant. But there's one positive side-effect everyone should be able to agree upon: fracking is an ideal vehicle for explaining key economic concepts of market failure and market power, including *externalities, asymmetrical information*, and *regulatory capture*, along with brand-new ones, like *science capture*. Let's start with the firewater.

## Liar Liar, Taps on Fire

In the fracking process, natural gas (methane) is released from shale rock strata up to a mile underground, by injecting millions of gallons of water, along with sand and a variety of synthetic chemicals. The huge pressure of the water makes new cracks in the rock, allowing the gas to dissolve and be extracted. Natural gas is now responsible for 30% of U.S. electricity production and for heating half of all U.S. homes. The national and business media have breathlessly reported huge growth in gas production, and the oil-and-gas industry projects that North America will return to exporting energy by 2025. Besides the sheer growth in production, the *Wall Street Journal* reported earlier this year, the fracking boom has brought other economic benefits, "improving employment in some regions and a rebound in U.S.-based manufacturing," and "greater defense against overseas turmoil that can disrupt energy supplies."

As made notorious by the documentary *Gasland*, water supplies are a major focus of concern about fracking, especially since the emergence of dramatic footage of a number of Pennsylvania homes, near fracking pads above the Marcellus Shale formation, producing fireballs from the kitchen tap. Duke University earth scientists conducted a more rigorous exploration of this phenomenon, published in the *Proceedings of the National Academy of the Sciences*. They surveyed rural Pennsylvanian water wells for residential use, measuring concentrations of methane, the main chemical component of natural gas. Concentrations rose far above natural levels closer to drill pads, spiking within one kilometer of active gas development sites to a level that "represents a potential explosion hazard." It was also found that the specific gas chemistry in the wells matched those produced through drilling, rather than through naturally occurring compounds. As the gas boom goes "boom," the cautious scientists conclude: "Greater stewardship, knowledge, and—possibly—regulation are needed to ensure the sustainable future of shale-gas extraction."

In parts of the country where water is scarcer, the issue is more ominous. The Environmental Protection Agency (EPA) and U.S. Geological Survey have found toxic alcohols, glycols, and carcinogenic benzene in underground aquifers in Wyoming, evidence that fracking has tainted precious underground water supplies. In press accounts, local residents who requested the study "expressed gratitude to the EPA, and perhaps a bit of veiled doubt about the zeal of local and state regulators." In parched Texas, the volume of water adequate for irrigating $200,000 worth of crops can be used to frack $2.5 billion-worth of gas or oil. The *Wall Street Journal* reports that "companies have been on a buying spree, snapping up rights to scarce river water—easily outbidding traditional users such as farmers and cities." A Texan rancher relates: "They're just so much bigger and more powerful than we are…We're just kind of the little ant that gets squashed."

## Top-Secret Ingredients

The heavy use of often-secret synthetic chemicals has also cast a shadow over the fracking debate. Bloomberg News reported in 2012 that energy companies and well operators were refusing to disclose the chemical formulas of thousands of substances used in the fracking process, enough to "keep [the] U.S. clueless on wells." Many states have instituted a self-reporting law, modeled on one first developed in Texas, allowing drillers to withhold the ingredients used in their chemical mixes. Bloomberg reports that drillers "claimed similar exemptions about 19,000 times" in the first eight months of 2012 alone. The congressional exemption of the industry from federal water requirements (discussed below) makes this non-disclosure possible, so that "neighbors of fracked wells … can't use the disclosures to watch for frack fluids migrating into creeks, rivers and aquifers, because they don't know what to look for."

This development is a perfect example of what economists call *asymmetric information*, where one participant in a transaction knows relevant information that is unknown to the other party. The lack of information on one side can put the other party at an advantage, like the seller of a used car who knows more about the car's problems than the prospective buyer. For example, a team of Colorado endocrinologists set out to catalogue these synthetic compounds used in wells across the country, based on regulatory filings. The survey was limited due to the "void of environmental authority" to compel chemical disclosure, and thus the data sheets and reports are "fraught with gaps in information about the formulation of the products." Many of these reports only specify the general chemical class or use the label "proprietary," providing no additional information. Ultimately, the scientists found that over 75% of the chemicals were harmful for the sensory organs, nearly half could affect the nervous and immune systems, and 25% could cause "cancer and mutations."

Another report by Colorado scientists observed that fracking development is increasingly located "near where people live, work, and play." The study used air sampling to find strongly elevated health risks within a radius of about half a mile from fracking sites. The effects ranged from "headaches and eye irritation" up to "tremors, temporary limb paralysis, and unconsciousness at higher exposures." A larger review by Pennsylvania scientists reached similar conclusions, based on local resident reporting and finding a match of over two-thirds "between known health effects of chemicals detected and symptoms reported."

The scientists caution that their findings "do not constitute definitive proof of cause and effect," but they do "indicate the strong likelihood that the health of people living in proximity to gas facilities is being affected by exposure to pollutants from those facilities." They frequently advocate the *precautionary principle*—that careful study showing that a product or process is *not* harmful should precede its use—as when they recommend "health impact assessments before permitting begins," and note that "scientific knowledge about the health and environmental impacts of shale gas development ... are proceeding at a far slower pace than the development itself." These conclusions contradict the industry's claim that fracking is both safe for public health and not in need of any further study. Especially considering the earthquakes.

## Tectonic Economics

Perhaps more alarming than the burning water and secret chemicals is the association of fracking with earthquakes. An early report of this development came from the Oklahoma Geological Survey, which surveyed the timing of tremors and their proximity to fracking sites and found a "strong correlation in time and space" and thus "a possibility these earthquakes were induced by hydraulic fracturing." Earthquake epicenters were mostly within two miles of wells, and any earthquake disruption or damage caused by fracking-related activities represents an *externality*, a side effect of an economic transaction that affects parties outside the transaction.

These findings are backed up by a review in the prestigious research journal *Science*, in which cautious scientists note that fracking *itself* is not responsible for "the earthquakes that have been shaking previously calm regions." Yet they find that the induced earthquakes do arise from "all manner of other energy-related fluid injection—including deep disposal of fracking's wastewater, extraction of methane from coal beds, and creation of geothermal energy reservoirs." A surveyed area in Arkansas typically had about two quakes a year, before the beginning of fracking-water disposal. The year water disposal began, the number rose to ten. The next year, to 54. After water injection was halted, the quakes tapered off. The *Science* authors observe the "strongly suggestive" correlation between water disposal and seismic activity: "The quakes began only after injection began, surged when the rate of injection surged, were limited to the vicinity of the wells, and trailed off after injection was stopped." The scientists' main conclusion is the adoption of the precautionary principle: "look before you leap ... Stopping injection has stopped significant earthquakes within days to a year. ... The new regulations in Ohio and Arkansas at least move in the direction of such a learn-as-you-go approach."

## Fracknapping

You might wonder why the EPA has not limited or regulated fracking operations, in light of the combustible water, cancer-causing chemicals, and earthquake clusters. The EPA might well have adopted significant national policies on fracking by now, had the practice not been made exempt from the main national environmental laws in the Energy Policy Act of 2005, an offspring of Dick Cheney's secretive energy committee. The exemptions from the Clean Water Act, the Safe Drinking Water Act, the Clean Air Act, and the Superfund law drastically limit the agency's authority to act on fracking.

The drive to limit even EPA *research* into fracking is decades old. An extensive *New York Times* report, based on interviews with scientists and reviews of confidential files, found that "more than a quarter-century of efforts by some lawmakers and regulators to force the federal government to police the industry better have been thwarted, as EPA studies have been repeatedly narrowed in scope and important findings have been removed." When Congress first directed the EPA to investigate fracking in the 1980s, the *Times* reported, EPA scientists found that some fracking waste was "hazardous and should be tightly controlled." But the final report sent to Congress eliminated these conclusions. An agency scientist relates, "It was like science didn't matter. ... The industry was going to get what it wanted, and we were not supposed to stand in the way."

Similarly, when an EPA public-advisory letter to the state of New York called for a moratorium on drilling, the advice was stripped from the released version. A staff scientist said the redaction was due to "politics," but could as well have said "business power." More importantly, the first major EPA review of fracking found "little or no threat to drinking water." This was an eyebrow-raising claim, given that five of seven members of the peer review panel had current or former energy industry affiliations, a detail noted by agency whistle-blower Weston Wilson. Other studies have been narrowed in scope or colored by similar conflicts of interest. More recently, the agency announced that its study finding contamination of Wyoming groundwater will not be subjected to outside peer review, and that further work instead will be funded directly by industry. As the EPA is presently drafting a brand-new report on the subject, these past embarrassments should be kept in mind.

This brings up the problem of *regulatory capture*, where an industry to be monitored gains major influence over regulators' policies. As mentioned above, fracking is very loosely regulated by the states, which is always a favorite outcome for corporate America since the regulatory resources of state governments are far smaller and the regulators are even more easily dominated than those of the federal government. The industry-sponsored FracFocus website is the state-sanctioned chemical-information clearing house, and a masterpiece of smooth PR design, suggesting clear water and full transparency. But Bloomberg News reports that "more than 40 percent of wells fracked in eight major drilling states last year had been omitted from the voluntary site."

Other state reactions have varied. In 2010, the New York State legislature voted to ban fracking, but then-Governor Paterson vetoed the bill and instead issued a temporary moratorium on the practice, though fracking remains illegal in the New York City watershed. Finally, while the EPA's main study is still pending, the agency has taken some steps, as in 2012 when it required well operators to reduce methane gas emissions from wells and storage pits to limit air pollution. But even here the regulation wears kid gloves: The new moves do not cut into industry profits. In fact, capturing the "fugitive" methane, the agency estimates, will *save* the industry $11 to $19 million annually. Also, the regulation won't take effect until 2015.

## Neoclassical Gas

Mainstream, or "neoclassical," economic theory considers itself to have solutions to these problems—solutions centered as always on "free markets." The idea is that if firms create chronic health problems or combustible tap water, market forces should drive up their costs, as landowners learn of these firms' practices and demand higher payment for drilling. But as seen above, even households that have already leased their land for gas development remain unaware of the identities and effects of the obscure synthetic chemicals to which they are exposed. This *informational asymmetry*—the firms know things the landowners don't—significantly attenuates the ability of landowners to make informed choices.

On the other hand, households that are located near a drill pad but uninvolved in licensing the drilling will experience the ill effects as externalities. Neoclassicals suggest these can be fixed through a better property-rights system, where surrounding individuals can sue drillers for injuring their health. But this solution runs up against another problem: proving cause-and-effect from a drilling pad to a particular individual's health problems is extremely difficult. The tobacco industry notoriously made this point in court for many years, arguing that it was impossible to prove if a man's lung cancer was caused by a four-pack-a-day cigarette habit, as opposed to, say, local auto exhaust. If cause-and-effect is hard to prove in court for cigarettes, doing so for air-delivered volatile organic compounds will be almost impossible.

This problem is aggravated by the use of corporate resources to influence research. The showcase example is a study produced by the University of Texas, "Fact-Based Regulation for Environmental Protection in Shale Gas Development." The study gave fracking a guardedly positive bill of health, finding no evidence of negative health impacts. The commercial media gave the study a good deal of favorable attention, until the revelation that the lead researcher, Dr. Charles G. Groat, formerly of USGS, sits on the board of the Plains Exploration & Production Company, a Houston-based energy firm heavily invested in gas development. His compensation from the board was several times his academic salary, and he also held 40,000 shares of its stock. An in-house review by the university was outspoken, saying "the term 'fact-based' would not apply" to the paper, which was "inappropriately selective ... such that they seemed to suggest that public concerns were without scientific basis and largely resulted from media bias." Groat retired from the university the day the review was released, but this practice has become increasingly common from industries under fire for environmental or public-health impacts. Bloomberg News flatly stated that "producers are taking a page from the tobacco industry playbook: funding research at established universities that arrives at conclusions that counter concerns raised by critics." This raises the ugly possibility of *science capture*.

## No Frackin' Way

Not that Americans are taking it lying down. A diverse popular coalition successfully fought to block a Gulf Coast gas terminal that stood to inflict major damage on local wildlife. The *Oil & Gas Journal* reports on the "firestorm" of activism: "In an unlikely but massive undertaking, environmental activists, sports fishermen, local politicians, media groups, and other citizens formed a coalition known as the 'Gumbo Alliance' that united opposition to the technology." The Louisiana governor vetoed the project "under considerable public pressure." Elsewhere, local residents have taken action to keep fracking and its negative externalities out of their communities. New York State "fractivists" have won an impressive 55 municipal bans and 105 local moratoriums against fracking, to date. The state's Court of Appeals—New York's highest court—recently upheld the bans against an industry lawsuit. These activist successes are an early challenge to what the *Wall Street Journal* called the new "shale barons."

American job markets remain highly depressed and state budgets are strained. What we need, instead of dogged extraction of every particle of fossil fuels from the ground, is a public employment program geared toward the construction of a new sustainable energy system. This would be a far superior alternative to fracking—on grounds of health, ecology, and employment. It could also serve as a springboard for a broader questioning of the suitability of capitalism for the challenges of the 21st century. That kind of radical approach would see the glass of water as half full, not half on fire. ❏

**Sources:** Russel Gold, "Gas Boom Projected to Grow for Decades," *Wall Street Journal*, February 28, 2013; Tom Fowler, "US Oil Sector Notches Historic Annual Gusher," *Wall Street Journal*, January 19, 2013; Stephen Osborn, Avner Vengosh, Nathaniel Warner, and Robert Jackson, "Methane contamination of drinking water accompanying gas-well drilling and hydraulic fracturing," *Proceedings of the National Academy of the Sciences*, Vol. 108, No. 20, May 17, 2011; Kirk Johnson, "EPA Links Tainted Water in Wyoming to Hydraulic Fracturing for Natural Gas," *New York Times*, December 8, 2011; Tennille Tracy, "New EPA Findings Test Fracking Site," *Wall Street Journal*, October 11, 2012; Felicity Barringer, "Spread of Hydrofracking Could Strain Water Resources in West, Study Finds," *New York Times*, May 2, 2013; Russel Gold and Ana Campoy, "Oil's Growing Thirst for Water," *Wall Street Journal*, December 6, 2011; Ben Elgin, Benjamin Haas and Phil Kuntz, "Fracking Secrets by Thousands Keep US Clueless on Wells," Bloomberg News, November 30, 2012; Theo Colborn, Carol Kwiatkowski, Kim Schultz and Mary Bachran, "Natural Gas Operations form a Public Health Perspective," *Human and Ecological Risk Assessment: An International Journal*, Vol. 17, No. 5, September 20, 2011; Lisa McKenzie,

Roxana Witter, Lee Newman, John Adgate, "Human health risk assessment of air emissions from development of unconventional natural gas resources," *Science of the Total Environment*, Vol. 424, May 1 2012; Nadia Steinzor, Wilma Subra, and Lisa Sumi, "Investigating Links between Shale Gas Development and Health Impacts Through a Community Survey Project in Pennsylvania," *New Solutions*, Vol. 23, No. 1, 2013; Austin Holland, Oklahoma Geological Survey, "Examination of Possibly Induced Seismicity from Hydraulic Fracturing in the Eolga Field, Garvin County, Oklahoma, August 2011; Richard Kerr, "Learning How NOT to Make Your Own Earthquakes," *Science*, Vol. 335, No. 6075, March 23 2012; Zoe Corbyn, "Method predicts size of fracking earthquakes," *Nature* News, December 9, 2011; Ian Urbina, "Pressure Limits Efforts to Police Drilling for Gas," *New York Times*, March 3, 2011; Devlin Barrett and Ryan Dezember, "Regulators Back 'Fracking' in New York," *Wall Street Journal*, July 1, 2011; John Broder, "US Caps Emissions in Drilling for Fuel," *New York Times*, February 4, 2012; Norman Augustine, Rita Colwell, and James Duderstadt, "A Review of the Processes of Preparation and Distribution of the report 'Fact-Based Regulation for Environmental Protection in Shale Gas Development,'" University of Texas at Austin, November 30, 2012; Jim Efsthathiou, "Frackers Fund University Research That Proves Their Case," Bloomberg News, July 23, 2012; Daron Threet, "US offshore LNG terminals face technical, legal maze," *Oil & Gas Journal*, December 24, 2007; Ellen Cantarow, "New York's Zoning Ban Movement Fracks Big Gas," Truthout, May 9, 2013 (Truthout.org); Alyssa Abkowitz, "The New Texas Land Rush," *Wall Street Journal*, April 25, 2013; Daron Threet, "US offshore LNG terminals face technical, legal maze," *Oil & Gas Journal*, December 24, 2007.

Article 6.4

# MAINE FARMERS AND CLIMATE CHANGE
*Reactive or Proactive?*

## BY STEPHANIE WELCOMER, MARK HAGGERTY, AND JOHN JEMISON
March/April 2015

Since the dawn of agriculture, the things farmers need from nature, like water and sunlight, have varied only within a relatively narrow, predictable range. This has changed in the last few decades. Now, climate change is affecting all farmers, increasing the risks they face and forcing them to adapt. The latest Assessment Report from the United Nations Intergovernmental Panel on Climate Change (IPCC) underlines the scope and breadth of the problem: "Human influence on the climate system is clear .... The atmosphere and ocean have warmed, the amounts of snow and ice have diminished, and sea level has risen." Climate change affects all farmers regardless of their location; their farming approach, conventional or alternative; their farm size, crop, or income. No farmer is exempt.

Climate change reshuffles the landscape that we count on to grow food. The shifts are accelerating and unpredictable, and farmers are on the front lines. How are they responding? Do they recognize changes in weather patterns? Do they attribute these shifts to climate change? Are they adapting their own agricultural practices in response? And are they advocating for policy to reduce greenhouse gas emissions—adopting a proactive stance, as opposed to a purely reactive one?

Our work suggests that farmers have a complicated relationship to climate change, recognizing its symptoms but not necessarily its causes. Yet, if farmers were to recognize the causes, they would be much more effective in adapting to climate change. Without this recognition, they will miss the chance to adjust their practices to protect land and water resources, and to reduce their own contributions to climate change. Agriculture's challenge is that it—like other sectors—has to change fundamentally to head off far more severe climate changes, which would require much more costly adaptations, or for which no adaptation is possible.

## Maine's New Climate Reality

According to the U.S. Department of Agriculture (USDA) 2012 census, Maine has about 1.45 million acres of farmland, and agriculture is estimated to generate over $750 million in annual sales. Maine farmers grow a wide variety of crops, including potatoes, beans, tomatoes, grains, livestock, apples, and blueberries, as well as aquaculture products (farmed fish and shellfish). Producers include conventional and alternative growers, and farm sizes range from less than one acre to over 3,000.

Although there are many commonalities between agriculture in Maine and the remainder of the nation there are some important differences. Maine appears to be

---

### "Assessing Maine's Agriculture Future": About the Study

The people interviewed included:
- A total of 199 Maine farmers and agricultural advisors
- Commodities farmers (apple, beef, blueberry, dairy, potato, and large vegetable producers)
- Small diversified farmers (farmers' market producers, organic farmers and gardeners, small vegetable producers)
- Tribal farmers (Micmac Nation)
- Agricultural consultants (extension-agency and industry crop advisors)

---

countering a national trend of declining numbers of farmers. Between 2007 and 2012, the state's number of farmers aged less than 35 increased by over 60%, from 336 to 551. Additionally, according to the New England Farmers Union, Maine has a higher percentage of farmers making direct sales. The state ranks fifth in percentage of farmers selling directly to the public, and third in percentage participating in community supported agriculture (CSA). (See Mark Paul and Emily Stephens, "Community Supported Agriculture: A Chance to Revitalize Farming?" Dollars & Sense, March/April 2015.) And Maine has a high and growing percentage of female farmers, with women accounting for 29% of "principal farm operators" (compared to 14% nationwide). Maine farms are also smaller, on average, 178 acres compared to the national average of 434.

The wide diversity in Maine's agriculture sector make the state an ideal "laboratory" for observing farmers' responses to climate change. According to the 2014 National Climate Assessment by the U.S. Global Change Research Program, Maine will experience rising temperatures, changing precipitation patterns, and increasing extreme weather events. Indeed, temperatures in the northeast United States are already increasing, by an average of half a degree per decade for the last 40 years, with bigger increases, over one degree per decade, for average winter temperatures. Scientists project increases in average temperatures between of 3°F and 10°F over the next century, along with increases in the total amount of precipitation, more rain (though less snow), and greater variability in precipitation. Already, the Northeast "has experienced a greater recent increase in extreme precipitation," according to the National Climate Assessment, "than any other region in the United States."

For farmers, rising temperatures do mean that the number of frost-free days increase and growing seasons expand. That might sound advantageous. But there are also big downsides: Pest varieties change, with the incursion of warm-weather tolerant insects. Soil run-off is more likely with more intense storms. Also, weather becomes harder to predict. For example, for the small northern Maine town of Caribou, the first half of July 2013 was one of the driest on record—with just 3/100 inch of rain. In the second half of the month, Caribou got enough rain—over 7 inches—to make the month the second wettest July in the town's history.

## How Do Farmers See It?

Maine's farmers are facing unprecedented challenges stemming from climate change, centered on the two key ingredients in agriculture—water and soil. Too much water can wash soil away, while too little limits crop production and dries the soil out. According to the University of Maine report *Maine's Climate Future*, the "high-intensity rainfall events" that are expected to accompany climate change are "less effective at replenishing soil water supplies and more likely to erode soil." Meanwhile, higher average temperatures mean that, for a given level of precipitation, less water will actually be available to crops, due to higher rates of moisture loss from the ground and from the plants themselves.

As part of the 2011 "Assessing Maine's Agriculture Future" study, we interviewed around 200 Maine farmers about changes in the climate and their expectations for the future of farming. We asked representatives and opinion leaders from a wide sampling of the state's farming sectors about their reasons for farming, their concerns, and their hopes for the future, as well as changes in weather patterns and their related adaptations. During the interviews, most farmers did not acknowledge that climate change was happening, only that weather was unpredictable. In the words of one farmer:

> *Well, talk about climate change. You have an early spring; you usually have an early fall. You have a late spring; the fall carries on three weeks, maybe sometimes even a fourth week. And, I've seen that happen time and time again, and that's, you know, that climate is changing all the time.*

Another farmer said:

> *I think we've been fighting weather forever and we always will. And there's never been two seasons alike and it's how you manage that weather.*

These farmers appear to argue that changing weather is nothing new, and that finding ways to manage the effects of the uncontrollable weather has always been inherent to agriculture. Still another farmer combines the recognition that adaptations are necessary with skepticism that there is actual human-caused climate change, or that it is a bad thing:

> *Yeah, I've read that and seen that. As far as what do we do? I order an extra pallet of plastic so I can put up more silage if it's a real rainy year. If it's a dry year, we make dry hay. It's all we can do. You ain't gonna change the weather.*

Then he continues:

> *If they say that the climate is changing due to —what's the big word?—"global warming." If this is global warming, I love every minute of it.*

This view suggests that at least some farmers see benefits to climate change. The additional carbon dioxide, indeed, positively impacts plant growth. The longer growing seasons and higher temperatures make additional crops and varieties viable. Yet most farmers express concern about how to manage changing and increasingly volatile weather patterns. In the "Assessing Maine's Agricultural Future" study, we found that farmers are using an array of adaptation strategies. Farmers are planting crops earlier, to take advantage of the shorter frost season, planting new crops, and even using genetically modified organisms to adapt to the new growing season. They are building structures to buffer crops from head-on exposure to the outside environment. One farmer says:

We're definitely going in the direction of doing more and more different things, building more hoop houses and greenhouses to have more control of the growing environment. As farmers discussed adaptation, they often acknowledged that weather was inextricably linked to soil structure, and to the lack of or over-abundance of water. They are turning to constructed ponds, irrigation, and new drainage systems to maintain crop and soil health. As one apple grower puts it:

Anything we can do to move Mother Nature out of the picture benefits us in the end. Not surprisingly, controlling the environment is a key part of dealing with climate change's related outcomes. One agriculture consultant explains:

I think whether people are doing it on a conscious level or it's just something that they have to deal with., The farmers I am working with are looking to have more control over different parts of their operations. They are definitely being impacted by it, whether or not they say, "Yes, this is climate change."

## A Sustainable Future?

Farmers interviewed in this study seem to be making adaptations to address day-to-day challenges they see in the field—drawing on techniques familiar to them, attempting to adapt their methods at the margins rather than at the deep structure. These adaptations prioritize maintaining short-term profitability and are not linked to a call for policies that could address the root causes of climate change. When asked about government policies or initiatives that they would like to see, none of the farmers argued for policies aimed at climate mitigation or supporting farmers' climate adaptations.

Yet farmers were not reluctant to advocate policy changes generally. They expressed a strong desire for policy to recalibrate agricultural regulations, and to influence other peoples' behavior. They argued for regulatory changes—reducing the regulatory burden and tailoring regulations according to farm size. They advocated for policy to create a cultural shift regarding food and the food system. They argued that the public is largely unaware of where its food comes from, and focuses on food prices rather than looking at the real costs to communities and farmers. They expressed a desire for policy that helps Maine farmers market and brand their products, and that opens new markets for their goods. They urged a significant overhaul of the food processing and transportation infrastructure, advocating for more local and regional processing centers for meat and other foods; "food hubs" for distribution and direct marketing; and more efficient transportation, including large trucks (for long and mid-distance routes) and light rail. (Currently, farmers use their own vehicles to haul their crops, often crossing scores and even hundreds of miles, within the state.) Additionally, farmers stressed the importance of research efforts from the USDA and Maine Extension to explore new effective farming methods. Overall, farmers emphasized public support to boost demand for their crops and lower processing and distribution costs—each of which aims to support the farming industry economically, but without addressing climate change. Environmental sustainability, including on climate, is scarcely on farmers' policy radar.

Though few farmers are thinking about policies to address climate change, clues to farmers' future practical approaches surfaced as they discussed their hopes for farming in 2025. Commodity-based farmers—large-scale, single-crop producers—tended to see farming in 2025 as based on ties to large corporate systems. The two largest groups of commodity producers in Maine, potato and blueberry growers, imagined a future characterized by fewer and larger farms, more food exported to non-Maine markets, and more genetically modified organisms (GMOs). In contrast, farmers in most of the other sectors imagined a more local and diversified food system, characterized by diversified farms, a mix of small and large farms, more farmers, increased interest in local foods, and more direct markets.

Because the farmers differ on the role of industrial technology, especially reliance on capital-intensive methods and synthetic (fossil-fuel based) fertilizers, their adaptation strategies diverge. More industrial approaches, such as petroleum-based fertilizers and GMO crops, will make farmers more vulnerable to the suppliers of these products, generally a few giant companies dominating entire industries. The smaller diversified farmers, in contrast, tend to advocate a farmer-controlled model that can adapt to the changes in soil and water associated with climate change. With their focus on building up the soil by non-synthetic means and on using human, animal, and alternative energy in place of petroleum-based inputs, these farmers will have more local control over their strategies.

Says one small diversified farmer:

> *You know, all the long-term ecological studies that are comparing conventional soil management with organic [or] for lack of a better word, ecological, really show that ecological soil management is really much less vulnerable to climate variability and unpredictability .... So I think that's really the best hedge that all of us can have.*

For the most part, farmers support practices and policies re-embedding the farm into the surrounding social communities. They are enthusiastic about farm-to-institution policies (linking farms directly to food programs in schools, colleges, prisons, and hospitals), about policies that allow the use of the Women, Infants, and Children program (WIC) and Supplemental Nutrition Assistance Program (SNAP) benefits at farmers' markets, about teaching community members how farming works and where food comes from. On the social and economic relationships in the food system, they are developing a clear policy agenda. On climate change, however, the understanding and policy advocacy are barely visible.

## System Change

Systems theorists, who study how organizations and systems change, offer some insight into farmers' minimal recognition of climate change, and their lack of advocacy for climate-mitigation policy. Management scholar Connie Gersick describes systems—such as the farming sector—as being in equilibrium until fundamental factors change. One key factor can be "environmental changes that threaten the system's ability to obtain resources." As the system's actors are faced with persistent, systemic problems, they experience mounting discomfort. Once key actors recognize that the system has become dysfunctional, they begin to search for new information about the sources of the problems and possible new steps. Newcomers enter the system and are enlisted or inspired to search for solutions. The entrenched understandings, relationships, and power dynamics of the system, finally, can be dismantled. Revolutionary change can happen and a new system can be created.

Climate scientists from all over the world are doing their best to raise the alarm that climate change is happening, that it will change our natural systems irrevocably, and that these changes are accelerating. Author Rebecca Solnit calls this a "slow-motion calamity." "Climate change is everything, a story and a calamity bigger than any other," she writes. "It's the whole planet for the whole foreseeable future, the entire atmosphere, all the oceans, the poles; it's weather and crop failure and famine and tropical diseases heading north and desertification and the uncertain fate of a great majority of species on earth."

A few of the farmers we interviewed do recognize the threat that climate change already poses. A blueberry grower commented:

*I think that the weather patterns are changing ... and I do believe global warming is going to have a very severe impact on the blueberry industry; even with irrigation because the heat in August has become so intense that they [blueberries] literally will cook in hours in the field. So I do think that that environmental aspect of global warming is something we're going to be dealing with in 20 or 30 years.*

Another farmer stated:

*Back to back, with these weather changes you saw probably our toughest year [in history] two years ago, the best growing year last year, and when you start getting a hundred year storms every four years, you begin to wonder, you know, that perhaps there is something to this sort of thing.*

An apple grower said:

*The problem with weather and growing food is that ... there's a very narrow window of stability there. I mean, we get outside that window very far and everything falls apart. And so yeah, I mean it's a real serious concern.*

Farmers, on the front lines of climate change, respond within their financial and knowledge constraints. Financial constraints dictate the ability to install greenhouses, wind power, irrigation, drains, etc. Knowledge constraints include limited access to the latest research on farming practices and climate adaptation, or on the relationship between micro-level season-to-season weather and macro-level climate change. That prevents the development of a long-term policy to address ever-increasing climate changes.

It is not that farmers are generally short-sighted, categorically resisting policies that deliver long-term benefits at the expense of short-term profits. Farmers support long-sighted policies like public spending for farmland availability and regulations that ensure food quality for consumers. But few have arrived at a consciousness of climate change like the farmers quoted above. Without a major shift in thought to acknowledge climate change, the farming community continues to suffer from an advocacy gap, putting mid- and long-term farm viability at risk.

The lack of a systematic approach to agriculture and climate change also risks exacerbating the problem. Agriculture is not just a passive victim of others' actions; it is a significant contributor of greenhouse gases. Globally, deforestation for farmland, conventional tillage, and the use of petroleum-based fertilizers, for example, are major sources of carbon dioxide emissions, while other agricultural practices are to blame for large methane and nitrous oxide emissions. All told, "agriculture is itself responsible for an estimated one third of climate change," according to the Climate Institute.

Farmers acting on individual interests, without policies incorporating common climate-related goals, may adapt to climate changes in ways that worsen the problem. They may till more, reducing carbon sequestration, and may turn to crops that increase greenhouse gas emissions. For instance, the northern U.S. grasslands are being converted to corn for ethanol production, even though this puts the soil at risk and releases more carbon into the atmosphere. An article in the *Proceedings of the National Academy of Sciences* concludes that "grassland conversion to corn/soy ... across a significant portion of the U.S. Western Corn Belt are comparable to deforestation rates in Brazil, Malaysia, and Indonesia." Not only can farmers benefit from acknowledging, studying, and responding to climate change, they can also reduce the negative impacts of agriculture on broader social and natural systems. For instance, converting a percentage of Midwestern corn production for ethanol into grass-based pasture systems could be a first step in carbon-emissions reduction.

As Rebecca Solnit points out, addressing climate change involves not only reworking the way we do things but also changing our understandings—our stories—about the weather, the soil and water, and our food, as well as our responsibilities to each other, future generations, and the earth's ecology. Responding to a failing system involves remaking existing relationships and formulating new narratives. By ignoring the reality of climate change and simply reacting, farmers are denying their own contribution to the problem. They are also ignoring the key role they have to play in solving it. ❑

*Sources:* David Abel, "In Maine, Scientists See Signs of Climate Change," *Boston Globe*, Sept. 21, 2014 (bostonglobe.com); Michael Jahi Chappell and Liliana A. LaValle, "Food Security and Biodiversity: Can We Have Both?" *Agriculture and Human Values*, 2011; Climate Institute (climate.org); Abigail Curtis, "USDA farming census: Maine has more young farmers, more land in farms 2014," *Bangor Daily News*, Feb. 23, 2014 (bangordailynews.com); P.C. Frumhoff, et al., Confronting Climate Change in the U.S. Northeast: Science, Impacts, and Solutions, Northeast Climate Impacts Assessment (NECIA), Union of Concerned Scientists (UCS), 2007; Connie J. G. Gersick, "Revolutionary change theories: A multilevel exploration of the punctuated equilibrium paradigm," *Academy of Management Review*, 1991; T. Griffin, et al., eds., Maine's Climate Future: An Initial Assessment, University of Maine, 2009 (climatechange.umaine.edu); Rajendra K. Pachauri, et al., eds., Intergovernmental Panel on Climate Change, Climate Change 2014 Synthesis Report: Summary for Policy Makers; Jerry M. Melillo, et al., eds., Highlights of Climate Change Impacts in the United States: The Third National Climate Assessment, U.S. Global Change Research Program, 2014; National Weather Service, July 2013 Climate Summary Caribou, Maine: Northern and Eastern Maine Monthly Climate Narrative (weather.gov); New England Farmers' Union, 2015 (newenglandfarmersunion.org); Rebecca Solnit, "Are We Missing the Big Picture on Climate Change?" *New York Times Magazine*, Dec. 2, 2014 (nytimes.com); USDA—NASS (2012), 2012 Census of Agriculture (agcensus.usda.gov); Christopher K. Wright and Michael C. Wimberley, "Recent Land Use Change in the Western Corn Belt Threatens Grasslands and Wetlands," *Proceedings of the National Academy of Sciences*, 2013

*Article 6.5*

# CLIMATE POLICY AS WEALTH CREATION

*The right policy would embody the principle that*
*we all own the earth's resources in equal and common measure.*

## BY JAMES K. BOYCE
*July/August 2014*

W*e know that climate change poses a grave threat to the earth and all who live on it. We also know, in the broadest sense, what we need to do to preserve a habitable planet: severely curtail greenhouse gas emissions from fossil fuels. The question of how to cure ourselves of our fossil-fuel dependence, however, has so far proven devilishly difficult. Possibilities like carbon taxes or carbon caps (and limited emissions permits) are widely discussed, but have so far run into political roadblocks: the power of vested interests like oil and coal companies, the attachment to fossil-fuel based ways of life, the fear of the economic costs involved, and the problem of coordinating national policies (and dividing up costs) to address a global problem. Economist James Boyce offers a policy proposal, based on the development of public-property rights over the atmosphere and the sharing of the proceeds from its use, which is both politically feasible and philosophically profound. This article is adapted from a lecture Boyce delivered, on March 31, as part of the "Climate Change Series" at the University of Pittsburgh Honors College. —Eds.*

## Why Climate Policies That Operate on the Supply Side?

Broadly speaking, there are two types of policies to reduce carbon emissions from fossil-fuel combustion. One set operates on the demand side of the picture, on the need for fossil fuels. These policies include investments in energy efficiency, alternative sources of energy, mass transit, etc.—investments that reduce our demand for fossil fuels at any given price.

I'm going to focus on the complementary set of policies that operate not on the demand side of the equation, but the supply side—policies that raise the prices of fossil fuels, resulting in lower use. Those policies raise prices either by instituting a tax on carbon emissions or, alternatively, by putting a cap on emissions and thereby restricting supply. In the same way that OPEC restricts supply when it wishes to increase the price of oil, a cap works to raise the price, too.

The policies that involve shifts in demand—investments in mass transit, clean and renewable energy, or energy efficiency— take time, possibly decades, to be fully implemented. In the short run, if we want to see immediate reductions in fossil-fuel consumption, we need policies in the mix that operate on the price today, and reduce consumption today. That's one reason I think that price-based policies can and should be part of the policy mix.

In addition, price-based policies themselves are critical to the reduction in demand. If consumers, households, firms, and public-sector institutions know that, over the next decade or two, the price of fossil fuels will inexorably rise due to policies purposely making that happen, they will have an incentive to make investments in energy efficiency and renewable energy sources. They will face price signals to push that investment along.

The easiest way to put a price on carbon emissions is through an "upstream" pricing system, which means that you apply the price where the carbon enters the economy, not where it comes out the tailpipe. So that would mean at the tanker terminals, the pipelines, the coal-mine heads, where fossil fuels are entering the economy. The Congressional Budget Office (CBO) estimates than an upstream system in a cap-and-trade or carbon tax regime would involve 2,000 "compliance entities"—that's the name for the folks who have to either pay the tax or surrender a permit for each ton of carbon they bring into the economy. If you tax carbon or price carbon upstream, those price increases become part of the price of the fuel and are passed along to business and consumers, thereby creating incentives for investments that reduce emissions over the longer haul.

There are two instruments that one can use to price carbon—one is a tax and the other is a cap. A tax sets the price and allows the quantity of emissions to fluctuate. A cap sets the quantity and allows the price of emissions to fluctuate. Other than that, they're basically the same thing. You can think of them both as involving permits. A tax says, "Here are permits, as long as you pay the price for them, you can have as many permits as you want." A cap says, "Here is the fixed number of permits, and we're going to let their price be determined at an auction or in a market."

If we had a tax to put a price on carbon emissions, I'd be all for it. But since the main policy objective is to hit the quantity target—to reduce the quantity of emissions—it seems to me that targeting the quantity rather than the price makes a lot of sense. We don't know for sure exactly what the relationship is between quantity and price. We know that a 10% increase in prices results in roughly

---

### Is Climate Change a "Tragedy of the Commons"?

Ecologist Garret Hardin coined the now-familiar phrase "the tragedy of the commons" in a 1968 article in the journal *Science*. Hardin argued that people inevitably deplete commonly held resources because they do not pay the full cost of using them. For example, livestock herders have an incentive to overgraze their own animals on common pasture— maximizing the benefits to themselves, while inflicting the costs of the overgrazing on others. Similar arguments have been made about the depletion of fisheries and many other environmental problems, among them climate change: each person enjoys the private benefits of fossil-fuel use, depleting the finite capacity of the atmosphere to absorb and recycle greenhouse gases, and inflicting damages on others. Mainstream economists have often seized upon this reasoning to argue that the solution to environmental problems is the division and enclosure of commons into private property, which would mean that each owner would bear the full cost of using his or her own property.

What economists are describing as "the tragedy of the commons," Boyce argues, would be better described as the "tragedy of open access." Open access allows individuals to appropriate resources at no cost, and when these resources are scarce, to inflict the costs of depletion on others. Understanding that a commons, however, can be "regulated through a system of common-property resource management," recasts the problem—and the solution. Protecting and preserving these resources does not require privatization: it can be achieved thought the development of public-property rights and regulations over their use. —*Eds.*

a 3% reduction in demand in the short run, but that relationship isn't precise. Moreover, it can change over time, particularly as more technologies are discovered. So if you want to hit the quantity target, it seems to me that setting a cap has advantages over setting a tax.

One way or another, however, what's important is to get a price on carbon. When we put a price on carbon, what we're doing is we're moving from an open-access regime, which is a situation where there are no property rights, to creating a set of property rights (see box). Regulations already assert a certain type of property right, the right of the public acting through the government to make rules about how the resource is used. Putting a price on emissions takes that process one step further. It not only sets rules about using the resource, but also charges a price for using that resource. So it moves along the spectrum from a complete absence of property rights towards a more full specification of property rights.

## Just How Much Would It Cost?

Back in 2009, the Speaker of the House of Representatives, John Boehner (R-Ohio), claimed in the debate running up to the vote on the American Clean Energy and Security Act— known as the Waxman-Markey bill, after its main sponsors, Henry Waxman (D-Calif.) and Ed Markey (D-Mass.)—that if this bill were passed, it would be the biggest tax increase on working families in American history. Now, that was probably political hyperbole, but Boehner wasn't entirely wrong. It would be like a tax increase, and it would be substantial. It has to be substantial if it's going to bring about the changes in consumption of fossil fuels that are needed to push forward the clean-energy transition. We're talking about big changes: an 80% reduction in our emissions by the year 2050. We're talking about an energy revolution, and the kinds of price increases that would be ultimately needed to drive that forward are not inconsequential.

What was the Democratic response? "No, no, it's not a tax, it's not a big price increase, and it's really not going to hurt people all that much. It's equivalent to a postage stamp a day." Now, that postage-stamp-a-day figure is an estimate of something quite different from the price increases that households would face. This is the estimated cost of abatement: how much it would cost to invest in energy-efficiency improvements to reduce fossil fuel consumption to 75% of the current level. That's not a huge cost because, in fact, there's a lot of low-hanging fruit out there in terms of investment opportunities.

The consulting firm McKinsey & Company produced a study a few years back that showed there are even investments that would have a negative cost. In other words, if you make that investment to reduce carbon emissions, you actually get money back because it's so efficient to make those investments. So overall, you can achieve reductions at a fairly modest cost.

But what I want to draw your attention to is the price of the emissions we're not reducing—the 75% that we're not cutting. That's the higher price consumers will be paying for their use of fossil fuels, and that's the primary reason for the price increases you will see at every gas pump, on every electric bill, and that you will see trickling through into the prices of other commodities in proportion to the use of fossil fuels in their production and distribution.

Let me remind you that gasoline prices are the most politically visible prices in the United States. They're advertised in twelve-inch-high numbers on street corners across America. During the 2008 Presidential campaign, when all the major candidates— including Hillary Clinton and John McCain—were talking about global warming and said they were in favor of limiting carbon emissions with a cap-and-trade policy, gas prices went up. And both Clinton and McCain said this was a terrible burden on the American people, that we needed to have a federal gas tax holiday for the summer to relieve this burden. Well, the federal gas tax is about 18 cents a gallon—it's really not that much. Compared to the price increases that we're going to see if we have a serious climate policy, I hate to tell it to you folks, but 18 cents rounds to about zero.

We're going to see gas prices going well above $5 a gallon in the first few years of the policy, and ultimately higher than that. How are you going to have a policy that squares the circle between, on the one hand, the need to price those emissions to address the problem of climate change and, on the other hand, even those politicians who see climate change as a problem saying, "We can't let the price of gas go up because it's going to hurt the American family"?

## Who Gets the Money?

How much money are we talking about when we put a cap on carbon emissions? What I want to share here are some "back of the envelope" calculations. Don't take these to the bank, but they'll give you some idea of the ballpark we're talking about.

These figures trace the trajectory if we're going to achieve an 80% cut in emissions by the year 2050. In the first six years of the policy, if we were to have such a policy in 2015, we'd be emitting on average about 6 billion tons of carbon dioxide per year, a little bit less than in the absence of a policy. The price associated with that reduction would probably be in the neighborhood of $15 a ton, so we'd be talking about $90 billion a year, or about $540 billion over those first six years. In the next decade, we'd be ratcheting those emissions down further to about 4.5 billion tons. To do so, the price would have to be about $30 a ton, generating a total cost to consumers and therefore a pot of money of about $135 billion a year, or $1.35 trillion over the decade. In the next decade, the 2030s, getting down to about 3 billion tons of carbon, we'd be raising the price to about $60 a ton, generating about $1.8 trillion over the decade. And the last decade, the 2040s, ratcheting down further to 1.5 billion tons, perhaps somewhat optimistically assuming here that the price needed would be only $120 a ton—this assumes that a lot of R&D has happened, a lot of new technologies come online, investments in public mass transit are online, etc., so you don't have to push the price through the roof—that would generate another $1.8 trillion.

You add it up and over that 35-year period, we're talking about something to the order of $5.5 trillion. Economists have a technical term for it—"a hell of a lot of money." The question is: Who owns the atmosphere and, therefore, who will get the money?

One possible answer is the fossil-fuel corporations. You could give them the money that consumers pay in higher prices. If you give the permits to the firms for free, on the basis of some allocation formula, then those permits have to be tradable,

---

### What Should We Make of the New EPA Rules?

This June, the U.S. Environmental Protection Agency (EPA) announced a new "Clean Power Plan" targeting a 30% reduction of carbon emissions from fossil-fuel-fired electrical power plants, relative to the 2005 level, by the year 2030. While we may think first of motor vehicles when we think about fossil-fuel use, electrical power generation actually accounts for more of our carbon emissions—over 2 billion metric tons, or nearly one-third of the U.S. total, each year. The EPA policy is not a new law (as climate legislation has been blocked in Congress), but a new set of rules that the Obama administration proposes to implement under the authority of the Clean Air Act.

The Clean Power Plan allows states to each develop their own paths to emissions-reduction targets. The EPA describes four ways to achieve reductions: increased efficiency of coal-fired power plants, a shift towards natural gasfired (away from coal-fired) plants, a shift toward renewables like wind and solar (away from fossil-fuel-based power generation), and increased energy efficiency in consumption. "States can meet their goal using any measures that make sense to them," the official EPA blog states. "They do not have to use all the measures EPA identified, and they can use other approaches that will work to bring down that carbon intensity rate."

One approach is to cap power plant emissions and auction the permits to the power companies. Nine northeastern states are already doing this under the Regional Greenhouse Gas Initiative (RGGI), and last year California began doing so under its Global Warming Solutions Act. Auction revenue can be returned to the people as dividends, or used to fund public investments, or some mix of the two as California is now doing.

"The Clean Power Plan offers every state the opportunity to institute cap-and-dividend climate policies," Boyce observes. "Earmarking some fraction of the auction revenue for public investment can make sense, too, but folks should understand that once we've capped emissions from the power sector, those emissions won't be reduced any further by public investments since the level has already been set by the cap. The biggest chunk of carbon revenue, I think, can and should be returned to the people as the rightful owners of our atmosphere." —Eds.

*Sources:* Carol Davenport, "Obama to Take Action to Slash Coal Pollution," *New York Times,* June 1, 2014 (nytimes.com); EPA News Release, June 2, 2014 (yosemite.epa.gov); EPA, National Greenhouse Gas Emissions Data (epa.gov); EPA, "Understanding State Goals under the Clean Power Plan," June 4, 2014 (blog.epa.gov).

---

because some firms end up being able to reduce emissions more cheaply while for others it's more expensive, so they need to be able to trade permits with each other. This is where the phrase "cap and trade" comes from. Cap and trade is really "cap and giveaway and trade." If you don't give away the permits, there's no need to make them tradable.

Who ultimately gets the resulting windfall profits? Well, they're distributed to whoever owns the firms, in proportion to stock ownership. Since stock ownership is very unequal and it's concentrated at the top of the wealth pyramid, most of the returns would go to those households. And some of the money would flow abroad to foreign owners.

A second possibility is cap and spend. It's analogous to tax and spend. In this case, the government doesn't give away the permits, but auctions them. There's an auction held monthly or quarterly. Only so many permits are on the table, and the firms bid for them. If they want to bring carbon into the economy, they need to have enough permits for the next month or the next quarter. The auction revenue is retained by the government, and it can be used to increase government spending on anything you want to imagine: on public education, on environmental C improvements, on foreign wars, you name it. It could be used to cut taxes. It could be used to reduce the deficit. All of those are possible uses of the revenue that comes from a cap-and-spend type policy.

The third possibility is what I'm going to call "cap and dividend." In this case, the money is recycled to the people on an equal per capita basis. In this case, too, permits are auctioned, but a week after the auction—every month or every quarter— you get your share of the money as your dividend. The result is that it protects the purchasing power of working families. The strongest instrumental appeal of a cap-and-dividend policy is that it would make working families whole. It would protect the middle class and working families from impacts of higher fuel prices and thus build in durable support for the climate policy for the decades it will take to achieve the clean-energy transition.

## How Would Cap and Dividend Work?

A carbon price is a regressive tax, one that hits the poor harder than the rich, as a proportion of their incomes. Because fuels are a necessity, not a luxury, they account for a bigger share of the family budget for low-income families than they do for middle-income families, and a bigger share for middle-income families than for high-income families. As you go up the income scale, however, you actually have a bigger carbon footprint—you tend to consume more fuels and more things that are produced and distributed using fuels. You consume more of just about everything— that's what being affluent is all about. So in absolute amounts, if you price carbon, high-income folks are going to pay more than low-income folks.

Under a policy with a carbon price, households' purchasing power is being eroded by that big price increase. But with cap and dividend, money is coming back to them in the form of the dividend. Because income and expenditures are so skewed towards the wealthy, the mean—the average amount of money coming in from the carbon price and being paid back out in equal dividends—is above the median, the amount that the "middle" person pays. So more than 50% of the people would get back more than they pay in under such a policy. As those fuel prices are going up, then, people will say, "I don't mind because I'm getting my share back in a very visible and concrete fashion." It's politically fantastical, I think, to imagine that widespread and durable public support for a climate policy that increases energy prices will succeed in any other way.

There are precedents for doing this kind of thing. The best known is the Alaska Permanent Fund. In the 1970s, the Republican governor of Alaska, Jay Hammond, instituted this policy when North Slope oil production was starting up. What they did in Alaska was impose a royalty payment on every barrel of oil being pumped out. They said that this oil belongs to every Alaskan in equal and common measure—current Alaskans and future generations, too. So what we're going to do is charge a royalty for extracting our oil, put it in what we'll call the Permanent Fund, and use that money in three ways: Part will go for long-term investment. Part will be put into financial assets, so that it will always be there, even after the oil is gone, for future Alaskans. And part of it will be paid out in equal per-person dividends to every man, woman, and child in the state of Alaska. That payment has been as much as about $2,000 a year. This way of providing dividends is not a complicated thing to do. It's not rocket science, folks. It's dead easy.

Apart from helping to support family incomes, I think that this policy has deep philosophical appeal, because it's founded on the principle that we all own the earth's resources, the gifts of creation, in equal and common measure. The planet's limited carbon absorptive capacity does not belong to corporations. It does not belong to governments. It belongs to all of us. Cap and dividend is a way of implementing that sense of common ownership, rather than abdicating ownership—giving it away for free—which we currently have under the open access regime.

Ask people, not only in this country but around the world, "Who owns the air? Who owns the gifts of creation?" The answer you will hear most often is that we all own them in equal and common measure. I think our challenge in addressing climate change is to translate this very widely held philosophical principle into actual policy by which we, as the owners of these gifts, use them responsibly. In the case of the atmosphere's ability to absorb carbon dioxide emissions, that means limiting the amount of carbon we put in the atmosphere. That's what we need to do. ❏

# Chapter 7

# LABOR MARKETS

## INTRODUCTION

**M**ainstream economics textbooks emphasize the ways that labor markets are similar to other markets. In the standard model, labor suppliers (workers) decide how much to work in the same way that producers decide how much to supply, by weighing the revenues against the costs—in this case, the opportunity costs of foregone leisure, and other potential costs of having a job, like physical injury. Workers are paid their marginal product, the extra output the firm gets from employing one extra unit (e.g., hour) of labor. Workers earn different wages because they contribute different marginal products to output. Of course, economists of every stripe acknowledge that, in reality, many non-market factors, such as government assistance programs, unionization, and discrimination, affect labor markets. But in most economics textbooks, these produce only limited deviations from the basic laws of supply and demand.

In "We're Not Lovin' It" (Article 7.1), Nicole Aschoff looks at the recent upsurge in protests and strikes against low wages and poor working conditions in the retail and fast-food sectors. Companies could raise wages and improve conditions, Aschoff argues, and still remain profitable.

Next, Alejandro Reuss addresses the reasons behind union decline in the United States (Article 7.2). While mainstream economists often attribute this trend to the inexorable forces of globalization, Reuss points out that unions have not declined to the same extent in other countries (including the United States' *more* globalized neighbor to the north). He emphasizes, instead, the differences between institutions and policies in different countries and their effects on the balance of power between workers and employers.

John Miller and Jeannette Wicks-Lim take apart the argument, increasingly heard in policy circles, that a large share of unemployment today is a result not of the generalized lack of demand caused by the recession, but of workers not having the skills that employers desire (Article 7.3). In this article, Miller and Wicks-Lim show that this argument has little empirical support and that it shifts the blame for unemployment onto workers themselves.

Next, Miller argues against the *Wall Street Journal* edtiors' view that the Affordable Care Act (ACA, or "Obamacare") wrongly "skews" labor-market decisions (Article 7.4). A Congressional Budget Office report does, indeed, say that some workers will drop out of the labor force as a result of the health-care reform law. The reason, however, is that they will no longer have to stay in bad jobs just to keep their health insurance. This new freedom to quit will, in turn, boost workers' bargaining power. A more comprehensive and universal health reform, such as a single-payer system, Miller argues, could do more.

Next, Gerald Friedman chronicles the rise of "contingent labor," or what he calls the "gig economy" in the United States. In "Dog Walking and College Teaching" (Article 7.5), Friedman shows how labor contracts with little job security have been on the rise in everything from construction and office work to higher education.

Dean Baker focuses, in his article "The False Libertarianism of the Silicon Valley Billionaires" (Article 7.6), on revelations that tech companies illegally conspired to hold down wages (by agreeing not to compete with each other for employees). This arrangement, Baker argues, is revealing, in that it shows the "Silican Valley billion-aires" do not believe that they operate in truly competitive labor markets.

Next, Dan La Botz (Article 7.7) explains what's happened to labor in U.S. truck-ing over the past few decades: shrunken and weakened unions, declining wages, and long work hours (not all of them paid). These trends parallel those that have swept across many U.S. industries.

Finally, David Bacon provides a vivid picture of the conditions and struggles of migrant farm workers in the United States today. Bacon gives an overview of this migrant work force—most of them indigenous people from Mexico, shuttling between the farms of California and Washington State—as a prelude to the poignant first-hand testimony of migrant farmworker and organizer Rosario Ventura (Article 7.8)."

## Discussion Questions

1.  (Article 7.1) What explains the recent upsurge in labor protests and strikes in the retail and fast-food sectors? Why have companies been so adamant on a low-wage strategy when there are examples showing how a high-wage approach can be consistent with profitability?

2.  (Article 7.2) Why has the number of workers represented by unions fallen in the United States over the last few decades? Is globalization, by itself, a plausible explanation?

3.  (Article 7.3) What data support the case that today's high unemployment rates can be attributed to a mismatch between job openings and workers' skills? How do Miller and Wicks-Lim respond to these arguments?

4.  (Article 7.4) Why would the availability of public benefits, like health cover-age, cause people to reduce their work hours? What positive effects does Miller believe would result?

5.  (Article 7.5) Why have "contingent" labor arrangements increased so much in recent decades? How do employers benefit from these arrangements? If workers, on balance, are harmed by reduced job security, why do employers not have a hard time finding people willing to work under such contracts?

6. (Article 7.6) Baker argues that, by their own behavior, Silicon Valley employers have shown that they do not believe they operate in competitive labor markets. What remedies might workers pursue when they are employed in an industry with a few dominant employers? Does the answer depend on whether those employers actively collude with each other or not?

7. (Article 7.7) Trucking is not impacted directly by import competition or global sourcing, yet changing labor conditions in trucking have paralleled those of manufacturing and other sectors. What are the implications for the claim, made by many economists, that globalization explains trends like wage stagnation and union decline?

8. (Article 7.8) Bacon and Ventura describes the low wages and harsh conditions faced by migrant workers in U.S. agriculture, and workers' own organization to try to improve their situation. What sorts of approaches can you think of for improving labor conditions in sectors like agriculture?

Article 7.1

# WE'RE NOT LOVIN' IT
*Low-wage workers fight to make bad jobs better.*

## BY NICOLE ASCHOFF
September/October 2013

There's a line in Johnny Paycheck's 1977 hit song that goes "I'd give the shirt right off my back, if I had the guts to say ... Take this job and shove it, I ain't working here no more." In the past year, fast-food, retail, and warehouse workers have shown they do have the guts—but instead of quitting, they're fighting back. From New York to California they're taking to the streets. They're fighting for a living wage, for respect from their bosses, and in some cases, for the right to form a union.

Back in June 2012, eight immigrant workers peeling crawfish under sweatshop conditions for C.J.'s Seafood (then a Walmart supplier) went on strike in Louisiana. They stayed out for weeks, demanding an end to forced labor, wage theft, and other unfair labor practices—and they won. Following up on the C.J.'s workers' successful action, Walmart warehouse workers in California and Illinois walked out in September, calling for improved workplace safety and a fair wage. A month later, Walmart associates walked out at 28 stores in twelve cities. The strikes marked the first time in history that Walmart retail workers had ever gone on strike, and were quickly followed by more strikes and demonstrations on Black Friday, the biggest shopping day of the year.

Walmart workers took a breather after the fall strikes, as they battled an NLRB lawsuit brought by the company and strategized their next action. But low-wage workers in other cities quickly picked up the baton. On November 29, hundreds of fast-food workers staged a one-day strike in New York City. The walkout marked the launch of Fast Food Forward, a new coalition of workers, unions, and community and civil-rights groups working to increase the wages of New York City fast-food workers. By April of this year, more workers were ready to join the fight. In a wave of strikes that would last through June, fast-food and retail workers in New York, Chicago, Seattle, Milwaukee, St. Louis, and Detroit walked off the job. Pickets popped up at KFC, Jimmy John's, Chipotle, Target, McDonald's, Burger King, Popeye's, Long John Silver's, Subway, Sears, Victoria's Secret, and dozens of other establishments. On August 29, a day after the fiftieth anniversary of the March on Washington, workers took to the streets again. Thousands of workers in nearly sixty cities participated in work stoppages, demanding $15 an hour, respect from management, safe working conditions, better hours, and the right to unionize.

What has sparked this upsurge? It's hard to say. Unions have been trying to gain a foothold in the low-wage service sector for decades—a task made more difficult by the declining bargaining power of unions like the United Food and Commercial Workers union (UFCW) in the face of grocery-industry restructuring. When unions were strong, their very presence pushed up wages and working conditions across the industry, and helped inspire workers hoping to organize a union, or move into existing union jobs in restaurants and supermarkets.

But those days are long gone.

Perhaps a major catalyst to the recent strikes is the nature of the "recovery" from the Great Recession. During the downturn, 78% of jobs lost were either mid-wage or high-wage jobs and, according to the Bureau of Labor Statistics (BLS), three out of five newly created jobs are part-time, low-wage jobs. A growing number of Americans is realizing that "good jobs" aren't coming back, and that for things to get better, they're going to have to fight to turn their McJobs into something better.

## Myths about Retail and Fast Food Jobs

Lousy jobs at fast-food joints and retail stores have been around for a long time. Sam Walton (of Walmart) and Ray Kroc (of McDonald's) designed their business models around underpaying their employees. But experts have always brushed off calls to improve these jobs, arguing that they were stepping-stones—summer jobs for teenagers; flexible, part-time jobs for moms; or extra-cash jobs for retirees. It didn't matter that the jobs paid low wages and offered little opportunity for advancement because they weren't designed to support a family or be a career.

But, as good jobs have steadily disappeared over the past three decades, these rationalizations are starting to sound pretty tired. A recent report by Catherine Ruetschlin at the think-tank Dēmos shows that more than 90% of retail workers are over the age of 20 and that, for the vast majority, this is their full-time, long-term occupation. Labor researchers Stephanie Luce and Naoki Fujita paint a similar picture in a study of New York City-area retail workers. According to their survey, the median age of retail workers in New York is 24 years and the average retail worker has been working in the industry for five years.

## The Hamster Wheel of Low-Wage Work

Widespread coverage of the strikes suggests growing public concern over the sustainability of a McJobs economy. Dozens of newspapers, magazines, and blogs have covered the walkouts and the plight of low-wage workers, with many telling a similar story: After working for years, or even decades, at the minimum wage, workers have little to show for their efforts. They make poverty-level wages. They don't make enough money to pay their bills and provide for their families. They have to beg their bosses for more hours to put food on the table and make them eligible for healthcare, but they are often rebuffed or told that hours are contingent on working harder. Many workers try to improve their job prospects by combining work and school, but in most cases, their wages don't pay enough for tuition, so they drop out or just take one class at a time.

And many retail and fast-food workers describe horrible working conditions. They get burned by the fryers, assaulted by customers, and humiliated by their bosses. If they ask for sick days or time off to heal from injuries, or speak up about unsafe working conditions, their hours are cut, they get harassed by their supervisors, they get demerits, or they get fired. At the recent Left Forum conference, a Brooklyn KFC worker described a common scenario: While covering a late-night shift, her boss would call her from home, screaming at her to get off the clock because there were not enough customers to justify paying her. The worker would have to finish her shift without pay.

This scenario is not unique to KFC. A recent report put out by Fast Food Forward shows that, of the 500 fast-food workers surveyed, nearly 85% had experienced some form of wage theft by their employer. The report corroborates the findings of a major study conducted by the National Employment Law Project (NELP) in 2008. The NELP study demonstrated severe and widespread workplace violations in low-wage industries across the United States, ranging from minimum wage, overtime, and "off-the-clock" violations, employer retaliation and discrimination, and straight-up theft through tip-stealing, illegal payroll deductions, and pay-stub violations (see sidebar, p. 14). Sophisticated workflow software exacerbates the problem. In recent years, companies like Microsoft have put out new software that enables managers to schedule workers down to the minute, calling them in for two-to-four-hour shifts once or twice a week, and telling them to be on call all other days.

## Does It Have to Be This Way?

Big companies and business organizations like the National Restaurant Association and the National Retail Association are vocal in their opposition to wage increases. Spokespeople for Walmart and Target argue that low wages are necessary to keep prices low and provide jobs in the communities where they operate. In a recent op-ed for the Washington Post, Walmart general regional manager Alex Barron argued against legislation to increase the pay of workers at big-box stores in Washington D.C., claiming higher wages would "result in fewer jobs, higher prices and fewer total retail options."

In fast food, the argument against increasing wages is slightly different. Companies like KFC (owned by Yum! Brands) and McDonald's are dominated by franchisees who rent their businesses from the parent corporation. These franchise owners claim that their margins are paper thin as a result of parent company demands, so they simply can't increase wages and stay in business. The Employment Policies Institute, a Washington, D.C., business lobbying group, reiterated this argument recently in a full-page scare ad published in USA Today. The ad warned workers that, if the $15 campaign was successful, owners would be forced to replace workers with "less-costly, automated alternatives like touch-screen ordering and payment devices."

A number of scholars have challenged these arguments, particularly Walmart's low-wages-for-low-prices ultimatum. University of Colorado-Denver management professor Wayne Cascio has shown, through a comparison of Walmart/Sam's Club and Costco, that low wages are not necessary for high profits and productivity. Costco employees average roughly $35, 000 per year ($17 per hour), while Sam's Club workers average roughly $21, 000 per year ($10 per hour) and Walmart workers earn an average of less than $9 an hour. Costco also provides it workers predictable, full-time work and health benefits. However, contrary to popular assumptions, Costco actually scores higher in relative financial and operating performance than Walmart. Its stores are more profitable and more productive, and its customers and employees are happier.

Costco is not exceptional. Zeynep Ton, of MIT's Sloan School of Management, has studied retail operations for a decade and argues that "the presumed trade-off between investment in employees and low prices can be broken." "High-road" employers like Trader Joe's, Wegmans, and the Container Store have all found ways to make high profits and provide decent jobs. Catherine Ruetschlin's research shows that a modest wage increase—bumping up the average annual salary of Walmart or Target workers to $25,000—would barely make a dent in big retailers' bottom line, costing them the equivalent of about 1% of total sales. Even if a company like Walmart passed on half the cost of the increase to customers, the average customer would pay roughly $17 more per year, or about 15 cents per shopping visit. And, considering most low-wage workers spend nearly their entire paycheck on necessities, the industry would see a boost in sales ($4 billion to $5 billion more per year) to its own workers. Fast-food companies are highly profitable. McDonald's alone saw profits more than double between 2007 and 2011. They could easily send some of these profits downstream to franchise owners and workers.

So why do most big retailers and fast-food chains insist on a bad-jobs or "low road" model? There are a few reasons. MIT's Ton argues that labor costs are a large, controllable expense, and retailers generally view them as a "cost-driver" rather than a "sales-driver." Store-level managers are pressured by higher-ups to control labor costs as a percentage of weekly or monthly sales. And because store managers have no control over sales (or merchandise mix, store layout, prices, etc.) they respond to pressure from above by cutting employment or forcing workers to work off-the-clock when sales dip. Another factor is financialization—the increasing dominance of finance in the economy. Firms feel a lot of pressure from Wall Street to be a Walmart and not a Costco. As Gerald Davis has argued, the rise of finance and the dominance of "shareholder value" rhetoric have resulted in an emphasis on short-term profits that register in increased share prices and big CEO bonuses.

---

### Rampant Wage-Theft and Abuse

A 2008 study by the National Employment Law Project (NELP) sought to uncover the scope of exploitative and coercive managerial practices that violate workers' legal rights. As expected, the abuses were myriad. The most common one? Wage-theft. According to the NELP report:
- Over 25% of workers interviewed were regularly paid below the minimum wage.
- Nearly 20% did not receive proper compensation for overtime.
- Nearly 17% had not been paid for off-the-clock work in the previous week.

The managers responsible for workplace abuses exhibit a disregard for labor rights that does not stop at under-payment of wages. The NELP study found many workers still remain in harm's way:
- 12% of tipped workers had experienced tip-theft within the previous week.
- 20% of workers had withheld complaints of wage-theft, dangerous conditions, or similar violations from their employer for fear of retaliation.
- 50% of workers who had filed for workers' compensation faced illegal managerial intimidation in reaction their claim. Common tactics include: denying the claim, calling immigration, or even firing the worker.　　　—Aaron Markiewitz

Perhaps the main reason why companies refuse to invest in creating good jobs is that they can. In this era of neoliberalism, there is little external pressure from unions, community groups, or the government forcing companies to create jobs that offer a predictable, full-time workweek paying decent wages and benefits. When ten Walmart butchers in Jacksonville, Tex., voted for a collective-bargaining agreement in 2000, the company simply negated their decision by eliminating delis from every one of its stores in the United States and switching to pre-packaged meat. Even companies with a positive image like Costco have dumped millions of dollars into fighting pro-worker legislation like the Employee Free Choice Act, preferring a paternalistic strategy over unionization.

## The Alt-Labor Upsurge

The organizations behind the recent fast-food and retail actions, and even the demands of the strikers themselves, vary considerably. However, one unifying characteristic across the movement is the absence of traditional union-organizing strategies, pushing many observers to classify the movement as an alternative labor, or "alt-labor" movement. "Alt-labor" is shorthand for organizations and campaigns that eschew old-school, one-worksite, one-union strategies, in favor of less risky, and often more effective, community-based methods of organizing and outreach.

Alt-labor strategies are not actually new. Workers adopted them in the 1930s, and organizations like New Labor in New Brunswick, N.J., have been around for years, fighting against wage theft and unsafe workplaces. But as labor scholar Janice Fine notes, non-traditional labor organizations have become increasingly important during the past two decades. New organizations like Brooklyn's New York Communities for Change (out of the ashes of ACORN) have appeared on the scene and are registering real gains. NYCC worked as part of WASH New York, a hybrid labor/community group organizing washeros at Astoria Car Wash & Hi-Tek in Queens. The groundbreaking campaign resulted in the first collective-bargaining agreement for New York car-wash workers. NYCC is also behind Fast Food Forward, another hybrid group that is organizing fast-food workers in Brooklyn, using community support networks to help workers stand up for better wages, hours, and working conditions.

The wave of fast-food and retail strikes that spread from New York to St. Louis, Detroit, Seattle, and other cities in April was spearheaded by broad coalitions like Fast Food Forward. These coalitions are comprised of unions like the Service Employees International Union (SEIU), religious organizations, alt-labor groups like Jobs With Justice, community groups, and immigrant-rights groups. They also share common goals—Fast Food Forward, the St. Louis Organizing Committee, the Workers Organizing Committee of Chicago, and other coalitions in Milwaukee, Detroit, and Seattle are all calling for $15 an hour and the right to organize a union. And rather than organizing through one union, one store at a time, the coalitions are targeting the industry as a whole, staging one-day protests designed to inspire other workers and call attention to their struggle.

The Organization United for Respect at Walmart (OUR Walmart) is the grass-roots organization behind the Walmart campaign. OUR Walmart gets much of its funding from UFCW and differs from the fast-food campaigns in that it is explicitly not seeking to form a union. Instead, OUR Walmart's goal is to build a worker-community support network that can pressure Walmart to improve its wages, hours, and working conditions without a collective-bargaining agreement. OUR Walmart has organized short (one-hour or one-day) simultaneous strikes that spotlight Walmart's abuses, while limiting the risk for workers involved. The strategy comes from decades of failing to crack Walmart using traditional organizing strategies.

Many labor scholars laud the actions of these coalitions, but don't see the alt-labor formations as a long-term solution. They argue that because the organizations are funded by external sources like unions, religious organizations, and grants, rather than by members, the organizations will eventually fade away after workers achieve initial successes and the public loses interest. Without a concerted, long-term strategy to unionize, workers will have no way to cement their gains, and will have to keep hitting the streets.

This may be the case, but for many workers, they've got nothing left to lose. There are so few good jobs out there that all strategies with the potential to make bad jobs better and increase wages need to be on the table. Fast-food and retail workers are showing they've got the guts to try something new, and if the past year is sign of things to come, one of these days we might finally have something to sing about on Labor Day. ❑

*Sources:* Catherine Ruetschlin, "Retail's Hidden Potential: How Raising Wages would Benefit Workers, the Industry and the Overall Economy," Dēmos, November 2012; Stephanie Luce and Naoki Fujita, "Discounted Jobs: How Retailers Sell Workers Short," Murphy Institute, City University of New York and Retail Action Project, 2012; Wayne F. Cascio, "Decency Means More than 'Always Low Prices': A Comparison of Costco to Walmart's Sam's Club," *Academy of Management Perspectives*, August 2006; Zeynep Ton, "Why Good Jobs are Good for Retailers," *Harvard Business Review*, January-February 2012; Gerald Davis, *Managed by the Markets: How Finance Re-Shaped America*, Oxford University Press, USA, 2009; Janice Fine, *Worker Centers: Organizing Communities at the Edge of the Dream*, ILR Press, 2006; Annette Bernhardt, et al., "Broken Laws, Unprotected Workers: Violations of Employment and Labor Laws in America's Cities," National Employment Law Project, 2008 (available at unprotectedworkers.org).

Article 7.2

# WHAT'S BEHIND UNION DECLINE?
*It's not just globalization, as a U.S.-Canada comparison shows.*

## BY ALEJANDRO REUSS
May 2015

The total number of union members in the United States peaked between the late 1970s and early 1980s, at over 20 million. As of 2010, it remained near 15 million. The story of union decline in the United States, however, does not begin in the 1980s, nor is it as modest as these figures would suggest. Union density (or the "unionization rate"), the number of workers who are members of unions as a percentage of all employed workers, has been declining in the United States for over half a century. The share of U.S. workers in unions peaked in 1954, at just over 25%. For nonagricultural workers, the high-water mark—at more than one third of employed workers—came even earlier, in 1945. It would reach nearly the same percentage again in the early 1950s, before beginning a long and virtually uninterrupted decline.

By 2010, the U.S. unionization rate was less than 12%. It would be even lower were it not for the growth of public-sector unions since the 1960s. For private-sector workers, the unionization rate is now less than 7%.

There are multiple reasons for union decline, including shrinking employment in highly unionized industries, falling unionization rates within these traditional bastions of unionism, and failures to unionize in new, growing sectors.

Employers' determination to rid themselves of unions has certainly played a major role in declining unionization rates. Where employers could not break unions, they were determined to find ways around them—even during the period of the so-called "capital-labor accord," from the 1940s to the 1970s. In reality, this was less a friendly relationship than a transition, on the part of employers, to low-intensity warfare when a frontal assault was not possible. Unionized companies established parallel non-union operations, a practice sometimes known as "double breasting," gradually shifting production and employment away from their unionized facilities. Some employers began contracting out work formerly done by union employees to non-union subcontractors (the original meaning of "outsourcing"). Some established new operations far from their traditional production centers, especially in less unionized and lower-wage areas. Many companies based in the Northeast and Upper Midwest, for example, set up new production sites in the South and West, and eventually in other countries. Finally, new employers entering highly unionized sectors usually remained non-union. The auto industry is a good example. So-called "transplants" (factories owned by non-U.S. headquartered companies) have accounted for an increasing share of the industry's shrinking labor force, and have remained overwhelmingly non-union.

Historically, union growth has come primarily in short spurts when unions expand into new industries. Since the 1940s, however, U.S. unions have failed to organize in growing industries to compensate for the declines in employment and unionization rates in traditional union strongholds. The public sector represents the one major exception. Since the early 1970s, union density for public-sector workers has increased from about 20% to over 35%. This has not been nearly enough, however, to counteract the decline among private-sector workers. To maintain the overall unionization rates of the 1950s or 1960s, unions would have had to enlist millions more workers in the private sector, especially in services.

## The Employers' Offensive

Since the 1970s, employers have fought unions and unionization drives with increasing aggressiveness, as part of what labor historian Michael Goldfield calls the "employer offensive." Many employers facing unionization drives fire vocal union supporters, both eliminating pro-union campaigners and spreading fear among the other workers. Researchers at the Center for Economic and Policy Research (CEPR) have found that, between 2001 and 2005, pro-union workers were illegally fired in around one-fourth of all union election campaigns. Meanwhile, during many unionization campaigns, employers threaten to shut down the facility (at least in part) if the union wins. Labor researcher Kate Bronfenbrenner reports, in a study from the mid 1990s, that employers threatened plant closings in more than half of all unionization campaigns, and that such threats cut the union victory rate (compared to those in which no such threat was made) by about 30%.

The employer offensive has unfolded, especially since the 1980s, against a backdrop of government hostility towards unions. The federal government has often turned a blind eye to illegal tactics (or "unfair labor practices") routinely used by employers to fight unionization drives. Employer retaliation against workers (by firing or otherwise) for union membership, union activity, or support for unionization is illegal. So is an employer threatening to close a specific plant in response to a unionization drive. However, since the 1980s, union supporters argue, the government agencies tasked with enforcing labor law have increasingly ignored such practices, imposed only "slap on the wrist" punishments, or delayed

**FIGURE 1: UNION MEMBERS AS A PERCENTAGE OF EMPLOYED WORKERS UNITED STATES, 1930-2003**

*Source:* Gerald Mayer, Union Membership Trends in the United States, CRS Report for Congress, August 31, 2004, Table A1, Union Membership in the United States, 1930-2003 (digitalcommons.ilr.cornell.edu/key_workplace/174).

## FIGURE 2: WORK STOPPAGES INVOLVING 1,000 OR MORE WORKERS
## UNITED STATES, 1947-2010

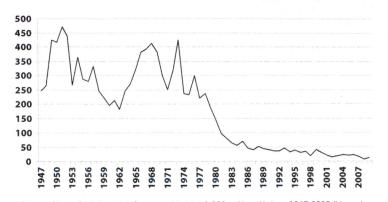

*Source:* Bureau of Labor Statistics, Work Stoppages Involving 1,000 or More Workers, 1947-2008 (bls.gov/news.release/wkstp.t01.htm).

judgment, sometimes for years, long after the unionization drive is over and done with.

Before the 1980s, it was relatively rare for employers to fire striking work-ers and hire "permanent replacements." (Sometimes, employers would bring in replacements during a strike, but striking workers would get their jobs back after a settlement was reached.) During the 1980s, private employers increasingly responded to strikes by firing the strikers and bringing in permanent replace-ments—a practice that is illegal in many countries, but not in the United States. Some labor historians point to the Reagan administration's mass firing of strik-ing air-traffic controllers (members of the Professional Air Traffic Controllers Organization, or PATCO) in 1981 as a deliberate signal to private employers that the government approved their use of permanent replacements (as well as other union-busting tactics). The number of large strikes, already in sharp decline during the preceding few years (possibly due to the employers' offensive, rising unemployment, and other factors), has since declined to microscopic proportions. People do not go out on strike if they feel that they are not only likely to lose, but to lose their jobs in the bargain.

At this point, union density in the United States—less than a tenth of all private-sector workers—is almost back down to its level on the eve of the Great Depression. An optimistic union supporter might note that the 1930s turned out to be the greatest period of union growth in U.S. history, with substantial additional growth in the 1940s and 1950s largely an aftershock of that earlier explosion. There is no guarantee, however, that history will repeat itself, and that the weakness of organized labor today will give way to a new burst of energy. In the midst of a deep recession, and now more than five years of a feeble recovery, there have been few signs of a labor revival. Ironically, only the recent attacks on public-sector workers and unions have provoked a mass-movement fight-back. Labor supporters, however, should understand this, soberly, as coming from a very defensive position.

## Is it Globalization?

Union size and strength have declined not only in the United States, but also in most other high-income countries. The reasons are complex, but globalization has surely played a role. Along with changing patterns of demand and increasing mechanization, global sourcing of production has contributed to employment declines in traditionally high-unionization industries. It has also provided employers with a stronger trump card when workers try to form new unions—the threat to relocate, especially to low-wage countries. To a greater or lesser extent, these effects are probably felt in all high-income countries.

Unionization rates, however, have declined in some countries much more than in others. According to data compiled by economist Gerald Friedman, the unionization rate for the United States peaked earlier, peaked at a lower percentage, and has declined to a lower percentage today, compared to those of most other high-income countries. Today, fourteen high-income countries (out of 15 listed by Friedman) currently have unionization rates higher than the United States' 14%. Ten have rates higher than the U.S. peak of about 26% (reached in 1956). Six have rates above 50%; three, above 80% (Gerald Friedman, "Is Labor Dead?" International Labor and Working Class History, Vol. 75, Issue 1, Table One: The Decline of the Labor Movement). (The declines in the unionization rates for ten of these countries, since each one's peak-unionization year, are shown in Figure 3.)

Let's compare, in more detail, the trajectories of unionization in the United States and its neighbor to the north, Canada (shown in Figure 4). Until the 1960s, the trends in the two countries were similar—declining in the 1920s, bottoming out in the early 1930s, growing dramatically through the rest of the 1930s, the 1940s, and into the 1950s. Since then, however, the two have diverged. The U.S. unionization rate has traced a long and nearly uninterrupted path of decline for the last half century. Meanwhile, the Canadian rate, which had gone into decline

**FIGURE 3: PERCENTAGE DECLINE FROM PEAK UNIONZATION RATE, SELECTED COUNTRIES (PEAK YEAR IN PARENTHESES**

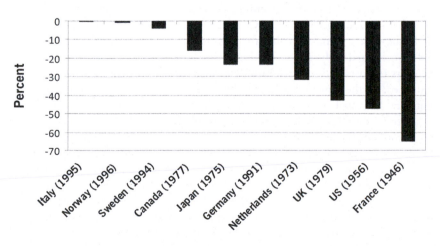

### FIGURE 4: UNIONZATION RATES, CANADA AND UNITED STATES, 1920-2009

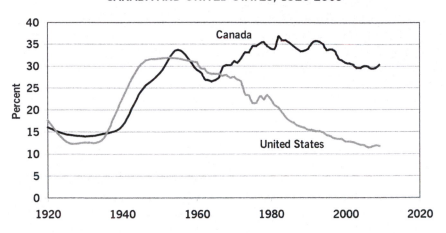

in the 1950s and 1960s, recovered between the 1970s and 1990s. It has declined somewhat since then, but remains nearly three times the U.S. rate (almost 30%, compared to just over 10% for the United States). It would be difficult, even ignoring the Canadian data, to attribute U.S. union decline just to international factors, such as import competition (which became a major factor in the 1970s) or global sourcing (which has been a major factor since the 1990s). These factors simply come too late to fully explain trends going back to the 1950s. Looking at the comparison with Canada, however, drives the point home: "globalization" is simply not the irresistible tidal wave, wiping out unions across the globe, that many commentators claim.

There are a couple of possible explanations for the divergence of U.S. and Canadian unionization rates (or, more generally, the divergence of the unionization rates in any two capitalist economies in the era of globalization).

First, perhaps it is possible for a country to effectively insulate itself from the global economy. That is, it may use controls on international trade and investment to prevent its economy from becoming "globalized" or, more likely, to regulate the ways that it is integrated into the world capitalist economy. That is, however, definitely not what is going on with Canada. It is a member of NAFTA; its economy is highly integrated with that of the United States, both in terms of trade and investment; its imports and exports, as a percentage of GDP, are actually much larger than those of the United States. By any standard Canada has a more globalized economy than the United States.

Second, even if a country's economy is highly integrated into the world capitalist economy, the political and legal environments for labor relations—as well as the history and culture of its labor movement—have tremendous effects on the ability of unions to survive in the age of globalization. A recent report from the Center for Economic and Policy Research (CEPR) attributes the much sharper decline of U.S. unions primarily to "employer opposition to unions—together with relatively weak labor law" in the United States compared to Canada, rather than "structural changes to the economy ... related to globalization or technological progress" (Kris

Warner, "Protecting Fundamental Labor Rights: Lessons from Canada for the United States," CEPR, August 2012, pp. 1, 4).

The report, in particular, focuses on two differences in labor law: In Canada, workers have card-check unionization, the right to form a union once most of the workers in a bargaining unit have signed a union card. This prevents employers from fighting unionization—including by firing union supporters or threatening shut downs, as are common in the United States—during a long, drawn-out period before a union election. (U.S. unions have proposed a similar legislation at the national level, but employers have so far prevented such a bill from passing.) Also, Canadian law requires, in the event that a union and employer cannot arrive at a first collective bargaining agreement, that the two parties enter arbitration. As the CEPR report put it, this "ensure[s] that workers who voted to unionize [are] able to negotiate a contract despite continued employer opposition" (Warner (2012), p. 21). In the United States, in contrast, employers often stonewall in initial negotiations, and many new unions never actually achieve a signed union contract.

A third factor, not discussed in the CEPR report, is the difference between the United States and Canada in laws governing the right to strike. In the United States, it is legal for employers to fire striking workers and hire permanent replacements. Since the late 1970s, when U.S. employers started routinely using permanent replacements, strikes have become much harder for workers to win and, as a result, much less frequent. This has deprived U.S. workers of their main form of bargaining power, the ability to withdraw their labor and shut down production, cutting off the source of the employer's profits. In contrast, most Canadian provinces ban employers from using permanent replacements.

Finally, the CEPR report does note the possibility that weaknesses of the U.S. labor movement itself—especially the "lack of focus on organizing new members" (p. 4)—accounts for at least part of the divergence. Indeed, the labor movements in most capitalist countries have faced changes in employment patterns, and the relative decline of traditional high-unionization industries. As Friedman notes, however, some have been able to make up for declining employment in their traditional strongholds by organizing workers in growing-employment sectors (Friedman, Reigniting the Labor Movement (Routledge, 2008)). The U.S. labor movement—mostly, to be sure, due to the hostile environment for new organizing—has not been able to do so. The Canadian labor movement also differs from U.S. labor in having created an explicitly labor-oriented political party, the New Democratic Party. (Most western European countries also have strong labor, social democratic, or socialist parties with institutional and historical ties to unions.) In many countries, such parties have played an important role in gaining favorable labor legislation, and more generally blunting attacks on labor by employers and governments.

Global economic forces affecting all countries cannot, by themselves, explain the various patterns of union decline across different capitalist countries (or the patterns would be more similar). The differing political environments in different countries—such as the laws protecting workers' rights to form unions, to go on strike, and so on—likely explain most of the differences in the degree of union decline in different high-income countries. ❏

**Sources:** Michael Goldfield, "Labor in American Politics—Its Current Weakness," *The Journal of Politics*, Vol. 48, No. 1. (Feb., 1986), pp. 2-29; Kate Bronfenbrenner, "Final Report: The Effects of Plant Closing or Threat of Plant Closing on the Right of Workers to Organize," *International Publications*, Paper 1, 1996 (digitalcommons.ilr.cornell.edu/intl/1); Gerald Friedman, *Reigniting the Labor Movement: Restoring Means to Ends in a Democratic Labor Movement* (New York: Routledge, 2008); Gerald Mayer, "Union Membership Trends in the United States," CRS Report for Congress, August 31, 2004, Table A1, Union Membership in the United States, 1930-2003 (digitalcommons.ilr.cornell.edu/key_workplace/174); Bureau of Labor Statistics, "Work Stoppages Involving 1,000 or More Workers," 1947-2008 (www.bls.gov/news.release/wkstp.t01.htm); John Schmitt and Ben Zipperer, "Dropping the Ax: Illegal Firings During Union Election Campaigns," Center for Economic and Policy Research, January 2007 (www.cepr.net/documents/publications/unions_2007_01.pdf).

*Article 7.3*

# UNEMPLOYMENT: A JOBS DEFICIT OR A SKILLS DEFICIT?

## BY JOHN MILLER AND JEANNETTE WICKS-LIM

*January/February 2011*

**M**illions of Americans remain unemployed nearly a year and a half after the official end-date of the Great Recession, and the nation's official unemployment rate continues at nearly 10%.

Why? We are being told that it is because—wait for it—workers are not qualified for the jobs that employers are offering.

Yes, it's true. In the aftermath of the deepest downturn since the Great Depression, some pundits and policymakers—and economists—have begun to pin persistently high unemployment on workers' inadequate skills.

The problem, in this view, is a mismatch between job openings and the skills of those looking for work. In economics jargon, this is termed a problem of "structural unemployment," in contrast to the "cyclical unemployment" caused by a downturn in the business cycle.

The skills-gap message is coming from many quarters. Policymaker-in-chief Obama told Congress in February 2009: "Right now, three-quarters of the fastest-growing occupations require more than a high school diploma. And yet, just over half of our citizens have that level of education." His message: workers need to go back to school if they want a place in tomorrow's job market.

The last Democrat in the White House has caught the bug too. Bill Clinton explained in a September 2010 interview, "The last unemployment report said that for the first time in my lifetime, and I'm not young … we are coming out of a recession but job openings are going up twice as fast as new hires. And yet we can all cite cases that we know about where somebody opened a job and 400 people showed up. How could this be? Because people don't have the job skills for the jobs that are open."

Economists and other "experts" are most likely the source of the skills-gap story. Last August, for instance, Narayana Kocherlakota, president of the Federal Reserve Bank of Minneapolis, wrote in a Fed newsletter: "How much of the current unemployment rate is really due to mismatch, as opposed to conditions that the Fed can readily ameliorate? The answer seems to be a lot." Kocherlakota's point was that the Fed's monetary policy tools may be able to spur economic growth, but that won't help if workers have few or the wrong skills. "The Fed does not have a means to transform construction workers into manufacturing workers," he explained.

The skills-mismatch explanation has a lot to recommend it if you're a federal or Fed policymaker: it puts the blame for the economic suffering experienced by the 17% of the U.S. workforce that is unemployed or underemployed on the workers themselves. Even if the Fed or the government did its darndest to boost overall spending, unemployment would be unlikely to subside unless workers upgraded their own skills.

The only problem is that this explanation is basically wrong. The weight of the evidence shows that it is not a mismatch of skills but a lack of demand that lies at the heart of today's severe unemployment problem.

## High-Skill Jobs?

President Obama's claim that new jobs are requiring higher and higher skill levels would tend to support the skills-gap thesis. His interpretation of job-market trends, however, misses the mark. The figure that Obama cited comes from the U.S. Department of Labor's employment projections for 2006 to 2016. Specifically, the DOL reports that among the 30 fastest growing occupations, 22 of them (75%) will typically require more than a high school degree. These occupations include network systems and data communications analysts, computer software engineers, and financial advisors. What he fails to say, however, is that these 22 occupations are projected to represent less than 3% of all U.S. jobs.

What would seem more relevant to the 27 million unemployed and under-employed workers are the occupations with the *largest* growth. These are the occupations that will offer workers the greatest number of new job opportunities. Among the 30 occupations with the largest growth, 70%—21 out of 30—typically do not require more than a high school degree. To become fully qualified for these jobs, workers will only need on-the-job training. The DOL projects that one-quarter of all jobs in 2016 will be in these 21 occupations, which include retail salespeople, food-preparation and food-service workers, and personal and home care aides.

In fact, the DOL employment projections estimate that more than two-thirds (68%) of the jobs in 2016 will be accessible to workers with a high school degree

---

### Labor Market Musical Chairs

To understand the data discussed here, try picturing the U.S. labor market as a game of musical chairs, with a few twists. At any time, chairs (job openings) can be added to the circle and players can sit down (get hired). When the music stops at the end of the month, not all the chairs are filled. Still, many people—far more people than the number of empty chairs—are left standing.

Each month, the Bureau of Labor Statistics reports on what happened in that month's game of labor market musical chairs in its various measures of unemployment and in the Job Openings and Labor Turnover Survey (JOLTS). Here's how the BLS scorecard for labor market musical chairs works.

- Job openings is a snapshot of the number of jobs available on the last day of the month—the number of empty chairs when the music stops.
- Hires are all the new additions to payroll during the month—the number of people who found a chair to sit in while the music was playing. Because many chairs are added to the circle and filled within the same month, the number of hires over a month is typically greater than the number of openings available on the last day of that month.
- Unemployed persons are those who looked for a job that month but couldn't find one—the number of people who played the game but were left standing when the music stopped at the end of the month.

or less. Couple this with the fact that today, nearly two-thirds (62%) of the adult labor force has at least some college experience, and an alleged skills gap fails to be convincing as a driving force behind persistent high unemployment.

## Low-Skill Workers?

If employers were having a hard time finding qualified workers to fill job openings, you'd think that any workers who are qualified would be snapped right up. But what the unemployment data show is that there remains a substantial backlog of experienced workers looking for jobs or for more hours in their existing part-time jobs in those major industries that have begun hiring—including education, healthcare, durable goods manufacturing, and mining.

Most telling are the *underemployed*—those with part-time jobs who want to work full-time. Today there are more underemployed workers in each of the major industries of the private economy than during the period from 2000 to 2007, as Arjun Jayadev and Mike Konczal document in a 2010 paper published by the Roosevelt Institute. Even in the major industries with the highest number of job openings— education and health services, professional and business services, transportation and utilities, leisure and hospitality, and manufacturing—underemployment in 2010 remains at levels twice as high or nearly twice as high as during the earlier period (measured as a percentage of employed workers).

Purveyors of the mismatch theory would have a hard time explaining how it is that underemployed workers who want full-time work do not possess the skills to do the jobs full time that they are already doing, say, 20 hours a week.

More broadly, workers with a diverse set of skills—not just construction workers—lost jobs during the Great Recession. Workers in manufacturing, professional and business services, leisure and hospitality, transportation and utilities, and a host of other industries were turned out of their jobs. And many of these experienced workers are still looking for work. In each of the 16 major industries of the economy unemployment rates in September 2010 were still far higher than they had been at the onset of the Great Recession in December 2007. In the industries with a large number of (cumulative) job openings during the recovery—education and health services, professional and business services, and manufacturing—experienced workers face unemployment rates twice what they were back in December 2007.

There are plenty of experienced workers still looking for work in the industries with job openings. To be faithful to the data, Kocherlakota and the other mismatch proponents would need to show that experienced workers no longer possess the skills to work in their industry, even though that industry employed them no more than three years ago. That seems implausible.

## Statistical Errors

Still, the statistical oddity that Bill Clinton and many economists have pointed to does seem to complicate the picture. If the number of job openings is rising at a good clip yet the number of new hires is growing more slowly and the unemployment rate is stagnant, then maybe employers *are* having trouble finding qualified folks to hire. Once you take a closer looks at the numbers, though, there is less here than meets the eye.

First, the *rate* at which job openings and new hires numbers change over time is not the right place to look. What we really need to know is how the number of unfilled job posts compares to the number of qualified workers employers hire over the same month. If employers in today's recovery are having a hard time finding workers, then the job openings left unfilled at the end of the month should be relatively high compared to the number of newly hired workers that month. In other words, if the number of positions left unfilled at the end of the month relative to the number of new hires rises *above* what we've seen during past recoveries, this would mean that employers are finding it harder to fill their positions with the right workers this time around.

But it turns out that the ratio of unfilled job openings to new hires is approximately the same during this recovery as in the recovery from the 2001 recession. In September 2010, fifteen months into the current economic recovery, the ratio of job posts left unoccupied at the end of the month to the number of monthly new hires stood at 69%—very close to its 67% level in February 2003, fifteen months into the

---

### Where Mismatches May Matter

The skills-mismatch theory does not go very far toward explaining stubbornly high U.S. unemployment. Still, there are unquestionably some unemployed and underemployed workers whose job prospects are limited by "structural" factors.

One kind of structural unemployment that does seem to fit the contours of the Great Recession to at least some degree is that caused by a mismatch of geography: the workers are in one part of the country while the jobs they could get are in another. The housing crisis surely has compromised the ability of unemployed workers to unload their single largest asset, a house, and move to another part of the country. Plus, job losses have been particularly heavy in regions where the housing crisis hit hardest.

But at the same time, lost jobs have been widespread across industries and there is little real evidence of geographic mismatch between job openings and unemployed workers. As labor economist Michael Reich reports, "economic decline and the growth of unemployment have been more widespread than ever before, making it unclear where the unemployed should migrate for greater job opportunities."

Even where there is a skills mismatch, that doesn't mean the government shouldn't get involved. On the contrary, government policies to boost economic demand can help significantly. When demand is high, labor markets become very tight and there are few available workers to hire. Workers previously viewed as "unemployable" get hired, get experience and on-the-job training, and see their overall career prospects brighten.

And, of course, government can fund expanded job-training programs. If the economy continues to slog along with low growth rates and persistent unemployment, the ranks of the long-term unemployed will rise. As they go longer and longer without work, their skills will atrophy or become obsolete and they will face a genuine skills-mismatch problem that will make job-training programs more and more necessary.

last recovery. In other words, today's employers are filling their job openings with the same rate of success as yesterday's employers.

Comparisons that focus on the unemployment rate rather than on the number of new hires are even less meaningful. As hiring picks up at the beginning of an economic recovery, workers who had given up the job search start looking again. This brings them back into the official count of the unemployed, keeping the unemployment rate from dropping even as both job openings and new hires rise.

## Not Enough Jobs

The reality of the situation—the widespread job losses and the long, fruitless job searches of experienced workers—make it clear that today's employment problem is a jobs deficit across the economy, not a skills deficit among those looking for work.

While it's true that any given month ends with some number of unfilled job openings, the total number of jobs added to the economy during this recovery has simply been inadequate to put the unemployed back to work. In fact, if every job that stood open at the end of September 2010 had been filled, 11.7 million officially unemployed workers would still have been jobless.

This recovery has seen far fewer job openings than even the so-called "jobless" recovery following the 2001 recession. Economists Lawrence Mishel, Heidi Shierholz, and Kathryn Edwards of the Economic Policy Institute report that cumulative job openings during the first year of this recovery were roughly 25% lower than during the first year of the recovery following the 2001 recession—that's 10 million fewer jobs. Even in the industries generating the most job openings in the current recovery—education and health services, professional and business services, leisure and hospitality, and manufacturing—the cumulative number of job openings has lagged well behind the figure for those industries during the first year of the recovery from the 2001 recession. (Only the mining and logging category, which accounted for just 0.5% of employment in 2007, has had more job openings during the first year of this recovery than during the first year of the 2001 recovery.)

Why has the pick-up in jobs following the Great Recession been worse than usual? The simple answer is that the recession was worse than usual. The sharp and extreme decline of output and employment in the Great Recession has severely dampened demand—that is, people have not had money to buy things. With the resulting lack of sales, businesses were not willing to either invest or hire; and this in turn has meant a continuing lack of demand.

If businesses have barely resumed hiring, it has not been for lack of profits. By the middle of 2010, corporate profits (adjusted for inflation) were about 60% above their low point at the end of 2008, well on their way back to the peak level of mid-2006. Also, in early 2010 non-financial firms were sitting on almost $2 trillion in cash. There was no lack of ability to invest and hire, but there was a lack of incentive to invest and hire, that is, a lack of an expectation that demand (sales) would rise. As is well known, small businesses have generally accounted for a disproportionately large share of job growth. Yet, since the onset of the Great Recession, small business owners have consistently identified poor sales as their single most important problem—and thus, presumably, what has prevented them from expanding employment.

## The Role of Demand

Regardless of the lack of evidence to support it, the skills-mismatch story has seeped into media coverage of the economy. Take, for example, National Public Radio's recent Morning Edition series titled "Skills gap: holding back the labor market." In one segment, reporter Wendy Kaufman presents anecdotes about employers turning down record numbers of applicants and leaving job openings unfilled. Economist Peter Capelli then comes on and remarks, "You know, a generation ago you'd never expect that somebody could come into a reasonably skilled, sophisticated position in your organization and immediately make a contribution. That's a brand new demand." Now, that comment does not point to today's workers possessing fewer skills or qualifications. Rather, it suggests that employers have raised the bar: they are pickier than in the past.

That makes sense. We've seen that employers are successfully filling positions at about the same rate as in the recent past. What's different this time around is that employers have had up to six unemployed workers competing for every job opening left vacant at the close of the month. This is by far the highest ratio on record with data back to 2000. During the 2001 recession, that ratio rose to just over two unemployed workers for each opening. (In the first years of the "jobless recovery" following the 2001 recession, the ratio continued to rise, but it remained below three to one.) Clearly, these numbers favor the alternative explanation. Unfortunately, Kaufman doesn't even consider it.

That's too bad. Recognizing that a lack of demand for goods and services is to blame for the severe crisis of unemployment puts the focus squarely back on the federal government and on the Fed, which could help to remedy the problem —*if* they had the political will to do so. Millions of unemployed workers, organized and armed with an accurate diagnosis of the problem, could create that political will— unless they are distracted by a wrong-headed diagnosis that tries to blame them for the problem. ❏

*Sources:* Bureau of Labor Statistics Table A-14, Unemployed persons by industry and class of workers, not seasonally adjusted, historical data (bls.gov); Lawrence Mishel, Heidi Shierholz, and Kathryn Anne Edwards, "Reasons for Skepticism About Structural Unemployment," Economic Policy Institute, Briefing Paper #279, September 22, 2010 (epi.org); Arjun Jayadev and Mike Konczal, "The Stagnating Labor Market," The Roosevelt Institute, September 19, 2010 (rooseveltinstitute. org); Bureau of Labor Statistics, Job Openings and Labor Turnover (JOLTS) Highlights, September 2010 (bls.gov); Michael Reich, "High Unemployment after the Great Recession: Why? What Can We Do?," Policy Brief from the Center on Wage and Employment Dynamics, Institute for Research on Labor and Employment, University of California, Berkeley, June 2010 (irle.berkeley.edu/cwed); Narayana Kocherlakota, President Federal Reserve Bank of Minneapolis, "Inside the FOMC," Marquette, Michigan, August 17, 2010 (minneapolisfed.org); Lawrence Mishel and Katherine Anne Edwards, "Bill Clinton Gets It Wrong," Economic Policy Institute, Economic Snapshot, September 27, 2010 (epi.org); "Remarks of President Barack Obama—Address to Joint Session of Congress," February 24, 2009 (whitehouse.gov); "The Skills Gap: Holding Back the Labor Market," Morning Edition, National Public Radio, November 15, 2010 (npr.org).

*Article 7.4*

# SKEW YOU!

**WSJ** *editors are upset that Obamacare makes workers less desperate.*

## BY JOHN MILLER
*March/April 2014*

No less than the Congressional Budget Office reported that the health law is causing Americans to work less or not at all. CBO says the economy will lose the equivalent of two million full-time workers by 2017 and 2.5 million over the next decade.

CBO's conclusion is that ObamaCare will encourage people to supply less labor by deciding not to take a job or by working fewer hours. CBO doesn't note, though we will, that simply extending "free" coverage skews job search decisions by offering an in-kind bonus for unemployment.

The White House seems to [think] that the report is positive because "individuals will be empowered to make choices about their own lives and livelihoods" and "have the opportunity to pursue their dreams." There you have it: the new American dream of not working.

—"The Jobless Care Act," Review and Outlook, *Wall Street Journal*, Feb. 4, 2014.

They just couldn't help themselves. It wasn't enough for the *Wall Street Journal* editors that the Congressional Budget Office (CBO) reported in February that the Affordable Care Act (ACA) was likely to reduce the size of the U.S. workforce by the equivalent of 2.5 million full-time workers in the next decade.

No, the *Journal* editors just had to add, "CBO doesn't note, though we will, that simply extending 'free' coverage skews job search decisions by offering an in-kind bonus for unemployment."

I guess we should be grateful. It's not that often that the *Journal* editors lay bare their dedication to maintaining the tremendous power enjoyed by owners and employers and the paucity of alternatives available to workers and job-seekers in today's labor market. The editors' conception of freedom for workers amounts to little more than nothing left to lose—the right to seek jobs under conditions dictated by employers and enforced by markets, without public-policy interventions, however modest, that might empower job-seekers.

The ACA is a largely pro-business type of reform. A conservative (Heritage Foundation) designed policy, the ACA built reform on the existing private employer-provided health insurance system, and protects the interests of all the big players in the industry (health-care providers, pharmaceutical companies, and especially insurance companies). So what is it, exactly, about the ACA—and the CBO report—that provoked the *Wall Street Journal* to lay bare the power relations of the labor market for all to see?

## Inside the CBO Report

To begin with, what the CBO report, "Labor Market Effects of the Affordable Care Act," didn't say seemed to tick off the editors as much as the White House's insistence that the report was good news. None of the CBO's projection of a smaller labor force comes from a decrease in the demand for labor or the numbers of available jobs—a finding that surely would have been a problem for workers and job-seekers, and would have helped the *Journal* editors build their case against the ACA.

The CBO could not be clearer on this point. Its estimate of the decline in number of hours worked over the next decade, in the words of the report, "stems almost entirely from a net decline in the amount of labor that workers choose to supply, rather than from a net drop in businesses' demand for labor." The CBO calculates that the expansion of Medicaid benefits and health-care subsidies for low-income households in the ACA will boost spending in the economy (net of higher taxes) and, in turn, "boost demand for labor over the next few years."

A decrease in the supply of labor is quite a different story than a decrease in the demand for labor. A decrease in the supply of labor says that workers will choose to work fewer hours, not that they will be unable to find work because of Obamacare.

Why would workers choose to work fewer hours over the next decade? Most fundamentally, fewer workers will be stuck in their jobs because they are afraid of losing their health insurance, as the White House emphasized. A *New York Times* editorial referred to this as just what it is: "freeing workers from the insurance trap." The ACA's subsidy for low-income individuals to purchase private insurance is the most important reason for this effect, according to CBO, followed by the health-care law's expansion of Medicaid.

## Skewing in the Right Direction

The CBO's empirical estimates are, as they admit, "subject to substantial uncertainty." But a reduction in the supply of labor, whatever its exact size, will surely alter labor-market outcomes. For the *WSJ* editors, that amounts to a "skewing" of job-seekers' decision making that needs to opposed. But those changes will empower workers, especially low-income workers.

The CBO's findings show that the ACA will reduce unemployment. The equivalent of 2.5 million full-time workers—counting both those who are unemployed and those who are employed but unable to find full-time work—are looking for jobs. Due to the ACA, the number of unemployed and involuntarily part-time workers will drop. And when full-time workers are harder for employers to come by, job-seekers should find their bargaining power enhanced.

This should also drive up wages of those who do have jobs. That's a result that most any introductory economics student would anticipate. A decrease in the supply of labor reduces the equilibrium quantity of labor (employment) and increases the equilibrium price (the wage rate). In addition, the ACA will reduce federal budget deficits. The report directs the reader to a letter the CBO sent to House Speaker Boehner estimating that the likely effect of repealing the ACA would be "a net increase in the in federal budget deficits of $109 billion over the 2013-22 period." The *WSJ* editors, who have spilled a lot of ink railing against budget deficits, never mention that the ACA will reduce the deficit.

All told, the access to health care afforded by Obamacare undoes the necessity for job-seekers to take undesirable jobs to get health coverage and for workers to stay in undesirable jobs to keep it. The ACA also lowers the unemployment rate, puts upward pressure on wages, and reduces the federal budget deficit.

That's hardly the jobless catastrophe the editors predict. The ACA, however, will "skew" the balance of decision making in favor of job-seekers at the expense of employers, just as the *Journal* editors complain it will. Coming in wake of over three decades of ever-worsening inequality, in which wages have stagnated and profits boomed, while the economy has faltered, a little skewing seems in order.

## Universal Health Care and Power

It will take more than the ACA to turn around the profound inequalities of income and power that plague today's economy and that are enforced by the free-market ideology espoused by the *WSJ* editors and their ilk. Surely a single-payer health-insurance system, or "Medicare for all," would have done more to right the imbalance of power that has crippled our economy and concentrated income gains almost exclusively among the most well-to-do.

While even genuinely universal social programs cannot do it alone—not without other equally fundamental changes, like bigger and stronger labor unions or checks on finance and globalization—they can do some real good for most of us.

Truly universal health care would tend to redistribute income and power in society because it provides all workers—not just low-income workers—with the option of switching jobs without risking the loss of health care. Workers with more options can push for higher wages. Universal health-care coverage would create a share of people's income that comes to them as members of society, and is not proportional to their market incomes or dependent on having a job. That contributes to greater income equality and economic security. And to the extent that people have greater economic security, their political as well as their economic power tends to grow.

Finally, a universal health-care program that, unlike the ACA, operates largely outside of the market would help to show that problems can be solved through shared responsibility. In that way, healthcare as a right—a service provided by all of us to all of us—would also contribute to undoing the notion, so prevalent for the last few decades, that just about everything should be "left to the market."

If Obamacare turns out to be the first step toward universal health care, then perhaps it truly is a threat to the powers-that-be and the free-market ideologues. Imagine that not only healthcare, but also things like education, from daycare to college, were provided universally—to all of us as a right. That just might usher in an era of economic security and well-being, dramatically reducing the desperate choices many face in today's labor market. Now that surely would render the *Journal* editors apoplectic.

But I say—skew them. ❏

*Sources:* Congressional Budget Office, The Budget and Economic Outlook: 2014 to 2024, Appendix B and Appendix C, February 2014; CBO, Letter to Honorable John Boehner, July 24, 2012; *New York Times*, "Freeing Workers From the Insurance Trap," Feb. 4, 2014.

Article 7.5

# DOG WALKING AND COLLEGE TEACHING
*The Rise of the American Gig Economy*

**BY GERALD FRIEDMAN**
March/April 2014

Growing numbers of Americans no longer hold a regular "job" with a long-term connection to a particular business. Instead, they work "gigs" where they are employed on a particular task or for a defined time, with little more connection to their employer than a consumer has with a particular brand of chips. Borrowed from the music industry, the word "gig" has been applied to all sorts of flexible employment (otherwise referred to as "contingent labor," "temp labor," or the "precariat"). Some have praised the rise of the gig economy for freeing workers from the grip of employers' "internal labor markets," where career advancement is tied to a particular business instead of competitive bidding between employers. Rather than being driven by worker preferences, however, the rise of the gig economy comes from employers' drive to lower costs, especially during business downturns. Gig workers experience greater insecurity than workers in traditional jobs and suffer from lack of access to established systems of social insurance.

## FIGURE 1: EMPLOYED WORKERS BY CONTRACT TYPE, 1999

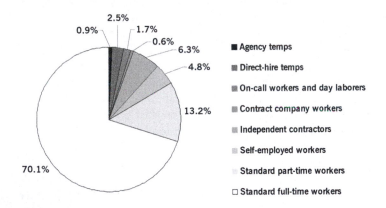

Special surveys by the Bureau of Labor Statistics in 1995, 2001, and 2005, and by the General Accounting Office in 1999, yielded widely varying estimates of the scale of the gig economy. The GAO estimated that as many as 30% of workers were on some type of contingent labor contract, including some categories of workers (self-employed and part-time workers) who are not counted as contingent workers by the BLS. According to BLS, 12% of workers were in "alternative work arrangements" (which includes independent contractors, temporary workers, on-call workers, and workers provided by contract firms) in 1999, similar to the number estimated from more recent surveys.

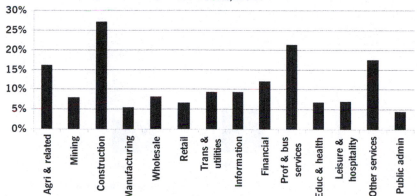

FIGURE 2: SHARE OF WORKERS IN ALTERNATIVE WORK ARRANGEMENTS, BY INDUSTRY, 2005

Contingent workers are employed throughout the economy, in all industries and in virtually all occupations. Workers in what the BLS terms "alternative work arrangements" made up over 11% of employed workers in 2005, according to BLS. Some workers in such arrangements do low-wage work in agriculture, construction, manufacturing, retail trade, and services; others are employed as highly paid financial analysts, lawyers, accountants, and physicians..

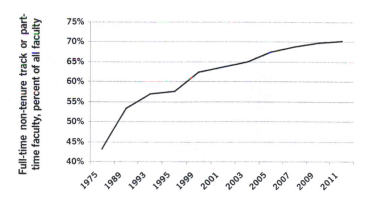

FIGURE 3: CONTINGENT LABOR, COLLEGE AND UNIVERSITY FACULTY

While many people may think of "day laborers" in construction or office "temps" when they think of contingent workers, few occupations have seen as sharp an increase in contingent labor as teaching in higher education. Full-time non-tenure track or part-time professors now account for the great majority of college faculty nationwide. Tenured and tenure-track faculty now comprise less than a third of the teaching staff, and teach barely half of all classes. Colleges and universities hire adjunct faculty because they make it possible to more precisely match faculty to the demand for classes, and because adjuncts are paid substantially less.

## FIGURE 4: AVERAGE COMPENSATION, TRADITIONAL VS. CONTINGENT EMPLOYMENT

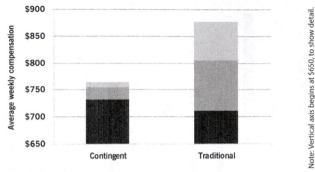

■ Cash wages ■ Government mandated benefits ■ Employer-provided benefits

Employers prefer contingent labor because it is more "flexible." Workers can be laid off at any time in response to a decline in sales. Employers can also pay contingent workers less by not offering benefits. By treating many contingent workers as independent contractors, employers avoid paying for government-mandated benefits (the employer's half of Social Security, unemployment insurance, workers' compensation, etc.). They also usually exclude contingent workers from employer-provided benefits such as health insurance and pensions. Counting wages and benefits, contingent workers are paid substantially less than workers in traditional jobs and are left much more vulnerable to illness or economic downturns.

## FIGURE 5: NET JOB GROWTH, TRADITIONAL VS. CONTINGENT, 1995-2013

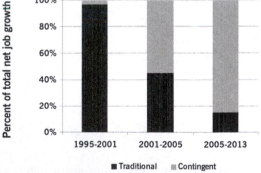

■ Traditional ■ Contingent

While a solid majority of workers is still employed under traditional arrangements, most new net job growth since 2001 has been under "alternative" arrangements. This is in sharp contrast to the late 1990s, when unemployment rates were low and employers had to offer workers more desirable long-term contracts. With the early 2000s recession, followed by the Great Recession and the anemic recovery (2007 to the present), however, employers have shunned long-term employment contracts and workers have had to settle. ❑

*Sources:* General Accounting Office (GAO), Contingent Workers: Incomes and Benefits Lag Behind Those of Rest of Workforce (gao.gov); Bureau of Labor Statistics (BLS), Contingent and Alternative Employment Arrangements, February 2005 and February 2001 (bls.gov); Sharon Cohany, "Workers in Alternative Employment Arrangements." *Monthly Labor Review* (October): 31–46; U.S. Department of Education, National Center for Education Statistics, National Study of Postsecondary Faculty; John Curtis, "Trends in Faculty Employment Status, 1975-2011" (aaup.org).

Article 7.6

# THE FALSE LIBERTARIANISM OF THE SILICON VALLEY BILLIONAIRES

**BY DEAN BAKER**
*January 2014;* The Guardian

Last week Mark Ames published an article that should forever destroy any connection between the Silicon Valley tech billionaires and libertarian worldviews. The article reports on a court case that alleges that Apple, Google, and other Silicon Valley powerhouses actively conspired to keep their workers' wages down. According to documents filed in the case, these companies agreed not to compete for each others' workers dating at least as far back as 2005. Workers in the industry have filed a class action suit that could lead to the payment of billions of dollars in lost wages.

This case is striking at many levels, the most obvious being the effective theft of large amounts of money by some of the richest people on the planet from their employees. This is pernicious, but not altogether surprising. After all, the boss stealing from the workers is as dog bites man as it gets. Few would be surprised that rich people were willing to break the law to get even richer.

The real news here is how the Silicon Valley barons allegedly broke the law. The charge is that they actively colluded to stifle market forces. They collectively acted to prevent their workers from receiving the market-clearing wage. This means not only that they broke the law, and that they acted to undermine the market, but that they really don't think about the market the way libertarians claim to think about the market.

The classic libertarian view of the market is that we have a huge number of people in the market actively competing to buy and sell goods and services. They acknowledge the obvious—some actors are much bigger than others—but there is so much competition that no individual or company can really hope to have much impact on market outcomes.

This point is central to their argument that the government should not interfere with corporate practices. For example, if we think our local cable company is charging too much for cable access, our libertarian friends will insist that the phone company, satellite television, or other competitors will step in to keep prices in line. They would tell the same story if the issue were regulating the airlines, banks, health insurance, or any other sector where there is reason to believe that competition might be limited.

They would tell the same story on the labor side. If we are concerned that workers are getting low wages then the answer is to improve their skills through education and training rather than raise the minimum wage. If workers were worth more than the minimum wage, then the market would already be paying them more than the minimum wage.

They have the same story when it comes to requiring family leave, sick days, or other benefits. Libertarians would say that if workers value these benefits they would negotiate for them and be willing to trade off wages. There is no reason for the government to get involved.

This story about the wonders of the free market is simple in its appeal and it has the great implication that nothing should be done to keep the rich from getting ever richer. However, the Silicon Valley non-compete agreements show that this is not how the tech billionaires believe the market really works. This is just a story they peddle to children and gullible reporters.

If they really believed the market had a deep sea of competitors in which no individual actor could count for much, then their non-compete agreements would serve no purpose. If Google, Apple, Intel, and the other biggies agreed not to hire each others' workers, it really wouldn't affect their pay since there would always be new upstarts ready to jump in and hire away underpaid engineers.

The fact the Silicon Valley honchos took the time to negotiate and presumably enforce these non-compete agreements was because they did not think that there were enough competitors to hire away their workers. They believed that they had enough weight on the buy-side of the market for software engineers that if they agreed to not to compete for workers, they could keep their wages down.

It shouldn't be surprising that the Silicon Valley billionaires really are not libertarians. After all, much of their fortunes rest on patents and copyrights, both of which are government granted monopolies: the opposite of a free market.

But for some reason, seeing the tech whiz-kids forming a cartel to keep down their workers' wages seems an even more direct violation of any belief in libertarian principles. This is the same sort of cartel behavior that we associate with the cigar-chomping robber barons of the late 19th century. It turns out that the biggest difference between the tech billionaires of the Internet Age and the high rollers of the railroad age is the cigars. ❑

Article 7.7

# FROM KINGS OF THE ROAD TO SERFS OF THE COMPANY

*How deregulation has left truck drivers in the dust.*

**BY DAN La BOTZ**
*September/October 2014*

The truck driver was once the king of the road, riding high from the 1950s through the 1970s. Sitting up in the tractor, pulling an eighteen-wheeler, looking out over America's city streets and country roads and highways, he—back then, the driver was almost always a he—earned good money, often had health benefits, and may well have had a pension plan. Hank Williams and Johnny Cash came in loud and clear over the radio, and the driver could see in his mind's eye the truck stop, cup of coffee, and slice of apple pie down the road. True, the hours were long and the work sometimes dangerous and unhealthy, but by and large, trucking was considered a good occupation. That was especially true for those drivers, nearly half a million, who were members of the International Brotherhood of Teamsters (IBT), covered by its freight contract, and who had enough seniority to protect them from layoffs in down times.

Trucking became the stuff of song and story, of legend. Dave Dudley's wonderful "Six Days on the Road"—the story of a truck driver who is a little overweight, way behind schedule, popping pills, and passing everything in sight, but happy because he's "gonna make it home tonight"—became a top hit in 1963. (Even better was the 1968 black blues version of the song by Taj Mahal—at a time when both employers and the union excluded African Americans from jobs as drivers.) A decade later C.W. McCall's song "Convoy" told the story of a mythical truck driver rebellion against the 55-mile per hour speed limit, a tale not so different from the real truckers' shutdown of 1974 over rising oil prices. "Convoy" became the number-one song in 1976 and later a bad movie. Truck drivers, popular culture told us, were lovers and fighters, independent working men in the mythic tradition of the pioneers and the cowpunchers. The romance of the road called to young men who sometimes spent a lifetime working for themselves or for the trucking company and retired with a company pin, a union pension, and nostalgia for their days behind the wheel.

Even back then, there were some serious problems in the trucking business. With recessions in 1975 and again in 1979, the companies began to press for higher productivity. With unemployment high, workers were reluctant to strike. The Teamsters fell under the control of a string of leaders—Frank Fitzsimmons, Jackie Presser, and Roy Williams—who had led the union into subservience to Richard Nixon, the mafia, and the FBI. Presser, whom the *New York Times* called a "Teamster union leader, lackey of the mob, Presidential adviser and top-level Government informer," collaborated with employers while ignoring the needs of rank-and-file union members. The rank-and-file of the 1970s rebelled, carried out wildcat strikes and organized Teamsters for a Democratic Union (TDU), and began a long battle for reform with some success. All these problems and conflicts notwithstanding, until 1980, working in the trucking industry meant a steady job, relatively high pay, and good benefits for hundreds of thousands of American workers.

Those were the days—and they are long over.

"The trucking industry is going to hell in a hand basket." That's what Ben Sizemore, a truck driver for over 35 years, told *Dollars & Sense*. Sizemore is a member of Teamster Local 407 in Cleveland, Ohio—he's one of the lucky ones who still has a union. "The laws have changed in favor of the corporations, and they're putting more of a burden on the driver. The employers today are trying to get more out of you for less. We have gone backwards in wages." Industry experts say that trucking workers' real wages have been driven back to the early 1950s, before there was a national freight contract.

When they don't have a labor union to represent them, drivers not only have low wages, but also work long hours—some of them unpaid. They often deal with difficult working conditions and face significant health and safety issues. Some of the jobs are so bad and pay so little that employers have a hard time filling the seats, with a turnover rate of more than 100% per year among large truck-load firms. If once they were kings of the road, today most truck drivers are serfs toiling on the vast corporate estate we call America. How did this happen? Where are we today? And what are the prospects for the future?

## The Great Depression Leads to Regulation

Truck transportation, replacing horse teams and wagons and supplementing the railroads, only really got rolling in the 1920s—just in time for the Great Crash of 1929 and the Great Depression. With 25% of the population unemployed, anyone and his brother modified their Model Ts, putting a box on the back, and went into the business, leading to fierce competition in local drayage (short-distance) as well as long-haul (intercity) trucking. Cutthroat competition led to the collapse of scores of trucking companies, forced down workers' wages, and made it difficult for shippers to find reliable service. Trucking was a mess.

In response, Congress passed and President Franklin D. Roosevelt signed the Motor Carrier Act of 1935, which regulated the trucking industry's routes and rates, while making it difficult for new companies to enter the business—thus ending the cutthroat competition that had prevailed earlier. The industry was more or less frozen in time as a collection of local cartage companies and regional carriers who moved freight through interline shipments; that is, breaking down and reassembling shipments, passing a barrel or a box from one company to another until it reached its final destination. The result was a government-supervised oligopoly, a legal cartel, but it brought an end to the chaos that the Depression had wrought on the industry.

At the same time the Teamsters succeeded in organizing both city and long-haul drivers in the East, Midwest, and West Coast, winning contracts that provided standard wages, hours, and conditions in numerous cities and even several regions of the country. And Teamsters organized not only the drivers, but also dockworkers and, later, clerical workers, becoming a national, industrial union. When the economy revived as a result of America's entry into World War II, trucking expanded to become a major transportation sector rivaling the railroads. Then, in the late 1950s, Teamster President Jimmy Hoffa began to bring all of the freight hauling companies into what became known as the National Master Freight Agreement. By the 1970s that "pattern agreement" covered 450,000 workers, and influenced—and tended to enhance—contracts covering hundreds of thousands of others.

With the American economy in its prosperous post-war years, the combination of government regulation and union organization created a stable and profitable trucking industry while also making it possible for the companies to pay higher wages and health and pension benefits for workers. We can now see, as economist Thomas Piketty has recently argued, that the "Golden Age"—1940-1970—was an exceptional period in American capitalism. The regulatory system tended to benefit the largest shippers (such as General Motors, Montgomery Ward, and Sears), and big regional trucking companies, as well as a group of highly paid workers, at the expense of smaller, would-be competitors and the general public to whom costs could be passed on. When that period ended, something had to change. The sun shining, the window open, and the breeze blowing in, truck drivers drove their rigs into the future—unaware of what it was to hold.

## The Return of Crisis and Deregulation

The reader may find it surprising that it was Ralph Nader and Ted Kennedy who pushed for deregulation of trucking (along with commercial air travel), setting off the revolution that ended government control of the industry and toppled the Teamsters from the union's stronghold. While Nader and Kennedy initiated the movement, they were part of a broader, bi-partisan consensus in favor of a deregulated economy. When he signed the Motor Carrier Act of 1980, Jimmy Carter promised that it would benefit all the nation's citizens—including labor. But that was not true. For labor it proved a disaster.

The 1980 Act was predicated upon the idea of the free market, removing barriers to the entry of new companies and dismantling regulated routes and rates. The earlier Freight Common Carrier sector now split into two parts: "truck-load" (TL) and "less-than-truck-load." (LTL). Very quickly, says Stephen V. Burks, professor of economics and management at the University of Minnesota in Morris, "companies fled the less-than-truck load freight industry while others flooded the truck-load sector." Existing trucking companies "double breasted"—opened non-union subsidiaries parallel to their existing union operations but paying lower wages, offering fewer benefits, and imposing poorer working conditions. More importantly, thousands of new non-union carriers entered the field. They grew and prospered as union companies collapsed. "The union got slaughtered," says Burks.

The less-than-truckload (LTL) sector of the industry began to shake out, with hundreds of companies failing. Sadly many of these companies first became Employee Stock Ownership Plan (ESOP) ventures that took truck drivers' and dock workers' savings and voluntary wage reductions before finally folding. Today there are about 60 LTL companies, but just a handful such as Conway, YRC Worldwide, Old Dominion, and Arkansas Best Freight (ABF) dominate the industry.

At the same time, other new non-union companies, eventually thousands of them, entered the truckload (TL) freight sector of the industry, where networks of terminals were not required. In fact, one could operate a trucking company with no terminals at all. Today, many drivers pick up freight at one location—an entire truckload—and deliver it to another. Drivers often go into the warehouse and pick up and load the freight themselves on their own unpaid time. This means that the company owner's only capital investment is the truck. It also means that there is no fixed base of operations, or one might say, no workplace. Truck drivers go to work all alone, sometimes at a different location every day, and might not have any contact with other drivers except at a truck stop. This makes it extremely difficult for the Teamsters to organize these workers, the great majority of whom remain non-union.

At the time of deregulation, there were perhaps 200,000 "owner-operators," self-employed drivers who owned their own trucks and worked for truck brokers, trucking companies, or shippers. While at one time the union had organized some owner-operators, by the time of deregulation there were few union members among them. Some of these drivers survived and some went under in the new competitive market, but there are still perhaps 300,000 owner-operators today, almost all non-union.

Finally there is the package sector—the government calls them "couriers"—which requires enormous capital for extensive networks of terminals and equipment. It became reduced to just three large corporations: United Parcel Service (UPS), Federal Express (FedEx), and the United States Postal Service (USPS). (I have not discussed here the private carriers such as Coca Cola and Pepsi Cola, firms with over a thousand trucks and drivers but not part of the for-hire industry.)

## Where Is the Industry and Where Are the Drivers Today?

What was the overall impact of deregulation? "It was effective at its goal," says Ken Paff, the national organizer of Teamsters for a Democratic Union (TDU), a reform group within the Teamsters union. "It drove down costs. The mainstream economists would say it became 'more efficient.' The biggest change was driving down labor costs, because the biggest bill is labor. Fuel is second. Trucks may be third. So that's how costs were driven down by deregulation: by cutting wages."

While the drivers' wages declined, the trucking companies have, by and large, done well. The total tonnage of freight being shipped by truck is up, the best year since 1998. Total trucking industry revenues for 2013, reports the *Journal of Commerce*, rose to $106.6 billion. UPS, the largest, had revenue of $25.6 billion, FedEx $15.4 billion, J.B. Hunt (the leading truck-load carrier), $5.0 billion, and YRC (the leading less-than-truck-load carrier), $4.8 billion. The average profit margin last year, according to *Forbes*, was 6%, compared to 3% to 4% in recent years. In terms of return on investment, profits are even higher. UPS, for example, had a return on investment of 14.62% in the first quarter of 2014, while its five-year return on investment through 2013 was 15.03%.

What did deregulation mean for the Teamsters and their historic freight contract that once covered 450,000 workers? Paff says, "There is no Master Freight Agreement today." Today the freight contract covers only about 35,000 workers, while the related UPS freight contract covers 13,000, and the carhaul (auto

### Truckers' Health Problems

"Long-haul trucking has been recognized as an occupation that is disproportionately det-rimental—when compared to other occupations—to the health, safety, and well-being of drivers." So argue Yorghos Apostolopoulos, Michael Lemke, and Sevil Sönmez in their re-cent article "Risks Endemic to Long-Haul Trucking in North America: Strategies to Protect and Promote Driver Well-Being," published in the environmental and occupational health journal *New Solutions*. "Tractor-trailer drivers function in a work context marked by high physical and psychological workload, erratic schedules, time pressures, disrupted sleep patterns, and resultant ramifications. These stressors have been linked with truckers' ex-cess cardio-metabolic disease, certain types of cancer, and musculo-skeletal and sleep disorders, along with highway crashes that carry serious repercussions not only for truck-ers but also for the general population."

These issues the authors note spill over into society in terms not only of accidents but other social costs. They call for an "Integrated Trucker-Health Protection and Promotion" approach that would focus on: "1) trucking work environment stressors (e.g., lack of healthful workplace resources, mile-based pay, fragmented sleep patterns, team driving); 2) non-work-environment stressors (e.g., absence of social capital and institutional protec-tions, absence of health insurance provision to drivers and their families); and 3) trucker health risk behaviors (e.g., unhealthy diets, lack of exercise)."

While these researchers call for "key stakeholders" to take an interest in this approach which could lead to both greater health and economic efficiency, it seems that for such a program to be successful, workers would need to be fully involved and have a union that they control with the power to make employers and the government treat driver health as the important issue that it is.

transporter) contract covers 7,000. UPS also has 250,000 package car drivers and loaders under union contract, though many of the warehouse workers are part-tim-ers. DHL has 2,000 union workers. Most long-haul freight drivers today have no union and no collective bargaining agreement—and their wages reflect that.

Some experts put the number of unorganized over-the-road drivers at about 800,000, though just how many truck drivers there are is a matter of great debate among the experts. According to the U.S. Bureau of Labor Statistics (BLS), there are about three million truck drivers in the United States. Of these, 1.7 million drive trac-tor trailers, while another 1.3 million or so drive box-style delivery trucks. The tractor drivers earn an average of $18.37 an hour or $38,200 a year for full-time work, says the BLS, while delivery truck drivers average $13.23 per hour or $27,530 per year.

What these statistics don't reveal is one of the biggest problems of truck drivers today: unpaid work. Under current safety regulations governing over-the-road truck drivers, drivers cannot drive more than eleven hours per day or work more than fourteen hours per day. What this means in practice is that drivers who are paid by the trip or the load—not by the hour—may spend anywhere from a half hour to several hours in a day either waiting in line at a warehouse or working loading the truck for no pay at all. The jobs in the truckload freight sector are so demanding and poorly paid that, according to the American Trucking Associations, companies have a nearly 100% turnover rate; that is, each year the company must hire the equivalent of an entire workforce. Companies complain that they can't even fill the seats, much less find enough well-qualified drives.

Michael Belzer, author of *Sweatshops on Wheels: Winners and Losers in Trucking Deregulation*, believes that the biggest reason for the tremendous turnover is unpaid working time. "You need to pay people," says Belzer. "The problem is economic. The driver shortage is not because people are sitting around collecting unemployment or welfare. The problem is that the job is now comparable to fast food or Walmart or ditch digger work. My solution is to pay people a decent living."

Belzer argues that because the companies don't pay workers for delays or non-driving work, there is an enormous loss of efficiency in the national economy while at the same time workers lose out in terms of wages. The answer, he says, is to combine full recording of all hours worked in "electronic logs" or "electronic on-board recorders" (EOBR), technology already produced by a variety of companies, and paying at least the minimum wage for what are currently unpaid hours. The result, he says, would be an increase in the efficiency of the economy and an increase in workers' wages, which would also make it possible to reduce driver turnover. Belzer confesses that while some large employers see the benefit in such an arrangement, there does not now exist the constellation of forces in government, society, and the industry to bring about such a limited re-regulation.

## Port Drivers: A Return to Union Organizing?

After deregulation, the Teamsters turned to organizing everyone from police officers to school employees. Their dues kept the union alive as an institution, but failed to increase workers' power in relation to the employers in the transportation sector which has been the union's heart for decades. TDU leaders, who are supportive of all Teamster organizing, criticize the union's leadership for a scattershot approach that has failed to focus on core Teamster industries, including trucking. The Teamsters union has in the last decade made several efforts to revive organizing in the trucking industry, though so far without much success. An organizing campaign at FedEx that began ten years ago fizzled.

The Teamsters' most recent attempt is a campaign among the 70,000 or more drivers who work in and around the country's seaports, hauling freight from docks to inland warehouses or other destinations. Teamster president Jimmy Hoffa, Jr., the son of past IBT president James R. Hoffa, named Fred Potter, an IBT vice-president and New Jersey Teamster leader to head the Ports Division. Potter, who earned $241,424 in 2012, told the press, "These are going to be nasty campaigns. Workers are going to be challenged, and we want to make sure they are up for the challenge. This is no different in many cases than preparing soldiers for war." So far there have only been skirmishes, though they seem to be growing in significance.

Still, there is certainly an army of low-paid and over-worked drivers out there who might be organized if the workers and the union can find the right strategy. Port drivers around the country are overwhelmingly among the people of color—Asian, Middle Eastern, Latino, and African American—who form part of America's enormous pool of low-wage workers. An in-depth study titled "Big Rig: Poverty, Pollution, and the Misclassification of Truck Drivers at America's Ports," which was produced in 2010 by the National Employment Law Project and Change to Win, a labor federation of which the Teamsters are a member, found, "Port truck drivers work long hours for poverty-level wage."

The authors of the report surveyed 2,183 port drivers in seven locations and found that average net earnings before taxes were $28,783 per year for contractors and $35,000 per year for employees. Contract drivers had to pay "for all truck-related expenses including purchase, fuel, taxes, insurance, maintenance, and repair costs." The report argued that many drivers were misclassified as contractors when in fact they were wage-earners, laying the basis for the Teamsters organizing strategy: turn contractors in wage-earners.

A 2014 update of the report sums up the current situation: "Powerful companies have moved core operations into nebulous networks of undercapitalized subcontractors, both domestic and overseas. And large numbers of workers find themselves beyond the reach of such core labor protections as a minimum wage, unemployment insurance, and Social Security." The report estimates that California port trucking companies are annually liable for between $787 million and $998 million each year for wage and hour violations. This is wage theft of enormous proportions.

Back in July 2008, Hoffa himself showed up at the Oakland Port at the head of a demonstration of 3,000 labor unionists and environmentalists. "Port drivers are on the front lines of this fight for clean air and good jobs," he said. "They toil away every day earning poverty level wages and can't earn enough to pay for the maintenance of their older trucks which are pumping out toxic pollution. This coalition of environmental, community and labor activists has come together for a common cause—to curb pollution in our ports and create good-paying jobs for port drivers."

The Teamsters have encouraged drivers to file complaints with the California State Department of Industrial Relations for wage theft, since they are not paid for all of the hours they work, and hundreds have done so. The Teamsters have also won court cases in various states ruling that so-called independent contractors were actually wage-earners. These cases are important because, as contractors, the drivers were not entitled to sick pay, vacation holidays, or severance pay.

The basis for such rulings has been the fact that the companies—which sometimes illegally required drivers to rent equipment from them—control every aspect of the workers' jobs: when and where they go, what they do, and how they do it. They are in no way independent. In addition to their court cases, the Teamsters have been pushing for several years at both the state and the federal level for new legislation that would in many situations classify owner-operators as employees because they do not really have any control over their jobs. Both trucking industry associations and broader business organizations have opposed such laws.

The second aspect of the Teamster campaign has been to use their alliances with community and environmental groups to push for regulations or legislation requiring cleaner trucks and better practices. Many port drivers had been driving old junk trucks and leaving them idling while standing in line. When the Teamsters pushed for, and won, new environmental regulations that would soon retire trucks built before 2008, the low-paid drivers could not afford to buy new ones—at a cost of $125,000 each. "The new rules forced some drivers out of the Port of Oakland," says Joe Keffer, a long-time labor organizer, now retired, who has worked as a volunteer with port drivers in their organizing efforts. "The company then came in and said, 'We'll buy your truck'." So employers loaned money to drivers for new trucks, turning the drivers into debt peons working to pay off their loans to the bosses. Two prominent blogs—the Working In These Times blog and the *Washington Post*'s Wonkblog—have called this "sharecropping on wheels."

Alex Cherin, executive director of the Harbor Trucking Association at the Port of Los Angeles, an employers' organization, has repeatedly claimed that most of the drivers want to be owner-operators, not wage-earners, and that those who want to be wage-earners can fill any of hundreds of positions available from the companies at the port. Volunteers working with port drivers also report some drivers don't want to be wage-earners and feel threatened by the Teamster strategy. They want to be owner-operators with whatever degree of independence they believe that gives them. Perhaps the Teamsters will have to try another strategy if they are going to organize the ports. Maybe they need to go back to their roots. When the union was founded in 1903, they represented drivers of horse teams, many of whom owned their own horses and wagons. Back in the 1950s and 1960s, the Teamsters succeeded in organizing some owner-operators when they agreed to negotiate both their wages and the costs of maintaining their equipment.

---

### Drivers Strike L.A.-Long Beach, Country's Largest Port, For Five Days

Workers associated with Justice for Port Drivers, a Teamster-backed group, struck at the adjoining ports of Los Angeles and Long Beach on Monday, July 7. The picket lines, at the largest seaport in the United States, handling most of the enormous trade from China, lasted for five days. The 120 drivers employed by Total Transportation Services Inc., Green Fleet Systems, and Pacific 9 were demanding to be treated as wage-earners rather than as independent contractors.

This was one of a series of small "demonstration strikes" calling attention to port truckers' issues, though this one had a larger impact than the others. The drivers picketed at four terminals, taking advantage of the fact that the contract between the Pacific Maritime Association (PMA), which represents shipping companies, and the International Longshore and Warehouse Union (ILWU), which represents all West Coast stevedores, had expired and negotiations were ongoing. With no PMA-ILWU contract in force, on their own initiative some ILWU members joined the picket line, at least at first. Their action briefly paralyzed Evergreen, APL, and Yusen terminals in Los Angeles and the Long Beach Container Terminal.

After a labor arbitrator ruled that the strike was not legitimate, employers and the union informed ILWU members that they had to return to work—breaking a long tradition of ILWU workers honoring others' picket lines. Los Angeles Mayor Eric Garcetti then intervened, holding a meeting with the port drivers who agreed to a "five-day cooling off period." The small strike had an equally slight impact on the movement of freight at the port, but it showed the drivers continued commitment to win their status as wage-earners.

When I talked to Ben Sizemore the other day, he was driving through West Virginia down to Charlotte, S.C. He told me in his twangy accent that things weren't right out there on the road. "These guys are working like they should to make a living, but they are not getting home time with their wives and families. They're not being paid what they deserve. That's what the American dream is all about, isn't it: a fair day's work for a fair day's pay—and it's gotten away from that."

What can be done to improve conditions for truck drivers? The most important thing is union organization and the use of union power to fight back against the companies that dominate the industry. While the Teamsters organizing deserves support, it is difficult to imagine that it will be successful without a truly democratic union movement that can tap the knowledge, creativity, and righteous indignation of both wage-earners and owner-operators. Even then the union will need allies in the social movements, such as we saw in the brief alliance between the ILWU in Longview and the Occupy movement. Only with such a broad class movement will it be possible to take on the industry. When that sort of alliance arises again—democratic, militant, and from below—there will be the possibility of lifting drivers out of serfdom. ❏

**Sources:** Dave Dudley, "Six Days on the Road," Grand Ole Opry live TV performance, October, 1966 (youtube.com); Taj Mahal, "Six Days on the Road," from the 1968 Columbia Records album Giant Step/De Ole Folks at Home, (youtube.com); Richard D. Leone, *The Negro in the Trucking Industry*, Industrial Research Unit, Wharton School of Finance and Commerce, (University of Pennsylvania Press, 1970); C.W. McCall, "Convoy" 1975 (youtube.com); Howard K. Smith (reporter), "Truckers' Strike Causes Widespread Unemployment and Shortages," ABC Evening News, February 6, 1974, Valderbilt Television News Archive (tvnews.vanderbilt.edu);. Ben A. Franklin, "Ex-F.B.I. Agent Links Teamsters' Chief to Crimes," *New York Times*, February 18, 1983; William Serrin, "Jackie Presser's Secret Lives Detailed in Government Files," *New York Times*, March 27, 1989; Thomas Piketty, Capital in the Twenty-First Century (Harvard University Press, 2014); John Berlau, "Ted Kennedy's Deregulatory Legacy on Airlines and Trucking," Competitive Enterprise Institute, August 26, 2009 (cei.org); National Center for Employee Ownership, "How an Employee Stock Ownership Plan (ESOP) Works" (nceo.org); William B. Cassidy, "Top 50 Trucking Companies Rode their Breaks in 2013," *Journal of Commerce*, April 16, 2014 (joc.com); Mary Ellen Biery, "U.S. Trucking Companies Deliver Sales, Profit Gains," Forbes, February 20, 2014 (forbes.com); "United Parcel Service's ROI per Quarter," CSIMarket.com, 2013 (csimarket.com); "UPS's ROI Over the Last Five Years," CSIMarket.com, 2013 (csimarket.com); "Occupational Outlook Handbook: Transportation and Material Moving Occupations," Bureau of Labor Statistics (bls.gov); "Summary of Hours of Service Regulations," Federal Motor Carrier Safety Administration (dot.gov); "Truckload Turnover Ticks Down in Third Quarter," American Trucking Association press release, December 11, 2013 (truckline.com); Michael H. Belzer, Sweatshops on Wheels: Winners and Losers in Trucking Deregulation (Oxford University Press, 2000); J.J. Keller & Associates website (jjkeller.com); Steven Greenhouse, "Teamsters Hope to Lure FedEx Drivers," *New York Times*, May 30, 2006; "Annual $150,000 Club Report, 2012," Teamsters for a Democratic Union (tdu.org); Brian Sumer, "Teamsters persist in drive to unionize truckers at L.A. and Long Beach ports," *Daily Breeze*, May 3, 2013 (dailybreeze.com); Rebecca Smith, David Bensman, and Paul Alexander Marvy, "The Big Rig: Poverty, Pollution, and the Misclassification of Truck Drivers at America's Ports," National Employment Law Project and Change to Win, December 2010 (nelp.org); Rebecca Smith, David Bensman, and Paul Alexander

Marvy and John Zerolnick,"The Big Rig Overhaul: Restoring Middle-Class Jobs at America's Ports Though Labor Law Enforcement," National Employment Law Project and Change to Win, March 2014 (justice4ladrivers.net); "Hoffa Joins Thousands of Workers to Support Clean and Safe Ports in Oakland ," Teamsters press release, July 22, 2008 (teamster.org); James Jaillet, "Federal court says fleet's drivers are employees, not contractors in Calif. Ruling," *Overdrive* magazine, June 17, 2014 (overdriveonline.com); Jill Dunn, "Federal, state governments review owner-operator status," *Overdrive* magazine, March 02, 2012 (overdriveonline.com); Jill Dunn, "Clean Ports bill floated in Congress," *Overdrive* magazine, August 29, 2013 (overdriveonline.com); Sarah Jaffe, "Sharecropping on Wheels," Working In These Times blog, May 15, 2013 (inthesetimes.com/ working/); Lydia DePillis "Teamsters score a win against 'sharecropping on wheels.' But will the trucking industry really change?" *Washington Post* Wonkblog, March 22, 2014 (washingtonpost. com/blogs/wonkblog/); Ricardo Lopez, "Port truck drivers launch strike to protest alleged labor violations," *Los Angeles Times*, April 18, 2014; Pacific Maritime Association (pmanet.org); International Longshore and Warehouse Union (ilwu.org); Robert Brenner and Suzi Weissman, "Unions that Used to Strike," *Jacobin* magazine, August 6, 2014 (jacobinmag.com); Karen Robes Meeks, "ILWU joins picketing truck drivers and Long Beach, LA ports," *Long Beach Press Telegram*, April 28, 2014 (presstelegram.com); Andrew Khouri, "Truckers strike briefly shuts 4 terminals at L.A., Long Beach ports," *Los Angeles Times*, July 8, 2014 (latimes.com); Bill Mongelluzzo, "Arbitrator Rules ILWU Workers Must Return to Work at LA," *Journal of Commerce*, July 8, 2014 (joc.com); Yorghos Apostolopoulos, Michael Lemke, and Sevil Sönmez, "Risks Endemic to Long-Haul Trucking in North America: Strategies to Protect and Promote Driver Well-Being," *New Solutions* magazine, January, 2014 (ncbi.nlm.nih.gov).

*Article 7.8*

# THESE THINGS CAN CHANGE

## BY DAVID BACON AND ROSARIO VENTURA
*March/April 2015*

In 2013, Rosario Ventura and her husband Isidro Silva were strikers at Sakuma Brothers Farms in Burlington, Wash. In the course of three months in 2013, over 250 workers walked out of the fields several times, as their anger grew over their wages and the conditions in the labor camp where they lived.

Every year, the company hires between 700 and 800 people to pick strawberries, blueberries, and blackberries. During World War II, the Sakumas were interned by the U.S. government because of their Japanese ancestry, and would have lost their land, as many Japanese farmers did, had it not been held in trust for them by another local rancher until the war ended. Today, the business has grown far beyond its immigrant roots, and is one of the largest berry growers in Washington, where berries are big business, with annual sales of $6.1 million, and big corporate customers like Häagen Dazs ice cream. Sakuma Farms owns a retail outlet, a freezer and processing plant, and a chain of nurseries in California that grow rootstock.

By contrast, Sakuma workers have very few resources. Some are local workers, but over half are migrants from California, like Ventura and her family. Both the local workers and the California migrants are immigrants, coming from indigenous towns in Oaxaca and southern Mexico where people speak languages like Mixteco and Triqui. While all farm workers in the United States are poorly paid, these new indigenous arrivals are at the bottom. One recent study in California found that tens of thousands of indigenous farm workers received less than minimum wage.

In 2013, Ventura and other angry workers formed an independent union, Familias Unidas por la Justicia—Families United for Justice. In fitful negotiations with the company, they discovered that Sakuma Farms had been certified to bring in 160 H-2A guest workers. The H-2A program was established in 1986, to allow U.S. agricultural employers to hire workers in other countries and bring them to the United States. In this program, the company first must certify that it has tried to hire workers locally. If it can't find workers at the wage set by the state employment department, and the department agrees that the company has offered the jobs, the grower can then hire workers from outside the country. The U.S. government provides visas that allow guest workers to work only for that employer, and only for a set period of time, less than a year. Afterwards, they must return to their home country. If they're fired or lose their job before the contract is over, they must leave right away. Growers must apply for the program each year. On hearing about the application, the striking workers felt that the company was trying to find a new workforce to replace them.

When I questioned someone from the company about why it needed guest workers, he said they couldn't find enough workers to pick their berries. But the farm was also unwilling to raise wages to attract more pickers. "If we [do], it unscales it for the other farmers," said owner Ryan Sakuma in an interview. "We're just robbing from the total [number of workers available]. And we couldn't attract them without raising the price hugely to price other growers out. That would just create a price war." He pegged his farm's wages to the H-2A program: "Everyone at the company will get the H-2A wage for this work."

"The H-2A program limits what's possible for all workers," says Rosalinda Guillén, director of Community2Community, an organization that helped the strikers. Community2Community, based in Bellingham, Wash., advocates for farm worker rights, especially those of women, in a sustainable food system. After the strikes, Sakuma Farms applied for H-2A work visas for 438 workers, saying that the strikers weren't available to work because they had all been fired. Under worker and community pressure, the U.S. Department of Labor (USDoL) did not approve Sakuma's application. Sakuma has still not recognized the union, and many workers feel their jobs are still in danger.

A decade ago there were hardly any H-2A workers in Washington State. In 2013, the USDoL certified applications for 6,251 workers, double the number in 2011. And the irony, of course, is that one group of immigrant workers, recruited as guest workers, is being pitted against another group—the migrants who have been coming to work at the company for many years.

As she sat in her home in Madera, Calif., Rosario Ventura described the personal history that led her to migrate yearly from California to Washington, and then become a striker: —*David Bacon*

## Rosario Ventura: In Her Own Words

I came from Oaxaca in 2001, from San Martín Itunyoso. It is a Triqui town [where the indigenous language Trinqui is spoken], and that's what I grew up speaking. My mother and father were farmers, and worked on the land that belongs to the town. It was just enough to grow what we ate, but sometimes there was nothing to eat, and no money to buy food.

There wasn't much work in Oaxaca, so my parents would go to Sinaloa [in northern Mexico]. I began to go with them when I was young, I don't remember how old I was. It costs a lot of money to go to school and my parents had no way to get it. In Mexico you have to buy a uniform for every grade. You have to buy the pencils, notebooks, things the children need. My brothers went to school, though. I was the only one that didn't go, because I was a girl.

When I told my dad I wanted to come to the U.S., he tried to convince me not to leave. When you leave, it is forever—that is what he said, because we never return. You won't even call, he said. And it did turn out that way. Now I don't talk with him because I know if I do, it will bring him sadness. He'll ask, when are you coming back? What can I say?

I would like to return to live with him, since he is alone. But I can't get the money to go back. There is no money, there is nothing to eat, in San Martín Itunyoso. I thought that I would save up something here and return. But it is hard here too. It's the same situation here in the U.S. We work to try to get ahead, but we never do. We're always earning just enough to buy food and pay rent. Everything gets used up.

It is easy to leave the U.S., but difficult to come back and cross the border. When I came, it cost two thousand dollars to cross, walking day and night in Arizona. We had to carry our own water and food. Out there in the desert it is life and death if you do not have any. It took a week and a half of pure walking. We would rest a couple of hours and get up to walk again.

Those who bring children suffer the most because they have to carry water and food for them, and sometimes carry the children themselves. Thank God we all crossed and were OK. But now that I'm here I'm always afraid because I don't have papers. I can never relax or be at ease.

When I crossed the border I came alone, and then found my brothers, who were already here in Madera. They took me to Washington State to work at Sakuma Farms. I met Isidro when I was working, and we got married in 2003. He speaks Mixteco and I speak Triqui, but that did not matter to us. In those times I hardly spoke Spanish, but now I know a little more.

When I came here, they were pruning the plants. That is very hard work because you get cut and the branches hit your face. When I was in Oaxaca, thinking of coming, I was expecting a different type of work. But this is all there is. People who know how to read and write or have papers can get easier jobs. The rest of us work in the fields.

At Sakuma Farms the company was always hard on us. They would tell us, "you came to pick, and you have to make weight." If you don't make weight they won't let you work for a few days. If you still can't make weight, they pull you out of the field and fire you. But when you're working, and you take what you've picked to be weighed, they always cheat you of two or three pounds.

I've always lived in the labor camp during the picking season. We decided to continue living in Madera, and never moved to Washington permanently. When it gets really hot in the San Joaquin Valley in the summer we go to Washington, where it's cooler. Then when it gets cold there and the work runs out, we come back to Madera. We go every season.

When we go to Washington we have to rent someplace in Madera to store our belongings, like our clothes. Then when we return we have to search for a new home again. It is a hassle. This year we left the house where we'd been living with my brother instead, because he didn't go to Washington. We all live here—Isidro, my four children, my brothers and sisters, and their children. The family pays two thousand a month for the whole house, and Isidro and I pay three hundred as our share.

When we're in Washington we have to save for the winter season, because there's no work until April. I don't work in Madera because I can't find childcare. The trip to Washington is expensive—about $250 in gas and food. If we don't have enough money, we have to ask for a loan. That's what we normally do, since by then we've used up what we saved from the previous year. There is a food bank in Washington, which helps when we get there.

With the strikes last year in Washington we were out of work for almost two months. We didn't save anything, so it was very hard for us afterwards. We didn't have enough to pay the bills, and we couldn't find work. The strikes started when the company fired Federico [a coworker]. We wanted Sakuma to raise the [piece rate] price, and the company refused. They told us if we want to work, work. Then they accused Federico of starting a protest. They went to his cabin, to kick him out of the camp. That's when we stopped work, to get his job back.

We were also upset about the conditions in the labor camp. The mattress they gave us was torn and dirty, and the wire was coming out and poked us. We're accustomed to sleeping with the children, but the bed was so small we couldn't even fit on it. There were cockroaches and rats. The roof leaked when it rained. They just put bags in the holes and it still leaked. All my children's clothes were wet.

They told us they would change things, and the county inspector would come check the cabin. But the company man in charge of the camp told me: "If the inspector comes, don't show him your bed. Don't say anything or you will have a lot of problems." So when the inspector came the company man followed him and didn't let me say anything.

They always try to make us afraid to speak up. If you ask for another five cents they fire you. They threatened to remove us from the camp because of the strikes, and said they'd fire us. They are always threatening us. They fired Ramón also [the leader of the strike and union] because he talked back to them. But thank God he had the courage to talk.

I think there will be strikes again this coming year, if the company doesn't come to its senses, and as long as we have support. We can't leave things like this. There is too much abuse. We are making them rich and making ourselves poor. It's not fair. I think these things can change if we all keep at it. We won't let them keep on going like this. We have to change them. It is important that they raise wages, treat us right, and help the farmworkers. All the mistreatment, threats, everything—it isn't fair.

I want to work, to have money, to be in a better place. I want a little house and to stay in one place with my kids. That's all I'm hoping for. I'd like to see my children reach high school and maybe college. If they don't, I want to go back to Mexico, if I can save money. My kids can go to school there too. I want them to continue studying. I don't want my children to work for Sakuma. ❏

# Chapter 8

# THE DISTRIBUTION OF INCOME AND WEALTH

## INTRODUCTION

For many mainstream economists, inequality in the distribution of income is a natural outcome of the functioning of markets. If workers get paid based on productivity, wage differences simply reflect underlying differences in productivity.

People who supply other inputs—investors or lenders supplying capital, landowners supplying land—are similarly rewarded according to the marginal products of those inputs. Even poverty is largely seen as a result of low productivity, which can be interpreted more compassionately as the consequence of a lack of education and training, or, at an extreme, as a result of shirking and a whole host of moral failings. President Reagan's deliberate use of the term "welfare queen" to cast poor, black women as undeserving of society's support is perhaps the most famous example of the latter. Indeed, in this view, a high degree of equality (or measures aimed at reducing inequality) would reduce the incentives for increasing productivity, slowing overall growth. Economists also argue that because the rich tend to save more (thus swelling the pool of resources available for investment), the larger the share of the economic pie that goes to them, the better the entire economy does. Trickle on down!

Chris Tilly, in his remarkable essay "Geese, Golden Eggs, and Traps" (Article 8.1), lays out the arguments for and against income equality and then takes down the rosy view of the economic benefits of inequality. His analysis shows how economies such as the United States' can end up in an "inequality trap" where high inequality leads to low growth, which in turn can lead to even higher inequality.

Dean Baker ("Inequality: The Silly Tales Economists Like to Tell," Article 8.2) rebuts mainstream economists' claims that globalization and technological change are the causes of rising inequality (and their implicit view that there is, therefore, nothing that can be done about it). Technological change, he argues, affects both lower-income and higher-income individuals. Meanwhile, the only reason that lower-income workers have borne the brunt of globalization is that, unlike high-income professionals, they lack the political power to secure protection from global competition.

The next two articles look at patterns of inequality along lines of gender and race. In his article "The Wages of Gender" (Article 8.3), Gerald Friedman reports that the gender income gap has narrowed in recent decades, owing to increased educational and work opportunities for women. There is still, however, a long way to go to achieve full equality. Meanwhile, Arthur MacEwan observes, in his article "Black-White Income Differences: What's Happened?" (Article 8.4), the income gap between African Americans and whites has hardly budged since 1970. This seeming lack of change, moreover, masks an increase in income inequality among African Americans—with a small number of success stories at the top hiding a worsening of the fortunes of low-income African Americans.

The next two articles return to the balance of power between workers and employers and its effects on the distribution of income. Arthur MacEwan points out that the income share of the richest 1% rose when the share of workers who were union members fell. To MacEwan it seems clear that restoring union size and strength would go a long way toward reducing inequality (Article 8.5).

For anyone who wants to explore questions of inequality and fairness, Gar Alperovitz and Lew Daly's article "The Undeserving Rich" (Article 8.6) provides some fascinating grist for the mill. They argue that growth is built on a base of collectively produced knowledge that each generation inherits—not merely on the efforts of individuals.

In his article "The Great Land Giveaway in Mozambique" (Article 8.7), Timothy A. Wise describes a recent government attempt to turn over small farmers' land to international investors. As he points out, however, the farmers themselves organized and fought off the attempted "land grab."

Finally, Gerald Friedman (Article 8.8) describes one of the most extreme manifestations of inequality and poverty in the United States today, widespread food insecurity. He notes that government nutrition programs have positive impacts both in terms of short-term alleviation of hunger and long-term health and economic benefits for recipients—but are just not extensive enough.

## Discussion Questions

1. (Article 8.1) According to Tilly, many of the mechanisms linking equality and growth are political. Should economic models incorporate political behavior as well as economic behavior? What are some ways they could do that?

2. (Article 8.1) Explain Tilly's metaphor about the "Goose that Laid the Golden Eggs." How is equality the goose?

3. (Article 8.2) Why does Baker think that increasing inequality is not simply due to unavoidable processes of globalization and technological change? How is economic inequality, in Baker's analysis, related to inequalities in political power?

4. (Article 8.3) What are the key factors explaining the decline of the wage gap between men and women? Has this always been because women's compensation has grown spectacularly?

5. (Article 8.3) According to Friedman, what have been the wider social consequences of the increase in women's educational and work opportunities, and in turn their increasing role as household "breadwinners"?

6.  (Article 8.4) MacEwan notes some spectacular African American "success stories" and, more broadly, an increase in opportunities for African American professionals. Nonetheless, the black-white income gap has hardly budged. Why not? What factors does he blame for the worsening fortunes of many African Americans?

7.  (Article 8.5) MacEwan shows that union strength and economic inequality are negatively associated (when one is high, the other is low). What possible explanations does MacEwan offer? Is there good reason to believe that higher unionization was the cause of greater equality in the past, and the decline of unions explains increased inequality in recent years?

8.  (Article 8.6) Consider the following quotation:

    > "I think we've been through a period where too many people have been given to understand that if they have a problem, it's the government's job to cope with it. ... They're casting their problem on society. And, you know, there is no such thing as society. There are individual men and women, and there are families."
    > —British Prime Minister Margaret Thatcher, talking to *Women's Own* magazine, October 31, 1987

    After reading Gar Alperovitz and Lew Daly's article "The Undeserving Rich," how do you think they would respond to Thatcher? How would you respond?

9.  (Article 8.7) According to Wise, why did the ProSAVANA project fail? Do governments in developing countries have to engage in large-scale land giveaways to international investors, in order to develop their agricultural sectors? What alternative approaches might they take?

10. (Article 8.8) If, as Friedman says, the United States is "wealthy enough that everyone could have enough to eat," why do people go hungry anyway? In your view, what could and should be done to remedy this situation?

# GEESE, GOLDEN EGGS, AND TRAPS

*Why inequality is bad for the economy.*

**BY CHRIS TILLY**
*July/August 2004*

Whenever progressives propose ways to redistribute wealth from the rich to those with low and moderate incomes, conservative politicians and economists accuse them of trying to kill the goose that lays the golden egg. The advocates of unfettered capitalism proclaim that inequality is good for the economy because it promotes economic growth. Unequal incomes, they say, provide the incentives necessary to guide productive economic decisions by businesses and individuals. Try to reduce inequality, and you'll sap growth. Furthermore, the conservatives argue, growth actually promotes equality by boosting the have-nots more than the haves. So instead of fiddling with who gets how much, the best way to help those at the bottom is to pump up growth.

But these conservative prescriptions are absolutely, dangerously wrong. Instead of the goose-killer, equality turns out to be the goose. Inequality stifles growth; equality gooses it up. Moreover, economic expansion does not necessarily promote equality—instead, it is the types of jobs and the rules of the economic game that matter most.

## Inequality: Goose or Goose-Killer?

The conservative argument may be wrong, but it's straightforward. Inequality is good for the economy, conservatives say, because it provides the right incentives for innovation and economic growth. First of all, people will only have the motivation to work hard, innovate, and invest wisely if the economic system rewards them for good economic choices and penalizes bad ones. Robin Hood-style policies that collect from the wealthy and help those who are worse off violate this principle. They reduce the payoff to smart decisions and lessen the sting of dumb ones. The result: people and companies are bound to make less efficient decisions. "We must allow [individuals] to fail, as well as succeed, and we must replace the nanny state with a regime of self-reliance and self-respect," writes conservative lawyer Stephen Kinsella in *The Freeman: Ideas on Liberty* (not clear how the free woman fits in). To prove their point, conservatives point to the former state socialist countries, whose economies had become stagnant and inefficient by the time they fell at the end of the 1980s.

If you don't buy this incentive story, there's always the well-worn trickle-down theory. To grow, the economy needs productive investments: new offices, factories, computers, and machines. To finance such investments takes a pool of savings. The rich save a larger fraction of their incomes than those less well-off. So to spur growth, give more to the well-heeled (or at least take less away from them in the form of taxes), and give less to the down-and-out. The rich will save their money and then invest it, promoting growth that's good for everyone.

Unfortunately for trickle-down, the brilliant economist John Maynard Keynes debunked the theory in his *General Theory of Employment, Interest, and*

*Money* in 1936. Keynes, whose precepts guided liberal U.S. economic policy from the 1940s through the 1970s, agreed that investments must be financed out of savings. But he showed that most often it's changes in investment that drive savings, rather than the other way around. When businesses are optimistic about the future and invest in building and retooling, the economy booms, all of us make more money, and we put some of it in banks, 401(k)s, stocks, and so on. That is, saving grows to match investment. When companies are glum, the process runs in reverse, and savings shrink to equal investment. This leads to the "paradox of thrift": if people try to save too much, businesses will see less consumer spending, will invest less, and total savings will end up diminishing rather than growing as the economy spirals downward. A number of Keynes's followers added the next logical step: shifting money from the high-saving rich to the high-spending rest of us, and not the other way around, will spur investment and growth.

Of the two conservative arguments in favor of inequality, the incentive argument is a little weightier. Keynes himself agreed that people needed financial consequences to steer their actions, but questioned whether the differences in payoffs needed to be so huge. Certainly state socialist countries' attempts to replace material incentives with moral exhortation have often fallen short. In 1970, the Cuban government launched the Gran Zafra (Great Harvest), an attempt to reap 10 million tons of sugar cane with (strongly encouraged) volunteer labor. Originally inspired by Che Guevara's ideal of the New Socialist Man (not clear how the New Socialist Woman fit in), the effort ended with Fidel Castro tearfully apologizing to the Cuban people in a nationally broadcast speech for letting wishful thinking guide economic policy.

But before conceding this point to the conservatives, let's look at the evidence about the connection between equality and growth. Economists William Easterly of New York University and Gary Fields of Cornell University have recently summarized this evidence:

- Countries, and regions within countries, with more equal incomes grow faster. (These growth figures do not include environmental destruction or improvement. If they knocked off points for environmental destruction and added points for environmental improvement, the correlation between equality and growth would be even stronger, since desperation drives poor people to adopt environmentally destructive practices such as rapid deforestation.)
- Countries with more equally distributed land grow faster.
- Somewhat disturbingly, more ethnically homogeneous countries and regions grow faster—presumably because there are fewer ethnically based inequalities.
- In addition, more worker rights are associated with higher rates of economic growth, according to Josh Bivens and Christian Weller, economists at two Washington think tanks, the Economic Policy Institute and the Center for American Progress.

These patterns recommend a second look at the incentive question. In fact, more equality can actually strengthen incentives and opportunities to produce.

## Equality as the Goose

Equality can boost growth in several ways. Perhaps the simplest is that study after study has shown that farmland is more productive when cultivated in small plots. So organizations promoting more equal distribution of land, like Brazil's Landless Workers' Movement, are not just helping the landless poor—they're contributing to agricultural productivity!

Another reason for the link between equality and growth is what Easterly calls "match effects," which have been highlighted in research by Stanford's Paul Roemer and others in recent years. One example of a match effect is the fact that well-educated people are most productive when working with others who have lots of schooling. Likewise, people working with computers are more productive when many others have computers (so that, for example, email communication is widespread, and know-how about computer repair and software is easy to come by). In very unequal societies, highly educated, computer-using elites are surrounded by majorities with little education and no computer access, dragging down their productivity. This decreases young people's incentive to get more education and businesses' incentive to invest in computers, since the payoff will be smaller.

Match effects can even matter at the level of a metropolitan area. Urban economist Larry Ledebur looked at income and employment growth in 85 U.S. cities and their neighboring suburbs. He found that where the income gap between those in the suburbs and those in the city was largest, income and job growth was slower for everyone.

"Pressure effects" also help explain why equality sparks growth. Policies that close off the low-road strategy of exploiting poor and working people create pressure effects, driving economic elites to search for investment opportunities that pay off by boosting productivity rather than squeezing the have-nots harder. For example, where workers have more rights, they will place greater demands on businesses. Business owners will respond by trying to increase productivity, both to remain profitable even after paying higher wages, and to find ways to produce with fewer workers. The CIO union drives in U.S. mass production industries in the 1930s and 1940s provide much of the explanation for the superb productivity growth of the 1950s and 1960s. (The absence of pressure effects may help explain why many past and present state socialist countries have seen slow growth, since they tend to offer numerous protections for workers but no right to organize independent unions.) Similarly, if a government buys out large land-holdings in order to break them up, wealthy families who simply kept their fortunes tied up in land for generations will look for new, productive investments. Industrialization in Asian "tigers" South Korea and Taiwan took off in the 1950s on the wings of funds freed up in exactly this way.

## Inequality, Conflict, and Growth

Inequality hinders growth in another important way: it fuels social conflict. Stark inequality in countries such as Bolivia and Haiti has led to chronic conflict that hobbles economic growth. Moreover, inequality ties up resources in unproductive uses such as paying for large numbers of police and security guards—attempts to prevent individuals from redistributing resources through theft.

Ethnic variety is connected to slower growth because, on the average, more ethnically diverse countries are also more likely to be ethnically divided. In other words, the problem isn't ethnic variety itself, but racism and ethnic conflict that can exist among diverse populations. In nations like Guatemala, Congo, and Nigeria, ethnic strife has crippled growth—a problem alien to ethnically uniform Japan and South Korea. The reasons are similar to some of the reasons that large class divides hurt growth. Where ethnic divisions (which can take tribal, language, religious, racial, or regional forms) loom large, dominant ethnic groups seek to use government power to better themselves at the expense of other groups, rather than making broad-based investments in education and infrastructure. This can involve keeping down the underdogs—slower growth in the U.S. South for much of the country's history was linked to the Southern system of white supremacy. Or it can involve seizing the surplus of ethnic groups perceived as better off—in the extreme, Nazi Germany's expropriation and genocide of the Jews, who often held professional and commercial jobs.

Of course, the solution to such divisions is not "ethnic cleansing" so that each country has only one ethnic group—in addition to being morally abhorrent, this is simply impossible in a world with 191 countries and 5,000 ethnic groups. Rather, the solution is to diminish ethnic inequalities. Once the 1964 Civil Rights Act forced the South to drop racist laws, the New South's economic growth spurt began. Easterly reports that in countries with strong rule of law, professional bureaucracies, protection of contracts, and freedom from expropriation—all rules that make it harder for one ethnic group to economically oppress another—ethnic diversity has no negative impact on growth.

If more equality leads to faster growth so everybody benefits, why do the rich typically resist redistribution? Looking at the ways that equity seeds growth helps us understand why. The importance of pressure effects tells us that the wealthy often don't think about more productive ways to invest or reorganize their businesses until they are forced to. But also, if a country becomes very unequal, it can get stuck in an "inequality trap." Any redistribution involves a tradeoff for the rich. They lose by giving up part of their wealth, but they gain a share in increased economic growth. The bigger the disparity between the rich and the rest, the more the rich have to lose, and the less likely that the equal share of boosted growth they'll get will make up for their loss. Once the gap goes beyond a certain point, the wealthy have a strong incentive to restrict democracy, and to block spending on education which might lead the poor to challenge economic injustice—making reform that much harder.

## Does Economic Growth Reduce Inequality?

If inequality isn't actually good for the economy, what about the second part of the conservatives' argument—that growth itself promotes equality? According to the conservatives, those who care about equality should simply pursue growth and wait for equality to follow.

"A rising tide lifts all boats," President John F. Kennedy famously declared. But he said nothing about which boats will rise fastest when the economic tide comes in. Growth does typically reduce poverty, according to studies reviewed by economist Gary Fields, though some "boats"—especially families with strong barriers to participating in the labor force—stay "stuck in the mud." But inequality can increase at the same time that poverty falls, if the rich gain even faster than the poor do. True, sustained periods of low unemployment, like that in the late 1990s United States, do tend to raise wages at the bottom even faster than salaries at the top. But growth after the recessions of 1991 and 2001 began with years of "jobless recoveries"—growth with inequality.

For decades the prevailing view about growth and inequality within countries was that expressed by Simon Kuznets in his 1955 presidential address to the American Economic Association. Kuznets argued that as countries grew, inequality would first increase, then decrease. The reason is that people will gradually move from the low-income agricultural sector to higher-income industrial jobs—with inequality peaking when the workforce is equally divided between low- and high-income sectors. For mature industrial economies, Kuznets's proposition counsels focusing on growth, assuming that it will bring equity. In developing countries, it calls for enduring current inequality for the sake of future equity and prosperity.

But economic growth doesn't automatically fuel equality. In 1998, economists Klaus Deininger and Lyn Squire traced inequality and growth over time in 48 countries. Five followed the Kuznets pattern, four followed the reverse pattern (decreasing inequality followed by an increase), and the rest showed no systematic pattern. In the United States, for example:

- incomes became more equal during the 1930s through 1940s New Deal period (a time that included economic decline followed by growth);
- from the 1950s through the 1970s, income gaps lessened during booms and expanded during slumps;
- from the late 1970s forward, income inequality worsened fairly consistently, whether the economy was stagnating or growing.

The reasons are not hard to guess. The New Deal introduced widespread unionization, a minimum wage, social security, unemployment insurance, and welfare. Since the late 1970s, unions have declined, the inflation-adjusted value of the minimum wage has fallen, and the social safety net has been shredded. In the United States, as elsewhere, growth only promotes equality if policies and institutions to support equity are in place.

## Trapped?

Let's revisit the idea of an inequality trap. The notion is that as the gap between the rich and everybody else grows wider, the wealthy become more willing to give up overall growth in return for the larger share they're getting for themselves. The "haves" back policies to control the "have-nots," instead of devoting social resources to educating the poor so they'll be more productive.

Sound familiar? It should. After two decades of widening inequality, the last few years have brought us massive tax cuts that primarily benefit the wealthiest, at the expense of investment in infrastructure and the education, child care, and income supports that would help raise less well-off kids to be productive adults. Federal and state governments have cranked up expenditures on prisons, police, and "homeland security," and Republican campaign organizations have devoted major resources to keeping blacks and the poor away from the polls. If the economic patterns of the past are any indication, we're going to pay for these policies in slower growth and stagnation unless we can find our way out of this inequality trap. ❑

*Article 8.2*

# INEQUALITY: THE SILLY TALES ECONOMISTS LIKE TO TELL

## BY DEAN BAKER
*October 2012; Al Jazeera English*

There is no serious dispute that the United States has seen a massive increase in inequality over the last three decades. However there is a major dispute over the causes of this rise in inequality.

The explanation most popular in elite and policy circles is that the rise in inequality was simply the natural working of the economy. Their story is that the explosion of information technology and globalization have increased demand for highly-skilled workers while sharply reducing the demand for less-educated workers.

While the first part of this story is at best questionable, the second part should invite ridicule and derision. It doesn't pass the laugh test.

As far as the technology story, yes information technologies have displaced large amounts of less-skilled labor. So did the technologies that preceded them. There are hundreds of books and articles from the 1950s and 1960s that expressed grave concerns that automation would leave much of the workforce unemployed. Is there evidence that the displacement is taking place more rapidly today than in that era? If so, it is not showing up on our productivity data.

More germane to the issue at hand, unlike the earlier wave of technology, computerization offers the potential for displacing vast amounts of highly skilled labor. Legal research that might have previously required a highly skilled lawyer can now be done by an intelligent college grad and a good search engine. Medical diagnosis and the interpretation of test results that may have previously required a physician, and quite possibly a highly paid specialist, can now be done by technical specialists who may not even have a college education.

There is no reason to believe that current technologies are replacing comparatively more less-educated workers than highly educated workers. The fact that lawyers and doctors largely control how their professions are practiced almost certainly has much more to do with the demand for their services.

If the technology explanation for inequality is weak, the globalization part of the story is positively pernicious. The basic story is that globalization has integrated a huge labor force of billions of workers in developing countries into the world economy. These workers are able to fill many of the jobs that used to provide middle class living standards to workers in the United States and will accept a fraction of the wage. This makes many formerly middle class jobs uncompetitive in the world economy given current wages and currency values.

This part of the story is true. The part that our elite leave out is that there are tens of millions of bright and highly educated workers in the developing world who could fill most of the top paying jobs in the U.S. economy: Doctors, lawyers, accountants, etc. These workers are also willing to work for a small fraction of the wages of their U.S. counterparts since they come from poor countries with much lower standards of living.

The reason why the manufacturing workers, construction workers, and restaurant workers lose their jobs to low-paid workers from the developing world, and doctors and lawyers don't, is that doctors and lawyers use their political power to limit the extent to which they are exposed to competition from their low-paid counterparts in the developing world. Our trade policy has been explicitly designed to remove barriers that prevent General Electric and other companies from moving their manufacturing operations to Mexico, China or other developing countries. By contrast, many of the barriers that make it difficult for foreign professionals to work in the United States have actually been strengthened in the last two decades.

If economics was an honest profession, economists would focus their efforts on documenting the waste associated with protectionist barriers for professionals. They devoted endless research studies to estimating the cost to consumers of tariffs on products like shoes and tires. It speaks to the incredible corruption of the economics profession that there are not hundreds of studies showing the loss to consumers from the barriers to trade in physicians' services. If trade could bring down the wages of physicians in the United States just to European levels, it would save consumers close to $100 billion a year.

But economists are not rewarded for studying the economy. That is why almost everyone in the profession missed the $8 trillion housing bubble, the collapse of which stands to cost the country more than $7 trillion in lost output according to the Congressional Budget Office (that comes to around $60,000 per household).

Few if any economists lost their six-figure paychecks for this disastrous mistake. But most economists are not paid for knowing about the economy. They are paid for telling stories that justify giving more money to rich people. Hence we can look forward to many more people telling us that all the money going to the rich was just the natural workings of the economy. When it comes to all the government rules and regulations that shifted income upward, they just don't know what you're talking about. ❑

*Article 8.3*

# THE WAGES OF GENDER

## BY GERALD FRIEDMAN
*September/October 2013 and November/December 2013*

Fifty years ago, in June 1963, President John F. Kennedy signed the Equal Pay Act, forbidding what he called the "unconscionable practice of paying female employees less wages than male employees for the same job." While acknowledging that "much remains to be done to achieve full equality of economic opportunity," he pronounced the law a "significant step forward."

Women have made much progress since then because of anti-discrimination legislation and the work of millions of activists to open occupations previously closed to women. The gap between men's and women's wages has narrowed significantly, and women have gained access to a broad range of professional and managerial occupations. With these economic gains, the balance of power between the genders and within families has changed because women can support themselves and their families even without a husband.

A great deal, however, still remains to be done. Women still earn less than men for reasons tied to gender—including outright discrimination in many occupations as well as the continued expectation that women will bear the primary responsibility for childcare and other household responsibilities. The great progress made in reducing gender disparities over the past decades shows the importance of maintaining political and social movements to eliminate remaining gender inequities.

FIGURE 1: WOMEN'S MEDIAN WEEKLY EARNINGS VS. MEN'S, FULL-TIME EMPLOYEES, 1979-2012

The median weekly wage for women employed full time is 81% of the figure for men. While this is a significant shortfall, it is also a significant improvement over the 1979 figure of 62%. While there has been progress in most years, improvement may have slowed. The ratio of women's earnings to men's increased by nearly eight percentage points in the 1980s, five points in the 1990s, and only four points since 2000.

## FIGURE 2: WOMENS MEDIAN WEEKLY EARNINGS VS. MEN'S, BY AGE AND YEAR

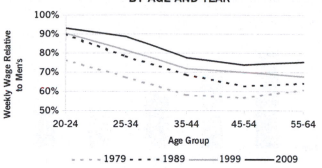

This graph shows median earnings for women compared to men, across different age groups, in 1979, 1989, 1999, and 2009. At least in part because of gender discrimination and the unequal burdens of family care work, women's wages grow more slowly with age than do those of men (reflected in the downward slope of each curve). This pattern has persisted even while women's wages have increased relative to men's for all age groups (reflected in the curve's consistent rise from one decade to the next).

## FIGURE 3: PERCENTAGE CHANGE IN INFLATION-ADJUSTED MEDIAN WEEKLY EARNINGS, BY GENDER AND EDUCATION, 1979-2011

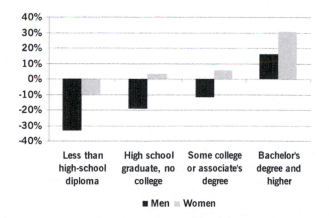

Rising relative earnings for women reflect both the entry of women into higher-paid occupations and rising earnings for women relative to men within occupations. Women's wages have risen relative to men's for all levels of education. For less-educated workers, however, much of the narrowing of the gender wage gap has come because women's wages have fallen less than men's have. Only among college graduates has the gender gap narrowed because wages have risen for both women and men, but have risen faster for women.

### FIGURE 4: WOMEN'S MEDIAN WEEKLY EARNINGS VS. MEN'S, BY POSITION IN FEMALE AND MALE INCOME RANKINGS

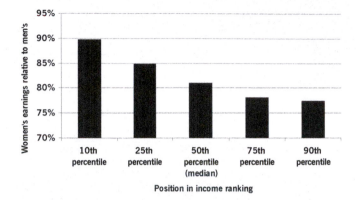

The gender pay gap is greater for higher-income workers. At low-paying jobs, women earn almost as much as men. (Women who are low in the female income ranking make almost 90% as much as men who are low in the male income ranking.) At higher income levels, however, women's pay lags further behind men's. This reflects the continuing exclusion of women from many of the highest-paid occupations and the top positions within occupations—the so-called "glass ceiling."

### FIGURE 5: MARRIED WOMEN WHO EARN MORE THAN THEIR HUSBANDS, 1947-2011

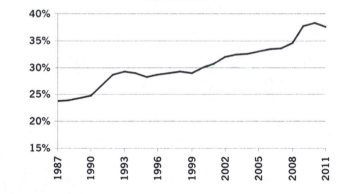

Women earn more than their husbands in a growing share of opposite-sex marriages. This increase is due not only to rising relative wages for women but also to an increase in the proportion of married women working outside the home. In addition, there has been a decline, especially since the beginning of the Great Recession, in the share of married men working outside the home—due both to higher male unemployment and more men dropping out of the labor force altogether.

## FIGURE 6: BA DEGREES BY GENDER, UNITED STATES, 1964-2006

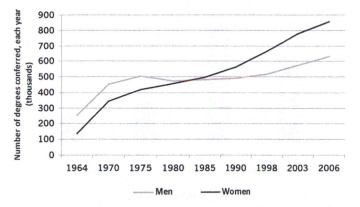

While barely a third of college degrees went to women in the early 1960s, the number of women earning BAs passed the number of men in the 1980s. Since then, college graduation numbers for women have continued to outpace the figures for men. With improvements in their educational attainment, women have gained access to more highly paid professions, like medicine and law, and their incomes have increased accordingly.

## FIGURE 7: OCCUPATIONAL DISTRIBUTION, BY GENDER, UNITED STATES, 2011

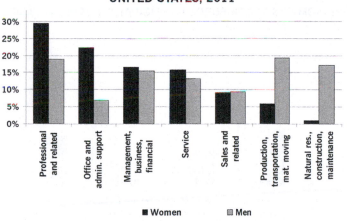

Compared to men, there are relatively few women employed in many traditional blue-collar occupations, including construction, manufacturing, mining, and transportation. To the extent that these jobs were relatively well-paid, the exclusion of women lowered their relative earnings. Over the past 40 years, however, more women have moved into higher paid professional and managerial occupations while wages for production workers have fallen relative to earnings in traditionally female service and office occupations.

## FIGURE 8: HOUSEWORK TIME, BY GENDER AND MARITAL STATUS, 1976-2005

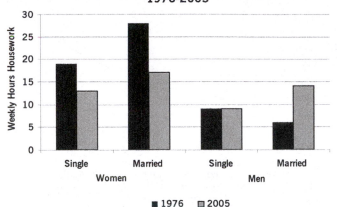

■ 1976    ▢ 2005

In the 1970s, marriage dramatically increased women's housework time while reducing men's. Since then, increasing women's economic equality has been associated with a change in the impact of marriage on housework. As of 2005, married men did more housework than unmarried men, rather than less. While married women still do more housework than men, marriage now causes a relatively small increase in the housework done by women, compared to what it did in the 1970s.

## FIGURE 9: WOMEN'S LABOR FORCE PARTICIPATION RATE, BY FAMILY STATUS

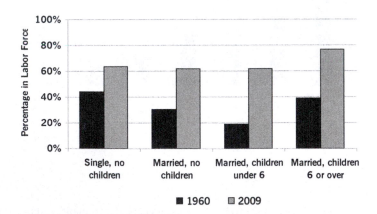

■ 1960    ▢ 2009

In 1960, fewer women were in the paid labor force, many left the labor force when they married, and most left when they had children. Family status has had much less effect on labor-force participation in more recent years. By 2009, few women left the labor force to marry and care for children. By continuing their paid employment, women are able to continue accumulating on-the-job training, remain part of work teams, and generally maintain their careers

**FIGURE 10: PERCENTAGE OF TOTAL EMPLOYEES, BY GENDER**

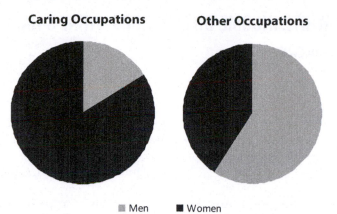

Caring Occupations          Other Occupations

■ Men    ■ Women

Women remain in a vulnerable economic position because their employment is concentrated in a particular subset of the economy. Women are disproportionately employed in "caring" occupations, including elementary school teachers (82% female), nurses (90%), housekeepers (90%), childcare workers (94%), and personal care attendants (87%). Cutbacks in government funding and social support for these occupations could undermine many of the economic gains made by women over the past decades. ❏

*Sources:* Bureau of Labor Statistics (BLS), Weekly and hourly earnings data from the Current Population Survey; BLS, "Highlights of Women's Earnings in 2011," October 2012; BLS, 1988–2012 Annual Social and Economic Supplements to the Current Population Survey (CPS); BLS, Current Population Survey, Labor Force Participation, Bulletin 2307; Department of Education, National Council of Education Statistics at (nces.ed.gov); Panel Study of Income Dynamics at University of Michgan, Institute for Social Research (www.nsf.gov).

*Article 8.4*

# BLACK-WHITE INCOME DIFFERENCES: WHAT'S HAPPENED?

**BY ARTHUR MacEWAN**
*July/August 2013*

> Dear Dr. Dollar:
> *There is a great deal of awareness of the general increase of income inequality in the United States. But what's happened to the income inequality between African Americans and European Americans (the "Black-White" inequality)?*
> —Andy Druding, Richmond, Calif.

With a president who is African-American and talk of a "post-racial" society, one might think that the economic position of African Americans relative to European Americans had improved significantly over the last 40 or so years. One would be wrong.

In 2011, the median income of Black households was about $32,000; that is, half of Black households had income above this figure, and half had incomes below this figure. This was 61.7% of the 2011 median income of White households. In 1970, before the general increase of income inequality, the figure was 60.9%, just a smidgen lower. Not much change. Also, there has been virtually no change if mean incomes are used for the Black-White comparison. (The "mean" is the average—the total income all households in the group divided by the number of households.)

This lack of change over the last 40 years might come as a surprise, contrary to visible indicators of improvement in the position of Black people. We see, for example, many Black professionals in fields where 40 years ago there were few. There are also more Black executives—even a few CEOs of major corporations. And there is Barack Obama. How do these visible changes square with the lack of change in the relative income positions of Blacks and Whites?

The answer to this question is largely that the distribution of income among Black households is very unequal, even more unequal than the distribution of income among White households. So, many of the prominent Black people who appear to be doing so well are indeed doing well. At the other end are the Black households that are doing worse. Between 1970 and 2011, the upper 5% of Black households saw their average (mean) incomes rise from about $114,000 to about $215,000 (measured in 2011 dollars), while the incomes of Black households in the bottom 20% saw their average income fall from $6,465 to $6,379.

Among White households, the pattern of change was similar but not quite so extreme. The average income of the top 5% of White households rose by 83% in this period, as compared to the 88% increase for the top Black households—though that elite White group was still taking in 50% per household more than their Black counterparts. The bottom 20% of White households saw a 13% increase per household in their inflation-adjusted incomes between 1970 and 2011.

So high-income Blacks have done pretty well—even slightly improved relative to the top White households. They have to a degree benefited from the social changes of recent decades. But for a very large segment of the Black population, not only that bottom 20%, their relative position has gotten somewhat worse, and for many their absolute incomes have actually fallen. The long-term reduction of the minimum wage (in real terms) has had an especially harsh impact on low-income Blacks, and the weakening of labor unions has also harmed a broad swath of the Black community. Add the mass incarceration of young Black men and their consequent exclusion from the economic mainstream, and it is not hard to understand continuing Black-White inequality.

Two other points should be kept in mind: First, the changes between 1970 and 2011 have not been smooth. Measured by either the mean or the median, the income position of Black households relative to White households was fairly stable in the 1970s, fell off sharply in the early 1980s, and rose again to a peak in the late 1990s before falling off to its current level.

Second, income distribution is only one measure of economic inequality. The Great Recession had a devastating impact on the wealth of Black households, largely explained by the impact of the housing crisis. In 2004, the net worth of White households was about eleven times that of Black households (bad enough), about the same as it had been since the early 1980s (with a slight improvement in the mid-1990s). But by 2009, though both Black and White net worth fell from 2004, White net worth was 19 times Black net worth.

The more things change, the more they stay the same—or get worse! ❑

*Sources:* U.S. Census Bureau, Historical Income Tables: Income Inequality (census.org).

*Article 8.5*

# UNIONS AND INCOME INEQUALITY

## BY ARTHUR MacEWAN
*November/December 2011*

Dear Dr. Dollar:
*I know unions have shrunk in the United States, but by how much? And how best to respond to my right-wing friends who claim that unions are bad for the economy?*
—Rich Sanford, Hardwick, Mass.

Take a look at the graph below. The two lines on the graph show for the period 1917 through 2007 (1) labor union membership as a percentage of the total U.S. work force and (2) the percentage of all income obtained by the highest 1% of income recipients. So the lines show, roughly, the strength of unions and the distribution of income for the past century. (John Miller and I developed this graph for our book *Economic Collapse, Economic Change.*)

The picture is pretty clear. In periods when unions have been strong, income distribution has been less unequal. In periods when unions have been weak, income distribution has been more unequal. In the post-World War II era, union members were about 25% of the labor force; today the figure is about 10%. In those postwar years, the highest-income 1% got 10% to 12% of all income; today they get about 25%.

### UNION MEMBERSHIP AND INCOME INEQUALITY, 1917-2007

*Source:* Arthur MacEwan and John A. Miller, *Economic Collapse, Economic Change: Getting to the Root of the Crisis* (M.E. Sharpe, 2011).

The causation between union strength and income distribution is not simple. Nonetheless, there are some fairly direct connections. For example, when unions are strong, they can push for higher wages and thus we see a more equal distribution of income. Also, strong unions can have an impact on the political process, bringing about policies that are more favorable to workers.

But causation can work in the other direction as well. Great income inequality puts more power in the hands of the rich, and they can use that power to get policies put in place that weaken unions—for example, getting people who are hostile to unions appointed to the National Labor Relations Board.

And then there are other factors that affect both union strength and income distribution—for example, the changing structure of the global economy, which places U.S. workers in competition with poorly paid workers elsewhere. Yet the structure of the global economy is itself affected by the distribution of political power. For example, the "free trade" agreements that the United States has established with other countries generally ignore workers' rights (to say nothing of the environment) and go to great lengths to protect the rights of corporations. So, again, causation works in complex ways, and there are certainly other factors that need to be taken account of to explain the relationship shown in the graph.

However one explains the relationship, it is hard to imagine that we can return to a more equal distribution of income while unions remain weak. This means, at the very least, that the interests of unions and of people at the bottom of the income distribution are bound up with one another. Building stronger unions is an important part of fighting poverty—and the hunger and homelessness that are the clear manifestations of poverty.

One important thing to notice in the graph: In the post-World War II years, economic growth was the best we have seen. Certainly no one can claim that it is impossible for strong unions and a more equal distribution of income to co-exist with fairly rapid economic growth. Indeed, we might even argue that strong unions and a more equal distribution of income create favorable conditions for economic growth!

Stronger unions, it turns out, could be good preventive medicine for much of what ails our economy. ❑

Article 8.6

# THE UNDESERVING RICH
Collectively produced and inherited knowledge and the (re)distribution of income and wealth.

BY GAR ALPEROVITZ AND LEW DALY
March/April 2010

Warren Buffett, one of the wealthiest men in the nation, is worth nearly $50 billion. Does he "deserve" all this money? Why? Did he work so much harder than everyone else? Did he create something so extraordinary that no one else could have created it? Ask Buffett himself and he will tell you that he thinks "society is responsible for a very significant percentage of what I've earned." But if that's true, doesn't society deserve a very significant share of what he has earned?

When asked why he is so successful, Buffett commonly replies that this is the wrong question. The more important question, he stresses, is why he has *so much to work with* compared to other people in the world, or compared to previous generations of Americans. Buffett asks: how much money would he have if he had been born in Bangladesh, or in the United States in 1700?

Buffett may or may not deserve something more than another person working with what a given historical or collective context provides. As he observes, however, it is simply not possible to argue in any serious way that he deserves *all* of the benefits that are clearly attributable to living in a highly developed society.

Buffett has put his finger on one of the most explosive issues developing just beneath the surface of public awareness. Over the last several decades, economic research has done a great deal of solid work pinpointing much more precisely than in the past what share of what we call "wealth" society creates versus what share any individual can be said to have earned and thus deserved. This research raises profound moral—and ultimately political—questions.

## Through No Effort of Our Own

Recent estimates suggest that U.S. economic output per capita has increased more than twenty-fold since 1800. Output per hour worked has increased an estimated fifteen-fold since 1870 alone. Yet the average modern person likely works with no greater commitment, risk, or intelligence than his or her counterpart from the past. What is the primary cause of such vast gains if individuals do not really "improve"? Clearly, it is largely that the scientific, technical, and cultural knowledge available to us, and the efficiency of our means of storing and retrieving this knowledge, have grown at a scale and pace that far outstrip any other factor in the nation's economic development.

A half century ago, in 1957, economist Robert Solow calculated that nearly 90% of productivity growth in the first half of the 20th century (from 1909 to 1949) could only be attributed to "technical change in the broadest sense." The supply of labor and capital—what workers and employers contribute—appeared almost incidental to this massive technological "residual." Subsequent research inspired by

Solow and others continued to point to "advances in knowledge" as the main source of growth. Economist William Baumol calculates that "nearly 90 percent . . . of current GDP was contributed by innovation carried out since 1870." Baumol judges that his estimate, in fact, understates the cumulative influence of past advances: Even "the steam engine, the railroad, and many other inventions of an earlier era, still add to today's GDP."

Related research on the sources of invention bolsters the new view, posing a powerful challenge to conventional, heroic views of technology that characterize progress as a sequence of extraordinary contributions by "Great Men" (occasionally "Great Women") and their "Great Inventions." In contrast to this popular view, historians of technology have carefully delineated the incremental and cumulative way most technologies actually develop. In general, a specific field of knowledge builds up slowly through diverse contributions over time until—at a particular moment when enough has been established—the next so-called "breakthrough" becomes all but inevitable.

Often many people reach the same point at virtually the same time, for the simple reason that they all are working from the same developing information and research base. The next step commonly becomes obvious (or if not obvious, very likely to be taken within a few months or years). We tend to give credit to the person who gets there first—or rather, who gets the first public attention, since often the real originator is not as good at public relations as the one who jumps to the front of the line and claims credit. Thus, we remember Alexander Graham Bell as the inventor of the telephone even though, among others, Elisha Gray and Antonio Meucci got there at the same time or even before him. Newton and Leibniz hit upon the calculus at roughly the same time in the 1670s; Darwin and Alfred Russel Wallace produced essentially the same theory of evolution at roughly the same time in the late 1850s.

Less important than who gets the credit is the simple fact that most breakthroughs occur not so much thanks to one "genius," but because of the longer historical unfolding of knowledge. All of this knowledge—the overwhelming source of all modern wealth—comes to us today *through no effort of our own*. It is the generous and unearned gift of the past. In the words of Northwestern economist Joel Mokyr, it is a "free lunch."

Collective knowledge is often created by formal public efforts as well, a point progressives often stress. Many of the advances which propelled our high-tech economy in the early 1990s grew directly out of research programs and technical systems financed and often collaboratively developed by the federal government. The Internet, to take the most obvious example, began as a government defense project, the ARPANET, in the early 1960s. Up through the 1980s there was little private investment or interest in developing computer networks. Today's vast software industry also rests on a foundation of computer language and operating hardware developed in large part with public support. The Bill Gateses of the world—the heroes of the "New Economy"—might still be working with vacuum tubes and punch cards were it not for critical research and technology programs created or financed by the federal government after World War II. Other illustrations range from jet airplanes and radar to the basic life science research undergirding many pharmaceutical industry advances. Yet the truth is that the role of collectively inherited knowledge is far, far greater than just the contributions made by direct public support, important as they are.

## Earned Income?

A straightforward but rarely confronted question arises from these facts: If most of what we have today is attributable to advances we inherit in common, then why should this gift of our collective history not more generously benefit all members of society?

The top 1% of U.S. households now receives more income than the bottom 120 million Americans combined. The richest 1% of households owns nearly half of all investment assets (stocks and mutual funds, financial securities, business equity, trusts, non-home real estate). The bottom 90% of the population owns less than 15%; the bottom half—150 million Americans—owns less than 1%. If America's vast wealth is mainly a gift of our common past, what justifies such disparities?

Robert Dahl, one of America's leading political scientists—and one of the few to have confronted these facts—put it this way after reading economist Edward Denison's pioneering work on growth accounting: "It is immediately obvious that little growth in the American economy can be attributed to the actions of particular individuals." He concluded straightforwardly that, accordingly, "the control and ownership of the economy rightfully belongs to 'society.'"

Contrast Dahl's view with that of Joe the Plumber, who famously inserted himself into the 2008 presidential campaign with his repeated claim that he has "earned" everything he gets and so any attempt to tax his earnings is totally unjustified. Likewise, "we didn't rely on somebody else to build what we built," banking titan Sanford Weill tells us in a *New York Times* front-page story on the "New Gilded Age." "I think there are people," another executive tells the *Times*, "who because of their uniqueness warrant whatever the market will bear."

A direct confrontation with the role of knowledge—and especially inherited knowledge—goes to the root of a profound challenge to such arguments. One way to think about all this is by focusing on the concept of "earned" versus "unearned" income. Today this distinction can be found in conservative attacks on welfare "cheats" who refuse to work to earn their keep, as well as in calls even by some Republican senators to tax the windfall oil-company profits occasioned by the Iraq war and Hurricane Katrina.

The concept of unearned income first came into clear focus during the era of rapidly rising land values caused by grain shortages in early 19th-century England. Wealth derived *simply* from owning land whose price was escalating appeared illegitimate because no individual truly "earned" such wealth. Land values—and especially explosively high values—were largely the product of factors such as fertility, location, and population pressures. The huge profits (unearned "rents," in the technical language of economics) landowners reaped when there were food shortages were viewed as particularly egregious. David Ricardo's influential theory of "differential rent"—i.e., that land values are determined by differences in fertility and location between different plots of land—along with religious perspectives reaching back to the Book of Genesis played a central role in sharpening this critical moral distinction.

John Stuart Mill, among others, developed the distinction between "earned" and "unearned" in the middle decades of the 19th century and applied it to other forms of "external wealth," or what he called "wealth created by circumstances." Mill's approach fed into a growing sense of the importance of societal inputs which produce economic gains beyond what can be ascribed to one person working alone in nature without benefit of civilization's many contributions. Here a second element of what appears, historically, as a slowly evolving understanding also becomes clear: If contribution is important in determining rewards, then, Mill and others urged, since society at large makes major contributions to economic achievement, it too has "earned" and deserves a share of what has been created. Mill believed strongly in personal contribution and individual reward, but he held that in principle wealth "created by circumstances" should be reclaimed for social purposes. Karl Marx, of course, tapped the distinction between earned and unearned in his much broader attack on capitalism and its exploitation of workers' labor.

The American republican writer Thomas Paine was among the first to articulate a societal theory of wealth based directly on the earned/unearned distinction. Paine argued that everything "beyond what a man's own hands produce" was a gift which came to him simply by living in society, and hence "he owes on every principle of justice, of gratitude, and of civilization, a part of that accumulation back again to society from whence the whole came." A later American reformer, Henry George, focused on urban land rather than the agricultural land at the heart of Ricardo's concern. George challenged what he called "the unearned increment" which is created when population growth and other societal factors increase land values. In Britain, J. A. Hobson argued that the unearned value created by the industrial system in general was much larger than just the part which accrued to landowners, and that it should be treated in a similar (if not more radical and comprehensive) fashion. In a similar vein, Hobson's early 20th-century contemporary Leonard Trelawny Hobhouse declared that the "prosperous business man" should consider "what single step he could have taken" without the "sum of intelligence which civilization has placed at his disposal." More recently, the famed American social scientist Herbert Simon judged that if "we are very generous with ourselves, I suppose we might claim that we 'earned' as much as one fifth of [our income]."

The distinction between earned and unearned gains is central to most of these thinkers, as is the notion that societal contributions—including everything an industrial economy requires, from the creation of laws, police, and courts to the development of schools, trade restrictions, and patents—must be recognized and rewarded. The understanding that such societal contributions are both contemporary and have made a huge and cumulative contribution over all of history is also widely accepted. Much of the income they permit and confer now appears broadly analogous to the unearned rent a landlord claims. What is new and significant here is the further clarification that by far the most important element in all this is the accumulated *knowledge* which society contributes over time.

All of this, as sociologist Daniel Bell has suggested, requires a new "knowledge theory of value"—especially as we move deeper into the high-tech era through computerization, the Internet, cybernetics, and cutting-edge fields such as gene therapy and nanotechnology. One way to grasp what is at stake is the following: A person today working the same number of hours as a similar person in 1870—working just as hard but no harder—will produce perhaps 15 times as much economic output. It is clear that the contemporary person can hardly be said to have "earned" his much greater productivity.

Consider further that if we project forward the past century's rate of growth, a person working a century from now would be able to produce—and potentially receive as "income"—up to seven times today's average income. By far the greatest part of this gain will also come to this person as a free gift of the past—the gift of the new knowledge created, passed on, and inherited from our own time forward.

She and her descendents, in fact, will inevitably contribute less, relative to the huge and now expanded contribution of the past, than we do today. The obvious question, again, is simply this: to what degree is it meaningful to say that this person will have "earned" all that may come her way? These and other realities suggest that the quiet revolution in our understanding of how wealth is created has ramifications for a much more profound and far-reaching challenge to today's untenable distribution of income and wealth. ❏

*Article 8.7*

# THE GREAT LAND GIVEAWAY IN MOZAMBIQUE

## BY TIMOTHY A. WISE
*March/April 2015*

I introduced myself to Luis Sitoe, economic adviser to Mozambique's minister of agriculture, and explained that I'd spent the last two weeks in his country researching the ProSAVANA project, decried as the largest land grab in Africa. This ambitious Brazil-Japan-Mozambique development project was slated to turn 35 million hectares (over 85 million acres) of Mozambique's supposedly unoccupied savannah lands into industrial-scale soybean farms modeled on—and with capital from—Brazil's savannah lands in its own southern Cerrado region.

Mr. Sitoe smirked. "Did you see ProSAVANA?" I hadn't, in fact. "So far there is no investment in Pro-Savana," he said, with surprising satisfaction considering that the project's most ardent supporter had been his boss, agriculture minister José Pacheco.

A firestorm of controversy had dogged the project since its "Master Plan" had been unceremoniously leaked in 2013. Farmers were actively resisting efforts by foreign investors and the government to take away their land. And Brazilian investment was almost nowhere to be found.

Had the land-grab boom gone bust? Was ProSAVANA's stuttering start a sign that African farmland had lost its luster? No, but it turns out to be easier to get a government to give away a farmer's land than it is to actually farm it.

## Reality Asserts Itself

Data from the Land Matrix project suggest that economic realities have begun to assert themselves. Commodity prices are down, speculative capital has returned to rebounding stock markets, low oil prices have cut the profit margins on biofuels. Oil and gas discoveries in some developing countries, meanwhile, have taken the wind out of the sails of domestic alternative energy projects which were fueling some land-grabbing.

As a result, the pace of large-scale land acquisitions has slowed, many projects have failed, and those underway often operate on a fraction of the land handed over to them.

National governments—perhaps the most willing negotiating partners in this often-ugly process—have ceded the rights to large tracts of land to foreign investors. As of mid-September 2014, Land Matrix had recorded 956 transnational land deals completed globally since 2000, with another 187 under negotiation. The completed agreements, most of which have taken place since 2007, cover 61 million hectares (about 150 million acres), with about half of that land under formal contract. Interestingly, of the 37 million hectares under contract, only 4.1 million (just 11%) are confirmed to be in production.

The much lower acreage contracted for production reflects how hard it can be to turn vague intentions, and government concessions into concrete business plans. Hardest of all is putting those plans into operation, which involves dealing with

---

### Introduction: Land Grabbing Around the World

The Land Matrix project, which tracks large-scale land acquisitions, defines a foreign land grab as a transfer of 200 hectares (500 acres) or more, via lease or sale, to a foreign entity intending to put the land to a new use. The project has compiled a database of such acquisitions since 2000, the vast majority of them since the food-price spikes of 2007–2008.

The picture of land grabbing that emerged in 2008 was of land or water-poor countries, panicked about their future food security, using sovereign wealth funds to snap up land to produce food for their domestic markets. China came in for particular scrutiny based on a series of highly publicized planned acquisitions. Most never materialized, and today's profile of grabbed land, from the Land Matrix project, looks quite different:

The majority of land grabs target lands in Africa. Six of the top ten target countries are South Sudan, the Democratic Republic of Congo, Mozambique, the Republic of the Congo, Liberia, and Sierra Leone. But Papua New Guinea, Indonesia, Brazil, and Ukraine are also in the top ten.

The investors are not mostly sovereign wealth funds from land-poor countries but investors from rich countries. Organization for Economic Cooperation and Development (OECD) countries—which include the United States, most of western Europe, and most other high-income countries—account for more than half of the deals.

The top land grabber—by far—isn't China but the United States, with 6.5 million hectares under contract, more than twice the level of the second-ranked investor country (Malaysia). China is eleventh on the list.

Food crops represent only about one-quarter of all acquired land. Biofuel crops or "flex crops" such as sugar—for either sweetener or ethanol—account for nearly as much acquired land, as do forestry projects. In Africa, only 13% of agricultural land-grab projects are for food.

Perhaps most importantly, the land targeted is not unoccupied. For land on which there are data about former use, the majority was in agriculture—with the majority of that being cultivated by small-scale farmers.

---

weak regional markets, poor infrastructure, and—most importantly—resistance from local residents currently using the land.

By all accounts, ProSAVANA stalled before it could even register as a productive project in the Land Matrix database. Mozambique is fifth among all target countries in the project's ranking by amount of land given away (behind Papua New Guinea, Indonesia, South Sudan, and the Democratic Republic of the Congo), with 99 concluded projects covering 2.2 million hectares. Three-quarters of that is for forestry projects. Of the agriculture projects, one finds just a few comparatively small soybean projects in the Nacala Corridor, ProSAVANA's target region.

Tucked in the database, one finds a grand "intended but not concluded" 700,000-hectare project that lists Brazilians as the investors and the Brazilian, Japanese, and Mozambican governments as partners. ProSAVANA. What happened to the 35 million hectares? That was the press release, the sales pitch to Brazilian investors. Only a fraction of that land is even suitable for agriculture; much is forested or degraded. Or occupied.

## Fundamentally Flawed

Frankly, I was surprised to find ProSAVANA to be such a bust. This wasn't some fly-by-night venture capitalist looking to grow a biofuel crop he'd never produced for a market that barely existed. That's what I saw in Tanzania, and such failed biofuel land grabs litter the African landscape.

ProSAVANA at least knew its investors: Brazil's agribusiness giants. The planners knew their technology: soybeans adapted to the tropical conditions of Brazil's Cerrado. And they knew their market: Japan's and China's hog farms and their insatiable appetite for feed, generally made with soybeans. That was already more than a lot of these grand schemes had going for them. But ProSAVANA foundered because its premise was fundamentally flawed. The Grand Idea was that the soil and climate in the Nacala Corridor were similar to those found in the Cerrado, so Brazilian technology could be easily adapted to tame an uninhabited region inhospitable to agriculture.

It turns out that the two regions differ dramatically. The Cerrado had poor soils, which is why it had few farmers. Technology was available, however, to address soil quality. The Nacala Corridor, by contrast, has good soils, which is precisely why the region is the most densely populated part of rural Mozambique. If there are good lands, you can pretty well bet people have discovered them and are farming them.

## Democracy and Resistance

Mozambique has one other thing Brazil didn't have when it tamed the Cerrado: a democratic government forged in an independence movement rooted in peasant farmers' struggle for land rights. At the time of Brazil's soybean expansion in the mid-1980s, a military dictatorship could impose its Cerrado project. Mozambique has one of the stronger land laws in Africa, which prevents private ownership of land and grants use rights to farmers who have been farming land for ten years or more—whether they have a formal title or not. Even if the government is now siding with foreign investors, it has laws through which an increasingly restive citizenry can hold it accountable.

What may end up dooming ProSAVANA is farmers' growing awareness of the threat to their land, and their capacity to resist. Spearheaded by União Nacional de Camponeses (UNAC), Mozambique's national farmers' union, the campaign to stop the project formed quickly, fueled by a Mozambican tour of the Cerrado organized with Brazilian farmer groups. The images of unending expanses of soybeans, without a small farmer in sight, and the tales of environmental destruction spread quickly through Mozambique.

Within months of the release of the Master Plan, a tri-national campaign in Japan, Brazil, and Mozambique formed. An open letter to the heads of government of the three countries caused a stir, particularly in Japan where the country's international development agency was accused of violating the long-standing separation of development assistance from commercial interests. Last year, the campaign adopted a firm "No to ProSAVANA" stance until farmers and local communities are consulted on development plans for the region.

Local resistance to specific land deals may have had an even greater impact. That certainly scared off some of the largest Brazilian investors, who complained not only that they couldn't own the land outright, but that it took a negotiation with the national government and then further negotiations with local governments just to get a lease. Even then, that lease was for land that was anything but unoccupied. Most packed up their giant combines and went home.

## No End to Land Grabbing

I asked Mr. Sitoe in the Ministry of Agriculture if the lesson of ProSAVANA was that agricultural development needed to be based on Mozambique's three million small-scale food producers. He smirked again. No, he assured me, the government is committed to foreign investment, with its capital and technology, as the path to agricultural development.

He pulled out a two-inch-thick project proposal for a 200,000-hectare foreign-funded scheme for irrigated agriculture along the Lurio River, on the northern edge of the Nacala Corridor. Was this part of ProSAVANA? No, he reassured me with another smile. That brand was clearly tarnished.

Had farmers and communities in the region been consulted about the Lurio River project? "Absolutely not," said Vicente Adriano of UNAC. In the words of the Mozambican independence movement, *A Luta Continua*—the struggle continues. ❏

*Article 8.8*

# FOOD INSECURITY IN AFFLUENT AMERICA

**BY GERALD FRIEDMAN**
*March/April 2015*

The United States is wealthy enough that everyone could have enough to eat. Nonetheless, millions of Americans go hungry each day, subsist on an unhealthy diet because they cannot afford healthier foods, or would go hungry except for social assistance, notably the Food Stamp program, now known as the Supplemental Nutritional Assistance Program (SNAP). Rising average income has done little to reduce the problem of food insecurity, and cutbacks in effective social welfare programs have added to the problems of hunger and malnutrition. SNAP and other safety-net programs are far too small to end hunger in America.

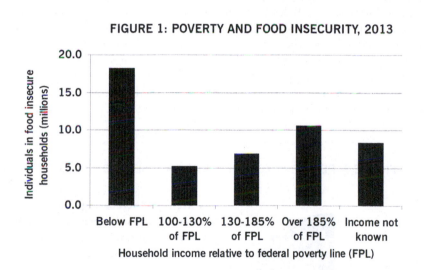

**FIGURE 1: POVERTY AND FOOD INSECURITY, 2013**

**Millions of Americans cannot afford adequate nutrition.** Nearly 50 million Americans are in "food insecure" households, which lack access to enough food for an active, healthy life for all household members. Food insecurity is most common in households under the federal poverty line. Insecurity is also more common in households with many children. While the urban poor dominate our images of hunger, rural residents actually have a slightly higher rate of food insecurity. (Data on food insecurity are based on an annual survey by the Current Population Survey. U.S. Department of Agriculture studies based on these data distinguish between low food security households ("reduced quality, variety, or desirability of diet") and very low food security households ("disrupted eating patterns and reduced food intake").)

## FIGURE 2: ECONOMIC GROWTH AND FOOD INSECURITY

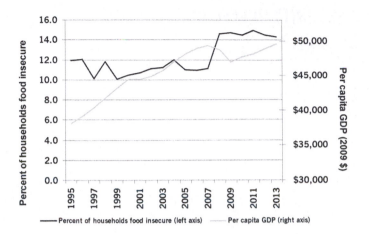

Percent of households food insecure (left axis) — Per capita GDP (right axis)

**Economic growth does not solve the problem of food insecurity.** Food insecurity has increased since the 1990s despite rising average income. A small decline in food insecurity during the boom of the late 1990s was largely reversed even before the Great Recession. Insecurity then soared with the economic crisis, beginning in 2007. High unemployment rates and stagnant or falling wages for working Americans have left illions hungry; cutbacks in social welfare programs have added to the burden of poverty. A dramatic increase in the size of the SNAP program, however, has helped prevent the problem from growing worse since 2009.

## FIGURE 3: PEOPLE IN FOOD INSECURE HOUSEHOLDS, 2013

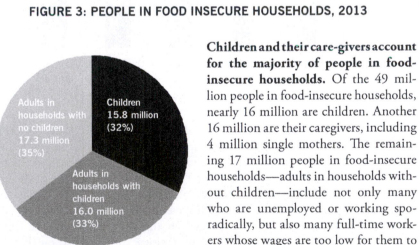

**Children and their care-givers account for the majority of people in food-insecure households.** Of the 49 million people in food-insecure households, nearly 16 million are children. Another 16 million are their caregivers, including 4 million single mothers. The remaining 17 million people in food-insecure households—adults in households without children—include not only many who are unemployed or working sporadically, but also many full-time workers whose wages are too low for them to afford adequate food.

## FIGURE 4: VERY LOW FOOD SECURITY HOUSEHOLDS, 2013

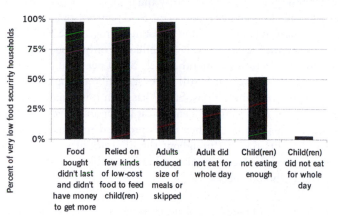

Type of food deprivation reported

**Food-insecure people go hungry, eat badly, and try to save food for their children.** Food insecurity means anxiety, stress, sacrifice, and real hunger for millions of Americans. Almost all "very low food security households"—including more than 17 million people—run out of food sometimes, even though they rely on low-cost foods, skimp on portion size, or skip meals. Adults in these households sacrifice so their children can eat. Almost all reported skipping meals, and over a quarter skipped eating for a whole day. Despite these sacrifices, children in over half the households at least sometimes did not get enough to eat. In over 400,000 very low food security households, at least one child did not eat at all for at least one day in the previous month.

## FIGURE 5: DIFFERENCES IN ADULT OUTCOMES, CHILDREN WHO RECEIVED SNAP COMPARED TO THOSE WHO DID NOT

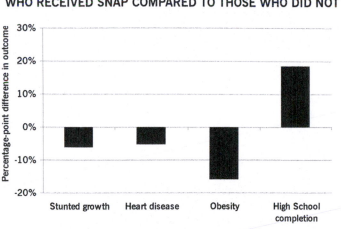

Outcome as adult

*Note:* From sample of individuals born 1956-1981 into "disadvantaged families" (household head had less than a high-school education).

SNAP (Food Stamps) increases food security and has lasting beneficial effects. While 26% of food-insecure households report using food pantries and 3% use soup kitchens, the federal Supplemental Nutrition Assistance Program (SNAP) is the largest source of food assistance. Even SNAP's $70 billion is only enough to provide $125 in food assistance per person per month, barely $1.30 per meal. SNAP reduces the incidence of food insecurity, but it still leaves 49 million people in food-insecure households. Despite these limitations, SNAP has both immediate and lasting benefits. Households that receive SNAP benefits eat better and have better health than similar households that do not. When aid is provided to households with young children, these benefits persist throughout the lifetimes of recipients. Those who receive assistance are healthier as adults and are more likely to finish high school, compared to those who do not. ❏

**Sources:** United States Department of Agriculture, Household Food Security in the United States (ers.usda.gov); Bureau of Economic Analysis (bea.gov); Federal Reserve Bank of St. Louis (FRED) (research.stlouisfed.org); Hilary W. Hoynes, Diane Whitmore Schanzenbach, and Douglas Almond, "Long Run Impacts of Childhood Access to the Safety Net," National Bureau for Economic Research (NBER), November 2012.

# Chapter 9

# TAXATION

## INTRODUCTION

"Only the little people pay taxes." —*Leona Helmsley*

"Taxes are the price we pay for civilization." —*Oliver Wendell Holmes, Jr.*

Taxation is a fascinating subject. It is perhaps the clearest manifestation of class struggle one can find. How a modern government funds itself in order to provide services is an elaborate study in power. The contentious tango of taxes and their inverse, subsidies, plays out daily at all three levels of government—federal, state and local. Who pays taxes and at what rates? What is taxed? Who bears the burden of taxation? And how are tax revenues collected? These are questions that this chapter will address.

In the Reagan era, "supply-side" economist Arthur Laffer famously claimed that high marginal tax rates discourage work and saving, and that cutting tax rates on the rich would spur investment and economic growth. We start the chapter with two articles on the subject: In "Can Tax Cuts Really Increase Government Revenue?" (Article 9.1), economist Ellen Frank reviews the basic arguments made by Laffer and the other supply-siders, and why there is reason to be skeptical. Gerald Friedman puts these arguments to the test, and finds that cutting taxes on the very rich, as the U.S. government has been doing for decades, has not led to the promised investment or economic growth (Article 9.2).

As John Miller points out in "No Fooling—Corporations Evade Taxes" (Article 9.3), *Forbes* magazine finally acknowledged a case of a large corporation gaming the tax code, reporting that General Electric generated $10.3 billion in pretax income but ended up owing nothing to Uncle Sam. What is worse, the company received a tax benefit of $1.1 billion from American taxpayers as gratitude for its clever accounting.

Next, economist Arthur MacEwan answers the question "What's Wrong With a Flat Tax?" (Article 9.4). As MacEwan points out, an income tax that takes the same percentage from everyone may sound even-handed. However, it would eliminate the main "progressive" federal tax (which takes a larger percentage from those with higher incomes), while leaving in place "regressive" taxes (that take a larger share of income from those with lower incomes) such as sales or payroll taxes. That, MacEwan argues, would just shift the tax burden from rich to poor.

Gerald Friedman (Article 9.5) argues that a focus on federal taxes creates the mistaken impression that the U.S. tax system is quite progressive, falling more heavily on high-income people than low-income people. In fact, he notes, the heavy reliance of state and local governments on regressive taxes and fees greatly reduces this progressivity.

Next, Friedman asks "Who Are the 47%?" (Article 9.6). Friedman refutes the view, first, that nearly half the U.S. population pays no taxes. The "47%" actually pay various state and local taxes, as well as federal taxes (especially payroll taxes) other than the income tax. Moreover, the main reasons that people do not pay federal income taxes are that they are elderly, disabled, or simply have very low incomes.

In "Transaction Tax: Sand in the Wheels, Not in the Face" (Article 9.7), economist John Miller makes the case for a tax on stock and other securities trades. This kind of tax, he argues, will not only raise revenue, but also reduce speculation in financial markets and help restore a focus on longer-term planning and job creation in the economy.

Steven Pressman (Article 9.8) analyzes the celebrated work of French economist Thomas Piketty on the growth of income inequality over the history of capitalism. Pressman summarizes Piketty's arguments that rising inequality is not a short-term anomaly, but a deep long-term trend in capitalist societies, then turns to a thoughtful discussion of Piketty's proposed policy responses.

## Discussion Questions

1. (Articles 9.1 and 9.2) What is the basis of supply-siders' claim that lowering the highest marginal tax rate will generate more tax revenue? What are the main arguments against this view?

2. (Article 9.2) In what way have tax policies contributed to growing inequality in the United States? Do you think there is a case for remaking tax policy to be more progressive?

3. (Article 9.3) What are the three key corporate "loopholes" from which corporations have traditionally avoided paying their full marginal tax rate?

4. (Articles 9.3) Why do corporations complain about a corporate marginal tax rate of 35% when in fact no company actually pays that rate?

5. (Article 9.4) In MacEwan's view, why is a "flat" income tax not desirable? What are some arguments in favor of progressive taxation?

6. (Article 9.5) Are state and local tax systems inherently more regressive than the federal system? Could state and local governments raise revenue in more progressive ways?

7. (Article 9.6) Is it bad that nearly half of the population does not pay federal income taxes? Does it affect your opinion to know that almost all of these individuals pay other kinds of (local, state, and federal) taxes?

8.  (Article 9.6) Are the reasons that people do not pay federal income tax justified? That is, would it be desirable to change the tax code to make sure more people did pay federal income taxes? To this end, would it be desirable to reduce other taxes?

9.  (Article 9.7) What is a "Tobin Tax"? Why is this a "two birds with one stone" form of taxation?

10. (Article 9.8) Economist Thomas Piketty proposes a global tax on wealth as a response to rising inequality. Do you think that his solution is feasible? Is it desirable?

Article 9.1

# CAN TAX CUTS REALLY INCREASE GOVERNMENT REVENUE?

**BY ELLEN FRANK**
*November/December 2003*

> Dear Dr. Dollar:
> *A Republican friend tells me that the huge new tax cuts will actually produce more revenue than the government would have collected before the cut, because once rich beneficiaries invest the money, they will pay taxes on every transaction. He suggested that the increase could be as much as 50% more than the originally scheduled revenues. Is this possible?*
> —Judith Walker, New York, N.Y.

**B**ack in the 1970s, conservative economist Arthur Laffer proposed that high marginal tax rates discouraged people from earning additional income. By cutting taxes, especially on those with the highest incomes, Laffer argued, governments would spur individuals to work harder and invest more, stoking economic growth. Though the government would get a smaller bite from every dollar the economy generated, there would be so many more dollars to tax that government revenues would actually rise. Ronald Reagan invoked the "Laffer curve" in the 1980s, insisting he could cut taxes, hike defense spending, and still balance the budget.

Bush's 2001 and 2003 tax packages are eerily reminiscent of the Reagan cuts. They reduce rates levied on ordinary income, with the largest rate cut going to the wealthiest taxpayers. They extend business tax write-offs and increase the child tax credit (though only for two years and only for families who earn enough to pay federal income taxes). They cut the tax on capital gains from 28% to 15%; dividend income, previously taxed at the same rate as ordinary income, now faces a top rate of 15%.

Citizens for Tax Justice estimates that two-thirds of the 2003 tax cut will accrue to the richest 10% of taxpayers. By 2006, the increased child credit will be phased out and nine out of ten taxpayers will find their taxes cut by less than $100. The top 1%, in contrast, will save an average $24,000 annually over the next four years, thanks to the 2003 cut alone.

Though inspired by the same "supply-side" vision that guided Reagan, Bush officials have not explicitly cited Laffer's arguments in defense of their tax packages. Probably, they wish to avoid ridicule. After the Reagan tax cut, the U.S. economy sank into recession and federal tax collections dropped nearly 10%. The deficit soared and economic growth was tepid through much of Reagan's presidency, despite sharp hikes in military spending. Some of the Republican faithful continue to argue that tax cuts will unleash enough growth to pay for themselves, but most are embarrassed to raise the now discredited Laffer curve.

The problem with your friend's assertion is fairly simple. If the government cuts projected taxes by $1.5 trillion over the next decade, those dollars will recirculate through the economy. The $1.5 trillion tax cut becomes $1.5 trillion in taxable income and is itself taxed, as your friend suggests. But this would be just as true if, instead of cutting taxes, the government spent $1.5 trillion on highways or national defense or schools or, for that matter, if it trimmed $1.5 trillion from the tax liability of low- and middle-income households. All tax cuts become income, are re-spent, and taxed. That reality is already factored into everyone's economic projections. But the new income, taxed at a lower rate, will generate lower overall tax collections.

To conclude that revenues will rise rather than fall following a tax cut, one must maintain that the tax cut causes the economy to grow faster than it would have otherwise—that cutting taxes on the upper crust stimulates enough additional growth to offset the lower tax rates, more growth than would be propelled by, say, building roads or reducing payroll taxes. Free-marketeers insist that this is indeed the case. Spend $1.5 trillion on highways and you get $1.5 trillion worth of highways. Give it to Wall Street and investors will develop new technologies, improve productivity, and spur the economy to new heights.

Critics of the Bush cuts contend, however, that faster growth arises from robust demand for goods and from solid, well-maintained public infrastructure. Give $1.5 to Wall Street and you get inflated stock prices and real estate bubbles. Give it to working families or state governments and you get crowded malls, ringing cash registers, and businesses busily investing to keep up with their customers.

Who is right? Die-hard supply-siders insist that the Reagan tax cuts worked as planned—the payoff just didn't arrive until the mid-1990s! But the Bush administration's own budget office is predicting sizable deficits for the next several years. Maybe, like your friend, they believe the tax cuts will pay for themselves—but they're not banking on it. ❏

*Article 9.2*

# THE GREAT TAX-CUT EXPERIMENT

*Has cutting tax rates for the rich helped the economy?*

## BY GERALD FRIEDMAN
*January/February 2013*

S ince the late 1970s, during the Carter Administration, conservative economists have been warning that high taxes retard economic growth by discouraging productive work and investment. These arguments have resonated with politicians, who have steadily cut income taxes, especially those borne by the richest Americans. The highest marginal tax rate, which stood at 70% by the end of the 1970s, was cut to less than 30% in less than a decade. (The marginal rate for a person is the one applied to his or her last dollar of income. A marginal rate that applies to, say, the bracket above $250,000, then, is paid only on that portion of income. The portion of a person's income below that threshold is taxed at the lower rates applying to lower tax brackets.) Despite increases in the early 1990s, the top marginal rate remained below 40%, when it was cut further during the administration of George W. Bush. These dramatic cuts in tax rates, however, have not led to an acceleration in economic growth, investment, or productivity.

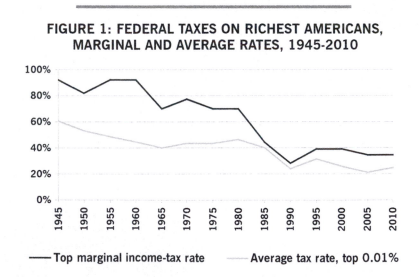

## FIGURE 1: FEDERAL TAXES ON RICHEST AMERICANS, MARGINAL AND AVERAGE RATES, 1945-2010

——— Top marginal income-tax rate ——— Average tax rate, top 0.01%

The federal government has been cutting taxes on the richest Americans since the end of World War II. The average tax paid by the richest taxpayers, as a percentage of income, is typically less than the top marginal rate. Some of their income (the portion below the threshold for the top marginal rate, any capital-gains income, etc.) is taxed at lower rates. Some is not subject to federal income tax because of deductions for state and local taxes, health-care costs, and other expenses. The decline in the average tax rate for the richest, however, does follow the cuts in the top marginal income-tax rate.

## FIGURE 2: TAX REVENUE AS A PERCENTAGE OF GDP, 2008

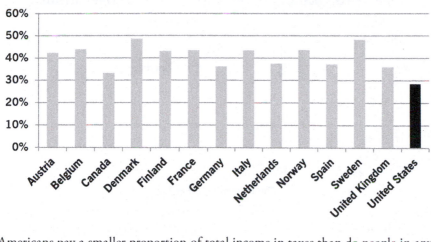

Americans pay a smaller proportion of total income in taxes than do people in any other advanced capitalist economy. As recently as the late 1960s, taxes accounted for as high a share of national income in the United States as in Western European countries. After decades of tax cuts, however, the United States now stands out for its low taxes and small government sector.

## FIGURE 3: AVERAGE TAX RATES ON RICHEST AND REAL GDP GROWTH, BY PRESIDENT, 1947-2010

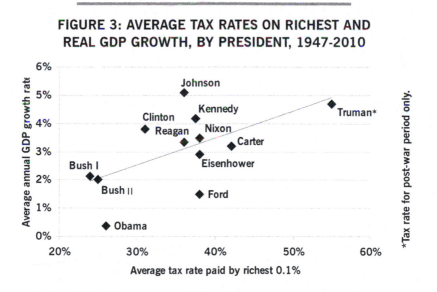

On average, the economy has grown faster during presidential administrations with higher tax rates on the richest Americans. Growth was unusually slow during George W. Bush's two terms (Bush II) and during Obama's first term, when the Bush tax cuts remained in effect. On average, every 10 percentage-point rise in the average tax rate on the richest has been associated with an increase in annual GDP growth of almost one percentage point.

## FIGURE 4: TOP MARGINAL TAX RATE AND INVESTMENT,1963-2011

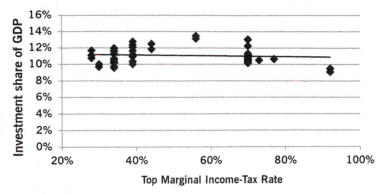

Cutting taxes on the richest Americans has not led them to invest more in plant and equipment. Over the past 50 years, as tax rates have declined, there has been no increase in investment spending as a percentage of GDP. (The flat trend line shows that changes in the highest marginal income-tax rate have not affected investment much, one way or the other.) Instead, the investment share of the economy has been determined by other factors, such as aggregate demand, rather than tax policy.

## FIGURE 5: TAX SHARE OF GDP AND PRODUCTIVITY GROWTH

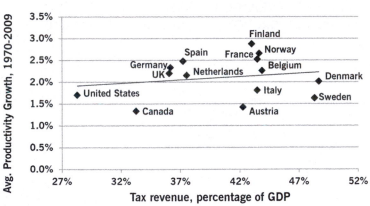

Despite lower and declining tax rates, especially on the rich, the United States has had slower productivity growth over the last several decades than other advanced economies. Overall, lower taxes are associated with slower growth in GDP per hour worked. A 10 percentage point increase in taxes as a share of GDP is associated with an increase in the productivity growth rate of 0.2 percentage points. ❏

***Sources:*** Tom Petska and Mike Strudler, "Income, Taxes, and Tax Progressivity: An Examination of Recent Trends in the Distribution of Individual Income and Taxes" (Statistics of Income Division, Internal Revenue Service, 1997); Thomas Hungerford, "Taxes and the Economy: An Economic Analysis of the Top Tax Rates Since 1945" (Congressional Research Service, 2012); Economic Report of the President, 2012; Bureau of Economic Analysis (bea.gov); Organization of Economic Cooperation and Development, OECD STAT.

*Article 9.3*

# NO FOOLING—CORPORATIONS EVADE TAXES

Forbes *finally notices what has been obvious for years.*

## BY JOHN MILLER
*May/June 2011*

<br>

WHAT THE TOP U.S. COMPANIES PAY IN TAXES

Some of the world's biggest, most profitable corporations enjoy a far lower tax rate than you do—that is, if they pay taxes at all.

The most egregious example is General Electric. Last year the conglomerate generated $10.3 billion in pretax income, but ended up owing nothing to Uncle Sam. In fact, it recorded a tax benefit of $1.1 billion.

Over the last two years, GE Capital [one of the two divisions of General Electric] has displayed an uncanny ability to lose lots of money in the U.S. (posting a $6.5 billion loss in 2009), and make lots of money overseas (a $4.3 billion gain).

It only makes sense that multinationals "put costs in high-tax countries and profits in low-tax countries," says Scott Hodge, president of the Tax Foundation. Those low-tax countries are almost anywhere but the U.S. "When you add in state taxes, the U.S. has the highest tax burden among industrialized countries," says Hodge. In contrast, China's rate is just 25%; Ireland's is 12.5%.

—Christopher Helman, "What the Top U.S. Companies Pay in Taxes," *Forbes*, April 1, 2011

When *Forbes* magazine, the keeper of the list of the 400 richest Americans, warns that corporations not paying taxes on their profits will raise your hackles, you might wonder about the article's April 1 dateline. If it turns out *not* to be an April Fool's joke, things must be *really* bad.

And indeed they are. As *Forbes* reports, General Electric, the third largest U.S. corporation, turned a profit of $10.3 billion in 2010, paid no corporate income taxes, and got a "tax benefit" of $1.1 billion on taxes owed on past profits. And from 2005 to 2009, according to its own filings, GE paid a consolidated tax rate of just 11.6% on its corporate rates, including state, local, and foreign taxes. That's a far cry from the 35% rate nominally levied on corporate profits above $10 million.

Nor was GE alone among the top ten U.S. corporations with no tax obligations. Bank of America (BofA), the seventh largest U.S. corporation, racked up $4.4 billion in profits in 2010 and also paid no corporate income taxes (or in 2009 for that matter). Like GE, BofA has hauled in a whopping "tax benefit"—$1.9 billion.

For BofA, much like for GE, losses incurred during the financial crisis erased it tax liabilities. BofA, of course, contributed mightily to the crisis. It was one of four banks that controlled 95% of commercial bank derivatives activity, mortgage-based securities that inflated the housing bubble and brought on the crisis.

And when the crisis hit, U.S. taxpayers bailed them out, not once but several times. All told BofA received $45 billion of government money from the Troubled

Asset Relief Program (TARP) as well as other government guarantees. And while BofA paid no taxes on their over $4 billion of profits, they nonetheless managed to pay out $3.3 billion in bonuses to corporate executives. All of that has made BofA a prime target for US Uncut protests (see p. 6) against corporate tax dodging that has cost the federal government revenues well beyond the $39 billion saved by the punishing spending cuts in the recent 2011 budget deal.

These two corporate behemoths and other many other major corporations paid no corporate income taxes last year, even though 2010 U.S. corporate profits had returned their level in 2005 in the midst the profits-heavy Bush expansion before the crisis hit.

## An Old Story

But why is *Forbes* suddenly noticing corporate tax evasion? After all, corporations not paying taxes on their profits is an old story. Let's take a look at the track record of major corporations paying corporate income before the crisis hit and the losses that supposedly explain their not paying taxes.

The Government Accounting Office conducted a detailed study of the burden of the corporate income tax from 1998 to 2005. The results were stunning. Over half (55%) of large U.S. corporations reported no tax liability for at least one of those eight years. And in 2005 alone 25% of those corporations paid no corporate income taxes, even though corporate profits had more than doubled from 2001 to 2005.

In another careful study, the Treasury Department found that from 2000 to 2005, the share of corporate operating surplus that that U.S. corporations pay in taxes—a proxy for the average tax rate—was 16.7% thanks to various corporate loopholes, especially three key mechanisms:

- Accelerated Depreciation: allows corporations to write off machinery and equipment or other assets more quickly than they actually deteriorate.
- Stock Options: by giving their executives the option to buy the company's stock at a favorable price, corporations can take a tax deduction for the difference between what the employees pay for the stock and what it's worth.
- Debt Financing: offers a lower effective tax rate for corporate investment than equity (or stock) financing because the interest payments on debt (usually incurred by issuing bonds) get added to corporate costs and reduce reported profits.

Corporate income taxes are levied against reported corporate profits, and each of these mechanisms allows corporations to inflate their reported costs and thereby reduce their taxable profits.

And then there are overseas profits. U.S.-based corporations don't pay U.S. corporate taxes on their foreign income until it is "repatriated," or sent back to the parent corporation from abroad. That allows multinational corporations to defer payment of U.S. corporate income taxes on their overseas profits indefinitely or repatriate their profits from foreign subsidiaries when their losses from domestic operations can offset those profits and wipe out any tax liability, as GE did in 2010.

# Hardly Overtaxed

Nonetheless, Scott Hodge, the president of the right-wing Tax Foundation, steadfastly maintains that U.S. corporations are overtaxed, and that that is what driving U.S. corporations to park their profits abroad (and lower their U.S. taxes). Looking at nominal corporate tax rates, Hodge would seem to have a case. Among the 19 OECD countries, only the statutory corporate tax rates in Japan surpass the (average combined federal and state) 39.3% rate on U.S. corporate profits. And the U.S. rate is well above the OECD average of 27.6%.

But these sorts of comparisons misrepresent where U.S. corporate taxes stand with respect to tax rates actually paid by corporations in other advanced countries. Why? The tax analyst's answer is that the U.S. corporate income tax has a "narrow base," or in plain English, is riddled with loopholes. As a result U.S. effective corporate tax rates—the proportion of corporate profits actually paid out in taxes—are not only far lower than the nominal rate but below the effective rates in several other countries. The Congressional Budget Office, for instance, found that U.S. effective corporate tax rates were near the OECD average for equity-financed investments, and below the OECD average for debt-financed investments. And for the years from 2000 to 2005, the Treasury Department found the average corporate tax rate among OECD countries was 21.6%, well above the U.S. 16.7% rate.

Current U.S. corporate tax rates are also extremely low by historical standards. In 1953, government revenue from the U.S. corporate income taxes were the equal of 5.6% of GDP; the figure was 4.0% of GDP in 1969, 2.2% of GDP from 2000 to 2005, and is currently running at about 2.0% of GDP.

By all these measures U.S. corporations are hardly over-taxed. And some major corporations are barely taxed, if taxed at all.

Closing corporate loopholes so that corporate income tax revenues in the United States match the 3.4% of GDP collected on average by OECD corporate income taxes would add close to $200 billion to federal government revenues—more than five times the $39 billion of devastating spending cuts just made in the federal budget in 2011. Returning the corporate income tax revenues to the 4.0% of GDP level of four decades ago would add close to $300 billion a year to government revenues.

The cost of not shutting down those corporate loopholes would be to let major corporations go untaxed, to rob the federal government of revenues that could, with enough political will, reverse devastating budget cuts, and to leave the rest of us to pay more and more of the taxes necessary to support a government that does less and less for us. ❑

*Sources:* "Corporate Tax Reform: Issues for Congress," by Jane G. Gravelle and Thomas L. Hungerford, CRS Report for Congress, October 31, 2007; "Treasury Conference On Business Taxation and Global Competitiveness," U.S. Department of the Treasury, Background Paper, July 23, 2007; "Six Tests for Corporate Tax Reform," by Chuck Marr and Brian Highsmith, Center on Budget and Policy Priorities, February 28, 2011; "Tax Holiday For Overseas Corporate Profits Would Increase Deficits, Fail To Boost The Economy, And Ultimately Shift More Investment And Jobs Overseas," by Chuck Marr and Brian Highsmith, Center on Budget and Policy Priorities, April 8, 2011; and, "Comparison of the Reported Tax Liabilities of Foreign and U.S.-Controlled Corporations, 1998-2005," Government Accounting Office, July 2008.

*Article 9.4*

# WHAT'S WRONG WITH A FLAT TAX?

## BY ARTHUR MacEWAN
*September/October 2012*

> Dear Dr. Dollar:
> *Today a minister asked me why a flat tax, where "everybody pays their fair share," is not the best idea. I did not have a short, convincing explanation. Can you help?* —Arthur Milholland, Silver Springs, MD

Although flat tax proposals differ, they have one basic thing in common: they would all reduce the tax rates for people with high incomes. Thus they would either shift the tax burden to people with lower incomes or lead to a reduction in government services or both.

Currently, the federal personal income tax is quite progressive on paper and somewhat progressive in fact. A "progressive" income tax system is one where people with higher incomes pay a larger percentage of their income as taxes than do people with lower incomes. (A "regressive" system is one where people with lower incomes pay a higher share of their income as taxes; a "proportional" system is one where everyone pays the same proportion of their income as taxes. A flat tax and a proportional tax are the same.)

The justification for a progressive tax system is fairness: people with higher incomes have a greater ability to pay taxes and therefore should be subject to a higher tax rate. For example (to take an extreme case), a family with an income of $2 million can pay $200,000 in taxes more easily (i.e., with less impact on their circumstances) than a family with an income of $20,000 can pay $2,000 in taxes. Also, the principle of fairness suggests that high-income families should pay higher rates to support a system that provides so well for them. These concepts of fairness have been long established in the U.S. personal income-tax system.

Even today, with rates for high-income people lowered from earlier years, the system still has a significant element of progressivity. For example, a family with taxable income of $20,000 would supposedly pay $2,150 (10.75%), while a family with taxable income of $1 million would supposedly pay $320,000 (32%). Of course many people, especially those with high-incomes, find various "loopholes," and do not end up paying as much in taxes as they otherwise would. Many loopholes are in the deductions that allow people to keep their taxable income—and therefore their taxes—down. At the same time, many people with low incomes have their taxes greatly reduced—sometimes resulting in payments *from* the government rather than tax payments *to* the government.

The Tax Policy Center has estimated that in 2010 people in the lowest 40% of the income distribution on average got money back from the government (because of the Earned Income Tax Credit and the Child Tax Credit), while people in the highest-income 20% on average paid taxes at a rate of 13.6%. People at the very top, the highest-income 1%, paid on average 18.6%.

Conservative ideologues like to jump on the fact that many low-income people pay no federal income tax at all. Yet federal income taxes are only part of the tax story. Low-income people still pay Social Security and Medicare taxes, sales taxes at the state level, and various other taxes. Overall, the U.S. tax system is hardly progressive at all, and may even be regressive.

Advocates of a flat tax claim it would be better to get rid of all the complications in the federal income tax—the adjustments, the credits, the deductions, etc.—and just charge everyone the same rate. Also, they argue that a flat tax would boost the economy because the current high rates on people with high incomes harm the incentive to invest and to work. Yet there is no way around the simple arithmetic: to lower the top rate and to obtain the same amount of revenue from a flat tax as from the current system, people below the top would have to have their tax rates increased. (While advocates of a flat tax generally reject the principles of fairness on which the progressivity of the U.S. tax code has long been based, it would be possible to introduce an element of progressivity into a flat tax by exempting all income below a certain level. Still, except for those people near the bottom, tax rates would have to be raised for most people—though not for those at the top.)

Furthermore, the claim that with a flat tax all the adjustments, credits, deductions, etc. would be eliminated is not credible. Indeed, since a flat tax would increase the after-tax income of those at the top, it would increase the amount of money they would have to buy influence to get their favorite "complications" reinstated (as if they didn't have enough influence already!). As to the argument that reducing the tax rate on people with high incomes would boost the economy, well, we have seen how well that has worked since the Bush tax cuts for the wealthy were put in place in 2001.

So a flat tax would be one more break for the rich, increasing their income on the backs of the great majority of the populace. Not fair at all. That's what's wrong with a flat tax. ❏

*Article 9.5*

# THE BURDENS OF AMERICAN FEDERALISM
*Income Redistribution Through Taxation*

## BY GERALD FRIEDMAN
*September/October 2015*

Because of increasing economic inequality, many scholars and activists have looked at tax policy both for changes that may explain widening income gaps and for reforms that might reduce inequality of market incomes. While it is appropriate to study the role of federal taxes, state and local governments take in nearly half of all government revenue. Non-tax revenues from fees and service charges account for nearly 15% of government revenue (all levels).

Americans are accustomed to thinking of the tax system as progressive, requiring higher-income people to pay a higher percentage of their incomes in taxes than lower-income people. Because the burden of state and local taxes and non-tax revenues is much heavier on poor people and the working class than it is on the rich, however, the fiscal system as a whole is much less progressive than it seems from looking only at federal-level taxation. While all states have regressive tax systems, requiring lower-income people to pay a higher percentage of their incomes than higher-income people, some states are more regressive than others. States that rely on sales taxes and user fees impose a heavier burden on poor and working people; states that rely more on income taxes do less to widen the income gap.

## FIGURE 1: TOTAL GOVERNMENT REVENUE BY LEVEL, 2012

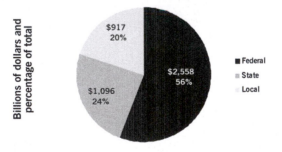

**The federal government collects only a little more than half of government revenues.** The federal government and its taxes—totaling just over $2.5 trillion (or 56% of government revenue)—have often been the focus of political attention and controversy. State and local governments, however, collect nearly $2 trillion in taxes and other types of revenue. (Non-tax revenue includes charges for services (such as water, the lottery, or college tuition) as well as fees (such as motor vehicle registration or licenses).) States and localities collect 44% of total government revenues. Therefore, to understand the distributional impact of government revenue policies in the United States, we have to consider all levels of government, not just the federal.

## FIGURE 2: GOVERNMENT REVENUE BY SOURCE, 2012

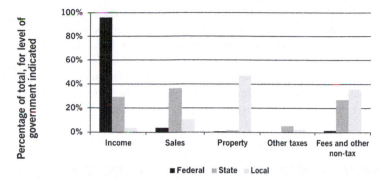

**Federal revenues are collected largely from income and payroll taxes; states and localities collect sales and property taxes, and charge fees.** There are three distinct tax systems in the United States, corresponding to the three levels of government. The federal government draws the vast majority of its revenue from taxes on income, including corporate and personal income taxes as well as Social Security and Medicare payroll taxes. In contrast, income taxes account for less than 30% of state tax revenue and virtually no local tax revenue. States are more likely to collect revenue from fees and from sales taxes, especially on material goods. (Business and consumer services usually go untaxed.) For their part, local governments rely little on sales taxes but draw most of their revenue from fees and from property taxes, mostly on real estate.

## FIGURE 3: DISTRIBUTION OF FISCAL BURDEN, 2011-2012

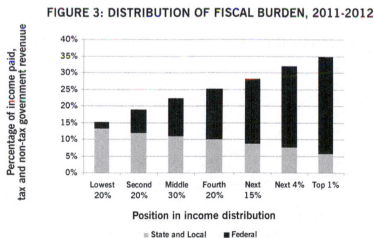

**The economic burden of state and local government falls most heavily on poor and working people.** Most Americans pay more in state and local government taxes and fees than they do in federal taxes. Because federal taxes fall more heavily on the rich than on the poor, they redistribute income "downwards." In contrast, state and local taxes and fees fall more heavily on the poor and the working class, while the richest Americans pay relatively little. (Property taxes, significant at the local level, are actually *regressive* on balance: While it depends somewhat on how one apportions the burden of property taxes between landlords and renters, the Intstitute for Taxation and Economic Policy calculates the bottom 20% pay 3.7% of their incomes in property taxes while the richest 1% pay only 1.6%.) The balance between state and local revenues, on the one hand, and federal revenues, on the other, is therefore important for understanding the impact of taxation on income distribution. The larger the share of state and local taxes and fees—apart from state and local income taxes—the less government redistributes income downward; and the larger the share of national taxation, the more the government does to equalize after-tax incomes.

### FIGURE 4A: DISTRIBUTION OF INCOME TAX BURDEN, 2011-2012

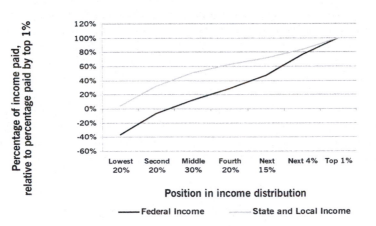

### FIGURE 4B: DISTRIBUTION OF SALES TAX BURDEN, 2011-2012

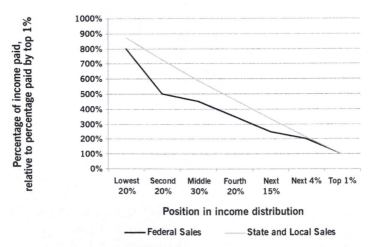

**Differences in the burdens of taxation between the federal government and states and localities result from the type of tax assessed.** Whether assessed on the state or on the national level, income taxes fall more heavily on the rich than on the poor.

Because of federal and state earned-income tax credits (tax exemptions on labor income that favor low-income people) and progressive income-tax rates, high-income people pay a much higher percentage of their incomes in income taxes than do lower-income people. This is true on both the state and federal levels. By contrast, sales taxes fall more heavily on lower-income people. This is because poor and working people spend higher proportions of their incomes on consumption than rich people do, and are more likely to consume material goods subject to sales taxes. Rich people spend more of their incomes on sales-tax-exempt services, such as legal services and personal care.

## FIGURE 5: PROGRESSIVITY OF STATE TAX SYSTEMS, 2012

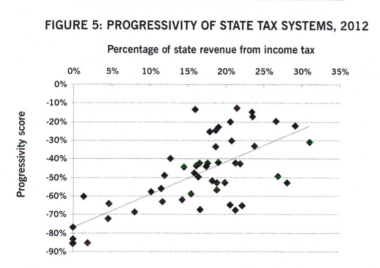

Percentage of state revenue from income tax

Note: Progressivity score = (percentage of income paid by top 1% - percentage of income paid by bottom 20%)/(percentage of income paid by bottom 20%). Only for state taxes (excludes local taxes and all fees).

**States that rely on income taxes have more equitable tax systems; those that rely on sales taxes and fees widen the gap between rich and poor.** While every state has a regressive tax system, some states are much more regressive than others. Regionally, southern states have more regressive tax systems, with the richest 1% paying only half as much of their incomes (in percentage terms) as do the poorest 20%; in northeastern states, by contrast, the richest 1% pay two-thirds as much as do the poor. The regressive effect of state and local revenue collection is not just a matter of region, but of policy. As with the federal government, progressivity in state and local taxation comes from reliance on income taxes. Whether in the North or the South, states without an income tax, like Texas, Washington, and Wyoming, or states where relatively little revenue comes from the income tax, have the most regressive revenue systems. By contrast, the states with the least regressive systems tend to rely more on income taxation and draw less of their revenue from sales taxes and fees. ❏

***Sources:*** Internal Revenue Service (irs.gov); The White House, Budget for Fiscal Year 2016 (whitehouse. gov); U.S. Bureau of the Census (census.gov); Institute for Taxation and Economic Policy (itep.org); Congressional Budget Office, The Distribution of Household Income and Federal Taxes(cbo.gov).

*Article 9.6*

# WHO ARE "THE 47%"?

*And why don't they pay (income) taxes?*

**BY GERALD FRIEDMAN**
*November/December 2012*

"There are 47% of the people ... who are dependent upon government, who believe that they are victims, who believe the government has a responsibility to care for them, who believe that they are entitled to health care, to food, to housing, to you-name-it .... These are people who pay no income tax."

While Mitt Romney did not intend for the general public to hear his candid remarks to his wealthy donors, his dismissal of nearly half of the American public as irresponsible dependents mooching off hard-working taxpayers is common among American conservatives. It is also wrong.

Virtually all of those who pay no federal income tax pay other taxes, including federal payroll taxes and state and local sales and property taxes, and many pay a higher share of their income in taxes than do Mitt Romney and his wealthy friends. (The latter avoid payroll taxes and much of their income tax by taking their salary as capital gains.) Furthermore, most of "the 47%" owe no federal income tax for good and sensible reasons: they are disabled, elderly, or have a very low income.

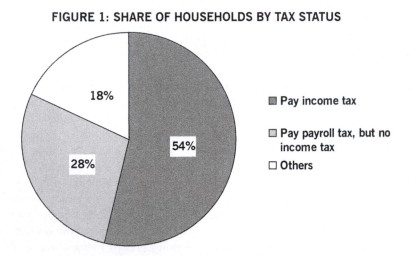

**FIGURE 1: SHARE OF HOUSEHOLDS BY TAX STATUS**

18%

54%

28%

■ Pay income tax

□ Pay payroll tax, but no income tax

□ Others

While just over 46% of Americans paid no income tax last year, over half of them (over 28% of the total) paid payroll taxes (e.g., Social Security and Medicare taxes), most paid federal excise taxes (on phones and other services), and almost all paid sales and other state and local taxes.

## FIGURE 2: REASONS FOR NOT PAYING INCOME TAX

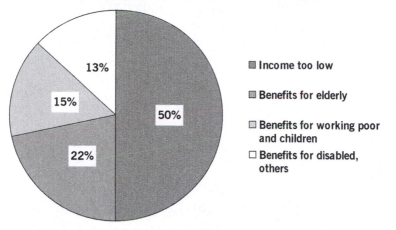

- Income too low
- Benefits for elderly
- Benefits for working poor and children
- Benefits for disabled, others

Those who are not paying income tax include the elderly, the disabled, many children, and the poorest Americans. Almost a third have household incomes under $10,000, and almost two thirds have incomes under $20,000. Only 5% have household incomes of as much as $50,000.

## FIGURE 3: PERCENTAGE NOT PAYING INCOME TAX, BY INCOME CLASS

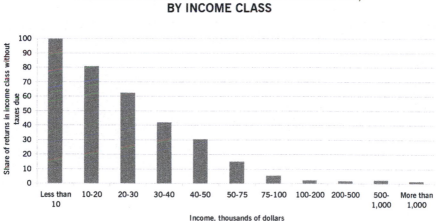

The proportion of returns without income tax liability falls quickly from almost 100% for the lowest incomes down to a negligible percentage for high income returns.

Many Americans do not pay income tax because of provisions inserted into the tax code, including some under Republican icons like Richard Nixon and Ronald Reagan, to encourage low-income Americans to seek paid work— such as the Earned

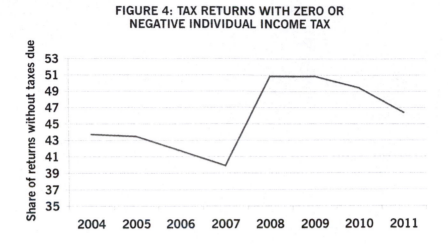

FIGURE 4: TAX RETURNS WITH ZERO OR
NEGATIVE INDIVIDUAL INCOME TAX

Income Tax Credit and the high minimum income threshold before income taxes are due. Because of provisions like these, when incomes fall, the income of a larger share of Americans falls below the level at which they pay income taxes. This is why the share not paying income tax increased sharply during the Great Recession, and has been decreasing (slowly) with the (slow) recovery since.

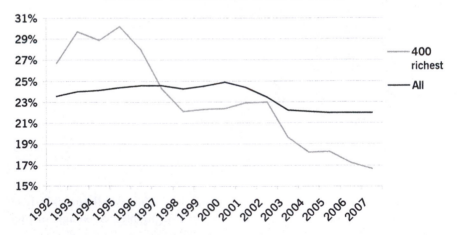

FIGURE 5: FEDERAL TAX RATES AS A SHARE OF ADJUSTED GROSS INCOME, 1992-2007 (INCOME AND PAYROLL TAXES)

The real tax evaders are not the disabled, elderly, or the poor who earn too little to pay federal income tax. They are the super-rich who shift income into tax shelters, offshore accounts, and get paid in capital gains taxed at a preferential rate. Such evasions have allowed the wealthiest Americans to lower their total federal tax bill to well below the rate paid by other Americans. ❑

*Source:* Tax Policy Center.

*Article 9.7*

# TRANSACTION TAX: SAND IN THE WHEELS, NOT IN THE FACE

*Why a transaction tax is a really good idea.*

**BY JOHN MILLER**
*March/April 2010*

> WHY TAXING STOCK TRADES IS A REALLY BAD IDEA
> [S]urely it is "socially useful" to let free people transact freely, without regulators and legislators micromanaging them. ... It's Economics 101 that the free actions of market participants cause supply and demand to reach equilibrium. And isn't that what investors—indeed even speculators—do? Can they do it as well when facing the dead-weight costs of a transaction tax?
>
> If not, then trading volume in our stock markets will fall. Beyond the tax, everyone—investors and speculator, great and small—who buys or sells stocks will pay more to transact in markets that are less liquid. In such a world, markets would necessarily be more risky, and the cost of capital for business would necessarily rise. The consequence of that is that innovation, growth, and jobs would necessarily fall. That would be the full and true cost of the trading tax.
> —Donald L. Luskin and Chris Hynes, "Why Taxing Stock Trades Is a Really Bad Idea," *Wall Street Journal*, January 5, 2010

"**S**ome financial activities which proliferated over the last 10 years were socially useless," Britain's Finance Service Authority Chairman Adiar Turner told a black-tie gathering of financial executives in London in September 2009. That is why he had proposed a transaction tax for the United Kingdom and why British Prime Minister Gordon Brown would propose an international transaction tax at the November G-20 summit.

The gathered bankers "saw red," as one report described their reaction. Investment bankers Donald L. Luskin and Chris Hynes are still irate.

In some ways their reaction is surprising. A financial transaction tax is nothing other than a sales tax on trading stocks and other securities. Transaction taxes are already in place in about 30 countries, and a transaction tax applied to the sale of stock in the United States from 1914 to 1964.

In addition, the transaction tax rates on a single trade are typically quite low. For instance, the "Let Wall Street Pay for the Restoration of Main Street Act of 2009," proposed by U.S. Representative Peter DeFazio (D-Ore.), would assess a one quarter of one percent (.25%) tax on the value of stock transactions, and two one hundredths of one percent (.02%) tax on the sale on a variety of derivative assets—including credit default swaps, which played such a large role in the mortgage crisis. To target speculators, the bill exempts retirement accounts, mutual funds, education and health savings accounts, and the first $100,000 of transactions annually.

In other ways, Luskin's and Hynes's reaction is not surprising at all. At its heart, a transaction tax is a radical measure. Its premise is that faster-acting financial markets driven by speculation don't bring relief to the economy—instead, they loot the economy. Its purpose, as Nobel Prize-winning economist James Tobin put it when he proposed his original transaction tax on international money markets during the 1970s, is to "throw sand in the wheels" of our financial markets.

Also, while its tax rate is low, the burden of a transaction tax adds up as securities are repeatedly traded, as is the practice on Wall Street today. For instance, even after accounting for its exemptions and allowing for a sizable decline in trading, the DeFazio bill would still raise $63.5 billion annually, according to the estimates of Dean Baker, co-director of the Center for Economic Policy Research.

Luskin and Hynes have two main objections to the transaction tax. The first is that a transaction tax would affect every single person who owns and invests in stocks, not just speculators. Customers would not have to pay a tax to buy or sell mutual funds, but, as Luskin and Hynes emphasize, the mutual funds themselves would have to pay a tax every time they trade stocks. So everyone holding mutual funds would still end up paying the tax.

What Luskin and Hynes don't say is this: Mutual funds that actively trade stocks would pay three times the transaction taxes of an average fund, as the Investment Company Institute, the fund industry trade group, reports. And stock index funds, which hold a sample of all stocks but seldom trade them, are taxed the least. Those funds have historically outperformed other mutual funds. So a transaction tax would work to push mutual fund customers to invest their savings more wisely, providing some with higher rates of return with a transaction tax than their previous funds provided without it. And that would mean fewer broker fees and lower profits for the fund industry.

But what really sticks in Luskin's and Hynes's craw is the assertion that financial trading is not socially useful. That claim flies in face of the long-held contention, buttressed by much of finance theory, that the equilibrium outcomes of financial markets are efficient. And if financial markets are efficient, there is no need for a tax that will reduce trading.

But much of what Luskin and Hynes have to say is not right. First, as anyone who *paid attention* in Economics 101 would know, reaching an equilibrium is not in and of itself desirable. To endorse the outcomes of today's speculative financial markets as desirable because they reach an equilibrium is the equivalent of describing a gambler in a poker game raking in a big pot as desirable because it clears the table. And the gamblers in our financial markets did rake in some awfully big pots betting that subprime borrowers would default on their loans. The last few years show us just how undesirable that equilibrium turned out to be.

Second, speculation dwarfs financing investment in U.S. stock markets. During the 1970s, for every dollar of new investment in plants and equipment, $1.30 in stocks were traded on the U.S. exchanges, reports Robert Pollin, co-director of the Political Economy Research Institute. But from 1998 to 2007, $27 in stocks were traded on the U.S. exchanges for every dollar of corporate investment in plant equipment. Such a rapid stock turnover has diverted the attention of managers of enterprises from long-term planning. Whatever damage that churning caused on Main Street, it paid off handsomely on Wall Street. From 1973 to 2007, the size of the financial (and insurance) sector relative to the economy doubled, financial sector profits went from one-quarter to two-fifths of domestic profits, and compensation in the finance industry went from just about average to 180% of the private industry average.

By counteracting these trends, a transactions tax can actually enhance, not diminish, the efficiency of financial markets. If it forces the financial sector to fulfill its function of transferring savings to investment with less short-term churning, then the tax will have freed up resources for more productive uses.

A transaction tax would surely be a step in the right direction toward reducing the bloat of the finance industry, righting the balance of speculation over enterprise, and restoring the focus on long-term planning and job-creation in the economy.

None of that will happen unless every last grain of the decades' worth of sand the bullies on Wall Street have kicked in our faces gets thrown into the wheels of finance. That is a tall order. But as DeFazio's and Turner's example shows, some of today's policymakers are up to the task. ❏

*Sources:* Dean Baker, "The Benefits of a Financial Transaction Tax," Center For Economic and Policy Research, December 2008; Robert Pollin and Dean Baker, "Public Investment, Industrial Policy, and U.S. Economic Renewal," Political Economy Research Institute, December 2009; Caroline Binham, "Turner Plan on 'Socially Useless' Trades Make Bankers See Red," Bloomberg. com; Yaiman Onaran, "Taxing Wall Street Today Wins Support for Keynes Idea (Update 1)," Bloomberg.com; Dean Baker, Robert Pollin, Travis McArthur, and Matt Sherman, "The Potential Revenue from Financial Transactions Taxes, Political Economy Research Institute, Working paper no. 212, December 2009; Donald L. Luskin and Chris Hynes, "Why Taxing Stock Trades Is a Really Bad Idea," *Wall Street Journal,* January 5, 2010; John McKinnon, "Lawmakers Weigh A Wall Street Tax," *Wall Street Journal,* December 19, 2009; Tobin Tax, freerisk.org/wiki/index. php/Tobin_tax; text of HR 4191—"Let Wall Street Pay for the Restoration of Main Street Act of 2009," www.govtrack.us.

*Article 9.8*

# WEALTH INEQUALITY AND WEALTH TAXATION
*A Primer on Piketty*

**BY STEVEN PRESSMAN**
*May 2014*

Great works in economics address important issues head-on, adopt a broad per-spective, and change our views regarding how economies work. Make no mis-take about it: Thomas Piketty's *Capital in the Twenty-First Century* is a great work. As an added bonus, it is extremely well written (and translated).

Given decades of rising inequality and its negative consequences and public concern about a disappearing middle class, this book is particularly timely. It relies on a wide array of data, collected by the author, showing long-term trends in income and wealth distribution. It explains the causes of these trends and ends by setting forth some bold policy solutions.

Still, the most important aspect of *Capital in the Twenty-First Century* is that it changes how we view the world. The following parallel might provide some histori-cal perspective on the book, and help understand its importance and the emotional reaction it has elicited.

Thomas Malthus became one of the most controversial figures in economics fol-lowing the publication of his *Essay on Population* in 1798. Despite much optimism at the time that ordinary people's lives could be improved, for Malthus poverty was inevitable due to the relationship between population growth and the growth of the food supply. His *Essay* argued (based on some empirical data) that population growth would outstrip food supply growth, resulting in famine and misery.

Piketty can best be understood as a sort of modern-day Malthus. Both doubt-ing Thomases sought to refute popular beliefs that life could easily be improved for most people, both used simple growth rates to do this, and both were criticized for their pessimistic conclusions.

Optimism regarding the future distribution of income stems from the work of Nobel laureate Simon Kuznets. In the 1950s, Kuznets examined U.S. income-tax data and saw income inequality improving over several decades. According to the standard interpretation of his work, he hypothesized that as capitalist economies developed, inequality first increases and then decreases. This message fit America's economic experience during the post-war years and its geo-political needs during the Cold War. Most economists came to accept this message of hope.

But times have changed. Inequality is rising in the United States and other high-income capitalist countries. Piketty explains why economists got it wrong. He argues that greater equality between World War I and the 1960s was not part of some positive long-term trend; rather, it stemmed from a unique set of factors—two wars (that destroyed much wealth), the very high marginal tax rates implemented to pay for these wars, plus a stock-market crash and Great Depression. Starting in the 1970s or 1980s (dates differ by country) the moneyed class revolted and began to influence policy. Top income-tax rates fell; income and wealth inequality rose rapidly. As a result, we seem headed toward another Gilded Age, similar to the late 19th century, where the fabulously wealthy live charmed lives and everyone else struggles to survive.

Piketty, like Malthus, draws his dismal conclusion from the relationship between two growth rates. In Piketty's case, they are the rate of return to wealth or capital (r) and the growth rate of the economy (g). When r exceeds g, more money flows to those at the top and inequality increases; when r is less than g, more benefits of economic growth flow to workers, making income and wealth distribution more equal.

One great virtue of Piketty's book is that it explains why income inequality has grown of late. First, the ratio of wealth to GDP declined in Europe from 6:1 or 7:1 around World War I to 2:1 in the 1960s. It has since rebounded to nearly 6:1. The United States experienced a smaller decline, since its factories were not destroyed by the two wars, but has also experienced a growing wealth-to-GDP ratio of late. Second, r has averaged around 5% over long periods of time in many different countries, while g cannot be expected to grow by much more than 1%.

Together these results create a distribution problem, which may be easiest to comprehend in personal terms.

Suppose you receive a $200,000 inheritance (your wealth) and you make $100,000 a year. If your wealth grows at 5% per year and your wages grow by 1%, after 35 years (a typical working life) your wages would be around $140,000 and your wealth (assuming no spending down of this wealth) over $1 million. After several generations, around 100 years, your great grandchild would have labor income of $268,000 and have $25 million in capital assets. With a 5% return, their capital income ($1.25 million) would dwarf their labor income. If some income from wealth gets consumed, which is likely, this process just takes a little longer to work out. At some point income from wealth will far exceed income from labor.

The problem is that we don't all begin with equal amounts of capital. Some start with large inheritances; most people begin with nothing. As a result, the incomes of the haves grow much more rapidly than those of the have-nots and wealth inequality soars.

Piketty's story is far superior to standard economic explanations of rising inequality, such as technological change and globalization. He rightly rejects these theories because they cannot explain national differences in rising inequality—technological change and globalization should have similar impacts on all developed nations.

Compiling the data to make this case has been a heroic endeavor. Piketty uses income tax returns to get data on the share of national income going to the top 10%, the top 1%, and the top 0.1% of households. Estate tax returns enable him to estimate wealth inequality. Substantial evidence supports Piketty's conclusion that income and wealth inequality have risen in the United States and elsewhere since the late 20th century.

Similar to Malthus's *Essay*, Piketty's *Capital* contains virtually no economic theory. It does not address what determines economic growth or the return to wealth. Its dismal conclusion stems from historic trends and Piketty's explanation of why high rates of return to wealth increase inequality.

## So Where Do We Go From Here?

The last part of Piketty's book discusses how to deal with rising inequality. Piketty is skeptical that institutional policies such as raising the minimum wage, or more generous government spending programs, will help much. It is not that he opposes such efforts. Rather, he thinks they are inadequate when wealth is so unevenly distributed and grows so rapidly. Government spending programs can help, but they cannot increase labor income by 5% annually over the long run.

Tax policy is all that is left (no pun intended). Piketty favors a more progressive individual income tax, with a 70% top rate. Corporations, he argues, also need to be taxed based on where they pay wages so they cannot book profits to subsidiaries in low-tax countries.

These policies would reduce income inequality and slow down, but not reverse, the more pressing issue of greater wealth inequality. To deal with this latter problem, Piketty advocates an annual wealth tax, imposed at very low rates—one or two percent on wealth in excess of 1 million euros (nearly $1.4 million). And it must be a global tax, so that it cannot be escaped by moving wealth abroad.

Those on the right objected to the tax rates that Piketty proposes as excessively high. The worst of these objections engaged in name-calling, deeming anyone a socialist who proposes higher taxes for whatever reason. Almost as bad have been the objections that higher taxes would give the government more money to waste— as if businesses never, ever wasted money and consumers always spent their money cautiously and rationally (e.g., they would never buy homes or be able to obtain mortgages that they couldn't possibly afford to repay). The more thoughtful and reasonable objections from the right have focused on the bad incentives to work hard, earn money, accumulate wealth, and provide for one's children and grandchildren as a result of higher taxes.

Those on the left and toward the center of the political spectrum have been fairly consistent in maintaining that the main policy proposal of Piketty was impractical because a global wealth tax would never get enacted. After making this point, the next sentence of these critiques typically push other policies (invariably the personal favorites of those criticizing Piketty), which are just as unlikely to get enacted given the current political situation in the United States and elsewhere.

I find all these criticisms both disturbing and a little bit off the mark. But before looking at his wealth tax proposals in greater detail, it is worth examining what Piketty has to say regarding monetary policy and fiscal policy, something which was not discussed in most of the prominent reviews of his book. Piketty downplays monetary policy in favor of fiscal policy. Monetary policy, he contends, cannot deal with the problem of rising inequality. In fact, he contends that we cannot know the impact of monetary policy on income and wealth distribution, although there is no argument for this. My gut instinct is that this is true, but I would have liked to see some data that supports this contention—say, looking at how income and wealth distribution vary based on interest rates. Such a study would make for a great thesis or doctoral dissertation, to say nothing about a nice professional paper.

Regarding fiscal policy, Piketty is fairly critical of government deficits. He spends a good deal of time focusing on the need to tax wealth so that we can repay existing government debt, but he fails to address the issue of whether government deficits and debt may be necessary at times. He also doesn't address the issue of whether government debt does any actual harm to overall macroeconomic performance. Rather, the focus is mainly (Surprise! Surprise! Surprise!) on the impact of debt on income distribution. Piketty's main point is that the large majority of government bonds created when the government goes into debt is owned by the very wealthy. They benefit greatly from government debt. With little risk, they receive positive returns on their money. This income generates part of their 5 percent rate of return on wealth or capital.

Unfortunately, the passages on fiscal policy and distribution are too brief. There are two key reasons I wish Piketty had written a good deal more on the relationship between fiscal policy and inequality. First, he argues throughout Capital that one main reason inequality declined from World War I through the 1950s was that there were high marginal tax rates on top incomes. This reduced the after-tax gains from owning wealth. Second, fiscal policy is central to Piketty's major policy proposals.

Writing more on fiscal policy and distribution would not have been all that difficult to do. Moreover, his entire case for changes in tax policy would have been considerably stronger had Piketty spent more time on this topic and then related it to the beginnings of the revolt of the rentiers in the United Kingdom and the United States when Margaret Thatcher and Ronald Reagan were elected heads of government.

The story in both cases is rather similar and involved several policy changes. There was a sharp cut in government spending (that hurt the poor and middle class more than wealthy households, which can provide their own benefits) and a sharp cut in taxes focused at the top of the income distribution. Overall, the cuts in government expenditures were less than the tax cuts, and the government had to borrow money by selling bonds. Abstracting a little from the overall process, the Reagan and Thatcher governments gave large tax breaks to the wealthy, and then borrowed the money back from them to pay for the tax cuts. Everyone else got small tax cuts that were funded by cutting the government benefits they received. Or in slightly bolder and simpler terms, the Reagan and Thatcher governments decided to fund a good deal of government spending by borrowing money from the wealthy rather than taxing the wealthy.

As Piketty's data demonstrate, these changes led to sharply rising inequality in the UK and U.S. over the past several decades. And it is no wonder why this occurred. Those earning high incomes got to keep a lot more of their income. Yet they had to do something with all this additional money. It could not be kept under the mattress, earning nothing. Bank deposits were insured, but not for balances of the sort that the very wealthy possessed. The result could only be that all this additional disposable income fueled rising asset prices, which also primarily benefited the wealthy.

According to the gospel of "supply-side" economics, which was used to justify these policy changes, the whole process should have resulted in much greater economic growth and enormous tax collections by the government so that there would be no deficit. However, this claim ignored the "balanced budget multiplier" described by the great 20th century U.S. economist Paul Samuelson. Samuelson showed that an equal cut in taxes and in government spending would slow economic growth or reduce GDP by an amount equal to the tax cut (or cut in government spending). The reason for this is very simple. A dollar less in government spending is a dollar less spending while a dollar tax cut was not an additional dollar in spending since some of the spending will be saved. Overall, this will reduce spending and economic growth. Yet ideology triumphed over economic knowledge. The U.S. government and the UK government gave huge tax cuts to the wealthy, and then borrowed the money back from them in order to fund the tax cut. Economic growth slowed as the balanced budget multiplier predicted it would. This made distributional matters even worse because it increased the gap between r and g by lowering g.

One last thing is worth some additional comments before getting to the issue of income and wealth taxes, especially since this has been one of the most frequent criticisms of Piketty. Many commentators complained that Piketty ignored alternative policies such as supporting unions and raising the minimum wage—but Piketty actually does discuss these policies. Chapter 9 of the book includes an extensive discussion of the minimum wage. The data Piketty presents and the written text both make it very clear that the distribution of wages has remained relatively equal in France because the French have continually increased the minimum wage and that the French minimum wage is rather high compared to average wages. Piketty even discusses why this happened—French President Charles de Gaulle (in office 1958-1969) was worried about the crisis of May 1968 and used higher minimum wages to deal with a problem that was more cultural and social than economic. Moreover, Piketty clearly supports raising the minimum wage and even provides several justifications for raising the minimum wage. So it is puzzling that so many people would criticize Piketty for not supporting higher minimum wages.

The real problem Piketty has with raising the minimum wage is not that it won't help equalize wage income, but that it won't deal with the problem of rising capital income in the long run. He is also skeptical that the minimum wage can be increased enough (5% per year in real terms) over the long haul without generating substantial unemployment. To try to make Piketty's point as simple and clear as possible, even if wages (and we can add rising union power here) were made completely equal across the board, inequality would be high and would continue to increase because of the immense wealth that is possessed by a few people.

It is wealth inequality for Piketty that is the main force driving inequality to rise under capitalism. A higher minimum wage can slow the process down. So too can stronger unions. So too can government spending policies that equalize after-tax incomes, such as paid parental leave, child allowances, generous unemployment insurance programs, and a large and sturdy social safety net. These are all policies that Piketty, I imagine, would support. But the key insight of Capital is this: the driving force of inequality is that we start with great wealth inequality and the high returns to wealth make things worse over time. Policies that equalize income distribution will help a little, but they ignore the main problem.

Still, Piketty does focus on tax policy to reduce the distribution of wage income. He argues first for a progressive income tax because this (along with inheritance taxes) is the only progressive form of taxation that governments have. Sales or indirect taxes are regressive in nature and social-insurance taxes (for retirement and for unemployment) tend to be proportional or regressive. Again, Piketty does not make either a strong or forceful case for this policy. I wish he had put a little more emphasis on the fact that high marginal tax rates during the war years and in the decade or so after World War II contributed to the falling inequality in this era. Historically, he contends that high marginal income tax rates have led to lower (before-tax) inequality. It is in the data; it should have been stressed more in the policy section of the book.

On the other hand, Piketty does worry about current trends in individual income taxation. In particular, by exempting capital income from the income tax (or taxing it at lower rates) the income tax becomes regressive at the very top (because that is where they get most of their income) and tends to make the entire tax system regressive in developed countries. But, again, the big issue for Piketty is that progressive income taxes cannot solve the wealth inequality problem. Like progressive spending programs, a progressive income tax would help reduce income inequality, but it does not solve the problem that wealth inequality tends to rise because of the high returns to wealth—much of it, such as stocks and homes that are not sold, are not taxed at all.

In a couple of pages that were pretty much ignored in the reviews of Capital, Piketty calls for a reform of corporate taxation. He proposes that corporate income taxes be assessed based on wages paid in different countries rather than on where in the world the multi-national firm declares its profits to come from (typically the country that has the lowest corporate income tax rate). This is not headline grabbing, and tax reform is never as exciting as proposing a new type of tax (this is why there are so many articles on the flat tax and the Tobin Tax and why reviews of this book focused on the global wealth tax), but it is something that needs to receive serious consideration and should be pushed more.

Again, the fact that Piketty does not focus a lot of attention on this proposal probably stems from the fact that (like higher marginal income tax rates) it will affect income distribution but not wealth distribution. When corporations pay higher taxes to governments there is less profit to distribute to the owners as dividends. This will reduce current incomes. However, higher corporate income taxes also reduce future profits after-taxes, which should affect the value of corporate stock. This will lower the price of shares of stock. Since it is mainly the very wealthy who own large amounts of stock, and whose wealth portfolio contains a higher percentage of stock compared to middle-income households, this policy should have significant and substantial effect on wealth inequality.

## Piketty and the Global Tax on Wealth

At last, we come to Piketty's main policy conclusion, his claim that the way to keep more and more income from going to those at the very top of the distribution is a global wealth tax. The tax needs to be global in order to keep wealth from moving to tax havens where it is not subject to the tax. Piketty also wants to keep the tax rate low (1-2%) in order to mitigate negative disincentives. His particular plan is that net assets worth between 1 million Euros ($1.35 million) and 5 million Euros

($6.75 million) be taxed at 1% and net assets worth more than 5 million Euros be taxed at 2%. The goal in all this, Piketty makes clear, is not to raise money for social programs but to tame the inequality that inevitably results under capitalism.

Piketty provides several different arguments for his progressive and global wealth tax.

First, he resorts to an appeal to authority. He invokes the 1918 American Economic Association Presidential address by Irving Fisher, in which Fisher worries about the fact that only 2% of the U.S. population owned more than 50% of the nation's wealth while two-thirds of the population had no net wealth. Fisher then went on to suggest a steeply progressive wealth tax to remedy this situation.

Second, Piketty argues that the rewards going to the very top are not justified by traditional economic arguments (that they depend on the marginal productivity of the worker). Instead, Piketty makes the case that CEO pay is due to luck to a large degree and that a bargaining model fits the data better than marginal productivity theory. He argues that when the government takes a very large chunk of any extra income, it is not worth it for a CEO to bargain with a compensation committee or shareholders to get higher pay. And he points to empirical evidence that high marginal tax rates keep down CEO pay while not hurting the economic performance of the firm.

Finally there is the main argument—that a global wealth tax is the only way to limit the growth of wealth accumulation and a return to 19th-century levels of inequality. Or, this is the only way we can avoid all the negative economic, social, and political consequences of great inequality. A tax on income will not achieve this end because much income is tied up in stocks and bonds and real estate that generally do not get taxed. The gains from these investments are taxed when assets are sold. This allows the gains to accumulate at the top and to keep doing so. Only a wealth tax can stop this process.

Finally, while his many critics fault Piketty for making such an unrealistic proposal, Piketty himself recognizes that a global wealth tax (or even higher taxes on income from capital in the United States) is not likely to happen anytime soon and perhaps will never happen. He has no unrealistic illusions about this policy being passed in the United States or Europe.

The alternative policy proposals made by critics of Piketty, as noted above, are probably as unrealistic as a global wealth tax. But the strong case against them, as Piketty points out, is that only a progressive wealth tax deals with the problem of rising inequality in income and wealth under capitalism. A higher minimum wage and greater support for labor unions cannot reduce the concentration of capital. Nor can progressive government programs such as paid parental leave and generous unemployment insurance. Even reforming individual and corporate income taxes will be of limited help (although, as I argue above, global corporate tax reform can do a lot of good). We are left with few options if we want to halt a return to the Gilded Age. ❑

# Chapter 10

# TRADE AND DEVELOPMENT

## INTRODUCTION

**G**iven the economic turmoil of the last decade in the developed world, it is ironic that the developing world is still being urged to adopt free markets and increased privatization as the keys to catching up with the West. These neoliberal policy prescriptions have been applied across the developing world, over the last few decades, as a one-size-fits-all solution to problems such as poverty, malnutrition, and political conflict. While spiking unemployment in the United States led to a (temporary) surge in government spending, developing countries with double-digit unemployment were routinely told that macroeconomic crises could only be dealt with by "tightening their belts." And while the West, having experienced a financial crisis, now embraced some new financial regulations, similar calls for more regulation from developing countries were dismissed as misguided.

The contributors to this section take on different aspects of the neoliberal (or "free market") policy mix, raising questions that recur through this entire volume. Where do the limits of the market lie? At what point do we decide that markets are no longer serving the general public, whose well-being economists claim to champion? And to what extent should communities, via politically representative bodies of all kinds, be able to regulate and control markets?

The first tenet of the neoliberal faith is the belief that openness to international trade is the key to growth and development. Ramaa Vasudevan, in the primer "Comparative Advantage" (Article 10.1), starts off this chapter with a critique of the Ricardian theory of comparative advantage that is central to the neoclassical argument for free trade.

Thomas Palley offers a concise and useful metaphor for the effect of globalization and outsourcing on productive industry in the United States. "The Globalization Clock" (Article 10.2) describes how globalization and outsourcing pick off domestic industries one by one, based on the relative exportability of the goods or services and the skill level of the workers. This metaphor also illustrates why, at any given period of time, there has not been a majority consensus against outsourcing: The majority of people (consumers) benefit through lower prices from the outsourced industry; only those acutely affected through the loss of their jobs are against it. But as the clock ticks forward, more and more industries at higher and higher levels of skill become outsourced.

The relationship between two economic giants, the United States and China, powerfully shapes the global economy. Exports are the engine of China's recent rapid growth, and the United States is its biggest customer. Arthur MacEwan examines accusations against the Chinese government of "currency manipulation"—a policy of actively pushing down the value of its currency, the yuan, relative to the dollar, and therefore keeping its exports cheaper. By examining why the United States, which has lost manufacturing jobs, does not protest more strenuously against this policy, MacEwan exposes the mutual dependence of Chinese and U.S. elites' economic strategies (Article 10.3).

Ellen Frank's "Should Developing Countries Embrace Protectionism?" (Article 10.4), points out that, contrary to the claims of globalization advocates and the theory of comparative advantage, the historical record suggests that protectionism may be a better strategy for economic development. In fact, it is hard to provide an example of successful economic growth and development from countries that "got prices right" as opposed to those that "got prices wrong"—but to their trading advantage.

Next, John Miller (Article 10.5) looks at the worker-safety accord put in place in Bangladesh in the wake of the 2013 Rana Plaza disaster, a factory collapse that killed over 1,100 workers. Miller argues that the legal liability of major clothing companies (who outsource clothing production to subcontractor companies) is a major positive step for worker safety. He also notes, however, that most major U.S. clothing companies have so far refused to sign onto the accord.

A major change in China's economy, and therefore in the entire global economy, may be coming from Chinese workers. Miller explains how the combination of tighter labor markets and labor militancy has been pushing up wages in China since 2009. Miller reports on the labor unrest in China's export factories and argues that improving conditions for workers in China is good news for factory workers around the globe (Article 10.6).

Finally, Elissa Dennis describes an intriguing policy proposal from the government of Ecuador, which would give the country needed funds for economic development in exchange for *not* extracting its oil (Article 10.7). Recognizing the environmental damage done by petroleum extraction (especially right around drilling sites) and consumption (globally), Ecuador has offered to "keep it in the ground." It would forego some of the revenues it could gain from extraction, while asking international contributors to pay the rest.

## Discussion Questions

1. (Article 10.1) Under what conditions might the mainstream argument about the advantages of specialization based on comparative advantage break down?

2. (Article 10.2) Thomas Palley argues that the relative benefits and costs of globalization are not evenly distributed. Some folks gain from globalization and others lose. What is "Palley's Clock"? Explain in detail the metaphor and mechanism.

3. (Article 10.2) Does Palley's assessment of globalization differ at all from your textbook's? What time is it in the United States according to "Palley's Clock"?

4.  (Article 10.3) How does China's government keep down the prices of its exports? Why does the U.S. government not protest more strenuously against this policy?

5.  (Article 10.4) What is the basic argument made by mainstream economists in favor of free trade? Ellen Frank argues that free trade can prevent poorer countries from developing, rather than helping them do so. (The same argument applies to poorer regions within richer countries like the United States.) What is her reasoning? How do you think a pro-free-trade economist would respond?

6.  (Article 10.5) Opponents of international labor standards argue that workers in very low-income countries just need jobs, and will only be hurt by well-intentioned efforts to raise wages or improve working condidtions. How do such arguments hold up to the experience in Bangladesh since the Rana Plaza disaster?

7.  (Article 10.6) What explains rising wages in Chinese export factories? How do Miller's and the *Wall Street Journal's* definition of the virtuous cycle of development differ?

8.  (Article 10.7) How does the development strategy proposed by the government of Ecuador differ from the neoliberal development path common in poor countries that possess valuable natural resources? How does it differ even from the paths of other countries in which the government plays a large role in resource development?

Article 10.1

# COMPARATIVE ADVANTAGE

### BY RAMAA VASUDEVAN

*July/August 2007*

Dear Dr. Dollar:

*When economists argue that the outsourcing of jobs might be a plus for the U.S. economy, they often mention the idea of comparative advantage. So free trade would allow the United States to specialize in higher-end service-sector businesses, creating higher-paying jobs than the ones that would be outsourced. But is it really true that free trade leads to universal benefits?*
—David Goodman, Boston, Mass.

You're right: The purveyors of the free trade gospel do invoke the doctrine of comparative advantage to dismiss widespread concerns about the export of jobs. Attributed to 19th-century British political-economist David Ricardo, the doctrine says that a nation always stands to gain if it exports the goods it produces *relatively* more cheaply in exchange for goods that it can get *comparatively* more cheaply from abroad. Free trade would lead to each country specializing in the products it can produce at *relatively* lower costs. Such specialization allows both trading partners to gain from trade, the theory goes, even if in one of the countries production of *both* goods costs more in absolute terms.

For instance, suppose that in the United States the cost to produce one car equals the cost to produce 10 bags of cotton, while in the Philippines the cost to produce one car equals the cost to produce 100 bags of cotton. The Philippines would then have a comparative advantage in the production of cotton, producing one bag at a cost equal to the production cost of 1/100 of a car, versus 1/10 of a car in the United States; likewise, the United States would hold a comparative advantage in the production of cars. Whatever the prices of cars and cotton in the global market, the theory goes, the Philippines would be better off producing only cotton and importing all its cars from the United States, and the United States would be better off producing only cars and importing all of its cotton from the Philippines. If the international terms of trade—the relative price—is one car for 50 bags, then the United States will take in 50 bags of cotton for each car it exports, 40 more than the 10 bags it forgoes by putting its productive resources into making the car rather than growing cotton. The Philippines is also better off: it can import a car in exchange for the export of 50 bags of cotton, whereas it would have had to forgo the production of 100 bags of cotton in order to produce that car domestically. If the price of cars goes up in the global marketplace, the Philippines will lose out in relative terms—but will still be better off than if it tried to produce its own cars.

The real world, unfortunately, does not always conform to the assumptions underlying comparative-advantage theory. One assumption is that trade is balanced. But many countries are running persistent deficits, notably the United States, whose trade deficit is now at nearly 7% of its GDP. A second premise, that there is full employment within the trading nations, is also patently unrealistic. As global trade intensifies, jobs created in the export sector do not necessarily compensate for the jobs lost in the sectors wiped out by foreign competition.

The comparative advantage story faces more direct empirical challenges as well. Nearly 70% of U.S. trade is trade in similar goods, known as *intra-industry trade*: for example, exporting Fords and importing BMWs. And about one third of U.S. trade as of the late 1990s was trade between branches of a single corporation located in different countries (*intra-firm trade*). Comparative advantage cannot explain these patterns.

Comparative advantage is a static concept that identifies immediate gains from trade but is a poor guide to economic development, a process of structural change over time which is by definition dynamic. Thus the comparative advantage tale is particularly pernicious when preached to developing countries, consigning many to "specialize" in agricultural goods or be forced into a race to the bottom where cheap sweatshop labor is their sole source of competitiveness.

The irony, of course, is that none of the rich countries got that way by following the maxim that they now preach. These countries historically relied on tariff walls and other forms of protectionism to build their industrial base. And even now, they continue to protect sectors like agriculture with subsidies. The countries now touted as new models of the benefits of free trade—South Korea and the other "Asian tigers," for instance—actually flouted this economic wisdom, nurturing their technological capabilities in specific manufacturing sectors and taking advantage of their lower wage costs to *gradually* become effective competitors of the United States and Europe in manufacturing.

The fundamental point is this: contrary to the comparative-advantage claim that trade is universally beneficial, nations as a whole do not prosper from free trade. Free trade creates winners and losers, both within and between countries. In today's context it is the global corporate giants that are propelling and profiting from "free trade": not only outsourcing white-collar jobs, but creating global commodity chains linking sweatshop labor in the developing countries of Latin America and Asia (Africa being largely left out of the game aside from the export of natural resources such as oil) with ever-more insecure consumers in the developed world. Promoting "free trade" as a political cause enables this process to continue.

It is a process with real human costs in terms of both wages and work. People in developing countries across the globe continue to face these costs as trade liberalization measures are enforced; and the working class in the United States is also being forced to bear the brunt of the relentless logic of competition. ❑

*Sources:* Arthur MacEwan, "The Gospel of Free Trade: The New Evangelists," *Dollars & Sense,* July/August 2002; Ha-Joon Chang, *Kicking away the Ladder: The Real History of Fair Trade,* Foreign Policy in Focus, 2003; Anwar Shaikh, "Globalization and the Myths of Free Trade," in *Globalization and the Myths of Free Trade: History, Theory, and Empirical Evidence,* ed. Anwar Shaikh, Routledge 2007.

*Article 10.2*

# THE GLOBALIZATION CLOCK
*Why corporations are winning and workers are losing.*

## BY THOMAS PALLEY
*May/June 2006*

Political economy has historically been constructed around the divide between capital and labor, with firms and workers at odds over the division of the economic pie. Within this construct, labor is usually represented as a monolithic interest, yet the reality is that labor has always suffered from internal divisions—by race, by occupational status, and along many other fault lines. Neoliberal globalization has in many ways sharpened these divisions, which helps to explain why corporations have been winning and workers losing.

One of these fault lines divides workers from themselves: since workers are also consumers, they face a divide between the desire for higher wages and the desire for lower prices. Historically, this identity split has been exploited to divide union from nonunion workers, with anti-labor advocates accusing union workers of causing higher prices. Today, globalization is amplifying the divide between people's interests as workers and their interests as consumers through its promise of ever-lower prices.

Consider the debate over Wal-Mart's low-road labor policies. While Wal-Mart's low wages and skimpy benefits have recently faced scrutiny, even some liberal commentators argue that Wal-Mart is actually good for low-wage workers because they gain more as consumers from its "low, low prices" than they lose as workers from its low wages. But this static, snapshot analysis fails to capture the full impact of globalization, past and future.

Globalization affects the economy unevenly, hitting some sectors first and others later. The process can be understood in terms of the hands of a clock. At one o'clock is the apparel sector; at two o'clock the textile sector; at three the steel sector; at six the auto sector. Workers in the apparel sector are the first to have their jobs shifted to lower-wage venues; at the same time, though, all other workers get price reductions. Next, the process picks off textile sector workers at two o'clock. Meanwhile, workers from three o'clock onward get price cuts, as do the apparel workers at one o'clock. Each time the hands of the clock move, the workers taking the hit are isolated. In this fashion globalization moves around the clock, with labor perennially divided.

Manufacturing was first to experience this process, but technological innovations associated with the Internet are putting service and knowledge workers in the firing line as well. Online business models are making even retail workers vulnerable—consider Amazon.com, for example, which has opened a customer support center and two technology development centers in India. Public sector wages are also in play, at least indirectly, since falling wages mean falling tax revenues. The problem is that each time the hands on the globalization clock move forward, workers are divided: the majority is made slightly better off while the few are made much worse off.

Globalization also alters the historical divisions within capital, creating a new split between bigger internationalized firms and smaller firms that remain nationally centered. This division has been brought into sharp focus with the debate over the trade deficit and the overvalued dollar. In previous decades, manufacturing as a whole opposed running trade deficits and maintaining an overvalued dollar because of the adverse impact of increased imports. The one major business sector with a different view was retailing, which benefited from cheap imports.

However, the spread of multinational production and outsourcing has divided manufacturing in wealthy countries into two camps. In one camp are larger multinational corporations that have gone global and benefit from cheap imports; in the other are smaller businesses that remain nationally centered in terms of sales, production and input sourcing. Multinational corporations tend to support an overvalued dollar since this makes imports produced in their foreign factories cheaper. Conversely, domestic manufacturers are hurt by an overvalued dollar, which advantages import competition.

This division opens the possibility of a new alliance between labor and those manufacturers and businesses that remain nationally based—potentially a potent one, since there are approximately seven million enterprises with sales of less than $10 million in the United States, versus only 200,000 with sales greater than $10 million. However, such an alliance will always be unstable as the inherent labor-capital conflict over income distribution can always reassert itself. Indeed, this pattern is already evident in the internal politics of the National Association of Manufacturers, whose members have been significantly divided regarding the overvalued dollar. As one way to address this division, the group is promoting a domestic "competitiveness" agenda aimed at weakening regulation, reducing corporate legal liability, and lowering employee benefit costs—an agenda designed to appeal to both camps, but at the expense of workers.

Solidarity has always been key to political and economic advance by working families, and it is key to mastering the politics of globalization. Developing a coherent story about the economics of neoliberal globalization around which working families can coalesce is a key ingredient for solidarity. So too is understanding how globalization divides labor. These narratives and analyses can help counter deep cultural proclivities to individualism, as well as other historic divides such as racism. However, as if this were not difficult enough, globalization creates additional challenges. National political solutions that worked in the past are not adequate to the task of controlling international competition. That means the solidarity bar is further raised, calling for international solidarity that supports new forms of international economic regulation. ❑

*Article 10.3*

# IS CHINA'S CURRENCY MANIPULATION HURTING THE U.S.?

## BY ARTHUR MacEWAN
*November/December 2010*

> Dear Dr. Dollar:
> *Is it true that China has been harming the U.S. economy by keeping its currency "undervalued"? Shouldn't the U.S. government do something about this situation?*
> —Jenny Boyd, Edmond, W.Va.

The Chinese government, operating through the Chinese central bank, does keep its currency unit—the yuan—cheap relative to the dollar. This means that goods imported *from* China cost less (in terms of dollars) than they would otherwise, while U.S. exports *to* China cost more (in terms of yuan). So we in the United States buy a lot of Chinese-made goods and the Chinese don't buy much from us. In the 2007 to 2009 period, the United States purchased $253 billion more in goods annually from China than it sold to China.

This looks bad for U.S workers. For example, when money gets spent in the United States, much of it is spent on Chinese-made goods, and fewer jobs are then created in the United States. So the Chinese government's currency policy is at least partly to blame for our employment woes. Reacting to this situation, many people are calling for the U.S. government to do something to get the Chinese government to change its policy.

But things are not so simple.

First of all, there is an additional reason for the low cost of Chinese goods—low Chinese wages. The Chinese government's policy of repressing labor probably accounts for the low cost of Chinese goods at least as much as does its currency policy. Moreover, there is a lot more going on in the global economy. Both currency problems and job losses involve much more than Chinese government actions—though China provides a convenient target for ire.

And the currency story itself is complex. In order to keep the value of its currency low relative to the dollar, the Chinese government increases the supply of yuan, uses these yuan to buy dollars, then uses the dollars to buy U.S. securities, largely government bonds but also private securities. In early 2009, China held $764 billion in U.S. Treasury securities, making it the largest foreign holder of U.S. government debt. By buying U.S. government bonds, the Chinese have been financing the federal deficit. More generally, by supplying funds to the United States, the Chinese government has been keeping interest rates low in this country.

If the Chinese were to act differently, allowing the value of their currency to rise relative to the dollar, both the cost of capital and the prices of the many goods imported from China would rise. The rising cost of capital would probably not be a serious problem, as the Federal Reserve could take counteraction to keep interest rates low. So, an increase in the value of the yuan would net the United States some jobs, but also raise some prices for U.S. consumers.

It is pretty clear that right now what the United States needs is jobs. Moreover, low-cost Chinese goods have contributed to the declining role of manufacturing in the United States, a phenomenon that both weakens important segments of organized labor and threatens to inhibit technological progress, which has often been centered in manufacturing or based on applications in manufacturing (e.g., robotics).

So why doesn't the U.S. government place more pressure on China to raise the value of the yuan? Part of the reason may lie in concern about losing Chinese financing of the U.S. federal deficit. For several years the two governments have been co-dependent: The U.S. government gets financing for its deficits, and the Chinese government gains by maintaining an undervalued currency. Not an easy relationship to change.

Probably more important, however, many large and politically powerful U.S.-based firms depend directly on the low-cost goods imported from China. Wal-mart and Target, as any shopper knows, are filled with Chinese-made goods. Then there are the less visible products from China, including a power device that goes into the Microsoft Xbox, computer keyboards for Dell, and many other goods for many other U.S. corporations. If the yuan's value rose and these firms had to pay more dollars to buy these items, they could probably not pass all the increase on to consumers and their profits would suffer.

Still, in spite of the interests of these firms, the U.S. government may take some action, either by pressing harder for China to let the value of the yuan rise relative to the dollar or by placing some restrictions on imports from China. But don't expect too big a change. ❏

*Article 10.4*

# SHOULD DEVELOPING COUNTRIES EMBRACE PROTECTIONISM?

## BY ELLEN FRANK
*July 2004*

> Dear Dr. Dollar:
> *Supposedly, countries should produce what they are best at. If the United States makes computers and China produces rice, then the theory of free trade says China should trade its rice for computers. But if China puts tariffs on U.S.-made computers and builds up its own computer industry, then it will become best at making them and can buy rice from Vietnam. Isn't it advantageous for poor countries to practice protectionism and become industrial powers themselves, rather than simply producing mono-crop commodities? I'm asking because local alternative currencies like Ithaca Hours benefit local businesses, though they restrict consumers to local goods that may be more expensive than goods from further away.*
> —Matt Cary, Hollywood, Fla.

The modern theory of free trade argues that countries are "endowed" with certain quantities of labor, capital, and natural resources. A country with lots of labor but little capital should specialize in the production of labor-intensive goods, like hand-woven rugs, hand-sewn garments, or hand-picked fruit. By ramping up produc-tion of these goods, a developing country can trade on world markets, earning the foreign exchange to purchase capital-intensive products like computers and cars. Free trade thus permits poor countries (or, to be more precise, their most well-off citizens) to *consume* high-tech goods that they lack the ability to *produce* and so obtain higher living standards. "Capital-rich" countries like the United States benefit from relatively cheap fruit and garments, freeing up their workforce to focus on high-tech goods. Free trade, according to this story, is a win-win game for everyone.

The flaw in this tale, which you have hit upon exactly, is that being "capital-rich" or "capital-poor" is not a natural phenomenon like having lots of oil. Capital is created—typically with plenty of government assistance and protection.

Developing countries can create industrial capacity and train their citizens to manufacture high-tech goods. But doing so takes time. Building up the capacity to manufacture computers, for example, at prices that are competitive with firms in developed countries may take several years. To buy this time, a government needs to keep foreign-made computers from flooding its market and undercutting less-established local producers. It also needs to limit inflows of foreign capital. Studies show that when foreign firms set up production facilities in developing countries, they are unlikely to share their latest techniques, so such foreign investment does not typically build local expertise or benefit local entrepreneurs.

The United States and other rich countries employed these protectionist strategies. In the 1800s, American entrepreneurs traveled to England and France to learn the latest manufacturing techniques and freely appropriated designs for cutting-edge industrial equipment. The U.S. government protected its nascent industries with high tariff walls until they could compete with European manufacturers.

After World War II, Japan effectively froze out foreign goods while building up world-class auto, computer, and electronics industries. Korea later followed Japan's strategy; in recent years, so has China. There, "infant industries" are heavily protected by tariffs, quotas, and other trade barriers. Foreign producers are welcome only if they establish high-tech facilities in which Chinese engineers and production workers can garner the most modern skills.

Development economists like Alice Amsden and Dani Rodrik are increasingly reaching the conclusion that carefully designed industrial policies, combined with protections for infant industries, are most effective in promoting internal development in poor countries. "Free-trade" policies, on the other hand, seem to lock poor countries into producing low-tech goods like garments and agricultural commodities, whose prices tend to decline on world markets due to intense competition with other poor countries.

In the contemporary global economy, however, there are three difficulties with implementing a local development strategy. First, some countries have bargained away their right to protect local firms by entering into free-trade agreements. Second, protectionism means that local consumers are denied the benefits of cheap manufactured goods from abroad, at least in the short run.

Finally, in many parts of the world the floodgates of foreign-made goods have already been opened and, with the middle and upper classes enjoying their computers and cell phones, it may be impossible to build the political consensus to close them. This last concern bears on the prospects for local alternative currencies. Since it is impos-sible to "close off" the local economy, the success of local currencies in bolstering hometown businesses depends on the willingness of local residents to deny themselves the benefits of cheaper nonlocal goods. Like national protectionist polices, local currencies restrict consumer choice.

Ultimately, the success or failure of such ventures rests on the degree of public support for local business. With local currencies, participation is voluntary and attitudes toward local producers often favorable. National protectionist polices, however, entail coerced public participation and generally fail when governments are corrupt and unable to command public support. ❏

*Article 10.5*

# AFTER HORROR, CHANGE?

*Taking Stock of Conditions in Bangladesh's Garment Factories*

**BY JOHN MILLER**
*September/October 2014*

On April 24, 2013, the Rana Plaza factory building, just outside of Bangladesh's capital city of Dhaka, collapsed—killing 1,138 workers and inflicting serious long-term injuries on at least 1,000 others.

While the collapse of Rana Plaza was in one sense an accident, the policies that led to it surely were not. Bangladesh's garment industry grew to be the world's second largest exporter, behind only China's, by endangering and exploiting workers. Bangladesh's 5,000 garment factories paid rock-bottom wages, much lower than those in China, and just half of those in Vietnam. One foreign buyer told The Economist magazine, "There are no rules whatsoever that can not be bent." Cost-saving measures included the widespread use of retail buildings as factories—including at Rana Plaza—adding weight that sometimes exceeded the load-bearing capacity of the structures.

As Scott Nova, executive director of the Worker Rights Consortium, testified before Congress, "the danger to workers in Bangladesh has been apparent for many years." The first documented mass-fatality incident in the country's export garment sector occurred in December 1990. In addition to those killed at Rana Plaza, more than 600 garment workers have died in factory fires in Bangladesh since 2005. After Rana Plaza, however, Bangladesh finally reached a crossroads. The policies that had led to the stunning growth of its garment industry had so tarnished the "Made in Bangladesh" label that they were no longer sustainable.

But just how much change has taken place since Rana Plaza? That was the focus of an International Conference at Harvard this June, bringing together government officials from Bangladesh and the United States, representatives of the Bangladesh garment industry, the international brands, women's groups, trade unions, the International Labor Organization (ILO), and monitoring groups working in Bangladesh.

## How Much Change On the Ground?

Srinivas B. Reddy of the ILO spoke favorably of an "unprecedented level of ... practical action" toward workplace safety in Bangladesh.

The "practical action" on the ground, however, has been much more of a mixed bag than Reddy suggests. In the wake of massive protests and mounting international pressure, Bangladesh amended its labor laws to remove some obstacles to workers forming unions. Most importantly, the new law bars the country's labor ministry from giving factory owners lists of workers who want to organize.

But formidable obstacles to unionization still remain. At least 30% of the workers at an entire company are required to join a union before the government will grant recognition. This is a higher hurdle than workers face even in the not-so-union-friendly United States, where recognition is based at the level of the workplace, not the company. Workers in special export-processing zones (the source of about 16% of Bangladesh's exports), moreover, remain ineligible to form unions.

The Bangladesh government did register 160 new garment unions in 2013 and the first half of this year, compared to just two between 2010 and 2012. Nonetheless, collective bargaining happens in only 3% of garment plants. And employers have responded with firings and violence to workers registering for union recognition or making bargaining demands. Union organizers have been kidnapped, brutally beaten, and killed.

After protests that shut down over 400 factories last fall, the Bangladesh government raised the minimum wage for garment workers from the equivalent of $38 a month to $68. The higher minimum wage, however, fell short of the $103 demanded by workers.

The government and the garment brands have also set up the Rana Plaza Donor Trust Fund to compensate victims and their families for their losses and injuries. But according to the fund's website, it stood at just $17.9 million at the beginning of August, well below its $40 million target. Only about half of the 29 international brands that had their clothes sewn at Rana Plaza have made contributions. Ineke Zeldenrust of the Amsterdam-based labor-rights group Clean Clothes Campaign estimates that those 29 brands are being asked to contribute less than 0.2% of their $22 billion in total profits for 2013.

## The Accord and the Alliance

Following Rana Plaza, a group of mostly European retail chains turned away from the business-as-usual approach of company codes that had failed to ensure safe working conditions in the factories that made their clothes. Some 151 apparel brands and retailers doing business in Bangladesh, including 16 U.S.-based retailers, signed the Accord on Fire and Building Safety in Bangladesh. Together the signatories of this five-year agreement contracted with 1,639 of the 3,498 Bangladesh factories making garments for export.

The Accord broke important new ground. Unlike earlier efforts:

It was negotiated with two global unions, UndustriALL and UNI (Global).

It sets up a governing board with equal numbers of labor and retail representatives, and a chair chosen by the ILO.

Independent inspectors will conduct audits of factory hazards and make their results public on the Accord website, including the name of the factory, detailed information about the hazard, and recommended repairs.

The retailers will provide direct funding for repairs (up to a maximum of $2.5 million per company) and assume responsibility for ensuring that all needed renovations and repairs are paid for.

Most importantly, the Accord is legally binding. Disputes between retailers and union representatives are subject to arbitration, with decisions enforceable by a court of law in the retailer's home country.

But most U.S. retailers doing business in Bangladesh—including giants like Wal-Mart, JCPenney, The Gap, and Sears—refused to sign. They objected to the Accord's open-ended financial commitment and to its legally binding provisions.

Those companies, along with 21 other North American retailers and brands, developed an alternative five-year agreement, called the Alliance For Bangladesh Worker Safety. Some 770 factories in Bangladesh produce garments for these 26 companies.

Unlike the Accord, the Alliance is not legally binding and lacks labor- organization representatives. Moreover, retailers contribute a maximum of $1 million per retailer (less than half the $2.5 million under the Accord) to implement their safety plan and needed repairs, and face no binding commitment to pay for needed improvements beyond that. The responsibility to comply with safety standards falls to factory owners, although the Alliance does offer up to $100 million in loans for these expenses.

Kalpona Akter, executive director of the Bangladesh Center for Worker Solidarity, told the U.S. Senate Foreign Relations Committee, "There is no meaningful difference between the Alliance and the corporate-controlled 'corporate social responsibility' programs that have failed Bangladeshi garment workers in the past, and have left behind thousands of dead and injured workers."

## Historic and Unprecedented?

Dan Mozena, U.S. Ambassador to Bangladesh, believes that, despite facing significant obstacles, "Bangladesh is making history as it creates new standards for the apparel industry globally."

While the Accord may be without contemporary precedent, joint liability agreements that make retailers responsible for the safety conditions of their subcontractor's factories do have historical antecedents. As political scientist Mark Anner has documented, beginning in the 1920s the International Ladies Garment Workers Union (ILGWU) began negotiating "jobber agreements" in the United States that held the buyer (or "jobber") for an apparel brand "jointly liable" for wages and working conditions in the contractor's factories. Jobber agreements played a central role in the near-eradication of sweatshops in the United States by the late 1950s. In today's global economy, however, international buyers are once again able to escape responsibility for conditions in the far-flung factories of their subcontractors.

Like jobber agreements, the Accord holds apparel manufacturers and retailers legally accountable for the safety conditions in the factories that make their clothes through agreements negotiated between workers or unions and buyers or brands. The next steps for the Accord model, as Anner has argued, are to address working conditions other than building safety (as jobber agreements had), to get more brands to sign on to the Accord, and to negotiate similar agreements in other countries.

That will be no easy task. But, according to Arnold Zack, who helped to negotiate the Better Factories program that brought ILO monitoring of Cambodian garment factories, "Bangladesh is the lynch pin that can bring an end to the bottom feeding shopping the brands practice." ❑

*Sources:* Arnold M. Zack, "In an Era of Accelerating Attention to Workplace Equity: What Place for Bangladesh," Boston Global Forum, July 8, 2014; Testimony of Kalpona Akter, Testimony of Scott Nova, Senate Committee on Foreign Relations, Feb. 11, 2014; Mark Anner, Jennifer Bair, and Jeremy Blasi, "Toward Joint Liability in Global Supply Chains," *Comparative Labor Law & Policy Journal*, Vol. 35:1, Fall 2013; Prepared Remarks for Rep. George Miller (D-Calif.), Keynote Remarks by U.S. Ambassador to Bangladesh Dan Mozena, Remarks by Country Director ILO Bangladesh Srinivas B. Reddy, International Conference on Globalization and Sustainability of the Bangladesh Garment Sector, June 14, 2014; "Rags in the ruins," *The Economist*, May 4, 2013; "Bangladesh: Amended Labor Law Falls Short," Human Rights Watch, July 18, 2013; Rana Plaza Donor Trust Fund (ranaplaza-arrangement.org/fund).

*Article 10.6*

# CHINESE WORKERS STAND UP
*What is the real cause of increasing wages in China?*

**BY JOHN MILLER**
*September/October 2010*

> ### "THE RISE OF CHINESE LABOR:
> ### WAGE HIKES ARE PART OF A VIRTUOUS CYCLE OF DEVELOPMENT"
>
> The recent strikes at Honda factories in southern China represent another data point in an emerging trend: Cheap labor won't be the source of the Chinese economy's competitive advantage much longer.
>
> The auto maker has caved and given workers a 24% pay increase to restart one assembly line. Foxconn, the electronics producer that has experienced a string of worker suicides, has also announced big raises. This is all part of the virtuous cycle of development: Productivity increases, which drive wages higher, forcing businesses to adjust, leading to more productivity growth.
> —*Wall Street Journal* op-ed, June 9, 2010

**W**ages in China are in fact rising. But that hardly constitutes a "virtuous cycle of development" that is the inevitable result of market-led economic growth, as the *Wall Street Journal* editors contend.

Rather, higher wages in China are the hard-fought gains of militant workers who have used tightening labor markets as a lever to pry wage gains out of employers whose coffers have long been brimming with cash.

Labor unrest taking advantage of tightening labor markets is the story in China today—not abstract economic forces lifting wages, the tale the *Journal's* editors want to pass off as a paean to free-market economics.

## A Changing Labor Outlook

In recent years rapid economic growth has indeed tightened the Chinese labor market, drying up the seemingly bottomless pool of jobseekers from the countryside. As of May 2010, job vacancies in China outnumbered the number of job applicants, according to the Chinese Labor Market Information Center.

And wages are rising for many. Pay for China's 150 million or so internal-migrant workers increased 16% in 2009 despite the global financial crisis, according to Cai Fang, head of the Institute of Population and Labor Economics at the Chinese Academy of Social Sciences.

Higher wages aren't about to break the corporate piggybank. In recent years the biggest increase in China's extraordinarily high national savings (which includes household and business savings) has come from retained earnings—the undistributed profits of Chinese corporations. Retained earnings did so much to boost the country's savings because low wages kept corporate profits high. For more than a decade, labor's share of national income has been on the decline in China as the corporate share has increased dramatically. On top of that, the strong productivity growth that the *Journal* editors laud has offset wage increases, keeping labor costs per unit of output in check. At the beginning of 2010 Chinese unit labor costs were no higher than in 2004.

Wage increases notwithstanding, working conditions in China remain oppressive, as even the *Journal* editors seem to recognize. In May 2010 a thirteenth worker attempted to commit suicide at a Foxconn factory in southern China. The world's largest maker of computer components, Foxconn supplies Apple, Dell, and Hewlett-Packard, among others. While working conditions at this Taiwanese-owned company are far from the worst in China, the hours are long, the assembly line moves too fast, and managers enforce military-style discipline.

Foxconn's string of suicides is just the tip of the iceberg. Early in 2008, the *New York Times* reported that worker abuse is still commonplace in many of the Chinese factories that supply Western companies. The *Times* quoted labor activists who reported unfair labor practices—child labor, enforced 16-hour days, and sub-minimum wages, among others—in factories supplying several U.S. firms including Wal-Mart, Disney, and Dell. The activists also reported that factories routinely withhold health benefits, employ dangerous machinery, and expose workers to lead, mercury, and other hazardous chemicals. According to government statistics, an average of 187 Chinese workers die each day in industrial accidents; the equivalent U.S. figure is three.

## The Real Virtuous Cycle

Rapid economic growth and rising productivity undoubtedly laid the groundwork for higher wages. But it is labor militancy that has exploited workers' improved bargaining position. The number of labor disputes in China doubled from 2006 to 2009. Workers have won wage increases in excess of 20% at several large export factories, including Foshan Fengfu Autoparts, the company that supplies exhaust pipes to Japanese automaker Honda, and Hon Hai Precision Industry Co., the Taiwan-based electronics manufacturer that supplies iPads and iPhones for Apple and a range of gadgets for Hewlett-Packard and Nintendo.

Predictably, the editors misrepresent how social improvement comes about with economic development. Not just in China but in the developed economies as well, improvements in working conditions have come about not due to market-led forces alone, but when economic growth was combined with social action and worker militancy.

The history of sweatshops in the United States makes that clear. The shirtwaist strike of 1909, the tragedy of the Triangle Shirtwaist fire two years later, and the hardships of the Great Depression inspired garment workers to unionize and led to the imposition of government regulations on the garment industry and other industries, beginning with the New York Factory Acts and extending to the Fair Labor Standards Act of 1938. The power of those reforms along with the postwar boom nearly eradicated sweatshops in the United States.

Since then, sweatshops have returned with a vengeance to the U.S. garment industry. Why? Declining economic opportunity is part of the answer. But severe cutbacks in the number of inspectors and a drop-off in union density paved the way as well. The U.S. experience confirms the take-away message from rising Chinese wages: Economic development by itself will not eliminate inhuman working conditions. Improve-ments in working conditions are neither inevitable nor irreversible.

Not only is labor organizing crucial for improving working conditions, but those organizing efforts need to be international if workers are to succeed in reaping durable gains from economic development.

China's case makes that clear. Rising wages in China have prompted footwear and apparel firms to shift their manufacturing elsewhere—to Indonesia, Bangladesh, and Vietnam, for example. Jim Sciabarrasi, head of sourcing and procurement at U.S.-based sneaker company New Balance, was clear about the reason for the firm's move. "Indonesia has a ready supply of workers and their wages are not going up as fast as in China," he told the *Boston Globe*.

Chinese workers attempting to organize and improve their situation always face the threat that their employer will simply pack up and depart for even lower-cost countries. This kind of threat, which helps employers resist demands for better wages and working conditions not just in China but elsewhere in global South and in the developed economies as well, has been increasingly effective as globalization has weakened limits on the mobility of corporations. It throws into sharp relief the common interests of workers in all countries in improving conditions at the bottom, in robust full-employment programs that raise their incomes and enhance their bargaining power.

In that way, the rise of China's workers and the bold labor unrest there should benefit manufacturing workers across the globe, a virtuous cycle the *Wall Street Journal* editors would not only be loathe to recognize but have gone out of their way to obscure. ❑

*Sources:* David Barboza, "In Chinese Factories, Lost Fingers and Low Pay," *New York Times*, Jan. 5, 2008; William Foreman, "13th worker attempts suicide at Foxconn tech factory in southern China, report says," *Los Angeles Times*, May 27, 2010; Jenn Abelson, "Local sneaker firms are making it in Indonesia," *Boston Globe*, May 29, 2010; Norihiko Shirouzo, "Chinese Workers Challenge Beijing's Authority," *WSJ*, June 13, 2010; Elizabeth Holmes, "U.S. Apparel Retailers Turn Their Gaze beyond China," *WSJ*, June 15, 2010; "NW: Wage disputes in China put world on notice," NIKKEI, June 14, 2010; Aileen Wang and Simon Rabinovitch, "Why labor unrest is good for China and the world," Reuters, June 2, 2010; World Bank, China Quarterly Update, June 2010; James Areddy, "Accidents Plague China's Workplaces," *WSJ*, July 28, 2010.

*Article 10.7*

# KEEP IT IN THE GROUND

*An alternative vision for petroleum emerges in Ecuador. But will Big Oil win the day?*

## BY ELISSA DENNIS
July/August 2010

In the far eastern reaches of Ecuador, in the Amazon basin rain forest, lies a land of incredible beauty and biological diversity. More than 2,200 varieties of trees reach for the sky, providing a habitat for more species of birds, bats, insects, frogs, and fish than can be found almost anywhere else in the world. Indigenous Waorani people have made the land their home for millennia, including the last two tribes living in voluntary isolation in the country. The land was established as Yasuní National Park in 1979, and recognized as a UNESCO World Biosphere Reserve in 1989.

Underneath this landscape lies a different type of natural resource: petroleum. Since 1972, oil has been Ecuador's primary export, representing 57% of the country's exports in 2008; oil revenues comprised on average 26% of the government's revenue between 2000 and 2007. More than 1.1 billion barrels of heavy crude oil have been extracted from Yasuní, about one quarter of the nation's production to date.

At this economic, environmental, and political intersection lie two distinct visions for Yasuní's, and Ecuador's, next 25 years. Petroecuador, the state-owned oil company, has concluded that 846 million barrels of oil could be extracted from proven reserves at the Ishpingo, Tambococha, and Tiputini (ITT) wells in an approximately 200,000 hectare area covering about 20% of the parkland. Extracting this petroleum, either alone or in partnership with interested oil companies in Brazil, Venezuela, or China, would generate approximately $7 billion, primarily in the first 13 years of extraction and continuing with declining productivity for another 12 years.

The alternative vision is the simple but profound choice to leave the oil in the ground.

Environmentalists and indigenous communities have been organizing for years to restrict drilling in Yasuní. But the vision became much more real when President Rafael Correa presented a challenge to the world community at a September 24, 2007 meeting of the United Nations General Assembly: if governments, companies, international organizations, and individuals pledge a total of $350 million per year for 10 years, equal to half of the forgone revenues from ITT, then Ecuador will chip in the other half and keep the oil underground indefinitely, as this nation's contribution to halting global climate change.

The Yasuní-ITT Initiative would preserve the fragile environment, leave the voluntarily isolated tribes in peace, and prevent the emission of an estimated 407 million metric tons of carbon dioxide into the atmosphere. This "big idea from a small country" has even broader implications, as Alberto Acosta, former Energy Minister and one of the architects of the proposal, notes in his new book, *La Maldición de la Abundancia* (*The Curse of Abundance*). The Initiative is a *"punto de ruptura,"* he writes, a turning point in environmental history which "questions the logic of extractive (exporter of raw material) development," while introducing the possibility of global *"sumak kawsay,"* the indigenous Kichwa concept of "good living" in harmony with nature.

Ecuador, like much of Latin America, has long been an exporter of raw materials: cacao in the 19th century, bananas in the 20th century, and now petroleum. The nation dove into the oil boom of the 1970s, investing in infrastructure and building up external debt. When oil prices plummeted in the 1980s while interest rates on that debt ballooned, Ecuador was trapped in the debt crisis that affected much of the region. Thus began what Correa calls "the long night of neoliberalism:" IMF-mandated privatizations of utilities and mining sectors, with a concomitant decline of revenues from the nation's natural resources to the Ecuadorian people. By 1986, all of the nation's petroleum revenues were going to pay external debt.

Close to 40 years of oil production has failed to improve the living standards of the majority of Ecuadorians. "Petroleum has not helped this country," notes Ana Cecilia Salazar, director of the Department of Social Sciences in the College of Economics of the University of Cuenca. "It has been corrupt. It has not diminished poverty. It has not industrialized this country. It has just made a few people rich."

Currently 38% of the population lives in poverty, with 13% in extreme poverty. The nation's per capita income growth between 1982 and 2007 was only .7% per year. And although the unemployment rate of 10% may seem moderate, an estimated 53% of the population is considered "underemployed."

Petroleum extraction has brought significant environmental damage. Each year 198,000 hectares of land in the Amazon are deforested for oil production. A verdict is expected this year in an Ecuadorian court in the 17-year-old class action suit brought by 30,000 victims of Texaco/Chevron's drilling operations in the area northwest of Yasuní between 1964 and 1990. The unprecedented $27 billion lawsuit alleges that thousands of cancers and other health problems were caused by Texaco's use of outdated and dangerous practices, including the dumping of 18 billion gallons of toxic wastewater into local water supplies.

Regardless of its economic or environmental impacts, the oil is running out. With 4.16 billion barrels in proven reserves nationwide, and another half billion "probable" barrels, best-case projections, including the discovery of new reserves, indicate the nation will stop exporting oil within 28 years, and stop producing oil within 35 years.

"At this moment we have an opportunity to rethink the extractive economy that for many years has constrained the economy and politics in the country," says Esperanza Martinez, a biologist, environmental activist, and author of the book *Yasuní: El tortuoso camino de Kioto a Quito*. "This proposal intends to change the terms of the North-South relationship in climate change negotiations."

As such, the Initiative fits into the emerging idea of "climate debt." The North's voracious energy consumption in the past has destroyed natural resources in the South; the South is currently bearing the brunt of global warming effects like floods and drought; and the South needs to adapt expensive new energy technology for the future instead of industrializing with the cheap fossil fuels that built the North. Bolivian president Evo Morales proposed at the Copenhagen climate talks last December that developed nations pay 1% of GDP, totaling $700 billion/year, into a compensation fund that poor nations could use to adapt their energy systems.

"Clearly in the future, it will not be possible to extract all the petroleum in the world because that would create a very serious world problem, so we need to create measures of compensation to pay the ecological debt to the countries," says Malki Sáenz, formerly Coordinator of the Yasuní-ITT Initiative within the Ministry of Foreign Relations. The Initiative "is a way to show the international community that real compensation mechanisms exist for not extracting petroleum."

Indigenous and environmental movements in Latin America and Africa are raising possibilities of leaving oil in the ground elsewhere. But the Yasuní-ITT proposal is the furthest along in detail, government sponsorship, and ongoing negotiations. The Initiative proposes that governments, international institutions, civil associations, companies, and individuals contribute to a fund administered through an international organization such as the United Nations Development Program (UNDP). Contributions could include swaps of Ecuador's external debt, as well as resources generated from emissions auctions in the European Union and carbon emission taxes such as those implemented in Sweden and Slovakia.

Contributors of at least $10,000 would receive a Yasuní Guarantee Certificate (CGY), redeemable only in the event that a future government decides to extract the oil. The total dollar value of the CGYs issued would equal the calculated value of the 407 million metric tons of non-emitted carbon dioxide.

The money would be invested in fixed income shares of renewable energy projects with a guaranteed yield, such as hydroelectric, geothermal, wind, and solar power, thus helping to reduce the country's dependence on fossil fuels. The interest payments generated by these investments would be designated for: 1) conservation projects, preventing deforestation of almost 10 million hectares in 40 protected areas covering 38% of Ecuador's territory; 2) reforestation and natural regeneration projects on another one million hectares of forest land; 3) national energy efficiency improvements; and 4) education, health, employment, and training programs in sustainable activities like ecotourism and agro forestry in the affected areas. The first three activities could prevent an additional 820 million metric tons of carbon dioxide emissions, tripling the Initiative's effectiveness.

These nationwide conservation efforts, as well as the proposal's mention of "monitoring" throughout Yasuní and possibly shutting down existing oil production, are particularly disconcerting to Ecuadorian and international oil and wood interests. Many speculate that political pressure from these economic powerhouses was behind a major blow to the Initiative this past January, when Correa, in one of his regular Saturday radio broadcasts, suddenly blasted the negotiations as "shameful," and a threat to the nation's "sovereignty" and "dignity." He threatened that if the full package of international commitments was not in place by this June, he would begin extracting oil from ITT.

Correa's comments spurred the resignations of four critical members of the negotiating commission, including Chancellor Fander Falconí, a longtime ally in Correa's PAIS party, and Roque Sevilla, an ecologist, businessman, and ex-Mayor of Quito whom Correa had picked to lead the commission. Ecuador's Ambassador to the UN Francisco Carrion also resigned from the commission, as did World Wildlife Fund president Yolanda Kakabadse.

Correa has been clear from the outset that the government has a Plan B, to extract the oil, and that the non-extraction "first option" is contingent on the

mandated monetary commitments. But oddly his outburst came as the negotiating team's efforts were bearing fruit. Sevilla told the press in January of
commitments in various stages of approval from Germany, Spain, Belgium,
France, and Switzerland, totaling at least $1.5 billion. The team was poised to
sign an agreement with UNDP last December in Copenhagen to administer the
fund. Correa called off the signing at the last minute, questioning the breadth of
the Initiative's conservation efforts and UNDP's proposed six-person adminis-
trative body, three appointed by Ecuador, two by contributing nations, and one
by UNDP. This joint control structure apparently sparked Correa's tirade about
shame and dignity.

Within a couple of weeks of the blowup, the government had backpedaled, withdrawing the June deadline, appointing a new negotiating team, and reasserting the
position that the government's "first option" is to leave the oil in the ground. At the same
time, Petroecuador began work on a new pipeline near Yasuní, part of the infrastructure
needed for ITT production, pursuant to a 2007 Memorandum of Understanding with
several foreign oil companies.

Amid the doubts and mixed messages, proponents are fighting to save the Initiative
as a cornerstone in the creation of a post-petroleum Ecuador and ultimately a post-
petroleum world. In media interviews after his resignation, Sevilla stressed that he
would keep working to ensure that the Initiative would not fail. The Constitution provides for a public referendum prior to extracting oil from protected areas like Yasuní,
he noted. "If the president doesn't want to assume his responsibility as leader…let's
pass the responsibility to the public." In fact, 75% of respondents in a January poll in
Quito and Guayaquil, the country's two largest cities, indicated that they would vote
to not extract the ITT oil.

Martinez and Sáenz concur that just as the Initiative emerged from widespread
organizing efforts, its success will come from the people. "This is the moment to
define ourselves and develop an economic model not based on petroleum," Salazar
says. "We have other knowledge, we have minerals, water. We need to change our
consciousness and end the economic dependence on one resource." ❏

**Resources:** Live Yasuní, Finding Species, Inc., liveYasuní.org; "S.O.S. Yasuní" sosYasuní.org;
"Yasuní-ITT: An Initiative to Change History," Government of Ecuador, Yasuní-itt.gov.ec.

## Update, November 2013

Declaring "the world has failed us," Ecuador's President Rafael Correa
signaled the termination of the Yasuní ITT Initiative in August 2013.
Citing a meager $116 million in pledges, he announced the decision to move
forward with the Plan B that was always in the background: extraction of oil
from the Ishpingo, Tambococha, and Tiputini fields in the eastern section of
Yasuní National Park. The drilling will only impact 0.1% of the parklands,
Correa contends, noting that the estimated value of oil in the targeted area has
increased from $7 billion to $18 billion. Despite street demonstrations in Quito
and Cuenca and calls for a national referendum, the National Assembly ratified
Correa's action in October 2013.

Correa, a U.S. trained economist, has consistently ridiculed "infantile" environmentalists, and is clearly most comfortable with a pragmatic economic development model of extractivism with equitable distribution of resources. Like his Bolivian counterpart Evo Morales, Correa has run afoul of indigenous communities and the environmental left through efforts to transform the nation from exploited exporter of raw materials into savvy user of natural resources to fuel economic growth and social programs.

"We can't be beggars sitting on a sack of gold," is Correa's constant refrain. The 2012 signing of a five-year $1.4 billion contract with the Chinese-owned mining company Ecuacorriente for development of the El Mirador copper mine in the southern Amazon is emblematic of this approach. While industry analysts cringed at the 52% of revenues slated for taxes and royalties to the state, advocates for the environment and indigenous Amazon community representatives took to the streets in protest at this launch of what the Correa government boasts will be a new era of mining in Ecuador.

Correa's critics say his government never wholeheartedly supported the Yasuní effort, and point to a growing Chinese political and economic influence. Since Correa's 2008 move to default on the nation's IMF debt, China has provided billions of dollars to Ecuador, with oil production pledged as repayment of some of that debt. China is also a key investor in Ecuador's oil industry, including links to ITT.

Ecuador's debt situation with China today is more "colonizing" than it was with the United States, says University of Cuenca professor Ana Cecilia Salazar, noting a $19 billion debt level in 2011 compared with $14.55 billion in 2004. She sees that as one reflection of a government long on populist rhetoric but short on progressive economic transformation. "We are living an illusion that has generated social backing for the government, but basically a policy of redistribution of wealth doesn't exist, rather a populist administration based on grants and subsidies that is not true social justice," she says.

Salazar acknowledges there has been some lessening of poverty during Correa's tenure, and some marginalized groups have benefited from government programs made possible by the high price of oil. But she notes "there is no change in the dynamics of concentration," with economic inequality growing, as 40% of the nation's wealth sits in the hands of 15% of the population. While 27,000 acres of land have been distributed to *campesinos*, millions of acres have been ceded to mining companies, she says.

Correa's strategy of moving from neoliberalism to "neo-Keynesianism," just creates a mirage of "green capitalism," Salazar says. With Yasuní, even if the drilling is contained in a small area, it is impossible to not impact the vulnerable megadiverse environment and the communities that have been living there in voluntary isolation. Opening up the area to oil necessitates new highways which expose the region to indiscriminate logging, a problem the government has not been able to control elsewhere in the Amazon region. With the end of the Yasuní initiative, the vision of a post-petroleum Ecuador is fading, Salazar says. "The government model that initially made us dream about overcoming the extractivist economy has disappeared." ❏

# Chapter 11

# POLICY SPOTLIGHT: GENERATIONAL WAR?

## INTRODUCTION

If you follow economic news and commentary, you will have heard arguments that there is a "generational war" afoot. What does this mean? Mainly, it is an argument that what we are doing economically today, especially what benefits the current working generation or the generation that has already retired, will harm the economic prospects of today's young people and those who are yet to be born. As some of the articles in this chapter argue, this view is very misleading when it comes to government debt (and has been used as a way to attack popular programs, like Social Security and Medicare, that ensure people will not be left destitute late in life).

The term "generational war" is certainly melodramatic. We would be better off referring to issues of "intergenerational distribution" or "intergenerational equity." While the notion that the current generation is doing future generations wrong may be incorrect when it comes to government finance, issues of intergenerational equity (whether the actions of the current generation are fair to future generations) are worth taking seriously. We do have to think about the world we will leave to our children, grandchildren, and so on.

The chapter begins with Dean Baker's refutation of the "generational war" idea, as it is commonly stated in relation to government spending. In "Are Our Parents Stealing From Our Kids? No, They Are Not" (Article 11.1), Baker points out that higher public spending on programs that benefit seniors actually goes hand in hand with higher spending on programs that benefit the young (both in U.S. history and across different countries). So much for a "zero-sum" game pitting one generation against the other.

The next three articles focus on education. To be sure, young people are getting short shrift in some ways, both in terms of the kind of education they are receiving and the ways it is paid for. (But seniors are not to blame.)

As Arthur MacEwan explains in "Education: Not Just 'Human Capital'" (Article 11.2), corporate-inspired education reforms are focused on making schools more effective "human capital" factories. The students should be tested, the "free market" reformers say, as a measure of quality. The teachers who do not perform should be fired, and "failing" schools should be shut down. This agenda,

MacEwan argues, reduces education to the production of an adequately skilled and obedient workforce, underestimates the successes of public schools (when they have adequate resources), and ignores the bigger social problems that impede greater educational achievement.

Instead of advocating for an education-financing system that would reduce this burden, explains John Miller (Article 11.3), the business press has been fighting for a further reduction in federal higher-education grants (Pell Grants) for low- and middle-income students. Far from being cut, Miller argues, Pell Grants should be made a "near universal" support for students.

In her article "The Student Loan Crisis and the Debtfare State" (Article 11.4), Susanne Soederberg argues that the "consumer protection" framing of the problem—that the solution is to get government involved to rein in the predatory practices of private educational lenders—is fundamentally flawed. The "debtfare state," in her view, has actively facilitated such practices. Government policy has pushed higher education into debt-based financing, and the state has acted as the enforcer of student debt obligations.

Meanwhile, seniors also find themselves under the gun, especially due to attacks on retirement security—from changes in pensions that shift risk from employers onto workers to attacks on Social Security and other federal "entitlement" programs. The next two articles tackle these issues.

In "What Happened to Defined-Benefit Pensions?" (Article 11.5), Arthur MacEwan takes on the dramatic shift from "defined-benefit" pensions, which guarantee workers' retirement income for life, to "defined-contribution" pensions, which make workers actual retirement incomes dependent on stock market returns. The shift in risk from employers to workers, MacEwan argues, reflects a larger shift in bargaining power in employers' favor.

Next, in "Myths of the Deficit" (Article 11.6), Marty Wolfson refutes the idea that federal budget deficits are creating a "burden" on future generations. Debts run up today will be paid back later. Those doing the paying, through future taxes, will be our grandchildren. But most of the people receiving the payments will also be our grandchildren, since most of the debt is owed to the U.S. public. (Current bond owners will leave these assets to their heirs.) The real distributional issues, in other words, are not really between, but within, generations.

Finally, Frank Ackerman puts intergenerational equity issues in a different light: focusing on the issue of long-term environmental sustainability and climate change. In his article, "Climate Economics in Four Easy Pieces" (Article 11.7), he argues that a key reason for aggressive action to avert climate change now is that "our grandchildren's lives are important."

## Discussion Questions

1. (Article 11.1) Baker argues that, far from being in opposition to one another, spending on programs for the young and for the old tend to go hand in hand. Why would this be the case? How does this fact relate to other articles in this chapter (which emphasize attacks on both affordable education and secure retirement)?

2.  (Article 11.2) Why does MacEwan argue that education is (and should be) about more than "human capital" formation? Why does he think that even employers are not interested only in the technical skills that future workers learn in school?

3.  (Article 11.2) Why does MacEwan think that the narrative about public schools failure is wrong? In what ways are public schools successful and in what ways not? How can we tell, if they are not completely successful, *why* this is the case?

4.  (Articles 11.3 and 11.4) Why have student debt burdens increased so much in recent years? What policy responses would you propose?

5.  (Article 11.4) Why does Soederberg argue that it is misleading to describe student debt as a "consumer protection" issue—where what is needed is government regulation to rein in private-sector abuses?

6.  (Article 11.5) Explain the contrast between "defined-benefit" and "defined-contribution" pensions. What does MacEwan mean when he argues that this is the result of a more general "power shift" in favor of employers and against workers?

7.  (Article 11.6) If Wolfson is right, and the main distributional effects of government debt are within (rather than between) generations, why is the "generational war" interpretation so widespread? Is this a simple mistake? Or does it reflect some political agenda?

8.  (Article 11.7) Ackerman argues that a key issue in making climate policy today is how we weigh the interests of future generations against those of the current generation. Why is this so important? What kind of formula would you use in weighing these different interests?

*Articke 11.1*

# ARE OUR PARENTS STEALING FROM OUR KIDS? NO, THEY'RE NOT

## BY DEAN BAKER
*October 2013; The Business Desk (PBS NewsHour)*

A common refrain in debates over Social Security and Medicare is that these programs are putting seniors ahead of children. The implication is that there is a fixed pool of tax revenue. If more of this revenue goes to seniors to pay for their benefits, there is less to cover the cost of child nutrition and health care, daycare, education and other programs that benefit the young. To put in crudely, in this view, a dollar spent on the elderly is a dollar taken away from spending on children.

There is an alternative perspective. The amount of money that the government collects in tax revenue may not be fixed. Understood this way, people's willingness to pay taxes may depend on their perception of the usefulness of the services provided. This could mean, for example, that if the public believes that the government services being provided to both seniors and children are valuable and should be expanded, they would be willing to pay higher taxes to support those services.

If we look at the situation historically in the United States, we have vastly increased the share of GDP going to government programs for both seniors and the young over the last 60 years. In 1950, Social Security payments were less than 1 percent of GDP and Medicare and Medicaid did not even exist. By comparison, we are now spending almost 5% of GDP on Social Security, and more than 5 percent of GDP on Medicare and Medicaid.

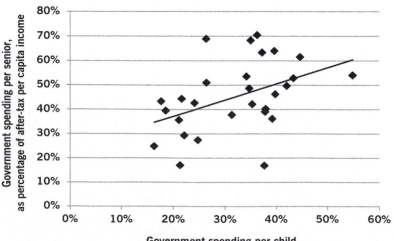

### PER PERSON SPENDING ON CHILDREN AND SENIORS, PERCENTAGE OF PER CAPITA INCOME

This growth in federal spending for programs that primarily benefit seniors has been accompanied by a huge expansion in programs intended to primarily benefit the young, such as Head Start; the Women, Infants and Children Nutrition Program; and the State Children's Health Insurance Program. In addition, state and local funding for education and other programs that benefit the young has also hugely increased relative to the size of the economy over the last six decades. People have been willing to pay more in taxes to finance programs that benefit both the elderly and the young.

There is a similar story if we look across countries. If the tradeoff view were correct, we should find that countries that are more generous in their support of seniors are stingier when it comes to public support for their children and vice versa. However, the opposite appears to be the case. If we control for the relative income of different countries, it turns out that a dollar of additional spending per kid is associated with 67 cents of additional spending for each senior. (This relationship is statistically significant at the 5% confidence level.)

In short, the data suggest that more spending on seniors is associated with more spending on kids. Presumably this indicates that countries where people rely on the government to ensure that their seniors have a decent standard of living are also inclined to provide the government with resources necessary to ensure that their children's needs are also met.

This evidence suggests that cuts to programs for seniors may be unlikely to end up benefitting our kids. Rather such cuts may be associated with reduced spending on kids as well. If the public does not trust the government to provide good care for seniors, it may also not trust the government to provide good care for children.

In that case, there would be no tradeoff between spending on seniors and spending on kids. If we care about both our seniors and our kids, and trust the government programs designed to provide support at both ends of life, then both sets of programs are likely to be adequately funded. In the opposite case, neither set of programs is likely to be adequately funded. The world where just one set of programs, either those supporting seniors or those supporting kids, receives adequate funding seems largely the invention of politicians. ❑

*Article 11.2*

# EDUCATION: NOT JUST "HUMAN CAPITAL"

**BY ARTHUR MacEWAN**
*January/February 2013*

> Dear Dr. Dollar:
> *What's going on with the economics of education? It all seems to be about impos-ing "standards" to motivate and punish educators. And then there is privatization, which is supposed to force schools to shape up or die. Help me out here!*
> —Nancy Hernandez, Colorado Springs, Colo.

A great deal of the economics of education reduces schooling to the creation of "human capital." Economists tend to view education as a way of making the individual more productive—like a better-functioning machine that can gener-ate more output. As with any piece of equipment coming off the production line, human capital is subjected to quality control—through standardized testing.

Of course, people are not machines, which presents employers with a problem. A good machine does what it is supposed to do and has no ideas about fair wages and decent working conditions. So in creating human capital, schools have the task of turning out well-behaved workers, people who follow orders and accept their employ-ers' authority. In other words, in economists' human-capital view of education, schools need to prepare pupils for the discipline of the capitalist workplace. Thus, testing is not simply quality-control for technical skills (reading and math) but also for test-taking ability, which teaches discipline, endurance, and not asking too many questions.

Education has—or should have—goals that are much more complex than those involved in building a machine. Education is about the passing on of culture. It is about preparing people both to get the most out of and make the greatest con-tribution to society. Enabling people to be more economically productive, while important, is only a part of this process. Reducing schooling to its narrowest eco-nomic function obscures and undermines the larger roles of education.

But from the perspective of business executives, the narrowest economic func-tion is the important thing, at least in the short run. Complaining that our public schools are failing, elite business groups have pushed an education agenda that would standardize the "products" of the schools, especially through high-stakes standard-ized testing. These groups (often private foundations, most prominently the Gates Foundation) and many economists argue that testing can create appropriate incen-tives for the students and their teachers. Students who fail the tests can't graduate and teachers whose students do poorly on the tests don't get raises or get fired.

Likewise, the argument continues, schools with low test scores should be closed down and replaced by other schools—just as private firms that don't produce good products are replaced by other firms. This is the root of the argument for school privatization—sometimes in the form of (formally public) charter schools and some-times through private schools. Privatized schools eliminate the supposed causes of public schools' failures—public bureaucracy and teachers' unions.

Beyond this ideological drive for privatization, there is also money to be made. For-profit firms such as EdisonLearning, Inc., and Educational Services of America, which run schools and provide services for school systems, are cashing in on the education market. As one consultant recently told a group of potential investors in education: "You start to see entire ecosystems of investment opportunity lining up. It could get really, really big."

There are many problems with the kind of school reform being pushed by many economists and elite business groups. For example:

Our public schools are not failing. We have some marvelous public schools. We also have some terrible schools. No surprise: the good schools tend to be in wealthy areas, the terrible schools in poverty-stricken areas.

To a large extent, the poor academic performance of many kids—in both traditional public schools and charter schools—is rooted in the larger problems of economic inequality and poverty. Poverty undermines children's ability to come to school ready to learn. Poor health, overworked parents, dangerous communities—all this undermines teachers' efforts.

In states where teachers unions exist, both good schools and terrible schools are unionized. Likewise, both good and terrible public schools operate under similar—sometimes the same—bureaucratic structures.

Incentives directed toward the wrong goal (the narrowest economic function) lead people in negative directions. Teaching to the test does not create students who are effective contributors to society.

Charter schools have been operating for decades. Yet there is no evidence that they produce better outcomes than traditional public schools.

Public schools are one of the great social support programs of our society. By themselves, they cannot eliminate poverty and other social ills, but they can move things in a positive direction. However, for the public schools to be an effective social support program, they need effective social support. ❏

*Article 11.3*

# PUTTING THE SCREWS TO GENERATION SCREWED
Wall Street Journal *editors oppose expanded Pell grants.*

## BY JOHN MILLER
*September/October 2012*

- Pell Grants are now so broad that more than half of all undergrads benefit.
- Better-off students often receive the large Pell Grants and apply them to more expensive schools.
- Pell Grants and other student aid are contributing to the ever-higher tuition spiral. Write 100 times on the chalkboard: Student aid raises tuition.
- Overall graduation rates were lower for students who received Pell Grants than for those who didn't.
- The best thing Mr. Obama could do for students, and taxpayers, is to get Pell Grants away from being a broad entitlement and back to their core mission of helping the poorest students.

> —Claims from "Pell Grants Flunk Out: The subsidy program has strayed far from its origins," *Wall Street Journal*, June 18, 2012.

More than $1 trillion of U.S. student debt. Better than nine of ten college graduates with student debt. Over one quarter of the repayments on those loans past due.

"A Generation Hobbled by the Soaring Cost of College" is how the *New York Times* put it in their recent exposé on college debt. And if you mix in the worst economy since the Great Depression, one that has hit those without a college degree especially hard and has left the employment prospects of even college graduates much diminished, this generation is not just hobbled but screwed. Apparently, however, not screwed enough for the editors of the *Wall Street Journal*. The editors rail against the ongoing expansion of Pell Grants, the chief form of federal aid to low- and middle-income students that can reduce the debt burden students incur.

The prospect of Pell Grants becoming an ever-more-universal entitlement must really have the *Wall Street Journal* editors spooked.

Below is a closer look at the predicament of students and former students burdened by debt and exactly why expanding Pell Grants should be supported, not opposed.

## Generation Screwed

The cost of college tuition and fees has skyrocketed and student debt along with it. Since 1978, the cost of college tuition and fees has increased eleven-fold, rising faster than even the cost of medical care, and many times faster than family incomes.

Since 1999, student loan debt has increased fivefold. It has eclipsed credit-card debt and is now second only to mortgage debt.

With bankruptcy not an option, borrowers can be stuck repaying their student loans long after leaving college. The federal government is now garnishing the Social Security benefits of an increasing number of retirees with student debt. The Treasury Department reports that in the first seven months of this year, the federal government withheld money from roughly 115,000 retirees' Social Security checks because they had fallen behind on federal student loans. That's nearly double the 60,000 cases in all of 2007. There were just six cases in 2000.

A college degree is now the minimum credential needed for entrance into much of today's economy. "In the mid 1970s, less than 30% of jobs in America required any education beyond high school," reports Jamie P. Merisotis, president and chief executive officer of Lumina Foundation, a private foundation dedicated to expanding higher-education opportunity. "Today, the majority of U.S. jobs require a postsecondary degree or credential." A recent study conducted by the Georgetown Center on Education and the Workforce projects that 63% of job openings in 2018 will require at least some college education.

On top of that, the penalty for not obtaining a college degree has increased dramatically over the last three decades. Beginning with the loss of manufacturing jobs beginning in the late 1970s, the gap between the earnings of college graduates and those with just high school education has steadily widened. The Georgetown study calculated that in 1980 college graduates' lifetime earnings were 44% higher than those of high-school graduates. In 2010 college graduates' lifetime earnings were nearly twice (97% more than) those of high school graduates.

At the same time, the employment prospects of even college graduates are far from bright. First off, having graduated from college is no guarantee of full-time employment. The Economic Policy Institute Briefing Paper on "The Class of 2012" found that the unemployment rate for young college graduates (ages 21 to 24) averaged 9.4% from April 2011 to March 2012. Another 19.1% of of this group was underemployed--unable to find full-time work--during that time period. Second, pay for college grads is down. On average, wages for full-time workers with four-year college degrees fell by 5.4% (adjusted for inflation) between 2000 and 2011. Finally, many graduates do not find the kinds of jobs they wanted. More than a third (37.8%) of college graduates under 25, reports a recent study by economist Andrew Sum of Northeastern University's Center for Labor Market Studies, were working at jobs that did not require a college degree.

For workers without a college degree the numbers are even worse. In May 2012 about one quarter (24%) of new high school graduates from 17 to 20 years old were unemployed, and about half (54% for April 2011 to March 212) were underemployed, unable to get a full time job. Finally, average hourly wages for young high-school graduates plummeted from 2000 to 2011, falling 11.1% after adjusting for inflation.

## Pell-Mell

The *WSJ* editors stand four square against providing relief for those hobbled by student debt, especially by expanding Pell Grants to an ever-wider swath of college students. But there is plenty wrong with the editors' long list of complaints about Pell Grants.

To start with, contrary to the editors' complaints, Pell Grants are well targeted. The evidence from a report by the conservative John William Pope Center, which is the source of many of the editors' claims, shows as much. In academic year 2009-2010, a year when the median household income was $51,190, some 94.2% of Pell grant recipients had a family income less than $50,000, and the majority (58.9%) had a family income of less than $20,000.

Nor is it surprising that the graduation rates for Pell Grant recipients are lower than other students. Proportionally, nearly twice as many Pell recipients have parents with only a high school diploma and nearly twice as many come from non-English-speaking homes as other undergraduates. Even the Pope Center recognizes that these are risk factors for dropping out.

The size of Pell Grants is another reason why it is hardly surprising that the graduation rates of Pell recipients are lower than those of other undergraduates. Award amounts for Pell recipients have remained relatively flat in real terms, but covered less and less of college costs. The $5,550 maximum Pell Grant in 2011 covered just one-third of the average cost of attending a public four-year college, just one half the level it covered in 1980-81, according to the Institute for College Access and Success. [Add something like: If Pell Grants covered more of college costs, students from lower-income families would be less likely to drop out due to economic hardship--like being unable to make tuition due to tight family budgets.

In addition, better-off students do not often receive large Pell Grants, as the editors contend. The College Board reports that in academic year 2010-2011 just 1.6% of recipients from families with an income above $60,000 received the maximum Pell Grant of $5,550, well below the 33.8% of the recipients from families with incomes between $15,000 and $20,000 who got the maximum grant. While a bit more than one-fifth of those high-income recipients did apply their Pell Grants to schools that cost $30,000 or more, that amounts to less than one half of one percent of all Pell Grants going to help these high-income recipients attend "more expensive" colleges.

Finally, writing 100 times on the chalkboard "student aid raises tuition," as the editors have suggested, might convince some readers that Pell Grants are driving up tuition. But the evidence is far from conclusive. The Pope Center report states that, "most studies show at least some effect of aid on tuition," which implies that other studies show that student aid has had zero effect on tuition. Indeed they do. For instance, David L. Warren, president of the National Association of Independent Colleges and Universities, reports, "Studies conducted during three successive administrations—Bill Clinton, George W. Bush, and Barack Obama—have found no link between student aid and tuition increases."

One must also ask how Pell Grants with a maximum grant that now covers just one third of the cost of attending a public four-year college, could have fueled the rise in college tuition. What's more, the College Board reports that the average inflation-adjusted net tuition and fees (published tuition and fees minus grants from all sources and federal tax benefits) at private, nonprofit colleges and universities actually dropped from 2006-07 to 2011-12, even as total Pell Grant expenditures more than doubled after correcting for inflation.

# A Universal Entitlement

The Obama administration has undertaken some positive steps to expand access to Pell Grants and toward providing debt relief for students. In 2010, the President signed legislation that converted all federally guaranteed student loans (loans issued by private banks to students, with the federal government promising to pay back the loan if the debtor failed to do so) to direct loans administered by the government. This change eliminated fees paid to the private banks that had acted as intermediaries, saving nearly $68 billion over the next 11 years, $36 billion of which is to be used to expand Pell Grants. This year, the Obama Consumer Financial Protection Bureau issued a report recommending that Congress enact legislation letting borrowers discharge their private student loans (those not backed by the federal government) through bankruptcy.

But much more needs to be done. Private student loans account for just 10% of student loans. A good first step toward genuine debt relief would be for Congress to pass the Student Loan Forgiveness Act of 2012, introduced by Representative Hansen Clarke, a Michigan Democrat, which would allow "existing borrowers" to be forgiven up to $45,000 in student debt after the borrower has made ten years of income-based payments (no more than 10% of income).

Pell Grants need to be not only a entitlement, but expanded to a near universal entitlement A recent report from the Pell Institute's newsletter, Postsecondary Education Opportunity, throws into to sharp relief the need to do yet more. Only 10.7% of students from families in the bottom fourth by family income, below $33,050, had attained a bachelor's degree by 24 years of age; among students from families in the second fourth by family income, with incomes between $33,050 and $61,600, only 15%. At the same time, 79.1% of students from the top fourth by family income, above $98,875, had a bachelor's degree by age 24.

As more and more families rely on Pell Grants to reduce the cost of a college education for their children, the more likely it is that Pell Grants will continue to withstand the budget cuts likely to come in the upcoming years. And more fulsome and the more universal Pell Grants will help make merit, not economic means, the determinant of who gets a college degree. ❑

*Sources:* Anthony Carnevale, Tamara Jayasundera, and Ban Cheah, "The College Advantage: Weathering the Economic Storm," Center on Education and the Workforce, Georgetown University, August 15, 2012; Jenna Ashley Robinson and Duke Cheston, "Pell Grants: Where Does All the Money Go?" John W. Pope Center for Higher Education Policy, June 2012; Rep. Hansen Clarke, The Student Loan Forgiveness Act of 2012; "Public Policy Analysis of Opportunity for Postsecondary Education," Postsecondary Education Opportunity newsletter, January 2012; Heidi Shierholz, Natalie Sabadish, and Hilary Wething, "The Class Of 2012: Labor market for young graduates remains grim," Economic Policy Institute Briefing Paper, May 3, 2012; Meta Brown, Andrew Haughwout, Donghoon Lee, Maricar Mabutas, and Wilbert van der Klaauw, "Federal Student Financial Aid: Grading Student Loans," Federal Reserve Bank of New York, March 05, 2012; Charley Stone, Carl Van Horn, Cliff Zukin, and John J. Heldrich, "Chasing the American Dream: Recent College Graduates and the Great Recession," Center for Workforce Development, May 2012.

*Article 11.4*

# THE STUDENT LOAN CRISIS AND THE DEBTFARE STATE

## BY SUSANNE SOEDERBERG

*May/June 2015*

Educational debt has become a ticking time bomb. With over $1 trillion in outstanding loan balances, the student loan industry has a lot in common with the sub-prime mortgage industry, which went into a devastating crisis in 2007-8. Both rely on a financial innovation called "asset-backed securitization" (see sidebar) to raise capital and to hedge risk—in other words, to raise money for loans and to reduce the likelihood that investors will lose their money. Student loans asset-backed securitization—or SLABS—means student loan agencies package student debts and sell them to investors who expect to get their money back, plus interest, as students pay back their loans. In theory, selling off nicely bundled packages of debt to investors allows these institutions to turn around more quickly and make new loans. For this reason, SLABS is touted as the main channel through which the lending industry moves funds from investors to students—and so is supposed to be of mutual benefit to students, lenders, and institutional investors such as hedge funds and pension funds.

Like the sub-prime housing industry, however, SLABS ultimately depends on the ability of borrowers to meet their debt obligations. Herein lies the rub. Since as far back as the recession of 2001, the majority of student debtors have not been able to get decent paying jobs upon leaving college.

Poor job prospects, as well as mounting costs of basic needs such as health care and housing, mean many college graduates have not been earning enough to pay back their loans. Default rates on student loans have been climbing since 2003. By 2012, student loans registered the worst delinquency rates in consumer credit, worse than even mortgage debts and credit cards.

Despite the uneasy relationship between the profitable student loan industry and growing student debt defaults, students continue to borrow to pay for college, and educational loans are the only form of consumer debt to increase markedly since 2008. The industry has grown steadily over the past several decades in lockstep with rapidly rising tuition and fees—and with the government's prioritization of loan-based funding over grants. To understand the growth of this risky business, we need to first grasp the basic alliance between government and finance in the profitable world of student debt.

## Sallie Mae and the Student Loan Industry

The student loan industry is made up of a wide array of overlapping public and private actors and institutions. There are two main categories of educational loans and lenders: public student loans, which are issued by the federal government and represent the largest category of loans (85%), and private student loans (15%), which are issued by a few large banks such as Wells Fargo and JPMorgan Chase.

---

### Student Debt Glossary

**Default** on a debt is the failure to make payment on interest or principal when it falls due.

**Dischargeable debt** is debt that can be cleared through bankruptcy proceedings. The federal government has enacted laws to prevent students from attempting to wipe out their education debt by filing for bankruptcy, unless they can prove "undue hardship"—and even then courts have been unwilling to discharge student debt.

**Federal Direct Loan Program (FDLP)** is a new law, enacted in 2010, under which public student loans originate directly from the U.S. Department of Education, effectively ending the ability of banks to issue federal government-backed student loans.

**Government Sponsored Enterprises (GSEs)** were created by Congress to enhance the efficiency of funds flowing between saving and borrowing in key areas of the economy. GSEs **Fannie Mae and Freddie Mac** are associated with housing, while GSE Sallie Mae deals with education. GSEs assist in the flow of funds by providing loan guarantees, reducing lenders' risk of losses due to borrower default.

**Stafford Loans** are a kind of fixed-interest-rate federal student loan. They are the most affordable type of student loan.

---

By far the most powerful private actor in the industry is Sallie Mae, a former government-sponsored enterprise, or GSE (see glossary). Sallie Mae's original role when it was founded in 1972 was to raise funds by selling student loans (also known as debt securities) on secondary markets, where investors buy securities from other investors. In this way, Sallie Mae could finance low-interest rate loans to increasingly more students by subsidizing and guaranteeing repayment to their private lenders. In 1996, Sallie Mae became the first GSE to be privatized and was subsequently renamed the SLM Corporation—although the moniker of Sallie Mae remains.

In 2010, the Federal Direct Loan Program (see glossary) assigned Sallie Mae and four other private educational lenders (FedLoan Servicing, Great Lakes Educational Loan Services, Nelnet, and Direct Loan Servicing Center) the role of federal loan servicers. These are companies that handle, for a fee, the billing and other services on federal student loans. By far the largest, Sallie Mae (or, more precisely, its offshoot company Navient), provides service to 3.6 million loan customers on behalf of the U.S. Department of Education. Sallie Mae has been growing at such a rapid pace that it has been diversifying into areas such as debt collection, insurance and consumer banking, and the issuing of credit cards to college students. Sallie Mae remains the main lender of private student loans and the largest issuer of SLABS.

## Raising Funds, Reducing Risks—for Whom?

SLABS is often presented by economists and neoliberal policy makers as a highly efficient method of raising capital and reducing risk for lenders, including the risks of default and bankruptcy. This view of SLABS conveniently ignores the unequal relations of power in the educational loan business—and how the business generates revenue from commissions, fees, and interest.

Consider, for example, a first-year undergrad at UCLA who gets a four-year, $25,000 student loan from Sallie Mae. Depending on the repayment schedule and an interest rate based on creditworthiness, this student could end up paying Sallie Mae anywhere from $50,545.95 (based on a 145-month repayment plan) to $70,259.07 (based on a 193-month repayment plan) to even $74,126.61 (based on a 144-month deferred repayment plan). The deferred repayment option costs more because the student is not required to make payments during school or, according to the Sallie Mae website, is allowed to "pay as much as you'd like." Sallie Mae's rosy language leaves out why student borrowers might choose loan terms that are more expensive in the long run: they are worried about their ability to repay, because their families have no extra resources and they may end up unemployed or underemployed after graduating from college.

Shortly after issuing the loan to the UCLA student, Sallie Mae securitizes the debt, packaging it with a bundle of other similar student loans. It then sells this debt bundle to an outside investor, like a pension or hedge fund, pocketing the total amount of the original loans plus fees and commissions. In doing so, Sallie Mae receives payment on its student loans immediately, as opposed to receiving small monthly payments for twelve to 16 years from students and bearing the risk that these students might default. Revenue is extracted in student debt collection, too. Thanks to amendments to the Higher Education Act in 1991, debt collectors that specialize in student debt are permitted to tack on hefty collection (25%) and commission fees (28%) to the outstanding loan, making debt collection a highly lucrative business.

Private lenders are not the only ones benefiting from the educational loan business. The Department of Education, which also securitizes its loans, is believed to have generated $101.8 billion in revenue from student loans from 2008 to 2013. It does so largely by exploiting a spread between the low interest rates it pays to borrow money (e.g., 2.52% based on the 10-year Treasury bond rate in 2013) and what it charges students (e.g., 6.8% for Stafford Loans (see glossary)).

The basic premise driving SLABS is that powerful financial actors and institutions are able, through regulatory and legal sanctioning by the government, to transform a debt obligation (student loan) into a financial asset (SLABS) that can be traded on the secondary markets. This can be understood as the "commodification of debt." The underlying assets for SLABS are student loans that have been sliced and diced to create packages of debt obligations that are then sold to investors such as pension funds. SLABS has proven to be a lucrative device to hedge risk for investors, raise capital, and even to generate income when student loan debtors default (through derivative contracts such as credit default swaps, which pay off in the event of default).

Once we peel away the complexities of SLABS, we are left with the basic problem: the success of the "investment" ultimately depends on the ability of the debtor to earn enough money to pay the principal of the loan, plus interest and fees. The alchemy of finance cannot erase the risk of how hard it may be for the student to ever repay the loan because the student will struggle to find gainful employment after graduation. From this angle, SLABS—like all forms of credit—rests on the ability of the state to ensure that debtors (students) will repay the loan—no matter what their incomes may be.

### Asset-Backed Securitization

Asset-backed securitization (ABS) is a financial technique used by governments and corporations to obtain funding on the basis of present and future revenue streams. It is classic financial alchemy: a special-purpose vehicle (a corporation, a trust, a limited liability company, or a partnership) is permitted to transform illiquid assets (mortgages, student loans, credit card receivables, song royalties, etc.) into tradable securities (bonds, swaps).

The use of ABS was first made famous by the recording artist David Bowie in 1997, when he turned to this method to raise $55 million. Bowie generated this vast amount of money by using current and future music royalties from his first 25 albums as collateral. These royalties were transformed into bonds with a maturity date of 10 years—"Bowie bonds"—that were then available for purchase by investors.

In 2001, a Greek finance minister suggested that the Parthenon should be securitized as a way of reducing Greece's large public debt. In this case, a securitization bond would be issued, backed by a stream of future revenues from annual ticket sales to tourists. The deal fell through, but the point remains: there are no limits to assets that can be repackaged and subsequently traded as securities (such as bonds) to raise capital.

ABS has been touted by its supporters as an efficient way of raising capital for corporations and governments (cheaper than turning to banks or other funders for loans) as well as an effective tool for managing risk of default, as it diversifies and thus spreads the risk. One way it is said to reduce risk on the underlying assets is by what is referred to as "tranching," or subdividing the assets into several classes of securities which are then tied to a large number of underlying loans—a process that has given it the moniker "slice and dice financing."

The 2008 sub-prime housing crisis revealed the dark side of this financial innovation. Mortgage-backed securities (MBSs) were used to raise capital to lend to people who wished to purchase a home but were categorized as high-risk (i.e., "sub-prime") borrowers. Instead of receiving small monthly payments for a period of 30 years, a bank may prefer to move the loan off its balance sheet by bundling it with other similar loans and—with the financial backing of a housing GSE (see glossary) such as Freddie Mac or Fannie Mae—selling it to an outside investor such as a pension or mutual fund. This method allows the bank to receive funds immediately by selling the loan (mortgage) and thus is motivated to issue more loans to more people, including sub-prime borrowers. Put differently, banks are given incentives to engage in risky "loan pushing," since they can securitize and sell off the loans, thereby avoiding exposure to the risk of default.

## Debtfare and Discipline

For the student loan industry to continue to expand and remain lucrative in the face of increasing rates of delinquency and default, the state must discipline the debtors. In my recent book, Debtfare States and the Poverty Industry (2014), I refer to this new feature of neoliberal governance—emerging alongside the rollback of the welfare state, dereliction of labor laws, and increased levels of precarity among working- and middle-class Americans—as "debtfarism."

Debtfarism represents a set of institutional and ideological practices aimed at regulating and normalizing the growing dependence on expensive consumer credit to meet basic needs, such as education. Personal bankruptcy law is a core regulatory feature of debtfarism, as it acts to deal with defaults in the student loan industry and to ensure the legal and moral obligation of debt—regardless of the borrower's ability to repay.

For many students, the draconian changes to the bankruptcy code with the enactment of the Bankruptcy Abuse Prevention and Consumer Protection Act (BAPCPA) of 2005 represented a major turning point. Among its notable features, the BAPCPA was designed to keep student debtors out of bankruptcy in three ways.

First, BAPCPA made relief under Chapter 7 (under which most debts are immediately cancelled) more difficult to access. Granted, federal student loans have long been exempt from discharge (the release of a borrower from the obligation to repay her/his student debt through bankruptcy) under Chapter 7, but some legal loopholes were available to highly distressed debtors, particularly holders of private student loans. The passage of BAPCPA makes it nearly impossible to pursue debt relief under Chapter 7.

Second, BAPCA made it more difficult for highly indebted students to qualify for the other remaining option for bankruptcy relief—Chapter 13 (adjustment of debts). Student debtors filing under Chapter 13 can only be granted bankruptcy protection if they prove "undue hardship." Undue hardship is determined through means-tested procedures making human suffering reducible to algebraic equations. (Congress refused to provide a clear and transparent definition of "undue hardship," opting instead to transfer responsibility for interpretation to the courts.) Chapter 13 also requires debtors to jump through more hoops, such as mandatory pre-bankruptcy credit counselling and a rigorous repayment plan for three to five years before the courts discharge "some" debt. Despite these obstacles, desperate student debtors continue to file under Chapter 13 to seek relief from dischargeable types of consumer credit, such as credit cards, medical debt, and auto loans.

Third, BAPCPA added private student loans to the types of educational loans that cannot be discharged without adequate proof of undue hardship. This means that private lenders such as Sallie Mae now enjoy the same state protection from debtor bankruptcy as the federal government. Moreover, private educational lenders such as Sallie Mae have been granted powers to garnish the wages, tax refunds, and even Social Security benefits of delinquent debtors with no statute of limitations.

The debtfare state's extension of super-creditor status to dominant private institutions like Sallie Mae deepens the hold corporations have over education financing. One out of every five students carries private loans, which have higher interest rates than government loans and carry fees that add to the balance. Many students are turning to private loans to augment their federal loans due to the increasing costs of living (health care and rent) and tuition (especially at for-profit colleges).

To manage the relentless wave of defaults, the government introduced the College Cost Reduction and Access Act in 2007 (effective July 1, 2009), which tweaked various aspects of the BAPCPA. While the law included some small victories for individuals holding public student loans, it also created a system of income-based repayment plans under which student debtors would be compelled to pay (through wage garnishment) 15% of their discretionary incomes (earnings available for savings or spending on non-essentials) for a period of 25 years. Only after this period would the borrowers be able to apply for cancellation of the remaining debt. It should be underlined that this system applies only to public educational loans (e.g., Direct Loan and the Federal Family Education Loan (or FFEL) programs) and to those student debtors who earn enough discretionary income to permit the garnishment. Moreover, it is an income-based repayment system that favours public-service employees over other workers. Under the Loan Forgiveness for Public Service program, for instance, public-service employees can apply for the remaining debt cancellation after paying 15% of their discretionary income for 10 years. All other student debtors are required to pay 15% of their discretionary income for 25 years before applying for the remaining balance of their debt to be cancelled.

## The Rhetoric of Consumer Protection

Framing private educational lending as a consumer protection issue makes it seem as if the root cause of the student debt problem is the predatory practices of private educational lenders, distorting the role of the debtfare state. The state has played a critical role in the construction and normalization of students' increased reliance on loans—both public and private—to fund their higher education. It has withdrawn funding for education, overseen the rise in student tuition and fees, and shifted from grant-based to loan-based financing. In other words, the consumer protection framing veils the role of the debtfare state in actively facilitating predatory practices.

Consumer protection has also remained largely rhetorical. Consumer protection for student loans does not deal with the social dimensions of student debt risk, such as defaulting, dropping out of college, moving back home, working two or more jobs, putting off marriage and starting families, and even—despite the long odds—filing for bankruptcy to reduce overall debt loads.

This has not been uncontested. Growing numbers of student debtors have channelled their anger and frustration with the management of these loans through numerous acts of protest, active lobbying, and advocacy to achieve debt justice. One of the more popular mobilizations has been the Occupy Student Debt Campaign—a loose network of several thousand student debtors and debt activists that sprang out of the Occupy Wall Street protests.

Occupy's Strike Debt Working Group and Rolling Jubilee Fund grabbed headlines with their "search and destroy" campaign in 2013. Using donated funds (largely through crowdsourcing), Rolling Jubilee located and purchased student debt at discounted prices and then abolished it. The campaign has cancelled $3.85 million of privately held debt through this approach. Rolling Jubilee acknowledges that this gesture was symbolic in that it sought to expose how debt operates and to empower student debtors.

The Debt Collective emerged from Rolling Jubilee and from growing student outrage with the exploitative strategies pursued by for-profit colleges. The group aims to create a platform for advocacy and for debtors to unite in collective action. One such act of resistance has been the country's first student debt strike, in which more than 100 former students of the for-profit Corinthian College system are refusing to pay their federal loans. For-profit colleges like Corinthian derive 66% of their revenues from federal student loans.

These activist organizations have been vital in exposing the injustices and exploitative nature of the student loan industry. One of their most important roles has been to politicize debt, convincing insolvent borrowers that they should move beyond the dehumanizing narrative of debt as an individual problem by collectively challenging the moral sanctity of debt.

Building on this momentum will require a focus on the powerful class interests that have benefited from student loans—from the issuance of private and public loans, to servicing and securitizing student debt, to collections. While protestors are right to vilify and target key corporate players such as Sallie Mae, more critical light needs to be cast on the role of the debtfare state in both legitimating the profitable "poverty industry" and failing to provide adequate public support for social programs, including education.

The poverty industry includes educational lending, but extends to other forms of consumer credit—such as payday loans, credit cards, sub-prime housing loans—all of which feed off of and reproduce marginalization and insecurity. The increasing reliance on expensive personal loans to replace or augment wages—as well as obtain an education—is not a natural phenomenon. Rather, it is a social construction that needs be revealed, attacked, and uprooted, not negotiated within the territory of consumer protection, which is sponsored by the debtfare state and the capitalist interests it represents. ❑

**Sources:** Consumer Financial Protection Bureau (CFPB) and Department of Education, Private Student Loans, 2012 (files.consumerfinance.gov/f/201207_cfpb_Reports_Private-Student-Loans. pdf); Ozgur E. Ergungor and Ian Hathaway, "Trouble ahead for student loans?" Federal Reserve Bank of Cleveland, Economic Commentary, May 2008 (files.eric.ed.gov/fulltext/ED505621.pdf); Federal Reserve Bank of New York, "Are Recent College Graduates finding Good Jobs?" *Current Issues*, Vol. 20(1), 2014 (newyorkfed.org/research/current_issues/ci20-1.pdf); Project on Student Debt, "Student Debt and the Class of 2012," The Institute for College Access & Success, 2012 (ticas.org/sites/default/files/legacy/fckfiles/pub/classof2013.pdf); Amy Traub, Tamara Draut, and David Callahan, "The Contract for College," *Demos*, 2012; U.S. Department of Education (www. ed.gov); Susanne Soederberg, *Debtfare States and the Poverty Industry: Money, Discipline and the Surplus Population* (Routledge, 2014).

*Article 11.5*

# WHAT HAPPENED TO DEFINED-BENEFIT PENSIONS?

## BY ARTHUR MacEWAN
*September/October 2013*

Dear Dr. Dollar:
*What has happened to the defined benefit pensions? Why are they being replaced by defined contribution programs? What are the implications for us (workers!) as we grow older and live longer?* —Susan A. Titus, Detroit, Mich.

In large part, the shift from defined benefit pensions to defined contribution pensions is explained by employers shifting risk from themselves to their employees. Increasingly, in recent decades, for the same reasons that employers have been able to hold down wages, employers have shifted pension plans because they have had the power to do so. (See box for definitions of the two types of plans.)

The shift has been dramatic. In 1975, 71% of active workers participating in pension plans had defined benefit plans, and 29% had defined contribution plans. By 2010, the figures had more than reversed: 19% were in defined benefit plans; 81%, in defined contribution plans. Even though the labor force grew by 64% over this 45-year period, the number of workers in defined benefit plans fell by 37%. (See graph.)

In a defined benefit pension system, the employer is obligated to pay the fixed pension regardless of what happens to the economy. The risk for the employer is that bad economic times can make it difficult to make the payments—because the

## PERCENTAGE OF NON-RETIRED PENSION-PLAN PARTICIPANTS, DEFINED BENEFIT (DB) VS. DEFINED CONTRIBUTION (DC) PLANS, 1975-2010*

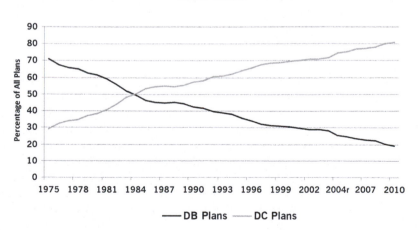

— DB Plans ⋯⋯ DC Plans

*Many people participate in more than one plan. In 2004 (shown twice) definitions changed.
**Sources:** U.S. Dept. of Labor, Private Pension Plan Bulletin Historical Tables and Graphs, Nov. 2012.

> **DEFINED BENEFIT:** Employer and employees make contributions to a general pension fund managed by the employer. Based on a formula including years of employment and level of salary, each employee receives a fixed annual amount of money after retirement; that fixed amount does not depend on how well the investment of the fund does. The quality of the plan from the perspective of the employee depends on the amount of employee and employer contributions and on the particulars of the formula for determining benefits.
>
> **DEFINED CONTRIBUTION:** Employer and employee make contributions to a fund that is identified with the individual and is managed by an investment firm. The money that the employee receives after retirement depends on the amount of money in the individual's fund. The quality of the plan from the perspective of the employee depends on the amount of employee and employer contributions and on how well the investment does, both up to and after the time of retirement.

investments made with the pension fund have done poorly, because the firm's revenues are less than anticipated, or both. Even if a private firm goes broke, defined benefit pensions are insured by the federal government, so the private-sector employee bears little or no risk. However, for public sector employees, who now account for most defined benefit plans, there is risk in extreme cases such as—you know it well!—Detroit in 2013. When a public employer goes bankrupt, the pensioners and active workers in the pension system are put in line behind the employer's creditors—mainly banks. (The Detroit situation is being disputed in the courts at this writing, but it does not appear likely that things will come out well for people in the public pension system.)

In defined contribution plans, the risk falls on the employee. The contributions (from both the employee and the employer) go into an investment fund for the individual worker, generally with taxes deferred until the money is taken out of the fund (as in a 401k). But if the economy goes sour— for example, if the stock market crashes—the employee has far less for retirement. This is exactly what happened with the crash of 2008.

There could hardly be a clearer case of conflict of interests between employees and employers. As employers have been able to hold down wages over the last several decades, they have shifted the burden of risk onto employees. There are several aspects of this power shift that have favored employers: the large decline in union membership, the way globalization has been structured to favor large firms, the general shift in political power (of which the decline in the minimum wage is a clear marker), and the way technological changes have been used to displace labor. The result has been a worsening of what workers get—stagnant wages and higher risk.

Social Security alone certainly does not provide a good standard of living. In 2012, the average annual Social Security payment from the Old-Age and Survivors Insurance trust fund was a little more than $14,000 per recipient. A person retiring in 2013 at age 65 who had been earning an annual salary of $70,000 (a bit more than the median family income), would receive about $21,000 annually. Even if all the efforts in Washington to cut Social Security benefits fail, it is easy to see why people need some additional form of retirement income to provide them with a reasonable standard of living during retirement.

Beyond Social Security, in 2010, active workers held 90.6 million pension plans, 17.2 million defined benefit plans and 73.4 million defined contribution plans. These figures involve some double counting, as many people have more than one pension plan, but, with a 2010 labor force of 153.9 million, this means that at least 41% of workers had no pension plan at all (other than Social Security). In fact, according to progressive pension expert Teresa Ghilarducci, a majority of workers do not have pension plans at work and over 75% of Americans nearing retirement age in 2010 had less than $30,000 in their retirement accounts.

While the pressure from business groups in Washington is to reduce Social Security, the current dismal state of retirement prospects for the majority of people in fact provides a strong case for a more extensive public pension system. ❑

*Sources:* Teresa Ghilarducci, "Don't Cut Pensions, Expand Them," *New York Times*, March 15, 2012; Teresa Ghilarducci, "Our Ridiculous Approach to Retirement, *New York Times*, July 21, 2012; Employee Benefit Research Institute, "The Basics of Social Security, Updated With the 2013 Board of Trustees Report," July 2013.

Article 11.6

# MYTHS OF THE DEFICIT

## BY MARTY WOLFSON
May/June 2010

Nearly 15 million people are officially counted as unemployed in the United States, and more than 6 million of these have been unemployed for more than 26 weeks. Another 11 million are the "hidden" unemployed: jobless workers who have given up looking for work and part-time workers who want full-time jobs. Unemployment has especially affected minority communities; the official black teenage unemployment rate, for example, stands at 42%.

The *moral* case for urgently addressing the unemployment issue is clear. The costs of unemployment, especially prolonged unemployment, are devastating. Self-worth is questioned, homes are lost, families stressed, communities disrupted. Across the land, the number one issue is jobs, jobs, jobs.

The *economic* case for how to address the jobs issue is also clear. As Keynes argued during the Great Depression, federal government spending can directly create jobs. And the $787 billion stimulus package approved by Congress in February 2009 did help pull the economy back from disaster, when it was shedding 20,000 jobs *a day* in late 2008 and early 2009.

But we still have a long way to go. To get back just to where we were when the recession began in December 2007, the economy would need to create 11.1 million jobs: 8.4 million to replace the jobs lost and 2.7 million to absorb new workers who have entered the labor market since then.

Despite a pickup of economic activity recently, long-term projections are that the unemployment rate will fall only gradually over the next several years. The Congressional Budget Office forecast for the unemployment rate for 2012 is a stubbornly high 8%. So why are we not moving more aggressively to reduce unemployment?

The *ideological* opposition to government spending remains a major obstacle. There are those who see an increase in the role of government as something to be avoided at all costs—even if the cost is the jobs of the unemployed.

Even among those who are not subject to such ideological blinders, there is still a *political* argument that resonates strongly. The argument is that government spending to create jobs will create large budget deficits, which will have terrible consequences for the American people. Politicians, pundits, and other commentators—in a frenzied drumbeat of speeches, op-eds, and articles—have asserted that the most urgent priority *now* is to reduce the budget deficit.

It is important to note that this argument is focused on current policy, not just the long-term budgetary situation. There is room for debate about long-term budget deficits, but these are affected more by the explosive growth of health-care costs than by government discretionary spending to create jobs.

Why, then, are people taken in by an argument that says it is more important to reduce the budget deficit now than for the government to spend money to create jobs? Two myths constantly repeated in the public debate have contributed to this situation:

### 1) Families can't spend more than they have; neither should the government.

It seems to be common sense that a family can't spend more than it has. But of course that is exactly what the family does when it takes out a car loan or a student loan, or does any other kind of borrowing. The government, just like families, should be able to borrow. The real issue is whether or not the debt is affordable. For families, and for the government, that depends on the size of the debt relative to the income available to service the debt; it also depends on the nature of the borrowing.

For the federal government, the relevant debt-income measure is the ratio of outstanding debt of the federal government to gross domestic product. (*Outstanding debt* is the total amount owed at a particular time, roughly the result of debt accumulated over time by annual budget deficits; GDP, the value of goods and services produced, is equal to total income.) In 2009, this ratio was 53%. Although higher than the recent low point of 33% at the end of the 1990s expansion, the ratio in 2009 was still far lower than the record peak of 109% in 1946—after which the U.S. economy in the post-World War II period experienced the strongest economic growth in its history.

The U.S. ratio of 53% actually compares favorably to those of other advanced industrial countries. For example, IMF data indicate the following debt-to-GDP ratios for 2009: France (67%), Germany (70%), Japan (105%), and Italy (113%).

The nature of the borrowing also affects affordability. If a family runs up credit-card debt to finance a lavish lifestyle, after the fancy dinners are eaten the family still needs to figure out how to pay its debt. But if a family member borrows to buy a car to get to work, presumably the job will help provide the income to service the debt.

Likewise for the federal government: If the government borrows to finance tax cuts for the rich, and the rich use their tax cuts to purchase imported luxury goods, then the government still needs to figure out how to pay its debt. On the other hand, if the government borrows to put people to work creating long-term investments that increase the productivity of the U.S. economy, like infrastructure and education, then it is in a much better situation. The income generated by the more productive economy, as well as by the newly employed workers, can help to provide the tax revenue to service the debt.

So it is a myth to say that families can't spend more than they have. They can, and so can the government. And both are justified in borrowing if the size of the debt is manageable and if so doing helps to provide the income necessary to service the debt.

### 2) Large budget deficits create a burden for our grandchildren.

This is the issue that probably resonates most forcefully with public opinion. If we in the current generation run up a big debt, it may be left to our grandchildren to repay. The only difficulty with this reasoning is that the grandchildren who may be asked to repay the debt are paying it to other grandchildren. When the government incurs a debt, it issues a bond, an obligation to repay the debt to the holder of the bond. If the holders of the bond are U.S. residents, then paying off the debt means paying money to U.S. residents. In other words, debt that is an obligation of future U.S. taxpayers is also a source of income to the U.S. holders of that debt. Thus there is not a generational burden that we today are imposing on "our grandchildren" as a collective entity.

Of course, the obvious exception to this reasoning is the debt held by non-U.S. residents. In that case, it is indeed true that future generations of Americans will need to pay interest to foreign holders of U.S. debt. But the basic reason for this situation is the trade deficit, not the budget deficit. When we pay more for imports than we receive from exports, and when U.S. multinational companies ship production abroad to take advantage of low-cost labor, foreigners are provided with dollars that they can use to invest in U.S. assets. And the real burden that this causes is the same whether foreigners invest in U.S. government debt or whether they invest in U.S. companies, real estate, the U.S. stock market, etc.

Borrowing by the federal government can in some situations create a real burden, but it has less to do with generational transfers and more to do with distributional issues and the nature of economic growth (discussed above). If the grandchildren who are taxed in the future to pay off government debt are poorer than the grandchildren who are paid, the distribution of income becomes more unequal.

Also, cutting taxes for the rich and spending money on wars in Iraq and Afghanistan do not lead to the kind of productive economic growth that generates strong tax revenue. So financing these by debt *does* create a real distributional burden: The rich and military contractors benefit, but the losers are those who might be taxed, or those whose government programs might be squeezed out of the budget, because of the need to pay interest on the debt.

Borrowing money to put people back to work does make sense. It helps people most in need, the unemployed. It provides them with income that they can use to pay taxes and to buy goods and services that create more jobs, more income, and more tax revenue. Indeed, our inability thus far to seriously tackle the unemployment problem is what has worsened the budget problem, as tax receipts have fallen and spending for unemployment benefits and food stamps have risen. An analysis by the Economic Policy Institute reveals that the largest source of the 2009 budget deficit (42%) was actually the recession itself.

We *will* leave a burden for our grandchildren if we don't address the urgent problem of unemployment, if we let parents and grandparents suffer the indignities and financial hardships of lost jobs. We *will* leave a burden for our grandchildren if we don't rebuild our aging infrastructure, break our reliance on fossil fuels, and provide all our children with an excellent education. It makes perfect sense to borrow money now to address these problems, and we shouldn't let myths about budget deficits get in the way of meeting these real needs. ❑

*Sources:* Congressional Budget Office, "The Budget and Economic Outlook: Fiscal Years 2010 to 2020," January 2010; John Irons, Kathryn Edwards, and Anna Turner, "The 2009 Budget Deficit: How Did We Get Here?" Economic Policy Institute, August 20, 2009; Dean Baker, "The Budget Deficit Scare Story and the Great Recession," Center for Economic and Policy Research, February 2010; Office of Management and Budget, "The President's Budget For Fiscal Year 2011, Historical Tables: Table 7.1, Federal Debt at the End of Year: 1940-2015," February 2010.

*Article 11.7*

# CLIMATE ECONOMICS IN FOUR EASY PIECES

*Conventional cost-benefit models cannot inform our decisions about how to
address the threat of climate change.*

## FRANK ACKERMAN
*November/December 2008*

Once upon a time, debates about climate policy were primarily about the science. An inordinate amount of attention was focused on the handful of "climate skeptics" who challenged the scientific understanding of climate change. The influence of the skeptics, however, is rapidly fading; few people were swayed by their arguments, and doubt about the major results of climate science is no longer important in shaping public policy.

As the climate *science* debate is reaching closure, the climate *economics* debate is heating up. The controversial issue now is the fear that overly ambitious climate initiatives could hurt the economy. Mainstream economists emphasizing that fear have, in effect, replaced the climate skeptics as the intellectual enablers of inaction.

For example, William Nordhaus, the U.S. economist best known for his work on climate change, pays lip service to scientists' calls for decisive action. He finds, however, that the "optimal" policy is a very small carbon tax that would reduce greenhouse gas emissions only 25% below "business-as-usual" levels by 2050—that would, in other words, allow emissions to rise well above current levels by mid-century. Richard Tol, a European economist who has written widely on climate change, favors an even smaller carbon tax of just $2 per ton of carbon dioxide. That would amount to all of $0.02 per gallon of gasoline, a microscopic "incentive" for change that consumers would never notice.

There are other voices in the climate economics debate; in particular, the British government's Stern Review offers a different perspective. Economist Nicholas Stern's analysis is much less wrong than the traditional Nordhaus-Tol approach, but even Stern has not challenged the conventional view enough.

What will it take to build a better economics of climate change, one that is consistent with the urgency expressed by the latest climate science? The issues that matter are big, non-technical principles, capable of being expressed in bumper-sticker format. Here are the four bumper stickers for a better climate economics:

1. Our grandchildren's lives are important.

2. We need to buy insurance for the planet.

3. Climate damages are too valuable to have prices.

4. Some costs are better than others.

# 1. Our grandchildren's lives are important.

The most widely debated challenge of climate economics is the valuation of the very long run. For ordinary loans and investments, both the costs today and the resulting future benefits typically occur within a single lifetime. In such cases, it makes sense to think in terms of the same person experiencing and comparing the costs and the benefits.

In the case of climate change, the time spans involved are well beyond those encountered in most areas of economics. The most important consequences of today's choices will be felt by generations to come, long after all of us making those choices have passed away. As a result, the costs of reducing emissions today and the benefits in the far future will not be experienced by the same people. The economics of climate change is centrally concerned with our relationship to our descendants whom we will never meet. As a bridge to that unknowable future, consider our grandchildren—the last generation most of us will ever know.

Suppose that you want your grandchildren to receive $100 (in today's dollars, corrected for inflation), 60 years from now. How much would you have to put in a bank account today, to ensure that the $100 will be there 60 years from now? The answer is $55 at 1% interest, or just over $5 at 5%.

In parallel fashion, economists routinely deal with future costs and benefits by "discounting" them, or converting them to "present values"—a process that is simply compound interest in reverse. In the standard jargon, the *present value* of $100, to be received 60 years from now, is $55 at a 1% *discount rate*, or about $5 at a 5% discount rate. As this example shows, a higher discount rate implies a smaller present value.

The central problem of climate economics, in a cost-benefit framework, is deciding how much to spend today on preventing future harms. What should we spend to prevent $100 of climate damages 60 years from now? The standard answer is, no more than the present value of that future loss: $55 at a discount rate of 1%, or $5 at 5%. The higher the discount rate, the less it is "worth" spending today on protecting our grandchildren.

The effect of a change in the discount rate becomes much more pronounced as the time period lengthens. Damages of $1 million occurring 200 years from now have a present value of only about $60 at a 5% discount rate, versus more than $130,000 at a 1% discount rate. The choice of the discount rate is all-important to our stance toward the far future: should we spend as much as $130,000, or as little as $60, to avoid one million dollars of climate damages in the early twenty-third century?

For financial transactions within a single lifetime, it makes sense to use market interest rates as the discount rate. Climate change, however, involves public policy decisions with impacts spanning centuries; there is no market in which public resources are traded from one century to the next. The choice of an intergenerational discount rate is a matter of ethics and policy, not a market-determined result.

Economists commonly identify two separate aspects of long-term discounting, each contributing to the discount rate.

One component of the discount rate is based on the assumption of an upward trend in income and wealth. If future generations will be richer than we are, they will need less help from us, and they will get less benefit from an additional dollar of income than we do. So we can discount benefits that will flow to our wealthier descendants, at a rate based on the expected growth of per capita incomes. Among economists, the income-related motive for discounting may be the least controversial part of the picture.

Setting aside changes in per capita income from one generation to the next, there may still be a reason to discount a sum many years in the future. This component of the discount rate, known as "pure time preference," is the subject of longstanding ethical, philosophical, and economic debate. On the one hand, there are reasons to think that pure time preference is greater than zero: both psychological experiments and common sense suggest that people are impatient, and prefer money now to money later. On the other hand, a pure time preference of zero expresses the equal worth of people of all generations, and the equal importance of reducing climate impacts and other burdens on them (assuming that all generations have equal incomes).

The Stern Review provides an excellent discussion of the debate, explaining Stern's assumption of pure time preference close to zero and an overall discount rate of 1.4%. This discount rate alone is sufficient to explain Stern's support for a substantial program of climate protection: at the higher discount rates used in more traditional analyses, the Stern program would look "inefficient," since the costs would outweigh the present value of the benefits.

## 2. We need to buy insurance for the planet.

Does climate science predict that things are certain to get worse? Or does it tell us that we are uncertain about what will happen next? Unfortunately, the answer seems to be yes to both questions. For example, the most likely level of sea level rise in this century, according to the latest Intergovernmental Panel on Climate Change reports, is no more than one meter or so—a real threat to low-lying coastal areas and islands that will face increasing storm damages, but survivable, with some adaptation efforts, for most of the world. On the other hand, there is a worst-case risk of an abrupt loss of the Greenland ice sheet, or perhaps of a large portion of the West Antarctic ice sheet. Either one could cause an eventual seven-meter rise in sea level—a catastrophic impact on coastal communities, economic activity, and infrastructure everywhere, and well beyond the range of plausible adaptation efforts in most places.

The evaluation of climate damages thus depends on whether we focus on the most likely outcomes or the credible worst-case risks; the latter, of course, are much larger.

Cost-benefit analysis conventionally rests on average or expected outcomes. But this is not the only way that people make decisions. When faced with uncertain, potentially large risks, people do not normally act on the basis of average outcomes; instead, they typically focus on protection against worst-case scenarios. When you go to the airport, do you leave just enough time for the average traffic delay (so that you would catch your plane, on average, half of the time)? Or do you allow time for some estimate of worst-case traffic jams? Once you get there, of course, you will experience additional delays due to security, which is all about worst cases: your *average* fellow passenger is not a threat to anyone's safety.

The very existence of the insurance industry is evidence of the desire to avoid or control worst-case scenarios. It is impossible for an insurance company to pay out in claims as much as its customers pay in premiums; if it did, there would be no money left to pay the costs of running the company, or the profits received by its owners. People who buy insurance are therefore guaranteed to get back less than they, on average, have paid; they (we) are paying for the security that insurance provides in case the worst should happen. This way of thinking does not apply to every decision: in casino games, people make bets based on averages and probabilities, and no one has any insurance against losing the next round. But life is not a casino, and public policy should not be a gamble.

Should climate policy be based on the most likely outcomes, or on the worst-case risks? Should we be investing in climate protection as if we expect sea level rise of one meter, or as if we are buying insurance to be sure of preventing a seven-meters rise?

In fact, the worst-case climate risks are even more unknown than the individual risks of fire and death that motivate insurance purchases. You do not know whether or not you will have a fire next year or die before the year is over, but you have very good information about the likelihood of these tragic events. So does the insurance industry, which is why they are willing to insure you. In contrast, there is no body of statistical information about the probability of Greenland-sized ice sheets collapsing at various temperatures; it's not an experiment that anyone can perform over and over again.

A recent analysis by Martin Weitzman argues that the probabilities of the worst outcomes are inescapably unknowable—and this deep uncertainty is more important than anything we do know in motivating concern about climate change. There is a technical sense in which the expected value of future climate damages can be infinite because we know so little about the probability of the worst, most damaging possibilities. The practical implication of infinite expected damages is that the most likely outcome is irrelevant; what matters is buying insurance for the planet, i.e., doing our best to understand and prevent the worst-case risks.

## 3. Climate damages are too valuable to have prices.

To decide whether climate protection is worthwhile, in cost-benefit terms, we would need to know the monetary value of everything important that is being protected. Even if we could price everything affected by climate change, the prices would conceal a critical form of international inequity. The emissions that cause climate change have come predominantly from rich countries, while the damages will be felt first and worst in some of the world's poorest, tropical countries (although no one will be immune from harm for long). There are, however, no meaningful prices for many of the benefits of health and environmental protection. What is the dollar value of a human life saved? How much is it worth to save an endangered species from extinction, or to preserve a unique location or ecosystem? Economists have made up price tags for such priceless values, but the results do not always pass the laugh test.

Is a human life worth $6.1 million, as estimated by the Clinton administration, based on small differences in the wages paid for more and less risky jobs? Or is it worth $3.7 million, as the (second) Bush administration concluded on the basis of questionnaires about people's willingness to pay for reducing small, hypothetical risks? Are lives of people in rich countries worth much more than those in poor countries, as some economists infamously argued in the IPCC's 1995 report? Can the value of an endangered species be determined by survey research on how much people would pay to protect it? If, as one study found, the U.S. population as a whole would pay $18 billion to protect the existence of humpback whales, would it be acceptable for someone to pay $36 billion for the right to hunt and kill the entire species?

The only sensible response to such nonsensical questions is that there are many crucially important values that do not have meaningful prices. This is not a new idea: as the eighteenth-century philosopher Immanuel Kant put it, some things have a price, or relative worth, while other things have a dignity, or inner worth. No price tag does justice to the dignity of human life or the natural world.

Since some of the most important benefits of climate protection are priceless, any monetary value for total benefits will necessarily be incomplete. The corollary is that preventive action may be justified even in the absence of a complete monetary measure of the benefits of doing so.

## 4. Some costs are better than others.

The language of cost-benefit analysis embodies a clear normative slant: benefits are good, costs are bad. The goal is always to have larger benefits and smaller costs. In some respects, measurement and monetary valuation are easier for costs than for benefits: implementing pollution control measures typically involves changes in such areas as manufacturing, construction, and fuel use, all of which have well-defined prices. Yet conventional economic theory distorts the interpretation of costs in ways that exaggerate the burdens of environmental protection and hide the positive features of some of the "costs."

---

### Average Risks or Worst-Case Scenarios?

You don't have to look far to find situations in which the sensible policy is to address worst-case outcomes rather than average outcomes. The annual number of residential fires in the United States is about 0.4% of the number of housing units. This means that a fire occurs, on average, about once every 250 years in each home—not even close to once per lifetime. By far the most likely number of fires a homeowner will experience next year, or even in a lifetime, is zero. Why don't these statistics inspire you to cancel your fire insurance? Unless you are extremely wealthy, the loss of your home in a fire would be a devastating financial blow; despite the low probability, you cannot afford to take any chances on it.

What are the chances of the ultimate loss? The probability that you will die next year is under 0.1% if you are in your twenties, under 0.2% in your thirties, under 0.4% in your forties. It is not until age 61 that you have as much as a 1% chance of death within the coming year. Yet most U.S. families with dependent children buy life insurance. Without it, the risk to children of losing their parents' income would be too great—even though the parents are, on average, extraordinarily likely to survive.

For instance, empirical studies of energy use and carbon emissions repeatedly find significant opportunities for emissions reduction at zero or negative net cost—the so-called "no regrets" options.

According to a longstanding tradition in economic theory, however, cost-free energy savings are impossible. The textbook theory of competitive markets assumes that every resource is productively employed in its most valuable use—in other words, that every no-regrets option must already have been taken. As the saying goes, there are no free lunches; there cannot be any $20 bills on the sidewalk because someone would have picked them up already. Any new emissions reduction measures, then, must have positive costs. This leads to greater estimates of climate policy costs than the bottom-up studies that reveal extensive opportunities for costless savings.

In the medium term, we will need to move beyond the no-regrets options; how much will it cost to finish the job of climate protection? Again, there are rival interpretations of the costs based on rival assumptions about the economy. The same economic theory that proclaimed the absence of $20 bills on the sidewalk is responsible for the idea that all costs are bad. Since the free market lets everyone spend their money in whatever way they choose, any new cost must represent a loss: it leaves people with less to spend on whatever purchases they had previously selected to maximize their satisfaction in life. Climate damages are one source of loss, and spending on climate protection is another; both reduce the resources available for the desirable things in life.

But are the two kinds of costs really comparable? Is it really a matter of indifference whether we spend $1 billion on bigger and better levees or lose $1 billion to storm damages? In the real-world economy, money spent on building levees creates jobs and incomes. The construction workers buy groceries, clothing, and so on, indirectly creating other jobs. With more people working, tax revenues increase while unemployment compensation payments decrease.

None of this happens if the levees are not built and the storm damages are allowed to occur. The costs of prevention are good costs, with numerous indirect benefits; the costs of climate damages are bad costs, representing pure physical destruction. One worthwhile goal is to keep total costs as low as possible; another is to have as much as possible of good costs rather than bad costs. Think of it as the cholesterol theory of climate costs.

In the long run, the deep reductions in carbon emissions needed for climate stabilization will require new technologies that have not yet been invented, or at best exist only in small, expensive prototypes. How much will it cost to invent, develop, and implement the low-carbon technologies of the future?

Lacking a rigorous theory of innovation, economists modeling climate change have often assumed that new technologies simply appear, making the economy inexorably more efficient over time. A more realistic view observes that the costs of producing a new product typically decline as industry gains more experience with it, in a pattern called "learning by doing" or the "learning curve" effect. Public investment is often necessary to support the innovation process in its early, expensive stages. Wind power is now relatively cheap and competitive, in suitable locations; this is a direct result of decades of public investment in the United States and Europe, starting when wind turbines were still quite expensive. The costs of climate policy, in the long run, will include doing the same for other promising new technologies, investing public resources in jump-starting a set of slightly different industries than we might have chosen in the absence of climate change. If this is a cost, many communities would be better off with more of it.

## Saving the Planet

A widely publicized, conventional economic analysis recommends inaction on climate change, claiming that the costs currently outweigh the benefits for anything more than the smallest steps toward reducing carbon emissions. Put our "four easy pieces" together, and we have the outline of an economics that complements the science of climate change and endorses active, large-scale climate protection.

How realistic is it to expect that the world will shake off its inertia and act boldly and rapidly enough to make a difference? This may be the last generation that will have a real chance at protecting the earth's climate. Projections from the latest IPCC reports, the Stern Review, and other sources suggest that it is still possible to save the planet—if we start at once. ❏

**Sources:** Frank Ackerman, *Can We Afford the Future? Economics for a Warming World*, Zed Books, 2008; Frank Ackerman, *Poisoned for Pennies: The Economics of Toxics and Precaution*, Island Press, 2008; Frank Ackerman and Lisa Heinzerling, *Priceless: On Knowing the Price of Everything and the Value of Nothing*, The New Press, 2004; J. Creyts, A. Derkach, S. Nyquist, K. Ostrowski and J. Stephenson, *Reducing U.S. Greenhouse Gas Emissions: How Much at What Cost?*, McKinsey & Co., 2007; P.-A. Enkvist, T. Naucler and J. Rosander, "A Cost Curve for Greenhouse Gas Reduction," *The McKinsey Quarterly*, 2007; Immanuel Kant, *Groundwork for the Metaphysics of Morals*, translated by Thomas K. Abbot, with revisions by Lara Denis, Broadview Press, 2005 [1785]; B. Lomborg, *Cool It: The Skeptical Environmentalist's Guide to Global Warming*, Alfred A. Knopf, 2007; W.D. Nordhaus, *A Question of Balance: Economic Modeling of Global Warming*, Yale University Press, 2008; F.P. Ramsey, "A mathematical theory of saving," *The Economic Journal* 138(152): 543-59, 1928; Nicholas Stern *et al.*, *The Stern Review: The Economics of Climate Change*, HM Treasury, 2006; U.S. Census Bureau, "Statistical Abstract of the United States." 127th edition. 2008; M.L. Weitzman, "On Modeling and Interpreting the Economics of Catastrophic Climate Change," December 5, 2007 version, www. economics.harvard.edu/faculty/weitzman/files/modeling.pdf.

# CONTRIBUTORS

**Frank Ackerman** is an economist with Synapse Energy Economics and a founder of *Dollars & Sense*.

**Gar Alperovitz** is a professor of political economy at the University of Maryland and co-author, with Lew Daly, of *Unjust Deserts: How the Rich Are Taking Our Common Inheritance and Why We Should Take It Back* (New Press, 2009).

**Nicole Aschoff** is a sociologist and writer living in the Boston area.

**David Bacon** is a writer and photojournalist based in California. He is an associate editor at Pacific News Service and writes for publications including *TruthOut, The Nation, The American Prospect, The Progressive*, and the *San Francisco Chronicle*.

**Dean Baker** is co-director of the Center for Economic and Policy Research.

**Peter Barnes**, co-founder of Working Assets, is a senior fellow at the Tomales Bay Institute.

**Sarah Blaskey** is a student at the University of Wisconsin-Madison and a member of the Student Labor Action Coalition.

**James K. Boyce** is a professor of economics at the University of Massachusetts-Amherst and co-director of the Political Economy Research Institute (PERI) Program on Development, Peacebuilding, and the Environment.

**Marc Breslow** is co-chair of the Massachusetts Climate Action Network and a former *Dollars & Sense* collective member.

**Marie Brill** is the executive director of ActionAid USA.

**Jim Campen** is professor emeritus of economics at the University of Massachusetts-Boston, and former executive director of Americans for Fairness in Lending.

**Lew Daly** is a senior fellow at Demos and co-author, with Gar Alperovitz, of *Unjust Deserts: How the Rich Are Taking Our Common Inheritance and Why We Should Take It Back* (New Press, 2009).

**Elissa Dennis** is a consultant to nonprofit affordable housing developers with Community Economics, Inc. in Oakland, Calif.

**Deborah M. Figart** is a professor or education and economics at the Richard Stockton College of New Jersey.

**Nancy Folbre** is a professor emerita of economics at the University of Massachusetts-Amherst. She contributes regularly to the *New York Times* Economix blog.

**Ellen Frank** teaches economics at the University of Massachusetts-Boston and is a *Dollars & Sense* collective member.

**Elizabeth Fraser** is an intern scholar at the Oakland Institute.

**Gerald Friedman** is a professor of economics at the University of Massachusetts-Amherst.

**Heidi Garrett-Peltier** is a research fellow at the Political Economy Research Institute at the University of Massachusetts-Amherst.

**Phil Gasper** teaches at Madison College and writes the "Critical Thinking" column for *International Socialist Review.*

**Mark Haggerty** is an associate professor in the Honors College at the University of Maine and a member of its Sustainable Foods Systems Research Collaborative.

**Lisa Heinzerling** is a professor of law at Georgetown University Law School, specializing in environmental law.

**Edward Herman** is an economist and co-author of *The Global Media: The New Missionaries of Corporate Capitalism* (Continuum, 1997).

**John M. Jemison, Jr.** is an extension professor of soil and water quality at the University of Maine.

**Dan La Botz** was a founding member of Teamsters for a Democratic Union (TDU), is the author of *Rank-and-File Rebellion*, and is a co-editor of *New Politics* and editor of *Mexican Labor News and Analysis.*

**Rob Larson** teaches economics at Tacoma Community College in Tacoma, Wash., and is the author of *Bleakonomics* (Pluto Press).

**Jonathan Latham,** PhD, is co-founder and executive director of the Bioscience Resource Project, publisher of Independent Science News (independentsciencenews.org).

**Arthur MacEwan**, a *Dollars & Sense* Associate, is professor emeritus of economics at the University of Massachusetts-Boston.

**John Miller,** a *Dollars & Sense* collective member, teaches economics at Wheaton College.

**Anuradha Mittal** is executive director of the Oakland Institute.

**Thomas Palley** is an economist who has held positions at the AFL-CIO, Open Society Institute, and the U.S./China Economic and Security Review Commission.

**Mark Paul** is a PhD candidate in economics at the University of Massachusetts-Amherst.

**Stephen Pressman** is a professor of economics and finance at Monmouth University and the author of *Fifty Major Economists*.

**Alejandro Reuss** (co-editor of this volume) is co-editor of *Dollars & Sense* and an instructor at the Labor Relations and Research Center at UMass-Amherst.

**Helen Scharber** is an assistant professor of economics at Hampshire College in Amherst, Mass.

**Juliet Schor** is a professor of sociology at Boston College and the author of *The Overworked American*, *The Overspent American*, and *True Wealth*.

**Zoe Sherman** is an assistant professor at Merrimack College and a member of the *Dollars & Sense* collective.

**Bryan Snyder** (co-editor of this volume) is a senior lecturer in economics at Bentley University.

**Susanne Soederberg** is a professor of political studies and global development studies at Queen's University, Canada.

**Emily Stephens** studies global women's health and international development at the University of Massachusetts-Amherst.

**Chris Sturr** (co-editor of this volume) is co-editor of *Dollars & Sense*.

**Chris Tilly** is a *Dollars & Sense* Associate and director of UCLA's Institute for Research on Labor and Employment and professor in the Urban Planning Department.

**Ramaa Vasudevan** teaches economics at Colorado State University and is a *Dollars & Sense* Associate.

**Rosario Ventura** is a migrant farm worker, moving between California and Washington State.

**Stephanie Welcomer** is an associate professor of management at the University of Maine.

**Jeannette Wicks-Lim** is an economist and research fellow at the Political Economy Research Institute at the University of Massachusetts-Amherst.

**Timothy A. Wise** is director of the Research and Policy Program at the Global Development and Environment Institute, Tufts University.

**Marty Wolfson** is a professor of economics at the University of Notre Dame.

Earn your **Master's Degree** in
# Applied Economics
at the University of Massachusetts Boston

Would you like to do applied economic research?
Our program will provide you with both critical analytical
thinking and quantitative problem-solving skills.

You will:

- Gain insights from alternative and traditional economic approaches.
- Learn and practice applied research techniques.
- Study with a progressive and diverse economics faculty whose interests include urban economics, political economy, feminist economics, and ecological economics.
- Pay affordable tuition at a great public university in a beautiful city.
- Study part-time or full-time in a 32 credit program designed for working adults.

Learn more at **www.economics.umb.edu**

UMASS
BOSTON